India Studies in Business and Economics

The Indian economy is considered to be one of the fastest growing economies of the world with India amongst the most important G-20 economies. Ever since the Indian economy made its presence felt on the global platform, the research community is now even more interested in studying and analyzing what India has to offer. This series aims to bring forth the latest studies and research about India from the areas of economics, business, and management science. The titles featured in this series will present rigorous empirical research, often accompanied by policy recommendations, evoke and evaluate various aspects of the economy and the business and management landscape in India, with a special focus on India's relationship with the world in terms of business and trade.

More information about this series at http://www.springer.com/series/11234

Pradip Kumar Biswas · Panchanan Das
Editors

Indian Economy: Reforms and Development

Essays in Honour of Manoj Kumar Sanyal

Springer

Editors
Pradip Kumar Biswas
Department of Economics
College of Vocational Studies
University of Delhi
Ghaziabad, Uttar Pradesh, India

Panchanan Das
Department of Economics
University of Calcutta
Kolkata, West Bengal, India

ISSN 2198-0012 ISSN 2198-0020 (electronic)
India Studies in Business and Economics
ISBN 978-981-13-8268-0 ISBN 978-981-13-8269-7 (eBook)
https://doi.org/10.1007/978-981-13-8269-7

This Springer imprint is published by the registered company Springer Nature Singapore Pte Ltd.
The registered company address is: 152 Beach Road, #21-01/04 Gateway East, Singapore 189721, Singapore

A Tribute to Manoj Kumar Sanyal

Professor Manoj Kumar Sanyal is currently working as an independent researcher and a writer. He has contributed to journals and edited volumes, and authored and co-edited books. He has also written articles in popular magazines on social history and cultural issues in Indian and global contexts. He, however, prefers to be known more as a teacher than as a professional researcher. His interest in cultural issues and social history culminated in publication of research papers on these topics in recent times.

A Ph.D. in economics from University of Calcutta, Professor Sanyal started his teaching career in the early 1960s with Krishnath College, Baharampur, West Bengal, one of the oldest teaching institutes of India. There he spent a large part of his service life. He joined the Centre for Economic Studies and Planning at Jawaharlal Nehru University, Delhi, in January 2001 as Senior (ICSSR) Fellow. He visited universities and research institutes, both in India and abroad, during and after his long tenure with Krishnath College. Four years ago, he visited the Monash Asia Institute of Monash University and spent quite some time to carry out research on social and economic issues in the South Asian context. This finally led to organizing the publication of, and co-editing (with Greg Bailey and David Templeman) an anthology, *Religion, Caste, Tribe and Gender* (2017: Delhi: MANAK) in the South Asian context. In this volume, he contributed a paper entitled 'Subaltern Peasants, Elite Society, and Socio-Religious Reforms: Discordant Notes of Nationalism in Colonial Bengal', Chap. 2, pp. 23–64. In another anthology that he co-edited with A. Ghosh in 2009 under the title *Culture, Society and Development in India—Essays for Amiya Kumar Bagchi* (Hyderabad: Orient Blackswan), he co-authored an article with Shantanu Bhattacharyya under the title *Wajid Ali Shah and his Culture of Music in Calcutta*, Chap. 7, pp. 89–100. In its prefatory note, this paper brings out that in any major writing on the colonial history of Calcutta, it is hardly mentioned that the city emerged as a major centre of Hindustani classical music in the second half of the nineteenth century. The historiography of Indian nationalism, as Sanyal believes, has been dominated by *bourgeois elitism*. In the same year (2009), one more anthology was published entitled *Post-reform Development In Asia—Essays for Amiya Kumar Bagchi*

(Hyderabad: Orient Blackswan). He co-edited this book with Mandira Sanyal and Shahina Amin. This volume addresses the development debate—whether neoliberal reforms in developing nations in Asia have raised poverty, inequality, food insecurity, hindered empowerment of women, aggravated agrarian distress and allocated resources for private gains. All these issues have definite social contents. He took a special interest in writing about the socio-economic problems in Bengali, and he wrote a number of special articles, including cover page stories, in *Desh* (ABP publication) in the 1990s. He also wrote for a few more magazines in Bengali.

As a student, he was worried about the border guards who tried to maintain the so-called sanctity of economics, by insulating it from other branches of social science. He recalls that a well-known teacher of a reputed college of his time addressed his students 'as the chosen people of God'. Now, he is happy to find that the barrier has disappeared and economists of this time contribute to a better understanding of social problems with their econometric tools. When we asked him about the lesson that one can draw from his long teaching experience, he was found to be critical about exclusive dependence on classroom lectures. He indicated his clear preference for interactive sessions between teachers and students. His passion for teaching made him spend hours with the students not only in classrooms but also at his residence, and occasionally at the residence of students with a weak foundation of the subject. Students from different colleges and universities used to attend his classes and discussion sessions at his home. He believes that, given a proper mindset, teachers could also learn a lot from interactive sessions with their students. Intellectually vibrant relations with students last long and work for mutual benefit. He recalls how one of his students drew his attention to the fact that we cannot arrive at national GDP by summing up the state GDPs, and there has been no systematic difference between those sets of time series. He took great interest in this problematic issue and worked together to publish a paper jointly with him (*Journal of Income & Wealth*, 2013, Vol. 35, No. 1). Among other collaborative papers with his students, he mentions one as the first attempt to estimate the effect of land reforms on agricultural output growth during the left front regime (published in *Economic and Political Weekly*, 1998, Vol. 33, Nos. 47–48).

He actually came to be known in the field of research in economics for providing a statistical framework for the study of debt and dispossession in the Bengal districts covering the first four decades of the twentieth century. He published the work (*Peasant Paddy Production, Indebtedness and Dispossession, Delhi: MANAK*, 2004) long after it was done. While doing this work, he found that the basic premise of revising official crop data for Bengal agriculture was questionable, and taking the cue from his earlier work, he reported his view in a paper in *The Indian Economic & Social History Review,* 'The peasant economy of East and North Bengal in the 1930s….'. He argued against the hypothesis that there was a systematic downward bias in official crop estimates (or anawari estimates) and the multiplication of official crop figures for each year by a constant factor is questionable. Among his other works that he did without collaboration, he prefers to mention two

(1) 'Policy Environment and Agricultural Trends: Post-Independence India' in Binay Bhusan Chadhuri edited *Economic History of India from Eighteenth Century*

to Twentieth Century, Vol. VIII, Part 3 of History of Science, Philosophy and Culture in Indian Civilization, General Editor; D. P. Chattopadhyaya, New Delhi: Centre for Study in Civilization.

(2) 2015. 'Social Science Research in India: Some Methodological Issues' in R. K. Mishra, Jayashree Raveendran and K. N. Jehangir edited *Social Science Research in India and the World*, Chap. 6, pp. 138–54, New Delhi: Routledge.

When asked about his fond memories that have had a lasting impact on his personality development, he narrated how some members of his family were involved in the activities of the *Azad Hind Fauj* (Indian National Army) led by Subhas Chandra Bose, popularly known as Netaji, and passed through an uncertain time in Rangoon (renamed Myanmar) during World War II. After Singapore, Rangoon became the operational hub of Bose when the war in the eastern theatre was closing. Professor Sanyal's father and paternal uncle were actively involved in the movement launched by Bose. His sister, Ava Sanyal (Bagchi), and his nearest cousin, Late Mrinalini Sanyal (Dasgupta), joined the *Rani of Jhansi Regiment*. Ava, nicknamed 'baby' by Bose, was too young to handle bayonet and other weapons. She was finally given a job of nursing where she excelled and won a prize from Netaji for her good work.

Growing up listening to these stories, he never lost his mental calm while narrating the horrific events of those days like rushing to the safety of trenches, getting accustomed to the deafening noise of the low flying sorties and sometimes witnessing burning war planes falling from the sky. As a young child, he often collected sprinters that scattered around the compound of their residence. He now believes 'uncertainties and exceptions are the joys of life'.

Acknowledgements

This volume is a tribute to our teacher Manoj Kumar Sanyal. It is a comprehensive study of the Indian economy in the context of policy reforms since 1991. The framework for the volume took shape in initial conversations with Amiya Kumar Bagchi, who has been its guiding spirit. Professor Bagchi was kind enough to comply with our request to take part in organizing the book and contribute. We are thankful to him. The volume would not have been possible without the generous efforts of students and friends of Professor Sanyal. It is a pleasure to acknowledge their contributions and to offer them our thanks.

The volume was planned roughly 3 years back by us. We organized a workshop to review the works by the contributors in the Department of Economics, University of Calcutta, on 6 July 2018. We are grateful to the Head of the Department for providing the auditorium and other facilities, and we also acknowledge the active participation of the faculty members of the department and other colleagues as chairperson of the sessions and as discussants. We are thankful to Bibekananda Raychaudhury for his valuable comments on several chapters of this book. Sanjib Pohit deserves special thanks for his suggestion at different stages of publishing the book.

We gratefully acknowledge the care taken by Springer in publishing the book.

Pradip Kumar Biswas
Panchanan Das

Contents

Editors and Contributors

About the Editors

Pradip Kumar Biswas is Associate Professor at College of Vocational Studies (CVS), Delhi University, where he has been teaching since 1990. He did his MSc in Economics from the University of Calcutta, and MPhil and PhD from Jawaharlal Nehru University (JNU), Delhi. He has worked as a Post-Doctoral Fellow at the university UTAD, Portugal during 2009-10 and as a Senior Principal Scientist at CSIR-NISTADS Delhi during 2011-13. His research areas include MSME, agriculture, organisation, innovation, rural development, environment and industry. His works have been published in several Indian and international refereed journals, edited books and reports. He has published a book, 'Rural Industrialisation in West Bengal: Institutions, Innovations and Growth' (Manak Publishers, Delhi), and co-edited a book, 'India: Science and Technology, Volume 3' (CSIR-NISTADS).

Panchanan Das is Professor of Economics at the Department of Economics of the University of Calcutta, and teaches advanced econometric theory and analysis of cross section, time series and panel data. Development economics, Indian economics, and applied macroeconomics are the broad research areas of Prof. Das. He has published several articles in referred journals like *Economic and Political Weekly*, *Asian Development Review*, *Indian Journal of Labour Economics*, *The Journal of Income and Wealth*, *Int. J. Management Concepts and Philosophy*, *The Bangladesh Development Studies*, *The Journal of Industrial Statistics*, and *Journal of Quantitative Economics*. He is a principal author of 'Economics I and Economics II', and 'Microeconomics I and Statistics', published by Oxford University Press, New Delhi. He is a major contributor of West Bengal Development Report – 2008, published by

Academic Foundation, New Delhi, in collaboration with the Planning Commission, Government of India. He has also contributed in edited volumes published by Routledge, Springer, Edward Elgar, and Science and Technology volume of the CSIR.

Contributors

Amiya Kumar Bagchi has been in the profession of teaching economics since 1958. He has taught and researched in many universities, including University of Calcutta, University of Cambridge, University of Bristol, Cornell University, Roskilde University, Denmark. He is Founder Director of the Institute of Development Studies Kolkata and currently at the Institute as Emeritus Professor. He has published many articles and books.

Parthasarathi Banerjee is Professor, International Management Institute, New Delhi, former Dean, Goa Institute of Management and former Director, CSIR-NISTADS; has been in teaching and research for longer than three decades; and has published several books, edited as well as authored, research papers and reports on the broad areas of technological change, innovation and developmental issues and in select areas of comparative thoughts especially from Indian vantages; a book in this area by him is 'Biomedical Innovation in India' published in 2007.

Samaresh Bardhan currently teaches economics in the Department of HSS, Indian Institute of Technology Ropar. Before joining IIT Ropar, he worked for few years as Research Officer in RBI Endowment Unit of Industrial Finance at Centre for Studies in Social Sciences, Kolkata, and also taught at Panchmura College, a government-aided college under The University of Burdwan, West Bengal. He did his Ph.D. from Jadavpur University, Kolkata. He works in the areas of growth and finance, credit-related issues, issues related to bank regulations and loan default with special reference to India, climate finance and sustainable development.

Saumen Chatopadhyay is Professor and the present Chairperson of the Zakir Husain Centre for Educational Studies (ZHCES), Jawaharlal Nehru University, and holds a Doctor of Philosophy in economics from JNU. He has been working at ZHCES since 2004. Earlier, he worked at the National Institute of Public Finance and Policy (NIPFP), New Delhi. He has worked in various projects—The Role of Tax Heavens: In Global Governance and Regulation in the External Finance Equation, as Principal Researcher in a project funded by the Global Development Network (GDN) on social science research in India and Bangladesh, and Equalities in Public Private Partnerships (EQUIPPPS) as a part of an international collaboration with funding support from ESRC.

His areas of interest and specialization include economics of education with a focus on education policy, governance and financing of education; public finance with a focus on tax evasion and the black economy. His books include *Education and Economics: Disciplinary Evolution and Policy Discourse* published in 2012 by Oxford University Press and *Macroeconomics of the Black Economy* published by

Orient Blackswan in 2018 among other co-authored books and reports. He was involved in various national and international projects.

Debashree Chatterjee Sanyal is affiliated with Deloitte Australia's Financial Risk Advisory practice. Her current work is in the modelling and measuring of risk in the context of credit portfolios in the financial sector. She holds a Ph.D. in economics from Indian Institute of Technology Bombay. Her area of doctoral research was a micro-study of industrial agglomeration and technical efficiency in the Indian organized manufacturing sector. She has published earlier in the area of agricultural productivity in the Indian states.

Sadhan Kumar Chattopadhyay has 25 years of experience in teaching and research. He is presently working in Reserve Bank of India as Assistant Adviser in the Research Department. Before joining RBI, he worked as Senior Research Fellow in National Institute of Science, Technology and Development Studies (NISTADS), New Delhi. He has got several publications in economics journals and edited books. He has authored one book also.

Shrabani Mukherjee completed her M.Phil. and Ph.D. from Jawaharlal Nehru University. She is currently working as Associate Professor at Symbiosis School of Economics (SSE), Pune, India. She is also the head of 'Centre for Quantitative Economics' at SSE. Prior to it, she was Assistant Professor at Madras School of Economics. She had also served the Department of Economics, Birla Institute of Technology & Science (BITS)—Pilani (K K Birla Goa Campus); National Council of Applied Economic Research (NCAER), New Delhi; NIPFP; the Economic Advisory Council to the Prime Minister (PMEAC); the Public Finance unit of the Government Reforms and Infrastructure Development (GRID) division of PricewaterhouseCoopers Pvt Ltd in various capacities. She has published a number of articles/chapters in peer-reviewed national and international journals and edited books and has been an anonymous reviewer of international journals. She has attended several national and international conferences and training on advanced econometrics conducted by renowned international experts on the subject and given talks as a resource person in UGC national-level seminars.

Subhankar Mukherjee is Doctoral Candidate in the Economics Group at Indian Institute of Management Calcutta. He holds a bachelor's in mechanical engineering from Jadavpur University, Kolkata, and a one-year full-time management diploma from Indian Institute of Management, Lucknow. His research interest is in the area of economics of development. In his doctoral thesis, he is investigating the barriers to and impact of the adoption of crop insurance among Indian farmers.

Nitya Nanda is a research professional with more than two decades of experience in research, consulting and teaching. He worked on international trade, geopolitics, investment, resources, environment and development issues the political economy and the legal aspects of these in particular. He has been involved with about 40 research/consulting projects and in about half of them as the principal investigator.

Currently, he is Senior Fellow and Associate Director in The Energy and Resources Institute (TERI) - a premier environment think tank based in India. He has about 120 research publications. He has authored two books and edited four volumes.

Srinibas Nandy is working as Associate Professor in Raghunathpur College, Sidho Kanho Birsa University, West Bengal. Prior to teaching at this college, he worked as Revenue Officer of the Government of West Bengal. He did his Ph.D. in GATT from Ranchi University. He has jointly edited a book and conference proceedings and published articles in journals and local magazines. His areas of research interest are agriculture and value education.

Parthapratim Pal is currently Professor in the Economics Group at Indian Institute of Management (IIM) Calcutta. He joined IIM Calcutta in 2006 as Assistant Professor. He has been Full Professor since April 2014. He has Master's, M.Phil. and Ph.D. in economics from the Center for Economic Studies and Planning of Jawaharlal Nehru University, New Delhi. He has also received education from University of Cambridge, UK, and Harvard Business School, USA. He is currently Coordinator of the Centre for Development & Environment Policy at IIM Calcutta. He has also been Chairperson of the PGPEX programme in the same institute. Before joining IIM Calcutta, he has worked with TERI, ICRIER, Indian Institute of Foreign Trade (IIFT), New Delhi. He has more than 20 years of research experience. His recent areas of interest include international trade, regional trade agreements and regional cooperation, development issues, WTO-related issues and international capital flows. He has several publications in nationally and internationally reputed journals and books.

Debarati Chatterjee Ray is currently associated with Department of Management, University of Calcutta, as Guest Faculty. Previously, she was attached with different institutions like Umes Chandra College under University of Calcutta, ICFAI National College and St. Xavier's College, Kolkata. She holds a Master's from University of Calcutta and M.Phil. from Jadavpur University. She is also pursuing her doctoral work in the Department of Economics, University of Calcutta.

Debarshi Sanyal is Head of the Risk Modelling Function at the Australia and New Zealand Banking Group's global retail portfolios. He is responsible for the modelling and management of financial risk that facilitates credit decisions and capital allocation. His team has a significant contribution to the bank's capital sufficiency and efficient decision management and in effect contributes to the financial stability in Australia and New Zealand. He holds a Ph.D. in economics from Northern Illinois University (NIU), USA. His area of doctoral research was in the dynamics of lifecycle consumption of households in the US context. During his postgraduate coursework at NIU, he had also researched on the labour market effects of alcoholism in the USA.

Aishna Sharma is Guest Faculty in the Department of Economics and Public Policy, School of Management and Entrepreneurship, Shiv Nadar University. Her Ph.D. is in the area of economics of education, broadly pertaining to university governance. She has previously worked with National Institute of Public Finance and Policy as Project Associate, in a project on Functioning and Finances of Urban Local Bodies in Jharkhand. She later joined Institute of Applied Manpower Research where she co-authored the Indian Human Development Report, 2011, published by Oxford University Press. Her other publications include research chapters in edited volumes published by Routledge and Springer, among others. She has published a research paper on financial autonomy of universities, published by University News, a journal of Association of Indian Universities. She has also co-authored working paper in the area of urban finances at Georgia State University. Her interest lies in the areas of development economics, human development and economics of education.

Rajesh Sharma is currently Assistant Professor in the Department of Economics at Delhi Technological University, East Delhi Campus. He has completed a Master's in economics from Panjab University. He has completed Ph.D. in economics from Indian Institute of Technology Ropar, Punjab. He has 2 years of experience in the banking sector. He has contributed several research papers/chapters in edited books published by Springer, Taylor & Francis and Public Library of Science (PLOS). His areas of research include health economics and development economics.

Debdulal Thakur completed his M.Phil. and Ph.D. from Jawaharlal Nehru University, New Delhi, and is a socio-economist by training. Currently, he is Deputy Director and Associate Professor at Symbiosis School of Economics. Prior to this, he had served NIPFP, BITS—Pilani (K K Birla Goa Campus) and PricewaterhouseCoopers in different capacities. He is Life Member of 'The Indian Econometric Society' (TIES). He has extensively worked in the areas of fiscal policy, budgets, urban finance and economics of education for the last 9–10 years. He has co-authored a number of project-based reports funded by UNDP, UNICEF, ADB and DFID related to budgets and public expenditure, especially related to strengthening the fiscal and governance position of the urban local bodies in India.

He has been trained (by invitation) at the 'Intermediate Budget Workshop' held at Dar es Salaam, Tanzania (2007), organized by IBP, Washington, D.C., and Fundar, Mexico. He has also been selected to attend the Roundtable on India Municipal Finance Study organized by KIPF-NIPFP-GOI at Seoul, Korea, and delivered a short lecture on designing methodologies for Indian municipal finance study.

Chapter 1
Introduction

Pradip Kumar Biswas and Panchanan Das

India's economic reforms of the 1990s represent a watershed in the country's policy approaches towards development. Initially, in 1991 some reform measures were introduced to overcome the economy's emergency-like situation arose due to fiscal imbalances, severe shortage of foreign exchange and the resultant balance of payment crisis, triggered by the Persian Gulf War. This was followed by a series of major policy changes in line with the Fund-Bank strictures advocating stabilization and structural changes, which covered almost all the major economic issues and domain of activities, notably trade, foreign and corporate investment, licensing, reservation for small industries, banking and finance, health, education, insurance, labour laws, bankruptcy, retail trade, pricing of and trade in agricultural commodities, taxation and subsidies, and the like. Although the crisis situation eased and the economy stabilized within two years, the process of economic reforms has been continuing unabated, even intensified in some fields like trade, foreign investment, land markets and taxation partly due to WTO requirements and partly due to internal dynamics of the economy which calls for high growth and high investment including FDI.

In general, these reforms intended to transform the economy through the unfettered interplay of the first-order economic principles, namely protection of property rights, contract enforcement, market-based competition, appropriate incentives, sound money, debt sustainability through creating/strengthening relevant institutions. In the beginning, stabilization policies, aimed at achieving macro-economic stability through controlling inflation with the deflationary strategies of reducing excess demand, reducing fiscal and current account deficits to sustainable levels, devaluation of rupee, abolition of export subsidies, were quite successful in the short run, which within a short period restored higher growth rate of the economy together with stability. The growth needed to be accelerated over a longer period without

P. K. Biswas (✉)
CVS, University of Delhi, New Delhi, India
e-mail: pkbiswas1963@gmail.com

P. Das
Department of Economics, University of Calcutta, Kolkata, India

P. K. Biswas and P. Das (eds.), *Indian Economy: Reforms and Development*, India Studies in Business and Economics, https://doi.org/10.1007/978-981-13-8269-7_1

falling back to the problems of fiscal imbalances or balance of payment crisis. For this, the commonly prescribed instruments by the international financial institutions were structural reforms which were catalogued under ten major points in Washington Consensus, although later on many more points are added to augment the original Consensus. India's attempt to structural reforms began with straight forward implementation of all these ten points with varied intensities without considering the specific requirements and constraints of the highly diverse/heterogonous country, and thereafter throughout the two and a half decades these reform measures continued with further modifications, refinement and addition of complementary policies, also termed as second generation reforms, depending on the political strength of/mobilization by the ruling party/coalition.

Indian policymakers thus expected that the policies of de-reservation, de-licensing and privatization would accelerate growth through supply-side responses such as through removal of distortions and inefficiencies, easing movement of resources from sectors/activities with low productivity to those with higher productivity, which in turn raise total factor productivity and competitiveness. This would be aided by financial deregulation for smoothening free flow of funds from various sources. As a result resources, including land, would flow from the small and marginal farmers, and small enterprises to the corporates adding to economic inequality and destitution.

Allowing FDI would add to the stock of capital as well as the latest technology and know-how from which the domestic producers would benefit through collaboration and thus inculcate a culture of industrial dynamism with frequent innovations, diffusion and growth. Development of technology not only requires R&D or FDI but also steady supply of skilled manpower for which higher education sector needed to be revamped. An easy solution would be opening up of the higher education sector for private investment making the sector most lucrative investment destination. Inflexibility or sluggishness in adjustment, high costs or inefficiency would be found in other public sectors as well, such as health, banking and finance, insurance, civil aviation, railways, and above all, many of these sectors would be highly profitable for private venture and therefore there would be a great demand for liberalization of these sectors. Once the liberalization process sets in, it need not be restricted to inefficient ones, rather all those with high potentiality for private profit-making would be liberalized one after another. Thus, in the name of efficiency, quick response and growth dynamism, avoiding inflation and crowding out of private investments, controlling fiscal deficits and balance of payments, state withdraws from undertaking its traditional and primary responsibilities. Private enterprises would no doubt thrive in all these sectors but only for a short to medium term, till the captive markets remained unsaturated. On the other hand, costs of health, education and other public utilities, which are largely public goods, would go up drastically adversely affecting the poor and common people. Competition from the corporates and multinationals would threaten survival of the small producers in almost all the fields. In the name of cost cutting or efficiency, corporates would employ a large proportion of contract workers/casual workers and wherever possible contract out part of the regular jobs to the SMEs who often employ low-cost female workers.

Reforms would definitely affect the Indian farmers as the government commits to fiscal consolidation and adheres to WTO agreements. Fertilizers subsidies, irrigation subsidies, MSPs, tariffs and other non-tariff restrictions on trade of agricultural commodities would all be withdrawn or reduced to minimal level. It would raise the costs of production of the Indian farmers weakening their competitiveness in the global market. Further, the Model APMC act 2003 including its emphasis on contract farming would eliminate the traditional traders enabling direct contacts between corporates and farmers who would be exposed to the highly volatile national and world market. These poor farmers are unlikely to benefit from this market integration because of their weak bargaining position vis-a-vis monopsonist buyer. Furthermore, demand for lands for non-agriculture uses has been increasing at rapid rates and most of the states have been trying to create free market for land including lease. In case the demand is not matched by supply, states often make special act/provision to expropriate lands from farmers (as in many SEZs or Singur), who would lose their traditional source of livelihood.

Reform policies implemented in India have created substantial growth opportunities which would be appropriated by those who are resourceful, highly educated and skilled, whereas the common people, particularly, the poor and unskilled, would be deprived of any benefit and some would even lose their livelihood in the face of competition. Growth would thus be accompanied by rising inequality leading to social tension, which in turn would chock the growth process itself making it unsustainable in the long run. Growth would also widen regional inequality, as only selected regions/states would be able to create necessary infrastructure to attract investments leading to the problem of migration, urban congestion and regional conflict. Along with sustaining growth over a long period requires taking appropriate care of the aspect of equity, both interpersonal as well as inter-regional, because the existing institutions evolved over the ages have inbuilt mechanism of segregation, discrimination, deprivation across social hierarchy perpetuating inequality and poverty at high levels. Reform measures designed for growth must be simultaneously targeting reforming these institutions.

The book provides a comprehensive study of the policy reforms implemented in India over the quarter century since 1991, impact of these reforms in terms of growth of output, employment and productivity, changes in economic, industrial and organizational structures, performance across major sectors, inequality and poverty outcome and linking them with institutional changes. The book contains fourteen chapters including the introductory one.

Although each chapter of the book analyses different aspects of the economy, these chapters together represent an integrated picture of the economy in the aftermath of reforms.

In Chap. 2, Amiya Kumar Bagchi begins with a distinction between classical liberalism and neoliberalism. He observes that neoliberalism is another name for free-trade imperialism, which first Britain, followed by the USA, has practised consistently. While the effect of neoliberalism may have been to raise the rate of economic growth, it has raised the degree of inequality to unprecedented heights. Bagchi argues that the neoliberal policy has also proved disastrous for ordinary people, leaving them hungrier than before and subject to illnesses which go untreated or badly treated.

The study by Parthapratim Pal and Subhankar Mukherjee traces some challenges relating to use of some important trade policy instruments by India (Chap. 3). Recently, the two sets of instruments which have been used frequently to manage trade more effectively are the ‘Minimum Import Prices’ (MIP) and trade remedial measures like anti-dumping duties. This chapter focusses on these two sets of trade policy instruments to analyse the rationale behind their use. It has been suggested that while these instruments provide protection to some domestic stakeholders, other domestic players in the value chains may get adversely affected by these policies. This leads to some inter- and intra-sectoral trade-offs. The discussion in this chapter will lead to a broader debate about the neoliberal policies propagated by the World Trade Organization (WTO) and their conflict with policy space available to developing countries for managing trade policies to suit their national objectives.

Chapter 4 by Srinibus Nandi analyses critically the Agreement on Agriculture and identifies several loopholes of the domestic subsidy provisions, which would tell upon Indian agriculture. Subsidies are categorized in a particular manner and concessions are given to specific category(ies) of subsidies, like those in green box which deliberately favour developed country members by providing them instruments of backdoor protection of agriculture through manipulation of subsidy cuttings. On the other hand, it increasingly corners the weak members of the WTO including India while fulfilling commitments. For India, it has serious implications on its food security or agricultural development. Nandy has argued that the domestic subsidy provisions will continue to limit the potential gains of India from its agriculture unless the necessary revision in the provisions is done, and therefore, the study has suggested that India and other developing country members jointly extert pressure for revision of the agreements.

In Chap. 5, Shrabani Mukherjee and Debdulal Thakur critically analyse the government policies and performance of the Indian agricultural sector during pre-reform and post-reform periods. This study describes systematically the factors for poor agricultural performance after liberalization. They have noted that there has been structural shift in cropping pattern from food grains to non-food grains during the post-reform period. The slowdown in agriculture productivity is caused mainly by the factors like withdrawal of state support, poor implementation of policies, lack of infrastructure, technological lock-in, over burden of imports.

Chapter 6 by Debashree Chatterjee Sanyal and Debarshi Sanyal looks into the performance of the manufacturing industries by analysing technical efficiency at the firm level, controlling for known or expected determinants of technical efficiency and in particular testing the influence of a wide array of state-specific infrastructure parameters. They examine the role of spatial concentration of firms within a state on the technical efficiency of those firms. The study observes that the size of the firm has a significant positive contribution to technical efficiency for all of the major industries analysed. Government-owned firms are seen to be less efficient compared to their privately owned counterparts. The age of firms has different impact on efficiency across industry groups. Younger firms are seen to be more efficient in sectors including textiles and the chemical industry which includes pharmaceuticals. However, in the cases of petroleum and coke, machinery and equipment, automobiles and other transport sectors, younger firms are seen to be less efficient, likely due to the longer span required to break-even in these sectors.

The study by Debarati Chatterjee Ray focusses on the prevalence of productivity differential among firms with different scales of production across manufacturing industries in India (Chap. 7). To analyse the existence of productivity dispersion across different firm sizes for the manufacturing sector, this study uses factory-level data from the Annual Survey of Industries, the primary data source for registered manufacturing in India, for the period 2009–2012. Factory units of similar industries are grouped by their firm size into four categories (micro, small, medium and large) at the two-digit level of NIC (2008) by following the definitions as provided in MSME Act 2006. The study observes that the productivity dispersion is a deep-rooted problem as total factor productivity of the firms is widespread not only within an industry but even within a firm size of a specific industry.

Performance of the services sector as compared to agriculture and industry has been investigated since the late 1960s in India in Chap. 8 by Nitya Nanda. The study observes a little transformative change, except in the cases of telecommunication and information technology services. Even after reforms, neither the access to services nor the quality of services has been found to improve to any significant extent. The improvements found in some sub-sectors are primarily due to technological changes. Nanda notes the contrasting patterns in India's service growth process—'cost disease' substantially raises money value of services adding to GDP without increase in quantity of services in selected sub-sectors while in many other sub-sectors despite substantial addition of real services actual producers get little due to a large number of them being disguised unemployed. He argues that it is not only difficult to claim that India had service-led growth, maintaining overall growth with excessive reliance on the service sector can become difficult in future.

Chapter 9 by Pradip Kumar Biswas traces the evolution of the concept of the unorganized sector and then analyses the pattern of growth of the sector at disaggregated levels identifying the factors responsible for the growth, and the associated changes in productivity, after reforms. Biswas finds that the sector started with moderate growth of employment and number of enterprises in the 1990s, then experienced high growth during 2000s, but slowed down considerably in the first half of 2010s. Labour productivity growth was, however, found to be faster when employment growth was slower and vice versa. Since efforts were made to improve the quality of employment, not just growth of employment, the latter is studied together with changes in productivity and other conditions. Size-class-wise estimates reveal that relatively larger-sized enterprises like directory establishments could benefit more than the own account enterprises (OAEs), both in terms of share of employment and number of enterprises, during the post-reform period. Many of the OAEs operating at subsistence level found it difficult to survive due to influx of goods and services from the formal sector. Another notable consequence of the reforms is the growth of subcontracting enterprises.

The study by Panchanan Das explores how wage inequality is associated with workers' human capital and employment status during the high growth regime that started in the early 1980s in India with household and personal-level information from different NSS rounds of employment and unemployment survey (Chap. 10). The study observes that 'within' group inequality declined very slowly, but the 'between' group inequality increased markedly during this period. Conditional wage earnings at different quantiles have been estimated to locate the possible effects of human capital, particularly education, and employment characteristics. The quantile regression analysis suggests that the wage gap between workers at different percentiles increased over time during the high growth regime, and at a higher rate at the upper end of the wage distribution. The workers' schooling has favourable effect on wage income as expected. Wage income is increased with higher level of education at a higher proportional rate at higher percentiles in the wage distribution. As returns to education have significant impact on wage income, the wage distribution became more unequal because of the difference in access to education.

In Chap. 11, Sadhan Kumar Chattopadhyay demonstrates that after reforms in the early 1990s, the Indian banking sector has been able to transform itself from a traditional banking set-up to a modern universal banking system with the help of new technology. Using accounting measures approach, Chattopadhyay finds substantial improvements as regards efficiency, productivity and soundness, which in fact have moved towards best global standards after adoption of Basel norms. Significant achievement was observed in case of public sector banks without diluting social obligations. Public sector banks are now competing with the new private sector and foreign banks which operate in free environment. It has placed itself into a global standard in many aspects, including new product, service quality and improved payment and settlement system. However, at the same time lot of challenges are also being faced by the banking sector, which needs special attention.

Chapter 12 by Samaresh Bardhan and Rajesh Sharma studies the relationship between finance and growth at decentralized level. The study covers 355 districts for the period 2004–05 to 2010–11 and observes that the districts with higher level of financial development also experience higher growth of per capita income. The authors notice the relatively stronger effect of deposit than credit on economic growth indicating the importance of branch access in unbanked locations in district economy. The study highlights the significance of bottom-up approach of decision-making in which local financial conditions are as significant as fostering financial development at macro-level in the process of economic development and economic reforms play a significant role to this effect through various policy instruments meant for local economy. They also observe positive and significant effect of human capital that may activate alternative growth and production channels that are less finance-intensive.

In Chap. 13, Saumen Chattopadhyay and Aishna Sharma analyse the series of higher education reforms which have been mooted and implemented since the beginning of the liberalization phase in India. They have attempted to figure out the extent of publicness in higher education and in that context looked at the policy of market creation, allowing private players and competition in higher education and changes in governance of public institutions. They particularly trace out the possible implications for the nature of expansion, inclusion and excellence, autonomy of the higher education institutions, and question the applicability of the neoliberal approach given the specificities of the higher education sector.

Finally, in Chap. 14, Parthasarathi Banerjee analyses the impact of reforms on healthcare industry, particularly through its newfangled linkages with finance. The business of health care is currently undergoing a profound transformation. Global finance is forcing transformation of the public policies as well as of the private business of health care. Key to this strategic leverage is financialization of the personal body. Drawing precedence from the early modern state in Europe, Banerjee states that under the received practices of health sciences, this would take hold of personal body for disciplining, regimenting and shaping the unseemly mass through public provisioning of health services. Public hygiene and public health provisioning with minimum health care attempted capture of massed bodies in order that the mass bodies could obey rules and codes of mass body politics. He analyses how personal health is reconstructed as emergent envelopes of information getting generated continuously with ever-increasing risks and uncertainty. Palliative goals are now replaced with elusive envelopes of probable health status. These bodily states of affairs being inherently risky are profoundly financializable. Postmodern state, postmodern business and postmodern person are no longer incorporated. They have translated into flux of finance. Inter-bodily relations are passe.

Part I
Neoliberalism: Some Conceptual Issues and Implications for India

Chapter 2
Neoliberalism and Globalisation in India

Amiya Kumar Bagchi

Abstract The chapter starts with a distinction between classical liberalism and neoliberalism. It also notes that neoliberalism is another name for free-trade imperialism, which first Britain, followed by the USA, has practised consistently. While the effect of neoliberalism may have been to raise the rate of economic growth, it has raised the degree of inequality to unprecedented heights. It has also proved disastrous for ordinary people, leaving them hungrier than before and subject to illnesses which go untreated or badly treated for ordinary people.

2.1 Introduction

Neoliberalism is radically different from classical liberalism. In classical liberalism, in the writings of Adam Smith, Jeremy Bentham, while the market was regarded as the best coordinating mechanism, the state had an important role to play. In Viner (1927), he showed that although he believed in a natural order of harmony, in his *Wealth of Nations*, he made many qualifications, including the recognition of the role of the state in regulating the market. In particular, Smith called on the state to play an important role in providing elementary education to the people (Zajda 2004).

The foundation of the theory of free-trade imperialism was laid by Josiah Tucker in the eighteenth century (Semmel 1970; Bagchi 2014a). The analytical model that he used was later known as the theory of cumulative causation. Both Adam Smith and Tucker were against establishment of colonies by monopoly companies through granting of charters by their governments. Further, they were also against the granting of special privileges to producers in the home governments as it adversely affected the economic development of colonies. They were also against the British government's strive to silence the revolt of the thirteen American colonies. However, Smith did not oppose the Europeans conquering non-European peoples. But, Tucker's opposition to colonialism was in some ways more fundamental, based as it was on what could be called the Hume–Tucker theory of economic development (Bagchi 1996). According

---

A. K. Bagchi (✉)
Institute of Development Studies Kolkata, Kolkata, India
e-mail: amiya.bagchi@gmail.com

P. K. Biswas and P. Das (eds.), *Indian Economy: Reforms and Development*, India Studies in Business and Economics, https://doi.org/10.1007/978-981-13-8269-7_2

to Tucker, "Hume's essays on money and the balance of trade … were being read as implying that a rich country, through free trade, would necessarily be brought down to the same level of income as a poor country. This reading suggested that when a rich country trades with a poorer country, it will gain gold or silver (virtually the only international currencies of the time) for the goods it sells to the poorer. The access to that bullion, coined or uncoined, would raise prices all round in the richer country and eventually make its exports uncompetitive, so that bullion will flow out of the richer country until the prices and, by implication, incomes were equalised in the two countries" (Bagchi 2014a).

Bagchi noted that Tucker worked out the mechanisms of cumulative causation that kept the richer country ahead of the poorer as follows: "(a) the richer country, with better implements, infrastructure, a more extended trading network and more productive agriculture, would be more productive overall; (b) it would be able to spend more on further improvements; and (c) the larger markets of the richer country would provide scope for greater division of labour and greater variety of products" (Bagchi 2014a). Further, Tucker also highlighted that the rich countries also enjoyed several advantages as regards human resources and knowledge generation: "(a) it would attract the abler and more knowledgeable people because of higher incomes and opportunities; (b) it would be better endowed with information and capacity for producing new knowledge; and (c) a greater degree of competitiveness gained through higher endowments of capital, knowledge, ability to acquire more knowledge and capital and the energy of people with more capital and ability to generate more capital and knowledge in the richer country would make products cheaper. Finally, the larger capital resources of the richer country would lower interest rates and render investable funds cheaper" (Bagchi 2014a).

In practice, that iconic liberal, William Gladstone, stepped forward to regulate the British railways: 'The Regulation of Railways Act 1844 (7 and 8 Vict. c85) was pushed through Parliament by W. E. Gladstone, President of the Board of Trade, despite fierce opposition from the railway companies' (McLean 2002, p. 2). Jeremy Bentham's earlier writings and his monumental code, published in 1841, had strong influence on regulation of health, education and labour and led to the centralised state, hallmark of classic liberalism, replacing the decentralised administration hitherto characteristic of Britain (Roberts 1959, p. 195): 'In 1834 Parliament established the Poor Law Commission, in 1839 the Education Committee of the Privy Council, and in 1848 a Board of Health, each with a staff of professional servants who were to inspect local authorities'. Bentham's secretary, Edwin Chadwick, was "the architect of most of [that] state intervention", and that even the aristocracy in imposing "intervention on nearly every economic activity … practically always [kept] as close as possible to Bentham's model of artificial identification of interests by central authority and local inspection." (Ibid., p. 196). Although Chadwick dragged his feet about restricting women's labour, ultimately other reformers prevailed. Benthamites in the House of Lords included Lord Brougham and Lord Shaftesbury, who played leading roles in regulating first women's and children's labour and then the hours of work of adult male labour. Freedom of contract was multiply constrained almost as soon as it was enacted (Atiyah 1979).

In France, in 1881, under Jules Ferry's administration, made education in all primary schools free (Price 1987, pp. 316–320). In England, in 1870, the Education Act, known as Forster's Act was passed, embodied a commitment to nationwide provision for elementary education (Sutherland 1990, p. 142). In 1872, the Meiji state introduced a system of compulsory education for the capital, which was soon extended to the rest of the country (Rohlen 1992, p. 330). As in the case of other imperialist countries, such as Britain and Germany, the concern of the rulers for the health of army recruits led to the adoption of welfare measures such as provision of better and more extended health care and introduced a degree of egalitarianism in such provisions' in Japan (Bagchi 2005a, p. 191; Kasza 2002, p. 423). The apogee of the liberal state was reached in Western Europe during the Golden Age of Capitalism from 1945 to 1971 (Marglin and Schor 1990).

All this changed with the global adoption of neoliberal policies from the 1970s. The state left the regulation activities, education and health care entirely to a free-wheeling market. The only constant that remained was a centralised state at the service of capital legally and militarily. It is not often realised that the ideological foundation of neoliberalism was laid by a series of books sponsored by the OECD before it was inaugurated in the advanced capitalist countries of the UK and the USA by the administrations of Margaret Thatcher and Ronald Reagan, respectively. There was a study of India by Bhagwati and Desai (1970), a series of books on Brazil, Pakistan, Mexico and the Philippines, and a summary volume by Little, Scitovsky and Scott (1970). All these books advocated free trade and the withdrawal of the state from economic activities, even though at the time most of the advanced capitalist countries were highly protectionist and countries like the UK, France, Germany and Italy had large public sectors (for a critique, see Bagchi 1971).

Neoliberal policies also promoted globalisation for the benefit of the capitalists, especially of the advanced capitalist economies. The word "globalisation" has no commonly accepted meaning, although it is constantly used by politicians, journalists and academics. As it is applied to an economy and society, the word might mean the process of connecting it with the world in an intricate two-way network of flows of information, trade, finance, productive assets and people. No economy of the world is fully globalised in this sense. The advanced capitalist economies may be said to globalise in respect of most of these attributes but they typically still impose severe restrictions on movements of commodities and people from less developed countries and do not permit full flow of information to other countries. The process of globalisation may be imposed from outside or it may be induced by developments within the country concerned. A typical third-world country has globalisation imposed on it (Bagchi 1994, p. 18).

But the imposition of globalisation on developing countries always requires local collaborators. In India, a group of capitalists had benefited from government patronage of various kinds—cheap loans, cheap energy and a protected domestic market and practically free infrastructure costs began to chafe against various restrictions. From the time of the emergency itself, some restrictions on foreign investment in Indian enterprises were relaxed and enterprises' restrictions on expansion were relaxed. A big push towards neoliberal policies was started in Rajiv Gandhi's budget of 1985, when the estate duty was abolished and taxes were lowered on all incomes, including corporate incomes. China and India were the only two less developed counties of the world which were not caught in a debt trap. International organisations such as the World Bank and the International Monetary Fund (IMF) encouraged India to borrow heavily in the world market. Rajiv Gandhi complied: all project imports were granted foreign exchange automatically and were made free of import duties. I had argued at that time (Bagchi 1985) that these measures would lead to unsustainable balance of payments deficit, lead India into a debt trap and proponents of neoliberal policies would argue that there was no alternative (TINA) to adopting free market policies. Sure enough, by 1989–1990 already, India was experiencing large balance of payments deficits and the foreign exchange holdings of public enterprises were being clubbed together with export earnings. In the middle of 1990, the then Secretary of the Ministry of Commerce was predicting a devaluation of the rupee.

India formally adopted neoliberal policies from 1991 with P. V. Narasimha Rao as Prime Minister and Dr. Manmohan Singh as Finance Minister in return for an IMF loan to bridge over the crisis. The features of the agreed package were: a substantial devaluation of the rupee; lifting of all controls over capital issues; the abolition of the Industrial Regulation Act, restricting expansion of the capacities of factories; substantial lowering of import duties; and a promise to gradually ease out quantitative restrictions.

Before we move to the effects of the neoliberal policies on India's economic growth and the welfare of common people, let me look at a key international development that impacted the freedom of manoeuvre of developing countries. This was the signing of the treaty for the World Trade Organization which was signed in Cancun in Mexico in 1994 and came into effect in 1995. India's Commerce Minister also signed that treaty before any discussion had taken place in the Parliament. This is one of the defects of the Indian Constitution that the executive can take momentous decisions without informing the Parliament.

Under this treaty, all countries were required to bring down their subsidies by certain required percentages in a time-bound fashion. The developed countries had already readied themselves by giving huge subsidies to their usually very rich farmers, so that the same percentage decline in their subsidies had affected them less than the much smaller subsidies the developing countries gave their much poorer farmers. Moreover, all counties had to give access to their markets of imports from all countries. This meant that the farmers of poor countries would be unable to compete with the highly subsidised imports from developed capitalist countries, so the food security of many countries, already under threat because of structural adjustment policies sweeping sub-Saharan Africa and Latin America would be further endangered (Gonzalez 2002). When the Uruguay Round of negations on GATT were coming to an end, it was obvious that the Dunkel Draft of agreement (predecessor of the Sutherland draft) would prove highly damaging to the welfare of the people of developing countries (Bagchi 1992). This was soon confirmed by the rigorous analysis of Helpman who concluded: "Who benefits from tight intellectual property rights in less developed countries? My analysis suggests that if anyone benefits, it is not the South" (Helpman 1993, p. 1274). UN DESA 1995 (p. 113) also pointed out that the developing countries lost much of the differential treatment they had enjoyed under GATT. Furthermore, they could no longer use quantitative measures and had to use only price-based measures for addressing balance of payments difficulties.

The WTO brought three other major areas under its purview that had not been part of the General Agreement on Trade and Services (GATT). These were Trade-related Intellectual Property Rights (TRIPs), Trade-related Investment Measures (TRIMs) and General Agreement on Trade in Services (GATS). There was a long conspiracy from 1975, when Ed Pratt, the CEO of Pfizer, the world's largest pharmaceutical company, threatened by new competitors in the industry, began his campaign to include intellectual property rights and brought in other large corporations with him (Braithwaite and Drahos 2002).

Globalisation was also accompanied by a radical financialisation of the economy. Anything that was fungible was floated on the maelstrom of finance, from production flows of all kinds, services including education, health care, care and nurture, security services, and women's wombs (Bagchi 2017, Chap. 4), digitisation pervaded the economy, stratosphere itself came under the purview of private markets. 'Underlying all the so-called innovations in the Indian financial system are the following assumptions. First, it is a good thing to link up the operations of financial intermediaries of different kinds. Second, diversification of all kinds of portfolios is good. Third, the only firebreaks needed to minimise the risk of a financial and economic meltdown are those of prudential regulation and market discipline. Fourth, the compounding of systemic risk through greater connectivity of financial intermediaries can be minimised without the public authorities being prepared to act as risk absorbers of last resort. Fifth, greater concentration of economic power in land, finance and industry is necessarily a good thing, and there is no threat of further marginalisation of the Indian economy in a world completely dominated by transnational financial and industrial corporations. Sixth, reforms in the financial sector can be discussed without taking into account what is happening to the real economy' (Bagchi 2005b, p. 42).

With the arrival of mobile phones, all the spectra of radio waves became subject to wheeling and dealing. Not only old assets but areas that had been hitherto regarded as public assets such as sources of water were privatised and sold in the market. Financial innovations leaped ahead with these innovations. Securitisation and futures trading reached new degrees of sophistication. But all these innovations rendered economic life much more uncertain than before. Not only developing countries but advanced capitalist countries became prey to repeated financial crises. The USA experienced the Savings and Loans Associations crisis, the blowing and bursting of the dotcom bubble, and the financial crisis beginning with the bankruptcy of Lehman Brothers in 2007 and spreading to practically the whole of the world, only a few economies escaping it more or less unscathed (Bagchi 1992; Rajan 2005). Then there was a long winter of asset bubble in Japan stretching from the 1980s to the decade of the 1990s, finally ending the Japanese miracle (BIS 2005; Shirakawa 2009; UN DESA 1996, pp. 94–98; Bagchi 2018, p. 155). Then there was the Asian Financial crisis starting in Thailand, again a result of an asset price bubble and then engulfing Malaysia and South Korea (Bagchi 1998; Furman et al. 1998).

2.2 Effects on India

The immediate effect of the economic reforms was a slow-down in economic growth especially in the primary and secondary sectors. While the trend rate of growth between 1980–1981 and 1990–1991 was 3.5% in the primary and 7.0% in the secondary sector, they were 3.3% in the primary and 6.5% in the secondary sector, respectively, between 1980–1981 and 1995–1996 (Nagaraj 1997, Table 3). The rate of growth of agriculture, especially of food grains, plummeted further. The growth was also polarising, both regionally and in class terms. The regional inequality, "measured by the coefficient of variation in per capita SDP across the major states, has nearly doubled in 25 years since 1970–1971, from about 0.2 to 0.4…, the divergence in per capita income between the top three and the bottom three states has widened sharply since 1986–1987" (Nagraj 2000) (after the first bout of reforms were carried out under Rajiv Gandhi). Further, "the share of wages in value added, in current prices, has fallen from about 35% in 1985–1986 to about 20% in 1996–1997. During the same period, the profit share (measured by profit before tax, after depreciation and interest) has gone up by about 15% points—roughly equal to the fall in the wage share" (ibid).

One of the key postulates of economic reforms was that it would reduce balance of trade deficits and the size of the external debt. The external debt grew from US$70.9 million in 1990–1991 to US$85.9 million in 1996–1997. While the deficit did go down from US$9438 million in 1990–1991 to US$2798 million in 1991–1992, it again grew fast to US$14815 million in 1996–1997. This is because with relaxed rules for imports, they grew much faster. That the current account deficit did not grow that much was due to the fact that the inward remittances, mainly from West Asia, increased from US$2083 million in 1990–1991 to US$12435 million in 1996–1997 (Nayyar 2001, Table 2.1). This had nothing to do with economic liberalisation. You could argue that the workers working in West Asia, often under deplorable conditions were paying for the luxury imports of the rich in a neoliberal India.

Financialisation accompanied other reforms. "The Indian experience with reform in the financial sector indicates that, inter alia, there are three important outcomes of such reforms. First, there is increased financial fragility, which the 'irrational boom' in India's stock market epitomises. Second, there is a deflationary macroeconomic stance, which adversely affects public capital formation and the objectives of promoting employment growth and reducing poverty. Finally, there is a credit squeeze for the commodity producing sectors and a decline in credit delivery in rural India and small-scale industry" (Chandrasekhar and Pal 2006).

2.3 Turmoil in Stock Markets

The stock market began to boom soon after the formal inauguration of economic reforms in mid-1991. As the regulation of capital issues was abolished, the share

Table 2.1 Health indicators for the total population, scheduled castes and scheduled tribes in India

	Total population	Scheduled castes (Untouchables)	Scheduled tribes (Adivasis)
Infant mortality rate (per 1000)	57	66.4	62.1
Under 5 mortality rate (per 1000)	74.3	88.1	95.7
% of children undernourished (weight for age)	42.5	47.9	54.5
% of children without full immunisation	56.5	60.3	68.7
% of women with anaemia	55.3	58.3	68.5
% of births not delivered by a skilled provider	54.4	59.4	74.6

Source International Institute for Population Sciences (IIPS) and Macro International (2007)

of many companies began to double and treble within a few months. The boom was fuelled by a small group of bull operators of whom the most prominent was Harshad Mehta, who were financed by a few foreign banks, such as ANZ Grindlays Bank, Citibank, Bank of America and two major public sector banks, the National Housing Bank and Bank of Baroda in violation of Reserve Bank of India guidelines and prudential norms. A sum of at least Rs 5000 crore lent by the banks remained unaccounted for. J. Pherwani, the then chairman of the National Housing Bank, who had been a key player in the extension of the stock market (having chaired two committees relating to it appointed by the Reserve Bank: Misra 1997, p. 353) died under mysterious circumstances as soon as the so-called bank scam came into public view.

After that, the government decided to endow the Securities and Exchange Board of India (SEBI), established in 1988, with some real powers of monitoring and regulation of stock markets. But that did not prevent bulls and bears from operating in the stock market necessarily causing unpredictable fluctuations. The Bombay Stock Exchange index of stock prices rose from 500.3 in 1990–1991 to 1051.3 in 1993–1994, to 1537.3 in 1994–1995 and slid to 1189.6 in 1995–1996 and to 1061.0 in 1997–1998 (Bagchi 1999, Table 6).

In the budget of 2004–2005, long-term capital gains, that is, all capital gains kept locked for more than 365 days were exempted from tax. Moreover, it was held that any company with a joint venture in Mauritius and paying the 10% tax on its earnings would not have to pay any tax in India. The government lacked either the will or the means for verifying the nature or reality of the joint venture. This meant that any firm could park its foreign earnings in Mauritius, bring it back to India, invest in the stock market and/or real estate, keep it locked for 366 days and get by paying 19% on its original foreign earnings and zero tax on its new Indian gains, instead of having to 30%+ corporate tax.

On 10 May 2006, the Bombay Stock Exchange's 30-share Sensex touched a new high of 12,612.38 on persistent buying by foreign funds (*Hindustan Times*, 11 May 2006). After that date, however, despite some ups and downs, the tendency of the Sensex was mostly downwards [on 5 June 2006, the Sensex had gone down to 10,213.48 (*Hindustan Times*, 6 June, 2006)]. This was despite the fact that many banks and mutual funds, flush with liquidity and urged by the Ministry of Finance, had made heavy purchases in falling markets from time to time. FIIs had been heavy sellers in most developing country markets in Asia, but the outflow from India had been particularly heavy: between 12 and 23 May the FIIs had withdrawn \$1.32 billion from India (*Indian Express*, 25 May 2006). According to a later estimate India had lost \$2.6 billion in FII outflows between 12 May and 1 June 2006 (*Hindustan Times*, 2 June, 2006). Since the so-called emerging markets had seen the withdrawal of \$5 billion over that period, India accounted for more than half of the outflow. This indicates how vulnerable to global financial movements emerging markets in general and India in particular remain, despite the lollipops extended to the FIIs by an indulgent Indian government. Chandra (2008) argued that India, along with other developing countries, had to invest in zero- or low-return foreign exchange or US treasury bonds as a firewall against such vulnerability.

The government, ignoring the protest note of the Reserve bank of India representative Vinay Baijal on the committee to examine the inflow of foreign investment, encouraged the indiscriminate entry of foreign investment flows. The result was naturally a stock market bubble. Even more seriously it badly dented the growth of Indian exports from 2005 to 2006. The Reserve Bank of India had to intervene repeatedly to prevent the rupee going through the roof. That added to the government's debt. On the other hand, following the Fiscal Regulation and Budgetary Management Rule, both the central government and the bullied state governments pursued fiscal austerity, even after the 2008 global financial crisis had erupted. This naturally depressed economic growth further.

2.4 Impact on India's Human Development

Almost three decades of economic reforms in India has left the majority of the people in India hungry, malnourished and substantially illiterate (only about 74% of the people can meet the minimum standard of literacy). From the very beginning of economic reforms, the food grain consumption of Indians began to decline. "In the course of 1998–2003, the population of the Republic of India has been sliding down towards sharply lowered levels of food grains absorption, levels so low in particular years that they have not been seen for the last half century. Between the early 1990s and at present, taking three-year averages, the annual absorption of food grains per head has come down from 177 to 155 kg" (Patnaik 2004). Patnaik commented that "[s]uch low absorption levels were last seen in the initial years of World War II—from where they had fallen further still. Again, after some recovery…the food crisis of the mid-1960s [was] comparable to present average absorption levels" (Patnaik 2004).

After this, the government and establishment economists spent all their energy not to reverse these trends, but arguing there was a substantial substitution of milk, fruits, vegetables and meat in people's consumption baskets, as if the earnings of the poor left a lot of leeway for spending on all those expensive items. The result was that the "2017 Global Hunger Index released by the International Food Policy Research Institute (IFPRI) labelled India's hunger levels 'serious' and ranked the country 100, sandwiched between Djibouti and Rwanda and worse than North Korea ranked 93. India's position on the index—where countries are ranked on the basis of undernourishment, child mortality, child wasting and child stunting—has fallen from 55 among 76 countries in 2014 to 80 among 104 countries in 2015 and to 97 among 118 countries last year" (Telegraph 2018).

We conclude this section by taking a summary look at the health situation of Indians. Binayak Sen, a brilliant paediatrician, a Gandhian activist, who condemned Maoist violence, was arrested and thrown into jail as a terrorist, because defying the norms of the upper caste oppressors of Adivasis, he dared to serve those Adivasis. The need for Sen's intervention will be evident from Table 2.1.

2.5 Neoliberalism and Inequality

Inequality of income and wealth has skyrocketed during the neoliberal regime. It was estimated by Oxfam in 2018 that "last year, one billionaire was created every two days. This is the biggest increase in the number of billionaires in history and a whopping 82% of all of the wealth generated between the second quarter of 2016 and the corresponding period last year went to the top 1%, according to the latest survey by Oxfam" (*Business Today (BT)* 2018). Last year's survey had further showed that "India's richest 1% held 58% of the country's total wealth, which was higher than the global figure of about 50%. According to the latest survey, the wealth of this elite group increased by over Rs 20.9 lakh crore during the period under review—an amount close to the total expenditure estimated in the Union Budget 2017. India's top 10% of the population now holds 73% of the wealth while 67 crore citizens, comprising the country's poorest half, saw their wealth rise by just 1%" (BT 2018).

The wealth of the Forbes list of the one hundred wealthiest Indians in 2017 totalled $468.74 billion. That list included only three Muslims and one lower caste man. The rest all belonged to upper castes. According to Credit Suisse, the value of India's total wealth in 2017 was $4987 billion. Thus, the wealth of these 100 billionaires was nearly equal to 10% of the total wealth of India. This degree of concentration of wealth in the pockets of mostly upper caste billionaires, generally with right-wing values, bodes ill for Indian democracy, and there is little doubt that almost complete deregulation of all markets contributed mightily to that outcome.

2.6 Workers Under the Neoliberal Regime

In India, workers only within a small well-defined organised sector enjoyed some degree of protection. In 1947, the Industrial Disputes Act (IDA) was passed, which required the permission of government for workers to be laid off in factories. A 1976 amendment, inserted in Chapter VB in IDA, restricted the employer's firing power in factories employing 300 workers or more. In 1982, another amendment brought down that threshold to 100. Although the whole organised sector, including government administration, large trading and financial organisations never employed more than 10% of the labour force, the little protection enjoyed by large industrial establishments came under attack under the neoliberal regime. It was argued that the rigidity of the labour market created by Chapter VB of the IDA dampened the incentive to invest in industry of capitalists in manufacturing and hampered economic growth. And mainstream economists came forth to support the official argument. Besley and Burgess (2004) constructed an index of employer-friendliness, in which a score of +1 was given if a state's laws were employer-friendly, a score of 0 if it was neutral and a score of −1 if it was judged to be worker-friendly. They came to the conclusion that states that were worker-friendly had lower rates of industrial growth.

Bhattacharjea (2006) critiqued the Besley–Burgess (BB) findings. It was shown that "BB misinterpreted several of the state-level IDA amendments; assigned identical scores to minor procedural amendments and major changes in job security rules; aggregated incommensurable pro-worker and pro-employer amendments occurring in the same year to give a summary score of +1 or −1 to a state for that year; used a misleading summation of these scores over time (so that a state that passed amendments in different years was assigned a higher score than one that passed the same amendments simultaneously); and ignored hundreds of other labour laws, including some whose provisions overlap with the IDA" (Bhattacharjea 2009). He also highlighted that BB strangely characterised Gujarat as pro-worker, and that the interpretation of their results in the World Bank's 2004 World Development Report was entirely unwarranted (2009, p. 55). Bhattacharjea "undertook a detailed assessment of state-level legislative and judicial changes which showed that attempts by earlier authors to quantify state labour regimes were riddled with errors. The earlier literature also overlooked some possibilities regarding the mode and timing of firms' adaptation to EPL, and also limitations in the data it relied upon" (2009, p. 61).

The government's attack on workers' earnings as a cost-minimising exercise is also ridiculous in a situation in which workers' share in value added in manufacturing enterprises has come down in registered manufacturing from about 25% in the 1980s to a little above 10%. In 2014–2015 it had declined to below 15% (Fig. 2.1).

Moreover, the Indian labour market has always been flexible. A principal instrument used by employers has been the wide-spread employment of contract labour in manufacturing. It increased from about 12% in 1990 to about 23% in 1992. In states like Andhra Pradesh, the increase was from 40% in 1990 to 62% in 2002 (Sharma 2006, p. 2081). Neoliberal reforms also impacted adversely on employment. Employment as a whole increased at an annual rate of 2% from 1961 to 1990, when the rate

Fig. 2.1 Labour share in GVA in registered manufacturing in India

Note: I am indebted to Panchanan Das for these calculations
Source: The figures are based on ASI data.

of GDP growth was only 3.5% per annum. It decelerated to 1.5% during 1990–1992 and further to 1% annually during 1993–2000 (Ibid, p. 2079).

2.7 Concluding Remarks

Neoliberalism thrives in practically in every country of the world, in spite of the fact that it has led to a greater inequality in every dimension of the human condition and led to enormous degree of underemployment and unemployment in the world, not only because the controllers of the state in every country use the repressive apparatus to coerce the revolting populace but also because it has a seductive appeal for the deprived. It has been well captured by Sukumar Roy's satirical poem, Chandikhurorr kal (the machine designed by Uncle Chandi) in which a banana is tied in front of a man, and the more he runs to get hold of the banana, the more it recedes before him. Albert Hirschman's tunnel parable (Hirschman and Rothschild 1973) analysed that the growth and inequality could substantially influence the evaluation by the people of their current and future economic opportunities at different stages of economic development. "The 'tunnel effect' describes the initial tolerance of increased inequality resulting from uneven economic growth processes on the part of relatively disadvantaged members of society, who, expecting to catch up and benefit in the near future, drew gratification from the improved income situation of others. If this moment of catching up did not arrive, however, the initial tolerance could switch, giving way to feelings of falling behind, envy and grievance and possibly resulting in social upheaval" (Flechtner 2013).

In a seminal article, Friedman and Savage (1948) had neatly captured the aspiration effect of the success of a few on the aspirations of the laggards. An individual may gamble for a large prize, knowing that the chance of obtaining that prize is slim. Thus, for example, in the lawyers' profession in India, only a few may earn crores of rupees a month, many individuals may enter it and do not do at all well. It will not deter the other aspirants who will crowd into the profession. Thus if we plot the lawyers' income on a two-dimensional diagram, it will have a very long tail at the end of which the curve will shoot upwards in almost in an unbounded fashion, with only a few individuals clustering there.

Neoliberal capitalism has made particular targets of children, stimulating their greed and often also rousing their violent instincts (Schor 2003, 2005). Thanks to the proliferation of electronic media portraying all kinds of sexual behaviour including child abuse, large numbers of children, especially in poor countries like India, are trafficked to satisfy the unnatural appetites of the customers. That kind of trafficking along with the trafficking of women has become a multi-billion dollar industry (Bagchi 2014b).

References

Atiyah, P. S. (1979). *Rise and fall of the freedom of contract.* Oxford: Clarendon Press.

Bagchi, A. K. (1971). The theory of efficient neo-colonialism. *Economic and Political Weekly, 6*(30–32), 1669–1676.

Bagchi, A. K. (1985, May). Hijacking the Indian economy. *The Herald Review.*

Bagchi, A. K. (1992, May 30). Transnational banks, US power game and global impoverishment. *Economic and Political Weekly*, 1130–1136.

Bagchi, A. K. (1994). Globalising India: The fantasy and the reality. *Social Scientist, 22*(7), 18–27.

Bagchi, A. K. (1996). Colonialism in classical political economy: Analysis, epistemological bradening and mystification. *Studies in History, N. S., 12*(1), 105–136.

Bagchi, A. K. (1998). Growth miracle and its unravelling in east and south-east Asia: Unregulated competitiveness and denouement of manipulation by international financial community. *Economic and Political Weekly, 33*(18), 1025–1042.

Bagchi, A. K. (1999). Globalisation, liberalisation and vulnerability: India and the third world. *Economic and Political Weekly, 34*(45), 3219–3230.

Bagchi, A. K. (2005a). *Perilous passage: Mankind and the global ascendancy of capital.* Lanham MD: Rowman & Littlefield.

Bagchi, A. K. (2005b). Rural credit and systemic risk. In V. K. Ramachandran & M. Swaminathan (Eds.), *Financial liberization and rural credit in India* (pp. 39–49). New Delhi: Tulika.

Bagchi, A. K. (2014a). Contextual political economy, not Whig economics. *Cambridge Journal of Economics, 38*(3), 545–562.

Bagchi, A. K. (2014b). An iron law of interconnectedness of child labour, bonded labour, and human trafficking. *Indian Journal of Labour Economics, 57*(1), 93–110.

Bagchi, J. (2017). *Interrogating motherhood.* New Delhi: Sage and Stree.

Bagchi, A. K. (2018). The 1990s: Fall of the Berlin Wall, globalization, and crises. In J. A. Ocampo, A. Chowdhury, & D. Alarcon (Eds.), *The world economy through the lens of the United Nations* (pp. 148–169). New York: Oxford University Press.

Bhagwati, J. N., & Desai, P. (1970). *India: Planning for industrialization and trade policies since 1951.* Oxford: Oxford University Press for OECD.

Bhattacharjea, A. (2006). Labour market regulation and industrial performance in India: A critical review of the empirical evidence. *Indian Journal of Labour Economics, 49*(2), 211–232.

Bhattacharjea, A. (2009). The effects of employment protection legislation on Indian manufacturing. *Economic and Political Weekly, 44*(22), 55–62.

Besley, T., & Burgess, R. (2004). Can labour regulation hinder economic performance? Evidence from India. *Quarterly Journal of Economics, 119*(1), 91–134.

BIS. (2005, April). *Real estate indicators and financial stability* (BIS paper no. 21). Bank for International Settlements.

Braithwaite, J., & Drahos, P. (2002). *Global business regulation*. Cambridge: Cambridge University Press.

Business Today. (2018). *Income inequality gets worse; India's top 1% bag 73% of the country's wealth, says Oxfam*. https://www.businesstoday.in/current/economy-politics/oxfam-india-wealth-report-income-inequality-richests-poor/story/268541.html.

Chandra, N. K. (2008). India's foreign exchange reserves: A shield of comfort or an albatross? *Economic and Political Weekly, 43*(14), 39–51.

Chandrasekhar, C. P., & Pal, P. P. (2006). Financial liberalisation in India: An assessment of its nature and outcomes. *Economic and Political Weekly, 41*(1), 975–988.

Flechtner, S. (2013). 40 years after Hirschman's tunnel parable: Income inequality, economic development and aspirations in Latin America. In *Paper Prepared for the IARIW-IBGE Conference on Income, Wealth and Well-Being in Latin America*, 2013, September 11–14. Rio de Janeiro, Brazil.

Friedman, M., & Savage, L. J. (1948). Utility analysis of choices involving risk. *Journal of Political Economy, 56*(4), 279–304.

Furman, J., Stiglitz, J. E., Bosworth, B. P., & Radelet, S. (1998). Economic crises: Evidence and insights from east Asia. *Brookings Papers on Economic Activity, 1998*(2), 1–135.

Gonzalez, C. G. (2002). Institutionalizing inequality: The WTO agreement on agriculture, food security, and developing countries. *Seattle University School of Law Digital Commons.*

Helpman, E. (1993). Innovation, imitation, and intellectual property rights. *Econometrica, 61*(6), 1247–1280.

Hirschman, A. O., & Rothschild, M. (1973). The changing tolerance for inequality in the course of economic development. *The Quarterly Journal of Economics, 87*(4), 544–566.

International Institute for Population Sciences (IIPS) and Macro International. (2007). *National family health survey, 2005–2006*. Mumbai: IIPS.

Kasza, G. S. (2002). War and welfare policy in Japan. *Journal of Asian Studies, 61*(2), 416–435.

Little, I., Scitovsky, T., & Scott, M. (1970). *Industry and trade in some developing countries*. Oxford: Oxford University Press for OECD.

Marglin, S. A., & Schor, J. (Eds.). (1990). *The golden age of capitalism*. Oxford: Clarendon Press.

McLean, I. (2002). The origin and strange history of regulation in the UK: Three case studies in search of a theory. In *Paper for ESF/SCSS Exploratory Workshop: The Politics of Regulation, Barcelona* (November 2002).

Misra, B. M. (1997). Fifty years of the Indian stock market. *Reserve Bank of India Occasional Papers, 18*(2 & 3), 351–363.

Nagaraj, R. (1997). What has happened since 1991? Assessment of India's economic reforms. *Economic and Political Weekly, 32*(44–45), 2869–2879.

Nagaraj, R. (2000). Indian economy since 1980: Virtuous growth or polarisation? *Economic and Political Weekly, 35*(32), 2831–2839.

Nayyar, D. (2001). Macroeconomic reforms in India: Short-term effects and long-term implications. In W. Mahmud (Ed.), *Adjustment and beyond: The reform experience in south Asia* (pp. 20–46). New York: Palgrave.

Patnaik, U. (2004). The republic of hunger. *Social Scientist, 32*(9/10), 9–35.

Price, R. (1987). *A social history of nineteenth-century France*. London: Hutchinson.

Rajan, R. G. (2005). *Has financial development made the world riskier?* (NBER Working paper 11728).

Roberts, D. (1959). Jeremy Bentham and the Victorian Administrative state. *Victorian Studies, 2*(3), 193–210.

Rohlen, T. P. (1992). Learning: The universalization of knowledge in Japanese political economy. In Kumon & Rosovsky (Eds.), (pp. 321–363).

Schor, J. B. (2003). The commodification of childhood: Tales from the advertising front. *The Hedgehog Review, 5*(3).

Schor, J. B. (2005). *Born to buy: The commercialized child and the consumer culture*. New York: Scribner.

Semmel, B. (1970). *The rise of free trade imperialism: Classical political economy, the empire of free trade and imperialism 1750–1850*. Cambridge: Cambridge University Press.

Sharma, A. N. (2006). Flexibility, employment and labour market reforms in India. *Economic and Political Weekly, 41*(21), 2078–2085.

Shirakawa, M. (2009, April 23). "Way out of Economic and Financial Crisis: Lessons and Policy Actions," Speech at Japan Society in New York. Available at http://www.boj.or.jp/en/type/press/koen07/ko0904c.htm.

Sutherland, G. (1990). Education. In Thompson (Ed.), (vol. 3, pp. 119–169).

Telegraph. (2018, October 13). Alarm as India skids on global hunger list. *The Telegraph (Kolkata)*.

Thompson, F. M. L. (Ed.). (1990). *The Cambridge social history of Britain 1750–1950* (Vol. 1–3). Cambridge: Cambridge University Press.

UN DESA. (1995). *World economic survey 1994*. New York: United Nations, Department of Economic and Social Analysis.

UN DESA. (1996). *World economic survey 1995*. New York: United Nations, Department of Economic and Social Analysis.

Viner, J. (1927). Adam Smith and Laissez faire. *Journal of Political Economy, 35*(2).

Zajda, J. (2004). Decentralisation and privatisation in education: The role of the state. In *AARE 2004*. University of Melbourne (November 29, Session 2 [2 p.m.–4 p.m.], pp. 1–20).

Chapter 3
You Win Some, You Lose Some, and Some Get Rained Out: A Study of Some Recent Trade Policy Instruments Used by India in the Context of Neoliberalism

Parthapratim Pal and Subhankar Mukherjee

Abstract In an era when free trade has been championed by neoliberal policies across the world, there is surprisingly high usage of trade-restricting measures adopted by developed and developing countries. While dissatisfaction with the neoliberal doctrine of free trade is the most important reason behind these policies, it also symbolizes a return of nation-states against the forces of globalization. Policymaking in international trade can be tricky as several trade policy instruments can have very different impact on different domestic stakeholder groups. This chapter discusses these challenges using a study of the usage of trade policy instruments by India. In the last few years, India is seen to be using a number of policies aimed toward managing trade more effectively. The two sets of instruments which have been used frequently are the 'Minimum Import Prices' (MIP) and trade remedial measures like antidumping duties. This chapter will focus on these two sets of trade policy instruments to analyze the rationale behind their use. Recent controversies around these instruments suggest that while they give protection to some domestic stakeholders, other domestic players in the value chains may get adversely affected by these policies. This leads to some inter- and intra-sectoral trade-offs. This discussion will lead to a broader debate about the neoliberal policies propagated by the World Trade Organization (WTO) and their conflict with policy space available to developing countries for managing trade policies to suit their national objectives.

3.1 Introduction

International trade and trade policy are going through major changes in the last few years. It appears that growing imbalances and tensions of globalization are leading to policy shifts in many of the developed countries. There is a strong belief among economists that these are reactions to a phase of fast and sometimes forced integration

P. Pal (✉) · S. Mukherjee
IIM Calcutta, Calcutta, India
e-mail: parthapal@iimcal.ac.in

P. K. Biswas and P. Das (eds.), *Indian Economy: Reforms and Development*, India Studies in Business and Economics, https://doi.org/10.1007/978-981-13-8269-7_3

of countries in a global economic network. Some economists, including Rodrik (2016, 2017) and Subramanian and Kessler (2013), call this 'hyper-globalization.' As Rodrik (2017) suggests, since the 1990s the world was pushed toward hyper-globalization. During this period, economic and political forces acted in a way that transformed globalization from being a means for national economic prosperity to becoming the end. Consequently, domestic priorities of countries gave way to the requirements of globalization. Financial institutions, multinational firms, and global multilateral organizations shaped the rules for globalization which often superseded national policy priorities. According to Rodrik, too much focus on free movement of capital and establishment of institutions like the World Trade Organization helped this period of hyper-globalization.

While globalization since the 1990s has yielded some benefits within and across countries, these benefits have not been evenly distributed. While it has benefited a group of people, it has also marginalized a significant part of the population. Inequality has increased alarmingly across the world, and the generation of remunerative employment in adequate numbers has become a challenge for domestic policymakers. Using a cross-country panel data with 147 countries and for the period 1970–2014, Lang and Tavares (2018) show that while globalization has benefited income of the countries in their early and medium stages of globalization, marginal returns from globalization diminish as the process moves on. More integrated countries benefit progressively less from further integration. This chapter also finds that the gains from globalization are concentrated at the top of national income distribution and in many countries have not helped the income of the poor in any significant way. The authors indicate that the process of globalization has led increased within-country inequality and higher global inequality of incomes between individuals.

Along with rising income inequality, there has been a rapid rise of market concentration among the firms engaged in international trade. The UNCTAD Trade and Development Report 2018 (UNCTAD 2018) highlights that in the era of hyper-globalization, expansion of trade has been driven to a large extent by the growth of global value chains (GVCs). These GVCs are mostly governed by lead firms headquartered in developed countries. According to TDR 2018, developing country shares in value added in manufacturing output have declined in all countries except for China. The report indicates that developed country firms are appropriating more and more value added from the GVCs and the distribution of benefits is getting more skewed against developing country firms participating in the GVCs. According to the estimates published in the report, 'after the global financial crisis, the 5 largest exporting firms, on average, accounted for 30% of a country's total exports, and the 10 largest exporting firms for 42%' (UNCTAD 2018, page v).

The rise of the power of large firms and pegging of the developing country firms at the lower end of the value chain has another profound implication. In a globalized world, restrictions on movement of tangible assets have gone down significantly. Technology and network of subsidiaries of multinational corporations (MNCs) has ensured that both tangible and intangible assets can be swiftly moved from one country to another without incurring significant cost. As most developing country firms are operating at the lower end of the value chain, search and training costs associated with such movements are also not very high. This ability to move capital countries has led to asymmetric power relations between lead firms and suppliers in the GVC. Workers have lost their bargaining powers, and it has allowed the creation of GVC-led enclave economies with very low spillover into the domestic market. Along with these, factors like strength of intellectual property rights, first mover advantage of the lead firms from developed countries, use of market power, and other uncompetitive practices by the dominant firms have further exacerbated the skewed income distribution pattern associated with globalization. The entry barriers caused by intellectual property rights, economies of scale and scope, and regressive taxation practiced by many countries have created an unequal playing field. UNCTAD (2018) suggests that the growing domination of the MNCs/TNCs has been instrumental in pushing down global labor income share.

The period of hyper-globalization has coincided with rising trade in services and rapid financialization and digitalization of international business. The problem of dominance of top firms is even more severe in these sectors. A glimpse of this dominance can be seen from the market capitalization numbers of these companies. Data published by UNCTAD (2018) show that share of top 1% companies from technology, software, and IT services sector in total market capitalization has increased from 27% in 1996–2000 to 52% in 2009–2015. Digital and financial services businesses are largely driven by knowledge and data, which are often protected by strong intellectual property rights. Along with this, the scale and network economies associated with these businesses create few highly profitable large firms with significant entry barriers for smaller firms. This leads to a market structure which can be summarized as 'winner-takes-most.'

The process of hyper-globalization coupled with extreme dominance of very large firms has started receiving some pushback in recent years. Growing inequality of income and opportunities has led to a popular backlash against the spirit of globalization. Strong social and political opposition are seen against the neoliberal doctrine of free movements of goods, services, and factors of production. For example, the UK has decided to move away from the European Union (BREXIT), the USA is increasing protection against imports from many countries and is actively renegotiating some of its free trade agreements (FTAs), and many developing countries are also adopting more interventionist trade policy measures. Sometimes the rules of international trade set by multilateral and regional institutions are being challenged and violated. Most countries are adopting mercantilist policies and are trying to maximize their net exports for their domestic gains.

It appears that there is a growing tendency to move away from neoliberal market fundamentalism. However, as many economists have pointed out, along with its dependence on 'free market,' neoliberalism has a second objective. It uses the state to engineer a redistribution of income and assets in favor of finance capital and big business (Chandrasekhar 2018). This is a trend which is becoming more visible globally. Big business and the super-elite are attempting to influence policymaking to their benefit. This is spilling over in the policy measures adopted by the countries. This includes selective incentives, allowing exploitation of government incentives and government inaction on deliberate rules violation by the big businesses.

India is also following a similar path. While incidence of trade restrictive measures has increased, many of these measures are allegedly benefitting the large corporations. During this period, India is seen to be using several policies aimed toward managing trade more effectively. After many years of unilateral liberalization, India has raised tariffs during the annual budget of 2018–19. There has been a marked increase in safeguard instruments to control imports. Even WTO incompatible measures like 'Minimum Import Prices' (MIP) have been introduced. India is also using various export incentive measures including interest rate subsidies for the exporters and direct export subsidies.

Against this backdrop, this chapter focuses on some trade policy instruments used by India to understand how these policies have affected different sectors in India. The study is structured in the following manner. Section 3.2 discusses some trade policy measures used by India and how effective those measures have been. Section 3.3 discusses import-restricting measure called minimum import price (MIP) imposed by India on the steel sector, and Sect. 3.4 analyzes the problems with special economic zone policy (SEZ) which was designed to be a policy to incentivize exports. Section 3.5 concludes the chapter.

3.2 Trade Policy Measures Adopted by India

After joining WTO in 1995, India had to reorient its trade policy to match its commitments made in the WTO. Normally, it would imply that India had to remove all its quantitative restrictions (QR) or quotas and tariffs would be the only allowed trade policy measure to protect its domestic market. However, due to the balance of payments problems faced by India, it was allowed to maintain QRs on some items. These were removed in 2011 after India lost a WTO dispute settlement case with the USA.[1] Since 1995, India also has signed a large number of free trade agreements (FTAs) and aggressively reduced its tariff rates. It can be said that after joining WTO, India tried to be part of the bandwagon of hyper-globalization. Rapid import liberalization by unilateral reduction of tariff and non-tariff barriers exposed Indian industries to international competition. Chaudhuri (2015) suggests that hasty import liberalization may have damaged the Indian domestic sector.

India's balance of payment data tends to support the claims by Chaudhuri (2015). Since India has officially moved to a tariff-only regime, it has faced chronic problems with its current account deficit (CAD). As Fig. 3.1 shows, India's CAD has been negative for most of the period and India's merchandise trade balance has always been negative since 1995. Also, the share of manufacturing sector in India's GDP is showing steady decline and reports indicate that it has reached an all-time low of

[1] DS90: India—Quantitative Restrictions on Imports of Agricultural, Textile and Industrial Products. Available at https://www.wto.org/english/tratop_e/dispu_e/cases_e/ds90_e.htm. Accessed 8th December 2018.

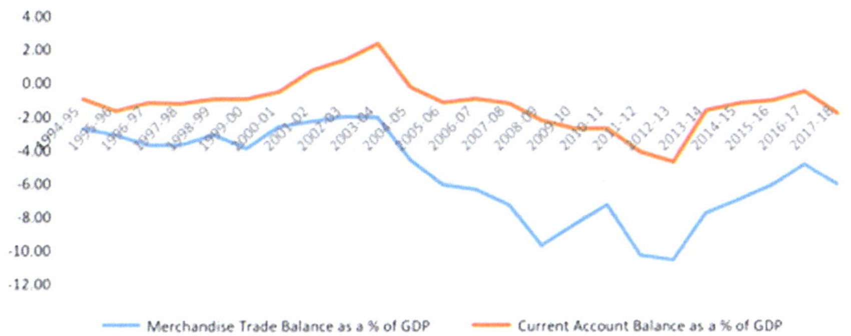

Source: Reserve Bank of India

Fig. 3.1 India's merchandise trade balance and current account balance as a percentage of GDP

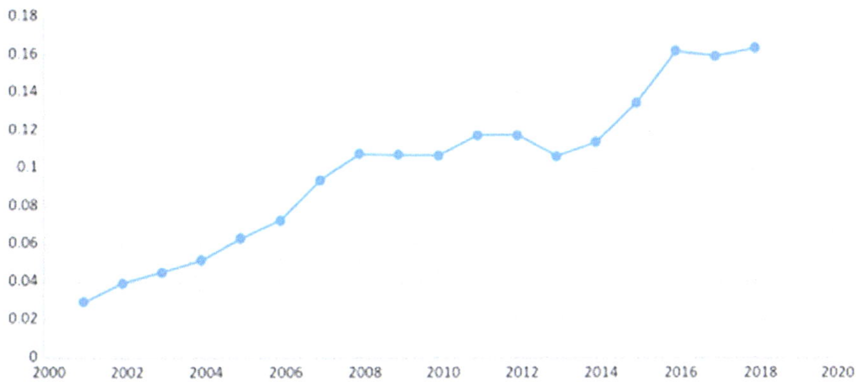

Source: CMIE Tradedx Database

Fig. 3.2 India's import from China as a ratio of total imports

15% in 2017.[2] Also, there has been a very sharp rise in imports of goods from China since its accession to WTO in 2001 (Fig. 3.2).

Faced with these problems, the government of India announced several steps to improve the manufacturing sector. The government announced a package called 'Make in India' in 2014 to incentivize the manufacturing sector and draw foreign direct investment (FDI) to India. A number of trade policy measures were also introduced to boost exports and protect the domestic economy from imports. After years of unilateral liberalization and reduction of tariff rates, the government started increasing tariffs on a number of items since 2017. The annual budget of 2018–19 increased most favored nation (MFN) tariff rates on around 50 products. But India did not

[2]https://www.cnbctv18.com/economy/share-of-manufacturing-in-indias-gdp-falling-despite-make-in-india-360521.htm. Accessed 8th December 2018.

change any preferential tariff rates and these tariff increases did not affect any of the countries that have entered into FTAs with India.

Along with increase in tariff rates on a number of products, India also used several trade remedial measures like the antidumping duties and countervailing duties. India, in fact, is one of the most prolific users of antidumping duty among the WTO member countries. Along with these, India has also used unconventional import-restricting measures like the minimum import price (MIP). As it will be discussed below, the MIP was not a WTO compatible measure and India was challenged by other WTO member countries when it imposed this measure.

On the export front, the government has tried to incentivize exports through a number of export promotion schemes. In 2006, the government introduced a new set of laws to promote special economic zones (SEZs) in the country. These laws allow units operating from SEZs a number of fiscal and non-fiscal incentives with the condition that these units should be net positive foreign exchange earners over a stipulated period of time. The government also tried to promote export using a plethora of fiscal subsidies for exporters like the interest equalization scheme, focus market scheme, focus product scheme, served from India scheme, etc.

These schemes have been controversial in many cases. It has been alleged that use of antidumping duty has specifically benefited certain big business houses. Any import duty that is imposed on primary or intermediary goods can have a positive impact on the domestic producer of the same good but can negatively affect other producers using that primary or intermediate good for further value addition. For example, as Thakurta (2014) says: ‘the central government on 25 July imposed an antidumping duty on imports of purified terephthalic acid (PTA), a critical intermediate that is used in the production of various polyester products. This decision will almost entirely benefit only one corporate entity, that is, RIL. The move to impose an antidumping duty was staunchly opposed, unsuccessfully, by at least 10 large companies in India, individually and through various industry associations.’ The author further points out that representations from domestic industry opposed the imposition of the antidumping duty on PTA as they thought it would be detrimental for 20,000 small- and medium-sized industrial units employing hundreds of thousands of workers across the country. These units use PTA to make various polyester products, and any antidumping duty on PTA would have made their final product more expensive.[3]

Similarly, there are allegations that a large Indian firm has misused various export incentive schemes by the government of India to launder huge amount of money and evade taxes worth more than Rs. 1000 crores (Thakurta 2017). Another businessman used diamond trading to defraud a public sector bank of more than Rs 11,400 crores.

On the other hand, export incentive schemes targeted toward the Micro, Small and Medium Enterprises (MSME) sectors have not fared well. In 2015, the government of India announced the interest equalization scheme on pre- and post-shipment rupee export credit to eligible exporters. The objective is to provide exporters a cheap source of working capital both for pre-shipment and post-shipment activities. This scheme

[3] Also see Iyengar (2016).

was designed to provide incentive to all manufacturer-exporters who are MSMEs across all products and to all manufacturer-exporters under 416 specific tariff lines at 4-digit HS codes. Through the IES, the government wanted to provide affordable credit to these exporters to enable them to become more competitive with the broader goal to promote export-led job growth in manufacturing.

However, the offtake of the scheme has not been up to the expectations. A government notification says: 'Financial implication of the proposed scheme is estimated to be in the range of Rs. 2500–2700 crore per year. However, the actual financial implication would depend on the level of exports and the claims filed by the exporters with the banks. Funds to the tune of Rs. 1625 crore under Non-plan Head of account are available under Demand of Grants for 2015–2016, which would be made available to RBI during 2015–16.'[4]

There are a number of possible reasons why the offtake has been less than expected. It is possible that the problems with the domestic banking industry are not allowing enough credit flow to the export sector which generally is treated as a more risky sector by the domestic banks. It is also possible that exports from MSME sector were adversely affected by the demonetization and the implementation of the GST and hence the demand for working capital credit were low (Behera and Wahi 2018).

Overall, it appears that the trade policy measures adopted by the government have not always performed the intended role. In the next sections, this chapter will have a more in-depth look at the MIP and the SEZ policies and evaluate its possible impact on different sectors of the economy.

3.3 Minimum Import Price and Its Impact on the Steel Sector in India

3.3.1 What Is a Minimum Import Price (MIP)?

A tariff rate is a markup over the international prices for a product on which the tariff is imposed. In most cases when a tariff rate is announced, it is a predefined rate which adds a markup over international prices to make the domestic landed price of the good higher than the international price. Tariffs can be specific tariffs—which are expressed as tariff per unit of a good—or ad-valorem tariffs—which are expressed as a percentage of international price. The primary objective of tariff is to increase the price of the imported good by a certain amount. This is predominantly done to protect domestic producers of the same or similar goods.

This method, however, has a weakness. If international price of the concerned product goes down significantly, then the protection offered by tariff rates may not be enough to protect the domestic producers from foreign competition. In such cases,

[4]http://pib.nic.in/newsite/PrintRelease.aspx?relid=131591. Accessed 8th December 2018.

countries have known to resort to alternate forms of tariffs. One such measure is the minimum import price or MIP. It is to be noted here that under the WTO regime, countries are generally not allowed to use quotas as trade control measures.

The term 'minimum import price' or MIP refers generally to the lowest price at which imports of a certain product may enter a member's domestic market. Under a minimum import price scheme, if the price of a product is below a specified minimum import price, an additional charge is imposed corresponding to the difference. MIPs act as a type of variable levy, and its impact in terms of protective and stabilization effects is very similar. In other words, an MIP is a measure which ensures that certain imported products will not enter a domestic market at a price lower than a certain threshold, normally by imposing an import duty assessed on the basis of the difference between such threshold and the transaction value of the imported goods. The import duty in case of MIP is inversely related to the international price as long as the international price is below the MIP.

3.3.2 Why Was the MIP Imposed in Steel Sector?

India imposed MIPs on imports of 173 steel products in February 2016. There were two main arguments that were put forth in support of this imposition. The first argument was that since steel producers employ a large labor force, protection of the domestic steel industry from unfair competition from foreign producers of steel was necessary for the interest of the country. The government felt that traditional trade remedial or safeguard measures were not providing adequate protection to the Indian steel producers.

The second argument of protecting the steel sector was the possibility of a banking crisis in case the large firms turned unviable. Many of the steel producers had large amount of debt from the banking system, and any negative impact on steel producers would have affected India's already troubled banking sector in a big way and therefore a systemic ripple effect in the economy as a whole. In fact, a newspaper report quoting a research paper by State Bank of India suggests that the steel industry is the largest contributor to the Indian banking system's overall non-performing assets (NPAs). According to the report, the top five steel companies viz. Essar Steel, Monnet Ispat, Bhushan Steel, Electrosteel Steels, and JSPL have large NPAs.[5] This observation is also supported by a RBI report which shows that only 12 companies are estimated to account for 25% of the total NPA of the banking sector and among them five are from the steel industry (Table 3.1).

However, the imposition of MIP on steel imports was not favored by the section within the steel industry which uses steel as an input for their manufacturing. MIPs pushed up the unit value of imported steel and therefore allowed domestic steel producers to charge higher prices. Consequently, downstream industries which

[5]https://www.thehindubusinessline.com/money-and-banking/steel-industry-is-the-largest-contributor-to-the-banking-systems-overall-npas/article9830403.ece. Accessed 8th December 2018.

Table 3.1 Non performing assets (NPAs) of top 12 firms accounting for 25% of total NPAs of the banking system

Company name	Loan default amount (in Rs crores)
Bhushan Steel Ltd.	*37,248*
Lanco Infratech	22,075
Essar Steel Ltd.	*14,074*
Bhushan power and Steel Ltd.	*12,115*
Alok Industries	22,075
Amtek Auto Ltd.	14,074
Monnet Ispat and Energy Ltd.	*12,115*
Electrosteel Steels Ltd.	*10,273*
Era Infra Engineering Ltd.	10,665
Jaypee Infratech	9635
ABG Shipyard	6953
Jyoti Structures	5165

Source As reported in Srivastava (2017)

consume steel as an input, such as engineering goods producers and automobile industries, started getting negatively affected due to the higher cost of production. On the other hand, countries protested against the imposition of MIP by India in the WTO. As variable levies are not allowed under WTO, pressure was built up on India to remove MIPs. Eventually in the middle of 2017, MIPs were withdrawn. In place of MIP, the government of India imposed safeguard duties and antidumping duties in most cases.

It is notable that only the steel industry received special and extensive protection from the government. Other metal sectors like aluminum, copper, and zinc did not receive such extensive level of protection. This has led to a disparate duty structure in the metal industry. For steel, the difference in duties between the raw material and the final products is around 7.5%. On the other hand, for aluminum and copper, the maximum difference is only 2.5%.[6]

However, recent news suggests that the government is planning to impose MIP on aluminum also.[7] It is probably not a coincidence given that aluminum has even higher degree of market concentration with two producers, namely Vedanta and Hindalco controlling over 90% of the output.

[6]https://www.financialexpress.com/opinion/a-better-duty-structure-needed/1312789/. Accessed 8th December 2018.

[7]https://economictimes.indiatimes.com/industry/indl-goods/svs/metals-mining/govt-considering-mip-on-some-aluminium-products-goyal/articleshow/57920616.cms. Accessed 8th December.

3.3.3 Analysis of Imports of Steel and Its Impact on Domestic Industry

Since 2014–15, Indian steel industry started facing import surges mostly in two broad categories of steel imports. These are HS 72 (iron and steel) and HS 73 (items of iron and steel). In the product category HS 72, imports were mainly happening from three countries, China, South Korea, and Japan. Together these three countries accounted for 40.4 and 48.5% of steel imports in 2013–14 and 2014–15, respectively. In HS 73, China, Japan, South Korea, and Germany have been the biggest source of imports and together these four countries have accounted for 61.03 and 59.67% of imports in 2013–14 and 2014–15, respectively.

This surge in cheap steel imports put pressure on large domestic steel manufacturers in India. Table 3.2 shows the distribution of share of sales among the top 12 firms. These firms together hold over 75% of total steel sales by domestic producers in India. The table shows that there is fairly high level of concentration in the steel industry in India. In fact, the share of sales by the top three firms in this industry is almost half of total sales by domestic producers. Not surprisingly, there are numerous accusations about the formation of price cartels in this sector.[8]

Figure 3.3 looks at the sales figures of the largest seven steel companies for the period 2000–2017. It shows that most of the firms suffered a decline in sales between

Table 3.2 Top firms with more than 1% market share in steel industry (annual data ending December 2017), sales in Rs million

Company name	Sales in 2017 (Rs million)	Share in total sales (%)
JSW Steel Ltd.	662,340.0	17.30
Tata Steel Ltd.	605,193.7	15.81
Steel Authority of India Ltd.	586,311.7	15.32
Essar Steel India Ltd.	217,860.4	5.69
Tata Steel B S L Ltd.	174,044.3	4.55
Rashtriya Ispat Nigam Ltd.	127,703.8	3.34
Jindal Stainless Ltd.	110,317	2.88
JSW Steel Coated Products Ltd.	97,410.6	2.54
Jindal Stainless (Hisar) Ltd.	95,497.2	2.49
Bhushan Power & Steel Ltd.	87,010.6	2.27
Posco Maharashtra Steel Pvt. Ltd.	69,690.7	1.82
Tube Investments of India Ltd.	46,824.2	1.22

Source CMIE Prowess Database

[8]See Sharma (2018) and https://economictimes.indiatimes.com/industry/indl-goods/svs/steel/gadkari-warns-steel-and-cement-firms-not-to-form-cartels/articleshow/63233219.cms. Accessed 8th December. See Mitra and Madhavan (2008) for a slightly older perspective on cement and steel cartels.

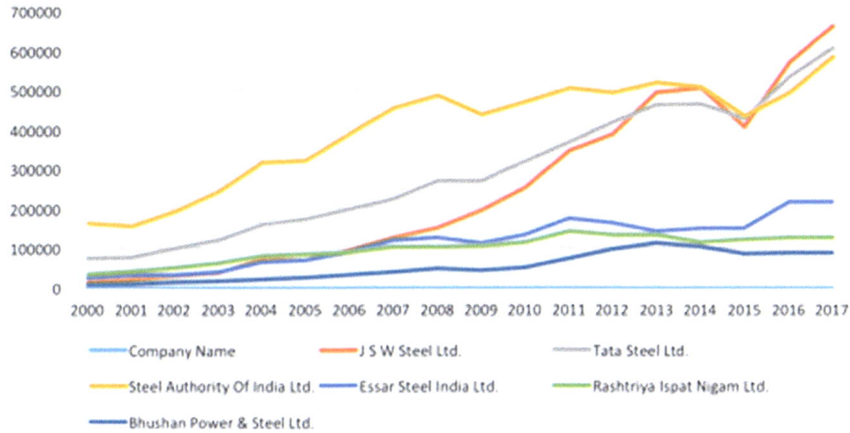

Source: CMIE Prowess Database

Fig. 3.3 Annual sales of top steel firms in India (2000–2017), sales in million rupees

2014 and 2016. The decline was particularly sharp for the top three firms. The steel lobby pushed the government for increased protection from foreign competition. As a result, the government started raising import duty on steel from 2015 to 2016. In a series of measures, the government pushed up protection on the iron and steel sector. Import duties were raised on a number of products, and antidumping duties were imposed on steel imports from a number of countries including China, Korea, Malaysia, Thailand, USA, and EU. The government also imposed standards (quality control measures) on steel imports to ensure that only good quality steel products can come into India. In short, a series of tariff and non-tariff measures were introduced to check imports of steel. A detailed account of these measures can be found here.[9]

These measures did not prove to be effective enough to dampen steel imports, and the government was forced to introduce minimum import price (MIP) on 173 steel products in order to 'provide a level playing field to domestic producers against the injury caused as evident from the decline in margins of the producers.'[10] Further, the government extended the MIP twice on 66 tariff lines which are not covered under the antidumping duty and safeguard measures for a period of 2 months (once in August, 2016 and again in October, 2016).

The official position adopted by India stated that some countries like China, Japan, and Korea (along with Russia and Ukraine) developed excess capacities to meet the steel demand in developed countries. According to India's submission to WTO, the world production capacity of crude steel was 2351 million tonnes as of December 31, 2014, which exceeded global demand by almost 30%. However, import demand

[9]The details of the measures can be found in the Rajya Sabha unstarred question no. 3813. The document can be found at http://steel.gov.in/sites/default/files/ru3813.pdf. Accessed on 8th December, 2018.

[10]http://pib.nic.in/newsite/PrintRelease.aspx?relid=158119.

for steel from traditional big importers like USA, EU, and China came down, and rather, exporters in these countries started looking for alternative markets for their steel exports. Given high and growing demand for steel in India, and due to its high domestic prices, India became 'the natural choice' for surplus steel manufacturers (WTO 2018a).

While the reasoning may be disputed, it is clear from Fig. 3.3 that Indian producers indeed faced high imports of steel and its high-cost domestic producers were put under pressure by these imports. The government sided with the domestic steel manufacturers and gave them series of protection. Along with other measures, minimum import prices of $445–$500 per ton was imposed in February 2016. Prices of imported steel went up due to the plethora of policies adopted by the government, especially after February 2016 (Fig. 3.3).

In international trade under WTO, countries are allowed to impose safeguards against unfair trade practices but they are not allowed to block imports from countries beyond the allowable use of bound tariff rates. After examining India's regime of protection for the steel industry, the WTO dispute settlement board (DSB) has ruled that during that time India behaved inconsistently with a number of WTO rules and provisions and that India's imposition of the anti-import measures is not justifiable. India had to eventually remove the MIPs but the government has imposed series of antidumping duties instead to keep the domestic steel industry insulated from international prices.

3.3.4 Impact of the MIP

Prima facie, the anti-import measures, were effective in bringing down imports quite substantially during the phase when MIP was in place (Figs. 3.4 and 3.5). MIP helped curb imports and improve pricing power for the domestic producers. Sales and profits before interest, tax, depreciation, and amortization (PBITDA) figures show a gradual rebound for the major domestic steel players (Figs. 3.3 and 3.6) since imposition of the policies. And as discussed before, the average unit value of imported steel also went up (Table 3.3).

It is notable from Figs. 3.3 and 3.6 that the bigger players in the domestic sectors managed to take advantage of the MIP regime and increased their sales and profit significantly. However, some other players like Essar Steel and Bhushan could not survive the period. Bhushan steel has been acquired by Tata Steel, and sale of Essar Steel is presently being negotiated.

Overall, it can be said that India's experience with minimum import prices shows that the MIP was able to fulfill its primary role of providing temporary protection to large domestic steel producers. However, India's policy of protecting an intermediate good like steel exacerbated the problem of inverted duty structure in India. Generally, it is expected that a country's tariff structure should exhibit tariff escalation. Tariff escalation essentially means that average tariff rates should increase with the level of processing. This is done to ensure that domestic industries focus more on higher

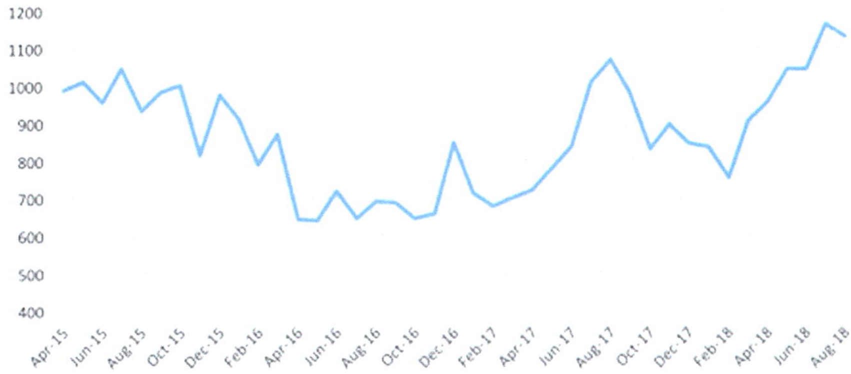

Source: DGCI&S, India

Fig. 3.4 Monthly import of iron and steel (HS 72) in million USD

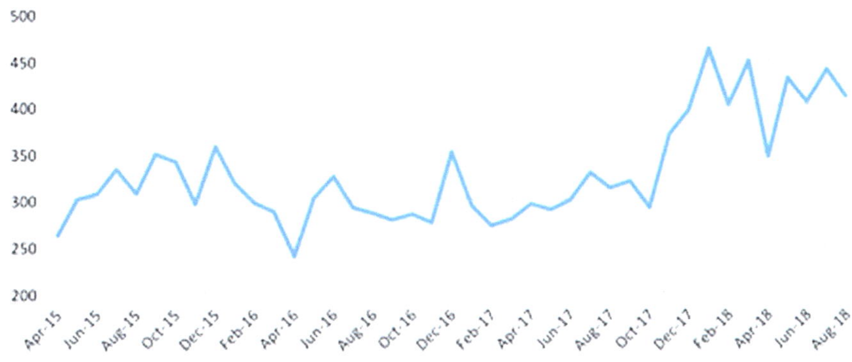

Source: DGCI&S, India

Fig. 3.5 Monthly import of items of steel (HS 73) in million USD

value-added products and the cost of imports for primary and intermediate goods are kept low. However, in India tariff structure shows pattern of inverted duty structure. The MIP on steel increased domestic protection of an intermediate good compared to the finished goods, giving rise to this inverted duty structure.

What is important here to highlight that the imposition of very high level of protection in steel may have benefited the large domestic steel manufacturers, a major penalty was imposed on the downstream producers who use steel as intermediate goods. This is especially true for HS 72, which has more products in the 'intermediate goods' category. A study by Engineering Export Promotion Council(EEPC) estimated that the introduction of minimum import price (MIP) on steel products raised the cost of raw materials for engineering products by about 6–10%. The subsectors which had to face the biggest challenges were auto and auto parts, industrial and electrical machinery and products of MSME sector. Capital goods industry and

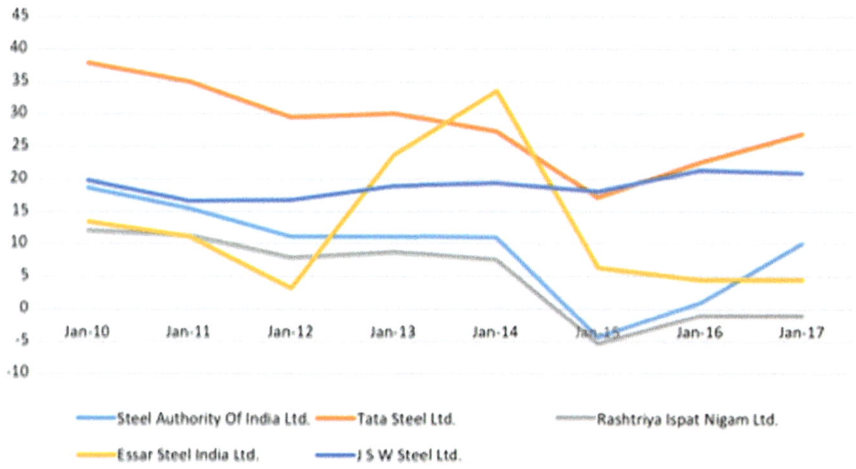

Data Source: CMIE Prowess Database

Fig. 3.6 PBDITA as a percentage of total income of some major domestic steel producers

Table 3.3 Average steel prices (US dollar/ton)

Average price: US dollar/ton						
HS code	Dec-15	Jan-16	Feb-16	Mar-16	April-16	May-16
7207	294.7	285.6	271.5	267.6	266.4	273.2
7208	402.4	344.2	397.6	388.4	407.7	426.3
7209	377.3	411.6	413.6	442.5	477.3	685.8
7210	647.8	567.5	573.6	630.7	825.5	814.8
7212	1464.0	1491.1	1378.4	1937.4	1860.3	1507.4
7213	434.2	504.1	620.3	475.1	532.6	549.6
7214	421.3	589.2	361.4	476.5	472.0	470.9
7224	415.6	439.1	369.4	390.6	410.4	718.8
7225	392.3	431.0	390.0	486.0	492.0	568.2
7227	384.0	360.3	339.5	354.7	398.3	480.2
Total price	415.4	402.4	410.7	441.9	475.2	506.3

Source DGCI&S, India

many infrastructure projects where steel is used extensively have also been affected quite significantly. Many of these sectors subsequently faced two more policy shocks through demonetization and imposition of Goods and Services Tax (GST). The net impact on these producers has been significantly negative. A report by the Reserve Bank of India has shown that exports by the MSME sector suffered significantly due to these policy shocks (Behera and Wahi 2018).

3.4 Special Economic Zones

Special economic zones (SEZs) are industrial enclaves within a country that primarily focuses on exports. These enclaves get some privileges and concessions that are not generally available to the rest of the economy. India was the first country in Asia to establish an export processing zone (EPZ) in 1965, and by the year 2000, India had seven EPZs that were owned by the central government with Ministry of Commerce and Industry's Department of Commerce as the nodal agency. In 2006, encouraged by the success of Chinese free zones and SEZs, the Indian government replaced the old EPZ policy with the new scheme of special economic zones.

After more than a decade of the SEZ policy, the special economic zones remain one of the most hotly debated issues in India. Since the inception of the SEZ policy, private SEZs proliferated in India and presently India has one of the largest numbers of approved SEZs in the world. According to the latest data, there are 420 approved SEZ in India now.[11] But among these, only 223 SEZs are in operation presently.[12] There are a number of reasons why many SEZs are not operating. Special economic zones are generally focused toward exports but in spite of a surge in the number of SEZs in India, exports from SEZs have almost stagnated. Figure 3.7 shows exports from SEZs of India. As it can be seen from the figure, since 2012–13, exports have decreased in nominal terms.

Here, it is worth mentioning that there is lack of transparency about data on SEZs. While export figures are readily available, import figures of SEZs are not published. As reported in Mukherjee et al. (2016), import intensity of exports of many SEZs is quite high. In some cases, net foreign exchange earnings (exports—imports) of some

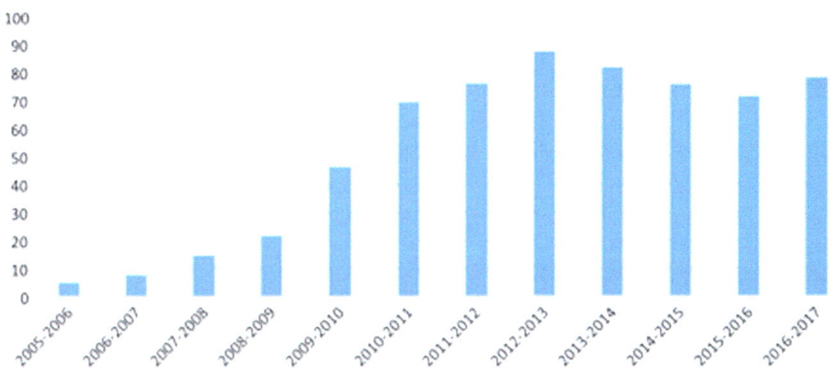

Source: Special Economic Zones in India. Ministry of Commerce and Industry, Department of Commerce. http://sezindia.nic.in/cms/export-performances.php

Fig. 3.7 Exports from SEZs of India (billion USD)

---

[11] http://sezindia.nic.in/upload/uploadfiles/files/Formal-Approval-list.pdf.

[12] http://sezindia.nic.in/upload/uploadfiles/files/Operational-SEZs-list.pdf.

SEZs have even been negative. Therefore, export performance of SEZs can be much worse than it appears from Fig. 3.7. Moreover, there have been numerous instances when duty-free imports allowed for the SEZs have been misused for smuggling activities.[13]

There are several reasons why Indian SEZs have not performed well. In India, approval to set up a large number of SEZs was given within a short time period. As a result, the 'special' nature of these zones was not established properly. Moreover, most SEZs in India do not have the scale and size to take advantage of economies of agglomeration and network benefits one generally associates with SEZs in countries like China. There are big question marks about why India approved so many sub-optimal SEZs across all over the country. And that leads to one of the biggest controversies about the SEZs. There are major concerns whether SEZs are used for land grabbing and windfall real estate gains (for details, see Levien 2011; Bhaduri 2007; Shiva et al. 2011). A Department of Revenue (DRA 2014) report has pointed out several cases where allotted land has not been put to the prescribed use by SEZs. It also highlights many cases where there are irregularities and non-transparencies in land allotments and usage (Mukherjee et al. 2016). In 2017, it was reported that of the almost 5000 ha (12,355 acres) of land acquired for SEZs in the last five years, only 362 ha (7.24%) have been used for their intended purpose. It is notable that much of the land acquired for SEZs were agricultural land. It is alleged that after the SEZ act many real estate developers and big players showed keen interest in the projects as it was perceived that such integrated zones with state-of-the-art facilities would lead to massive increase in real estate prices around the SEZ areas. Also, the SEZ act allowed dual use of the non-processing area of SEZs where developers are allowed to set up social infrastructure like schools, hospitals, and hotels which can be accessed by people within and outside these conclaves. In many cases, real estate development became the primary objective and the SEZ law was used to grab the land from its alternate use. There are allegations of forceful acquisition of agricultural land and/or low compensation for farmers and those dependent on such land. It is rumored that some SEZs licenses were distributed as political favors as it was expected that such land acquisitions would lead to windfall gains.

Another big problem faced by the SEZs is that it requires cooperation between the center and the state. However, the SEZ act and rules are not conducive for such cooperation with state governments. State government officials are often not taken on-board by the Department of Commerce when projects are approved.

Along with these massive problems with land acquisitions, concerns have been raised if SEZs have become tax havens where units operate in SEZs for availing the tax and other fiscal sops associated with it. Given their poor growth and stagnating exports, there is a feeling that SEZs are leading to a loss of revenues. It is also possible that existing units in the non-SEZ area have shifted to SEZs to avail of

[13]https://www.ndtv.com/india-news/india-finds-new-gold-smuggling-route-tax-free-special-economic-zones-646607 and https://www.hindustantimes.com/delhi-news/rs-150-cr-fraud-by-jewellery-unit-in-noida-unearthed-says-dri/story-OKLKUfbC0zWa8LUP6LiAHP.html.

the fiscal benefits, thereby not adding to the productive capacity of the country but leading to a revenue loss for the government.

Overall, the SEZ policy in India has not worked the way it was perceived. A large number of SEZs are in IT and IT services where the benefits from being in an SEZ are somewhat questionable. Manufacturing-oriented SEZs have not performed well as it is evident from poor export figures. But on the other hand, the SEZ policy has been severely misused for land grabbing and illegal imports. It is another example of trade policy instruments used for passing on benefits to a few private sector players without bringing in significant benefit to the country.

3.5 Conclusion

Trade policies across the world seem to be moving away from the doctrine of free trade. More and more countries are adopting policies which have inter-elements. This may seem like a move away from neoliberalism but there is another trait which is important to highlight. There is a strong evidence that in the last few years, there has been a growing concentration of economic power. The latest UNCTAD Trade and Development report has pointed out that economic power concentration of large companies has increased significantly over the last few years. The role of state and use of state policies to help this power concentration is one of the defining features of the present period.

It appears that some of the policies adopted by the policymakers in India are also following a similar trend. There is increased intervention by the state in international trade. The government is actively using policy instruments to restrict imports and promote exports. However, the implementation of these policy measures seems to benefit the bigger players more. Use of trade remedial measures like antidumping duties on intermediate goods has been used when it is known to adversely affect large number of downstream small producers only because it benefits a few large domestic producers. Similarly, the MIP policy has helped the large domestic steel manufacturers to recover from a sharp downturn. But the resultant higher domestic steel prices have caused injury to a large number of manufacturers including many smaller domestic producers in the MSME sectors. Presently, domestic steel prices are high and there are accusations of steel cartel being formed. There are now talks of imposition of MIP in the aluminum industry where cartelization is also a possibility because if its oligopolistic market structure. The imposition of MIP is clearly driven by pressures from large domestic firms, and this is part of a global trend where the big business is influencing economic decision making in a significant way.

India's export incentive measures like the SEZ or the interest equalization schemes (IESs) had limited success in helping the target exporters. For a number of reasons, the offtake of IES has been disappointing. The SEZ policy, on the other hand, shows the precise problem highlighted above. The state-formulated SEZ policy is being used to grab land from other uses. Majority of the land acquired for SEZs are from the agricultural sector. There are major complains with the compensation package offered to the stakeholders who are associated with such land transfers. The acquired land in many cases is not used for the original purpose, and a significant part of these lands are used for making windfall gains from real estate development.

The SEZs which are operational are not without their pitfalls. As discussed above, there are instances of misusing the duty-free import facility of SEZs. More importantly, the SEZ policy allows the units operating within SEZs to have certain laws including labor laws which are different from the laws of the land. Not all states in India have allowed the SEZs to have a different labor law, but the pressure of competitiveness may be used by the policymakers to push more flexible laws within SEZs.

Internationally, there is a growing tendency to defy WTO rules and commitments. The MIP and the IES are clear violations of WTO rules. Yet India went ahead and imposed them. Though India had to remove the MIP subsequently, India willingly defied the WTO rules till it was challenged in the dispute settlement board. Similarly, the USA has blatantly violated many basic WTO rules and provisions, and some of these violations are also being challenged under the WTO. As a part of this trend, it will not be surprising if India backs out from some of the free trade agreements it has signed. This will be a similar move like the USA renegotiating the North American Free Trade Agreement (NAFTA) deal.

The implication of these will be interesting to follow as the global trade seems to have entered an uncertain period. The rise of general protectionist tendency across the countries is highlighted in a recent WTO report which shows a sharp rise in trade restrictive measures from the G-20 countries (WTO 2018b). The estimated coverage of the new protectionist instruments used by the G-20 countries is around US$481 billion which is the largest since this measure was first calculated in 2012. The rise of protectionism, a move away from hyper-globalization and increased dominance of the global economy and policymaking by big business and the so-called 'superstar' firms, is a new phenomenon that will chart an interesting course for the global economy in the next few years. India seems to be very much aligned with this pattern of big business policymaker nexus that we are observing globally.

References

Behera, H., & Wahi, G. (2018). How have MSME sector credit and exports fared? Reserve Bank of India Mint Street Memo No. 13. https://m.rbi.org.in/Scripts/MSM_Mintstreetmemos13.aspx#C7a.

Bhaduri, A. (2007). Development or developmental terrorism? Countercurrents.org. http://www.countercurrents.org/ind-bhaduri070107.htm. Accessed December 8, 2018.

Chandrasekhar, C. P. (2018). The indiscreet aggression of the bourgeoisie. International development economics associates. https://www.networkideas.org/featured-articles/2018/07/the-indiscrete-aggression-of-the-bourgeoisie/. Accessed December 8, 2018.

Chaudhuri, S. (2015). Import liberalisation and premature deindustrialisation in India. *Economic and Political Weekly, 50*(52), 60–69.

Department of Revenue. (2014). Report of the comptroller and auditor general of India for the year 2012–13 on performance of Special Economic Zones (SEZs). Union Government,

Department of Revenue (Indirect Taxes—Customs), Ministry of Finance, Government of India, No. 21 of 2014. Available at http://www.saiindia.gov.in/english/home/Our_Products/Audit_Report/Government_Wise/union_audit/recent_reports/union_performance/2014/INDT/Report_21/21of2014.pdf. Accessed October 4, 2018.

Iyengar, S. P. (2016). Key input shortage strands polyester-makers. *The Hindu Business line*, June 01.

Lang, V. F., & Tavares, M. M. (2018). *The distribution of gains from globalization* (Working Paper No. WP/18/54). International Monetary Fund.

Levien, M. (2011). Special economic zones and accumulation by dispossession in India. *Journal of Agrarian Change, 11*(4), 454–483.

Mitra, A., & Madhavan, M. (2008). Commodity cartels: Fact or fiction? *The Hindu business line*, May 18.

Mukherjee, A., Pal, P., Deb, S., Ray, S., & Goyal, T. M. (2016). *Special economic zones in India*. Springer, Berlin.

Rodrik, D. (2016). Put globalization to work for democracies. *New York Times*, September 17.

Rodrik, D. (2017). *Straight talk on trade: Ideas for a sane world economy*. Princeton University Press.

Sharma, Ch. R. S. (2018). Builders complain of high cement, steel prices. *The Hindu business line*, August 03.

Shiva, V., Jani, S., & Fontana, S. M. (2011). The great Indian land grab. Navadanya, New Delhi. http://www.navdanya.org/attachments/RFSTE_The%20Great%20Indian%20Land%20Grab_28-9-2011%20(1).pdf. Accessed December 8, 2018.

Srivastava, P. (2017). India's bad loans: Here is the list of 12 companies constituting 25% of total NPAs. *Financial Express*, October 23, 2017.

Subramanian, A., & Kessler, M. (2013). *The hyperglobalization of trade and its future* (Working Paper No. 13-6). Peterson Institute for International Economics.

Thakurta, P. G. (2014). Polyester prince revisited. https://www.paranjoy.in/article/polyester-prince-revisited. Accessed December 8, 2018.

Thakurta, P. G. (2017). Did Adani Group evade ₹1,000 crore taxes? *Economic and Political Weekly, 52*(2), 35–40.

UNCTAD. (2018). Trade and development report 2018: Power, platforms and the free trade delusion. Available at https://unctad.org/en/PublicationsLibrary/tdr2018_en.pdf.

WTO. (2018a). India—Certain measures on imports of iron and steel products. *World Trade Organization*. https://www.wto.org/english/tratop_e/dispu_e/518r_e.pdf. Accessed December 8, 2018.

WTO. (2018b). Report on G20 trade measures: Mid-May 2018 to Mid-October 2018. *World Trade Organization*. https://www.wto.org/english/news_e/news18_e/g20_wto_report_november18_e.pdf. Accessed December 9, 2018.

Part II
Globalisation, Reforms and Indian Agriculture

Chapter 4
Indian Agriculture in the Perspective of the Provisions of Domestic Subsidies in the Agreement on Agriculture Under WTO

Srinibas Nandy

Abstract Several loopholes lie in the domestic subsidy provisions under the Agreement on Agriculture (AoA) which tell upon the health of the agricultural sector of India. Classification of subsidies deliberately favours developed country members by providing them with backdoor-protection mechanism for their agriculture through manipulation of subsidy cuttings and at the same time increasingly corners the weak members of the World Trade Organization (WTO) including India while fulfilling commitments. It also threatens the Indian food security programmes. Agricultural prospects of the country will be further worsened if the developed country members use their policy space to their fullest extent. The domestic subsidy provisions will continue to limit the potential gains of India from its agriculture unless the necessary revision in the provisions is done. The Peace Clause is neither a permanent solution nor a solution ensuring any legal rights. Increase in production efficiency of the Indian agriculture through technological upgradation and side-by-side exertion of continuous pressure jointly by India and other developing country members for necessary revision can help India get rid of the situation of slowdown in its agriculture.

4.1 Introduction

A large majority of the Indian people is still dependent on agriculture despite substantial decline of the share of agriculture in GDP over the past seven decades. As in the most other developing countries, Indian agriculture serves the economy through multiple ways, such as (i) providing employment opportunities to its vast population [total agricultural workers including cultivators and agricultural labourers constitute 54.6% of total work force in 2011 (GoI, Department of Agriculture, Cooperation & Farmers Welfare 2017, Table 2.9)], (ii) contributing to the country's GDP though the share is gradually falling, (iii) achieving self-reliance and providing food security, (iv) bringing about equity in income distribution, (v) reducing countrywide poverty levels, (vi) serving as raw material base for the country's industrialization and a

S. Nandy (✉)
Raghunathpur College, Sidho-Kanho-Birsha University, Purulia, West Bengal, India
e-mail: srinibasprl@gmail.com

P. K. Biswas and P. Das (eds.), *Indian Economy: Reforms and Development*, India Studies in Business and Economics, https://doi.org/10.1007/978-981-13-8269-7_4

market for the manufactured goods. Most importantly, it provides food and nutrition to the country's 1.3 billion people. Thus, the importance of agriculture in India can hardly be underestimated. On the other hand, India has entered the Agreement on Agriculture (AoA) in the GATT 1994 which imposes some complicated restrictions on providing domestic subsidies in agriculture. As a consequence, like other member counties, India is also no longer allowed to extend domestic subsidy support to its farm producers beyond the cap limit fixed in the AoA. But in India most of the subsidies are provided generally in the form of supplying subsidized inputs such as fertilizers, irrigation, power (electricity, diesel, etc.) and seeds and a measure of support price to the farm producers. However, in the agreement these supports are classified as the amber box support which is mostly targeted for reduction over a period of time. Hence, it becomes an increasing threat to our agricultural economy with the passage of time.

Under these perspectives, India's agriculture needs to be paid in-depth and careful attention for its rapid growth to feed its huge population and to fulfil other objectives mentioned above. This becomes a growing challenge to India particularly in view of the implementation of the national food security programmes under the National Food Security Act 2013. India has been striving for its agricultural development since the very beginning of the First Five-Year Plan through increasing investment and introducing new technology, particularly in the third and the successive plans. Along with these developmental measures, India has been providing subsidies to its agriculture sector to boost up production and thereby to achieve self-reliance in foodgrains. Self-reliance in food is also a country's precondition for attaining a milestone in its way to economic development. So it is easy to understand how important the agriculture is in the country! Under these circumstances, whether this agreement on subsidies tells upon the agricultural health of the Indian economy today or tomorrow is a matter of concern.

Scheme of the chapter is as follows: Section 4.2 provides a brief review of the agricultural sector focusing on food production and contribution to GDP. Section 4.3 discusses the theoretical logic put forward by the developed countries for the inclusion of agriculture in the Uruguay Round of GATT. The main characteristic features of the AoA, classification of domestic subsidies and loopholes lying in the provisions of domestic subsidies in the AoA are analysed in Sect. 4.4. Finally, Sect. 4.5 discusses the likely effects of the AoA on Indian agriculture.

4.2 A Brief Review of Food Production and the Contribution of Agriculture to the Country's GDP

During the period from 1951 to 2014, India's population has increased about 3.6 times from 361 to 1296 million (Census of India 1951; Population Reference Bureau 2014), while India's foodgrain production has increased more than five times from

50.83 to 265.04 million tonnes during the period from 1950–51 to 2013–14 (GoI, Department of Agriculture, Cooperation & Farmers Welfare 2016). Table 4.1 shows the increase in food during the said period. India has achieved self-reliance in food due to this substantial increase in food production.

Nadkarni (2018) has analysed that the increase in foodgrain production has been possible due to an increase in net sown area under cultivation (about 18% in 62 years) and irrigation (by 4 times) and increased diversification in agriculture in post-independence India. According to Nadkarni, this has changed India's status from being a net importer to a net exporter of foodgrains (ibid, p. 28). This growth of food production and self-sufficiency no doubt would make us complacent but what about the growth of overall agriculture?

A glimpse may be had from Table 4.2 which portrays an unhappy picture, as the growth rate of this sector lagged far behind overall GDP growth rate and the gap has been widening. Further, Table 4.2 shows that after 1980s till date, the average growth rate of agriculture per annum has been decelerating, whereas that of GDP shows an increasing trend except in the incomplete decade from 2011 to 2017.

Table 4.1 Foodgrain production in India from 1950–51 to 2013–14 (million tonnes)

Years	Rice/wheat	Total foodgrain (rice, wheat, cereals, pulses, etc.)
1950–51	20.58	50.83
1960–61	34.58	82.02
1970–71	42.22	108.42
1981–82	53.25	133.30
1990–91	74.29	176.34
2000–01	84.98	196.81
2010–11	95.98	244.49
2013–14	106.65	265.04

Source Compiled from Government of India (GoI), Department of Agriculture & Farmers Welfare (2017), Table 2.9

Table 4.2 Growth rate of agriculture and growth rate of GDP of the economy

Periods	Average growth rate of agriculture (% per annum)	Average growth rate of GDP of the economy (% per annum)
1975–80	3.25	4.22
1981–90	3.51	5.22
1991–2000	3.35	5.59
2001–10	3.32	7.55
2011–2017	2.80	6.85

Source Author's calculation based on pincodeindia.net/agriculture-growth-rate.php and pincodeindia.net/gdp-growth-rate.php (accessed on 26/11/18)

Moreover, the study on the performance of agriculture at the state level during the post-reform period (1990–93 to 2003–06) and the immediate prereform period (1980–83 to 1990–93) by Bhalla and Singh (2009) has also shown that the growth of agricultural production has decelerated during the post-reform periods. However, it is observed that the starting of deceleration in the growth of agriculture has coincided with the beginning of the World Trade Organization's (WTO) functioning since mid-1990s. It is also true that the domestic supports provided by the government to the agriculture sector have also significant roles to play in increasing agricultural production when agricultural prices are volatile in nature. One may wish to know what happens to Indian agriculture in the WTO regime when India as a member follows the commitments of reduction on domestic subsidies. This issue is addressed in the present exercise.

4.3 Theoretical Basis of Inclusion of Agriculture in the Uruguay Round of GATT

It is the Uruguay Round of GATT which first considered agriculture for inclusion in the trade negotiations. The agriculture was included, and ultimately, the AoA was reached in the Marrakesh Agreement of GATT 1994. This Agreement (AoA) mainly aims at removing almost all domestic subsidies in the form of input subsidies, minimum support price (MSP) and export subsidies in agriculture that do cause distortions and affect the optimal allocation of the world resources. Various earlier studies measured the extent of trade distortions caused by domestic supports in agriculture. The studies by Johnson (1973, 1991), Tyers and Anderson (1992) and Islam and Valdes (1990) indicated that the direct and the indirect subsidies in agriculture distort the world prices and trade in agricultural commodities and thereby lead to inefficient allocation of world resources and losses in total world welfare. These theoretical explanations strongly acted behind the inclusion of agriculture in the WTO.

4.3.1 Genesis of Supports to Farmers

In order to protect agriculture, the USA first started giving subsidy supports to their agricultural sector during the periods of 1950s and 1960s. Then came Japan, EU and the Republic of Korea to strengthen their own agriculture through providing subsidies. However, this practice later on appeared as their fundamental means to overcome the glut in the supply of agricultural products in their home markets leading to plummeting prices. In these countries, the price elasticities of demand for farm products at some higher level of income were very low. As a result, a little increase in the supply of agricultural commodities often led to a more than proportionate fall in farm product prices for market clearing and thus farm income declined. 'This was the genesis of support prices to the farmers' to overcome the vulnerable situation in agriculture (Rao 2001). Now, it has become an instrument of the developed country members of the WTO to exploit gains from international trade in agriculture.

However, by giving subsidies in agriculture, developed countries were able to keep the agricultural prices artificially at very low level in the international market and thereby disposed of their surplus agricultural products in the world market. Hence, it was expected that reduction in agricultural subsidies would raise the price of the agricultural products in the international market and also ensure the level playing field for those who are really efficient producers of agricultural commodities through free and fair play in the trade (Rao 2001). But this had not come true in reality. The picture was reverse. Immediately in the periods of post-Uruguay Round negotiations, the share of advanced countries in global exports had risen significantly and that of developing countries had fallen due to sharp fall in the farm product prices in the world market (Rakshit 2000) and it became a matter of great concern to the developing countries. Where loopholes lie in the AoA and why the developing countries like India are pushed back and left at a disadvantageous position in the spectrum of trade in agricultural commodities will also be focused here. For that, the characteristic features of the AoA need to be analysed first.

4.4 Characteristic Features of Agreement on Agriculture (AoA)

The following characteristic features constitute the fundamental part of the AoA under WTO:

(a) All kinds of domestic supports in agriculture must be reduced by 20% in 6 years (1993–99) by member countries. Of course, there are certain exceptions allowed to some countries.
(b) It is mandatory for developed countries that budgetary outlays on direct export subsidies and the volume of exports that receive export subsidies are to be reduced by 36 and 24%, respectively, in the same period from 1993 to 1999.
(c) Non-tariff barriers of all forms such as quantitative import restrictions, variable import levies, minimum import prices, voluntary export restraint (VER) and discriminatory import licensing will have to be replaced by tariffs.
(d) On the market access issue, each member country of the WTO must provide a market access measuring at least 3% of its domestic consumption of some agricultural goods in the base year 1993. But in those countries where this market access is more than 3%, it will have to be increased up to 5%. All these attempts aim at expanding the agricultural trade in the international market.

There are, of course, certain other provisions regarding Trade-Related Intellectual Property Rights (TRIPs), and provisions related to sanitary and phytosanitary matters in the AoA, but the present analysis will be carried on only in the perspective of the provisions of domestic subsidies agreed upon in the AoA. Special attention will be given to the classification of domestic subsidies, as the classification was very important from the point of view of trade distortion. In the following part, this classification is analysed in detail.

4.4.1 Classification of Domestic Subsidies: Why Needed

Under the AoA, all domestic supports are classified mainly into three categories in accordance with their trade-distorting nature. They are as follows:

(1) **Most Trade-Distorting Subsidies**

Aggregate Measure of Supports (AMS). The most trade-distorting subsidies are the Aggregate Measure of Supports comprising (i) total subsidies on inputs, i.e. on fertilizer, irrigation, credit and power (electricity, diesel, etc.); and (ii) market price support measured by the difference between domestic market price and world price multiplied by the quantities of exports. This support is also known as the amber box supports.

(2) **Non-Trade-Distorting Subsidies**
These are divided into two subgroups:

(a) **Green Box Supports**. These supports comprise of different forms of direct payment to farmers, subsidy on general research and development, infrastructural services, pest and disease control programmes and trainings, research in connection with environment programmes, inspection and market intelligence. These measures are not only exempted from reduction commitments, but they can also be increased without any limit in WTO as they have no or minimal trade-distorting effects on production. There will be no violation in WTO rules whatever be the increase in the amount of subsidies given in this category.

(b) **Blue Box Supports**. The supports in this category do not have any direct effects on increase in the volume of production. They include direct payments to farmers such as deficiency payments and compensation payments in agriculture, and these payments are made after production is over.

(3) **Less Trade-Distorting Subsidies**
The following two categories of supports fall under the less trade-distorting category:

(a) **De Minimis Supports**
These are trade-distorting but are not required to be reduced if they lie under the specified limit as per de minimis provisions of the AoA. A WTO member can provide trade-distorting domestic subsidies to its agriculture sector up to a certain limit. The ceiling limit for a developed country for trade-distorting subsidies under the AMS is 5% of its agricultural GDP in

a year in question, whereas in the case of developing countries this limit is 10% of their agricultural GDP. So long as the agricultural supports are within their specified limits, they are called the de minimis supports and they will be treated as less trade-distorting. For a developed country, the de minimis supports, for both product-specific and non-product-specific, must not exceed 5% of the total value of agricultural products of that country in a year in question. Similarly, for a developing country, the same will not exceed 10% of the total value of the agricultural production of that country in a year in question. But when they exceed their specified limits, they will be no longer treated as de minimis supports; rather, they will fall in the amber box category and will be included in the calculation of Aggregate Measure of Support (AMS).

b) **Special and Differential Treatment Box Subsidies**
The developing and the low-income countries are only allowed to provide these domestic subsidies to their low-income and resource-poor farmers for the purpose of development of their agricultural sector. These are the special rights conferred on only the poor countries. No other countries can exercise these rights except the poor and developing ones. The 'special and differential treatment' box subsidies include some concessions and special provisions in the following forms: (i) a longer time period for implementation of commitments made in the AoA; (ii) measures which particularly aim at increasing trade opportunities of developing and poor countries; (iii) necessary helps and supports to the developing and low-income countries so that they can build up their capacity and function well under the WTO, etc.

Among these categories of measures, only the category 2 measures are non-trade-distorting, the category 3 measures are considered to be less trade-distorting, and the category 1 (AMS) measures are considered to be the most trade-distorting subsidies.

In course of analysis, it will be clear that the classification of domestic subsidies is so designed in the AoA that though it appears to be favouring the developing countries, actually it is biased towards favouring developed country members of the WTO and they have been able to exploit more benefits from the international trade in agricultural commodities by manipulating these provisions. This classification aims at easy manipulation of the provisions in the agreement and maximum gains from the trade in agriculture.

4.4.2 Intension Behind Classification of Domestic Subsidies

As the direct and indirect domestic subsidies in agriculture distort the world prices and trade in agricultural commodities and thereby lead to inefficient allocation of world resources and cause a net loss in total world welfare, the agreement on reduction commitments on subsidies and its gradual removal has had a definite theoretical and economic basis. It is good for the world as a whole. Initially did this raise our hope that the poor and developing countries would certainly gain more benefits from the international trade in agriculture when subsidies would be removed because the prices of the agricultural commodities in the international market which have so far been kept artificially very low would go up and thereby result in the increased capability of the developing country members to compete with the developed nation members of the WTO in the international market. But the provisions of agricultural subsidies have been so designed in the AoA that it would deliberately serve the greater interest of the big and powerful members of the WTO through increasing their competitive power in the world market in an unfair way. They had a hidden game while designing the provisions of domestic subsidies to serve their vested interests. There is none to refute the argument for removal of domestic subsidies as it is based on some economic principles. But which economic theory can be forwarded in favour of the classification of agricultural subsidies? Patnaik (undated) has righteously stated that the classification of agricultural subsidies is based neither on any credible economic principle nor on any theoretical foundation. It is quite arbitrary and deliberately biased to protect the interest of the economically developed nation members of the WTO. The USA and other developed countries can derive much more benefits from the world trade in agriculture simply by transferring their subsidies from the amber box to the green box/blue box as no restriction is imposed on green box/blue box supports by the WTO. But reduction in amber box supports is a mandatory both for developed and developing member nations as they are considered to be trade distorting in nature. Thus, amber box subsidies can easily be shifted to the green box or blue box causing no violation of WTO rules.

The maximum permitted amount of amber box subsidies that a member country can provide to agriculture has been determined considering the value of agricultural production of 1986–88 as the base year's production value of that nation. The maximum permitted limit of subsidies in the amber box for developed countries is 5% of their agricultural production value in the year in question, and for developing countries, it is 10% of their production value in the relevant year. Apparently, it seems that developing countries are much favoured by giving them more concessions in respect of agricultural subsidies than the developed countries, but the picture is quite reverse. One can notice some disguised intensions of the developed country members of the WTO behind the provisions of classification of the subsidies as noted below:

(i) Transfer of subsidies from the prohibited box (amber box) to green box or blue box has been made possible and easy without violation of the WTO rules. This classification of agricultural subsidies provides a **backdoor-protection mechanism** through which huge amount of subsidies can be provided to agriculture. It is no doubt a big loophole in the agreement.
(ii) As the production value of the USA or any other developed nation members were much higher than that of India or any other developing countries in 1986–88, the absolute amount of subsidies calculated for the developed countries on the basis of 5% of their production value were much higher than the absolute value of subsidies for India and other developing countries calculated on the basis of

10% of their production value in the same year. This is **another mechanism** through which developed countries can maintain much higher absolute amount of subsidies in their agriculture without violating the WTO rules, which will be further discussed below. Thus, it turns out to be another major loophole in the agreement.

4.5 Effects of AoA on Indian Agriculture

(a) **Manipulation of Subsidy Cuttings and Depression of International Prices of Agricultural Goods**
As per provisions of the AoA, the WTO member countries are required to reduce their domestic supports under the amber box category if the amount of support exceeds the de minimis level because the amber box subsidies are said to be the most trade distorting in nature. However, it is seen that many developed countries have resorted to manipulating subsidy cuttings and have been able to maintain high amount of subsidies in their agriculture just by shifting the subsidies from amber box to green box or blue box. Most of their subsidies are given in the form of cash transfer under green box or blue box which are characterized as non-distorting. Hence, by doing so, the USA and EU have been able to bring down and keep the amber box subsidies within the WTO specified limit. Sharma and Das (2017) observed that in accordance with the latest domestic support notifications of the USA and EU, they are utilizing merely 20 and 8% of their AMS entitlement, respectively. As a consequence, developed countries have had their huge policy space to distort agricultural trade without violating their commitments under the WTO. This can further worsen the Indian agriculture in future when 100% of their AMS entitlements will be utilized.

Tables 4.3, 4.4 and 4.5 present the trends of annual international prices of some agricultural commodities. Table 4.3 shows the changes of US wheat prices. The movement shows a declining trend during the period from 1981 to 1887, then a mild upward trend till mid-1990s, but the prices were still lower in the period from 1998 to 2001 than that in 1980. During the period from 2005 to 2012, prices went up except the years 2009 and 2010, and after 2012, they started declining continuously. Manipulation of subsidy cuttings by USA from amber box to blue box or green box may have contributed to this declining trend in international prices. The movement graph of the prices is depicted in Graph 4.1.

Graph 4.2 shows the price movement of US soya bean during the period from 1981 to 2017. In 1981, it was \$7.1668/bushel. In 1996, it rose to \$7.5348. Then, it continuously fell and reached its minimum, i.e. \$4.5965 in 2001. After that, price movement shows an upward trend with a slight decline in the span of 2004–2006 and 2008–2009 and reaches its highest in 2012. After 2012, price fell continuously up to 2015.

Table 4.3 US wheat price historical annual data, 1981–2017, price in US Dollars/Bushel

Year	1981	1982	1983	1984	1985	1986	1987	1988
Average closing price	4.2817	3.5092	3.5670	3.5086	3.2565	2.8086	2.8573	3.7030
Year	1989	1990	1991	1992	1993	1994	1995	1996
Av. closing price	4.0967	3.1868	3.0476	3.6521	3.3035	3.5871	4.2164	4.7452
Year	1997	1998	1999	2000	2001	2002	2003	2004
Av. closing price	3.6793	2.9395	2.6215	2.6053	2.7417	3.2541	3.3615	3.4785
Year	2005	2006	2007	2008	2009	2010	2011	2012
Av. closing price	3.2152	4.0607	6.4086	7.9908	5.3381	5.8712	7.1443	7.5412

Year	2013	2014	2015	2016	2017
Av. closing price	6.8608	5.8908	5.0836	4.3945	4.4014

Source https://www.macrotrends.net/2534/wheat-prices-historical-chart-data

Table 4.4 US soya bean price historical annual data, 1981–2017, price in US Dollars/Bushel

Year	1981	1982	1983	1984	1985	1986	1987	1988
Average closing price	7.1668	6.0458	7.1249	7.0394	5.5310	5.1159	5.3193	7.6539
Year	1989	1990	1991	1992	1993	1994	1995	1996
Av. closing price	6.7076	5.9959	5.7057	5.7153	6.2728	6.2379	6.1240	7.5348
Year	1997	1998	1999	2000	2001	2002	2003	2004
Av. closing price	7.4906	6.0477	4.7752	5.0033	4.5965	5.1316	6.3340	7.4371
Year	2005	2006	2007	2008	2009	2010	2011	2012
Av. closing price	6.0987	5.9494	8.6682	12.3199	10.1956	10.4889	13.1852	14.6226

Year	2013	2014	2015	2016	2017
Av. closing price	13.8587	12.2850	9.4242	9.8753	9.7820

Source https://www.macrotrends.net/2531/soyabean-prices-historical-chart-data

Graph 4.3 displays the pattern of price movement of rice in Japan. It is clear that there is a continuous rise in price during the period from 1981 to 1994. After 1994, the picture is quite reverse showing a continuous fall in price except a slight rise in 2004.

In Japan, rice, wheat, beef, sugar and dairy are called the 'sacred' five and they have been kept insulated and protected from international free market competition through providing them heavy subsidies and imposing tariffs on foreign imports, often upwards of 100%. 'Tariffs on rice imports may be the most egregious example at 778%' (nbakki, at http://nbakki.hatenablog.com/entry/Changes_in_Rice_Price) (posted on 22.06.2015 and accessed on 23/11/2018).

Table 4.5 Changes in prices of rice in Japan, 1970–2014, price in Yen/5 kg rice, index (2010 = 100)

Year	1970	1975	1980	1981	1982	1983	1984	1985
Price of 5 kg rice	1080	1790	2512	2611	2713	2766	2865	2955
Year	1986	1987	1988	1989	1990	1991	1992	1993
Price of 5 kg rice	2974	2974	2926	2969	3003	3001	3120	3212
Year	1994	1995	1996	1997	1998	1999	2000	2001
Price of 5 kg rice	3519	3083	3006	2981	2863	2909	2790	2703
Year	2002	2003	2004	2005	2006	2007	2008	2009
Price of 5 kg rice	2639	2795	3066	2659	2577	2531	2500	2509
Year	2010	2011	2012	2013	2014			
Price of 5 kg rice	2422	2325	2538	2589	2424			

Source www.stat.go.jp/data/cpi/historic.htm. Also available at http://nbakki.hatenablog.com/entry/Changes_in_Rice_Price

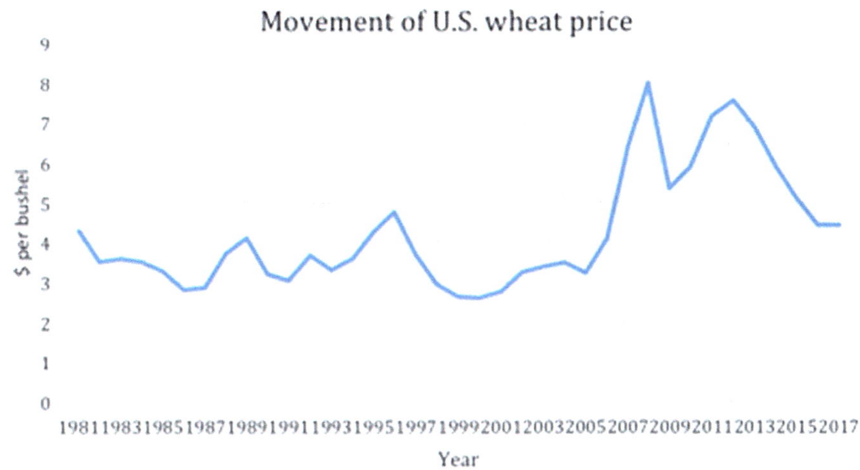

Graph 4.1 Movement of US wheat price, 1981–2017

(b) **Worsening Terms of Trade in Indian Agriculture**
If this trend of manipulations of subsidy cuttings leading to depression of international prices of agricultural commodities by developed countries continues, they will not only go on distorting agricultural trade in disguise, but also certainly produce negative effects on the Indian agriculture through worsening terms of trade. In this connection, we may have a glimpse of the terms of trade in Indian Agriculture and its movements before and after economic liberalization. De Roy (2017) has clearly shown that the movements of the terms of trade were in favour of Indian agriculture during the entire decade of 1980s and more or less the same trend continued up to 1994–95. After that, it remained stagnant

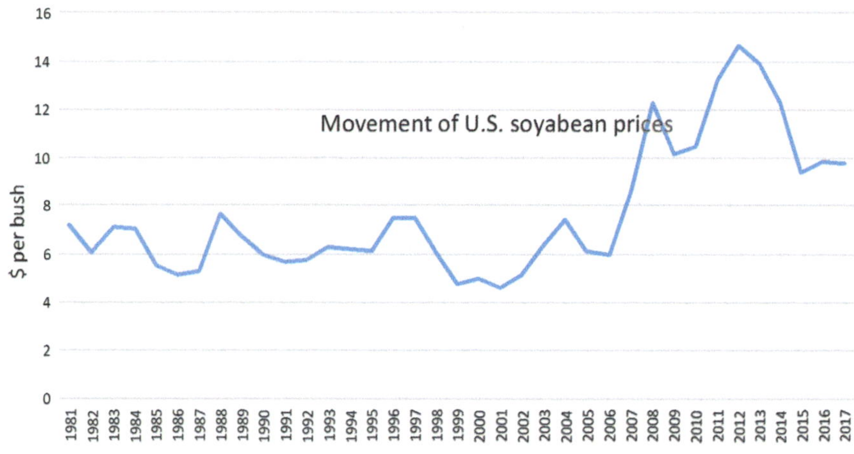

Graph 4.2 Movement of US soya bean prices, 1981–2017

up to 1998–99. Then, the terms of trade had a mild fall till 2008–09. During the period from 2009–10 to 2011–12, the terms of trade slightly improved and then it started declining again till 2013–14 (ibid, p. 68). If this declining term of trade continues, it will lead to negative effects on Indian agriculture by destroying competitive power of the Indian agricultural products in the international market and India will lose its potential gain from the trade.

(c) **Helping Top Corporations in Agribusiness**

According to the WTO Annual Reports in 2003, the agricultural subsidies provided by the developed countries in their agriculture were not merely to help the poor and vulnerable farmers; rather, it was meant for helping the top corporations in agribusiness (WTO Annual Report 2003, p. 22). It is evident from this report that by helping the top corporations in agribusiness the USA and other powerful members of the WTO fix their targets at grabbing the international market through displacement of India and other developing countries instead of removing distortions in trade and world resource allocation. They are really not aiming at optimal allocation of resources on global basis. If they had a noble desire, they would not help the top agribusiness corporations and rather would help only the poor and vulnerable farmers.

(d) **Peace Clause and India**

The maximum permissible 10% limit on agricultural subsidies in the AMS group needs analytical views specially in respect of developing countries. This limit is critically insufficient for developing countries particularly for India, while it determines to provide food security to its poor people and to provide income support to the resource-poor farmers. So, before the Doha Round, India considering the importance of subsidies in food security programme raised demand for a provision of 'Food Security Box' so that developing countries can ensure food security to their poor people. In the 4th Ministerial Conference

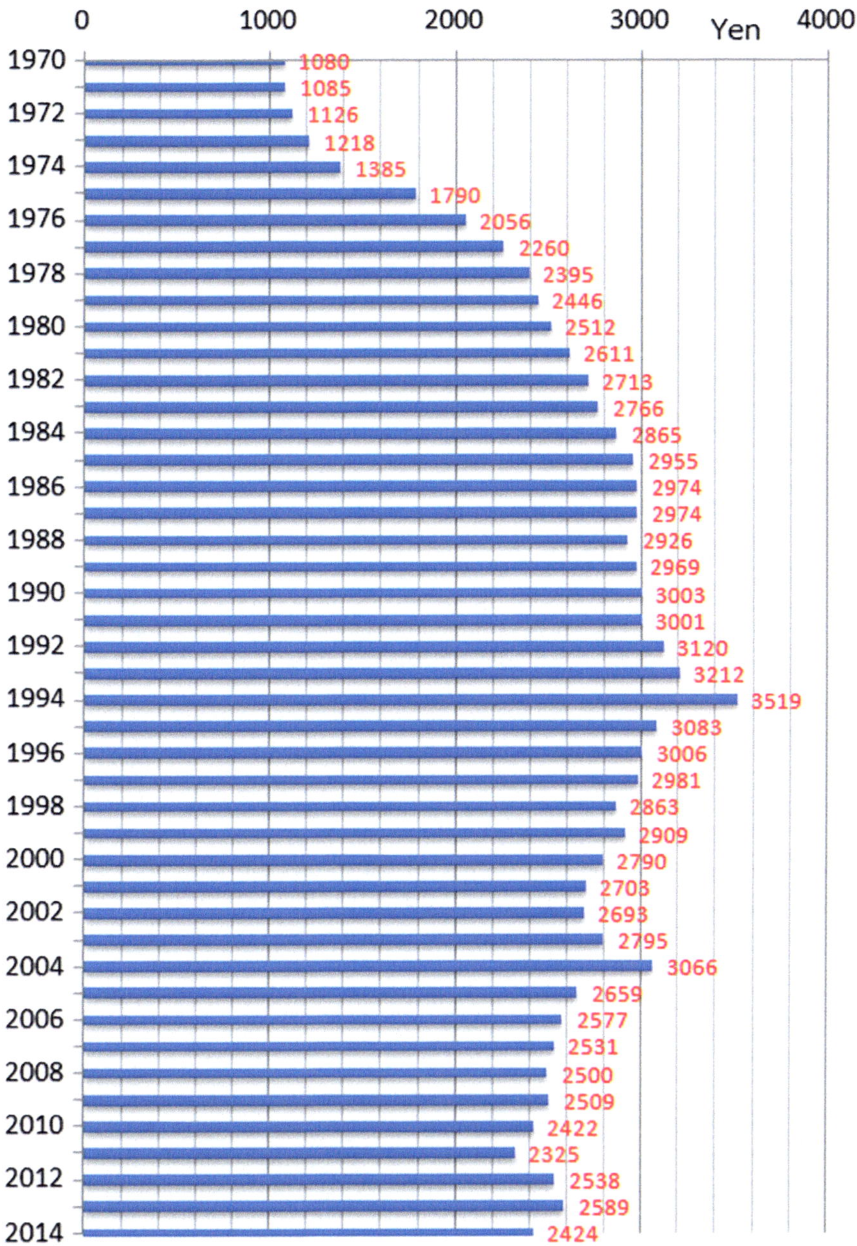

Graph 4.3 Price movement of rice in Japan, 1970–2014 (Yen per 5 kg of rice)

in Doha in 2001, on agricultural subsidy issue, the member countries of WTO were divided into two groups: the developed countries led by EU, USA, Canada and Japan were grouped in one group, and the developing countries led by India, China, Brazil and South Africa were grouped in another. In spite of the multiple efforts made by the developing countries to resolve this issue, no solution was reached for a long time. Then in 2012, the G-33 group being led by India created a pressure on WTO and submitted a proposal to them for exemption from the 10% subsidy limit in the amber box subsidies for the sake of ensuring food security. Developing countries immediately after the Doha Round demanded that the subsidies provided through procurement of foodgrains at administered price for the purpose of food security must not be accounted in the calculation of amber box subsidies. So, in response to this demand of developing countries, an interim solution was resolved in the 9th Ministerial Conference held in Bali in 2013 and it is known as the 'Peace Clause'. This Peace Clause is a mere temporary solution to the subsidy issue in agriculture which states that developing countries will be allowed to provide subsidies more than 10% of their agriculture GDP in the amber box and no country can complain against this to WTO for the next 4 years, i.e. till 2017. In this clause, it is clearly stated that such subsidy must be aiming at ensuring food security and or at helping the poor only. Some people are of the opinion that it is neither a permanent solution nor does it give any legal rights to resolve food security issue in the platform of WTO.

However, it was decided that the permanent solution would be sought in the 11th Ministerial Conference of the WTO in Buenos Aires in Argentina from 10 to 13 December 2017. But no such permanent solution was reached there, and hence the Prime Minister of India refused to sign the Trade Facilitation Agreement (TFA). But to pass the TFA, obtaining signature (positive consent in writing) of all the 160 WTO member nations is a mandatory. So having such a scope India exerted a pressure on this issue and the 'Peace Clause' issued in 2017 ultimately provides a temporary protection to the developing countries from breaching the 10% subsidy limits for the food security programmes. Sharma and Das (2017) have shown that in case of rice and wheat though India has been able to be within the de minimis level till 2015–16, there is every possibility of crossing the cap limit in near future particularly in case of rice. In their paper, they have worked out that product-specific support of rice as a percentage of value of production in fluctuated between 5.45 and 7.68% during 2010–11 to 2015–16. The figure 7.68% in 2012–13 was about to approaching the maximum permissible cap limit, i.e. 10% of the value of production. The possibility of breaching the cap limit is going to be a reality soon. Any time it may breach the cap limit if attempts are taken for widening the food security programme to cover more and more people. Other than the food security programme what does it imply? First, due to insufficient supports to agriculture, India cannot realize its potential growth in agriculture in future. Second, India no longer can use the food procurement process as its one of the important instruments to its fullest extent for stabilizing prices in its domestic market. These two factors will limit the future agricultural growth if permanent solution is not reached on this issue.

In that case, neither the interest of the resource-poor farmers nor that of poor consumers will be protected permanently. Moreover, the Peace Clause provides a temporary solution to the subsidy issue subject to the fulfilment of several conditions tied up with it. One such condition is that the subsidies allowed under the Peace Clause must be for the purpose of helping only the poor and vulnerable farmers not others. Developing countries are also required to make domestic support notifications for the preceding five years as one of the necessary conditions for having benefits under the Peace Clause. Thus, the Peace Clause is so tied up with many such conditions that there is doubt about its effectiveness. It is relevant to point out here that India has already made its domestic support notifications up to 2013–14. On the contrary, most actions of the developed countries in respect of giving subsidies to their agriculture are not in tune with the removing of trade distortion and ensuring efficient world resource allocation.

(e) **Calculation of AMS and India**
The method used for calculation of AMS also has a serious negative effect on Indian agriculture as majority of subsidies given by Indian Government to their agriculture fall within the amber box category. In such calculation, a fixed external reference price (ERP) from a base year (1986–88) is used to assess the support price. India wants to be allowed to take ERP in the base year in the domestic currency because the measure used now is not perfect and not without flaws. It considers neither inflations nor exchange rate fluctuations in the calculation of AMS as ERP is three decades old. If the ERP is taken in the domestic currency in the base year, India would have a greater range of de minimis level of subsidies producing better effects in the Indian agriculture.

(f) **Food Security in India and Farm Producers: Are They to Face a Challenge?**
According to the National Food Security Act (NFSA) 2013, the Indian Government is to ensure the availability of subsidized foodgrains to its two-thirds population. Implementation of the food security programme in India accordingly involves three-tier functioning, namely (i) procurement of food, (ii) stockholding of food and (iii) distribution of food through PDS. Further, public distribution system is to ensure 5 kg foodgrains per person per month at a highly subsidized price and for that public stockholding of food commodities is a must. Again, procurement of foodgrains is a necessary precondition for public stockholding, but under the AoA, the procurement process gets severely constrained by the provisions of domestic subsidies when it is done through providing minimum support price (MSP) to the farmers in developing countries including India. Public stockholding is needed to serve the two-fold purposes in the economy. First, it can act as an instrument for stabilization of prices by removing fluctuations of agricultural commodities in its supply. At the time of harvest, generally the supply of agricultural commodities surges the market on the one hand. On the other, farmers are often compelled to sell their goods immediately after their harvest to clear their loan dues to money lenders and financial institutions. Due to excess supply, prices start falling and come down below the cost price. In this situation, the government intervention is needed to create artificial demand

Table 4.6 Expenditure on Supplemental Nutrition Assistance Program (SNAP) by USA

Year	Total annual benefit/expenditure (in million $)	No of beneficiaries (in million)	Benefit/expenditure per beneficiary (in $)
1995	22,764.07	26.61	855.47
2000	14,983.32	17.19	871.63
2005	28,567.88	25.62	1115.06
2010	64,702.16	40.30	1605.51
2015	69,645.14	45.76	1521.96
2016	66,539.35	44.21	1505.07
2017	63,603.66	42.12	1510.05

Source US Department of Agriculture, Data as of September 7, 2018

and that can be done through procurement of food stock. Thus, procurement of food stock helps eliminate excess supply in the market. Further, supply of agricultural goods is not available throughout the year as its production is seasonal. So when its supply is far below the demand or artificially supply shortage is created, prices of foodstuff start rising very fast leaving adverse effects on the economy. In this volatile situation, more or less the equality between supply and demand can be restored through release of food commodities from the public stock. Thus, procurement of foodgrains at the time of harvest and release of the same at the time of supply shortage should not only be considered as a part of food security programme of India but **as an important instrument for stabilizing prices** in the Indian economy. Secondly, public stockholding is also necessary to provide support price (minimum cost price) to the farm producers in developing countries when socio-economic factors compel them to sell their products at very low prices. Therefore, food security programme is urgently necessary in India when the farm producer class includes a large number of small and marginal farmers and huge people yet live below the poverty line. But here lies the problem. As this minimum support price falls under the amber box subsidies, the FCI can provide product-specific subsidy up to a maximum of 10% of the value of agricultural production in the relevant year. Hence, this maximum cap limit (10%) on the amber box subsidies puts a constraint to the procurement process through providing MSP to the farmers in India. On the other side, the provisions of AoA allow a country to spend as much as it can on stockholding and distribution without any limit as these expenditure falls under green box supports. If India aims at ensuring food security to the majority of its people through PDS, breaching the cap limit on the AMS is inevitable in near future. Side by side a picture of trend of expenditure done by USA on their food assistance programme can be portrayed in Table 4.6 just to make it easy to understand their motive.

Before going to discuss about implications of Table 4.6, India's picture needs to be referred to here. Sharma and Das (2017) have shown that the total annual food subsidy provided by India on the programme of National Food Security Act 2013 amounted to 19,482.49 million dollars in 2016–17. Total number of beneficiaries was 813.40 million, and subsidy per beneficiary stood at 23.95 dollars.

It may be noted in Table 4.6 that the total expenditure on food assistance done by USA in 2017 is 63,603.66 million dollars. The US food assistance is more than 3 times the total annual food subsidy provided by India in 2016–17 (19,482.49 million dollars). The beneficial expenditure/subsidy per beneficiary in USA is $1510.05, whereas in India it amounts to only $23.95 stating that the US amount is about 63 times larger than the Indian amount in 2016–17. Further, it is found that the food assistance provided by the USA increased from 22,764.07 million dollars in 1995 to 63,603.66 million dollars in 2017. The increase is about 3 times during the said period instead of any cut in food assistance. Other developed countries also follow the same path. These actions of 180° reverse direction reveal their real intension. In spite of this excessive expenditure on food assistance, the developed countries are exerting mounting pressure on the developing countries for reduction of subsidy in agriculture and food. This expenditure by USA is also a kind of domestic supports provided to their agriculture not in the form of MSP through procurement but in the form of deficiency payment to their eligible farmers.

The table also presents us a very clear scenario that helps us understand how tactfully the USA provided such a large chunk of agricultural supports to their agriculture simply by shifting them from the amber box to the green box/blue box. Their expenditure per beneficiary increased from $855.47 to $1510.05 during the period from 1995 to 2017. The developed country members have been using this classification of domestic subsidies as their **backdoor-protection mechanism** to provide greater amount of subsidies in aggregate. Is it not really trade-distorting directly or indirectly? Is it not leading to a loss in total world welfare through inefficient allocation of world resources? These questions need to be paid a deeply analytic attention.

If these provisions of subsidies continue to be unaltered in the AoA, not only the procurement level and the food security programmes to cover more people will be thwarted in near future but millions of farmers will be adversely affected in India. The small farmers will get frustrated when they fail to cover the cost of their produce. This will definitely increase their social and financial burden manifold.

Recently, the growing incidence of farmers' suicide seriously draws our attention as to why the number of suicide has been increasing so fast since 1995. According to National Crime Records Bureau of India, about three lakh farmers committed suicide in India during the period from 1995 to 2013. The actual number may have been much higher because in some states suicide reports have not been recorded properly and in some cases reports have been deliberately suppressed by state governments (Ballabh and Batra 2016). Moreover, people not owning land but farming on informal leasing in of land are not recorded as farmers. So their suicidal cases have not been counted as farmer's suicide. Unfortunately, this incidence has coincided with the implementation of the commitments in the AoA under WTO. So there is left enough room for pursuing investigation to correlate the farmers' suicide and agricultural subsidies under WTO. Nadkarni (2018) has clearly stated that subsidization and support would be inevitable no matter what the WTO might say.

4.6 Conclusion and Suggested Measures

Though the objective of the provisions of the AoA is to do away with all sorts of protectionist approaches of development and to ensure a competitive, free and efficiency-based growth, developed countries have tactfully managed to maintain high subsidies in their agriculture in the WTO regime. At the same time, pressure is mounting on the developing countries to follow strictly the provisions of AoA. This is a gross duality. As a consequence, the expectation of improving the trade efficiency and the terms of trade of the developing countries including India through reduction of subsidies remains as distant reality to them yet.

However, one can realize the importance of agriculture in India. It continues to be the main source of livelihood for the majority of its people. So, those provisions in the AoA which go against the interest of the developing countries should immediately be revised properly so that the duality designed at the time of framing these provisions is removed. A concerted effort for creating pressure for such necessary revision will have to be organized by the developing countries.

The process of conversion of non-tariff barriers to tariff barriers is not specified in the AoA. As a result, high equivalent tariff conversion is there leading to distortions in the trade and inefficient world resource allocation. It should be clearly specified.

India has to get the maximum 10% cap limit on agricultural subsidies relaxed through permanent solution; otherwise, its food security programmes under the NFSA 2013 will not be materialized and small farmers will suffer the most. There might happen increasing suicidal trend of the poor and marginal farmers in India in the absence of adequate agricultural supports. This tendency may be intensified if the food security programme fails in such a vast country where the majority of population depends on agriculture.

Moreover, the Indian agriculture has been put into the framework of unfair global competition through AoA. Export competitiveness of the Indian agricultural commodities is being deliberately destroyed by the developed countries as world prices of agricultural goods are not only artificially kept very low by them but are falling continuously. In such a regime of more open and competitive economy, if India wants to have considerable gains from international trade in agriculture, it has to enhance its export competitiveness and efficiency in production of agricultural goods up to the required degree. In order to reach the target, the following steps are suggested:

i. Indian agricultural economy suffers from some infrastructural weaknesses that have to be overcome with a view to attaining the long-term gains. It is clear from Tables 4.7 and 4.8 that the public investment as percentage share of total GDP shows a little rise from 0.5% in 2004–05 to 0.6% in 2005–06 and 2006–07 and thereafter it shows a declining trend. In the case of private investment, though

Table 4.7 Public and private investment in agriculture and allied sectors as percentage share of total GDP at market prices (2004–05)

Year	% share of public investment	% share of private investment	Total % share
2004–05	0.5	1.8	2.3
2005–06	0.6	1.9	2.4
2006–07	0.6	1.8	2.4
2007–08	0.5	1.9	2.5
2008–09	0.5	2.4	2.9
2009–10	0.5	2.3	2.8
2010–11	0.4	2.1	2.5

Source Govt. of India (GOI), Department of Agriculture, Cooperation & Farmers Welfare, Pocket Book of Agricultural Statistics 2016, Table 2.9. Accessed on 22/11/2018

Table 4.8 Public and private investment in agriculture and allied sectors as percentage share of total GDP at market prices (based on 2011–12 series)

Year	% share of public investment	% share of private investment	Total % share
2011–12	0.4	2.7	3.1
2012–13	0.4	2.4	2.7
2013–14	0.3	2.6	2.9
2014–15	0.3	2.3	2.6
2015–16	0.4	1.9	2.3
2016–17	0.4	1.8	2.2

Source GOI, Dept. of Agriculture, Cooperation & Farmers Welfare, Pocket Book of Agricultural Statistics 2017, Table 2.8. Accessed on 22/11/2018

percentage share shows an increasing trend from 2004–05 up to 2010–11, it fell more or less steadily after 2011–12.

For long-term gain from agriculture, public investment has to be increased for extension of road networks, irrigation and other infrastructural facilities. Further, it can also be shown that the investment in agriculture has also been lesser in amount in comparison with non-agriculture sector. For this scanty attention of the government to agriculture, the latter has to suffer. Public investment should be increased significantly to enhance efficiency in agriculture to cope up with the situations emerging from the AoA.

ii. Adequate measures for extension of irrigation facilities should be taken by the government on priority basis. As stated by De Roy (2017), the growth rate of gross irrigated area was not satisfactory; rather, it declined during the period from 1981–82 to 2012–13. He has shown that the growth rates of gross irrigated area were 2.07% in the period from 1981–82 to 1989–90, 1.11% in the period from 2000–01 to 2009–10 and 1.36% in the period from 2010–11 to 2012–13.

In order to combat the unfavourable situations in agriculture under the WTO regime, production efficiency must be increased through increased irrigation facilities.

iii. Chand and Kumar (2004) have analysed that providing subsidies leads to a temporary gain in agriculture but the long-term beneficial effects can only be realized from the increase in public investment in agriculture. It is estimated by them that if one rupee is spent on public sector capital formation, it will raise agricultural GDP by Rs. 35.21 over a span of 58 years. They have further observed that diversion of 1% resources from agricultural subsidies to public investment can increase output by more than 2% and advocated for greater emphasis on the matter. But the Indian context should be considered differently when developed country members of the WTO are supporting their agriculture by providing huge subsidies through manipulation of subsidy cuttings. So, increase in public investment in agriculture should not be encouraged at the cost of agricultural subsidies unless the necessary revision in the provisions of AoA is done. But increase in public investment from other resources in this sector is always welcome for ensuring greater efficiency.

iv. Increasing emphasis has to be put on the expansion of agro-based industries so that perishable vegetables can be converted into processed ones like soya chunks, potato chips, tomato sauce, chilli sauce, processed mushroom, etc.

v. Domestic subsidy relaxation should be determined in maximum absolute amount, for example, per acre of cultivated land, but not in terms of the percentage of value of agricultural production. It may also consider total agricultural land size, population of a country, percentage of population engaged in agricultural activities, share of total capital engaged in agriculture, etc., as factors determining subsidies. In this case, maximum absolute amount will act as a ceiling and transfer of subsidies from prohibited box to non-trade-distorting box can be totally stopped. No country can manipulate subsidy cuttings any further. Then, WTO can give out more justice to its member countries.

Despite the above loopholes and flaws associated with the provisions of agricultural subsidies in the AoA, India cannot leave the WTO. According to the WTO Report (2015), 98% of the global trade takes place among the WTO member countries. In case of going out of the WTO, India's international market will shrink badly and it will lose potential gains from international trade. Increasing strength and efficiency is one of the important solutions instead of leaving WTO. Continuous efforts will have to be made for upgrading the technology in agriculture so that production efficiency is increased at a maximum. Side by side India and other developing countries must organize themselves so effectively that they can exert the required pressure to the WTO for necessary revision in the provisions of the AoA.

References

Ballabh, V., & Batra, P. (2016). Farmers in distress and resources under stress: A completely neglected subject. In C. Ramasamy & K. R. Ashok (Eds.), *Vicissitudes of agriculture in the fast growing Indian economy* (pp. 377–400). New Delhi: Academic Foundation.

Bhalla, G. S., & Singh, G. (2009). Economic liberalization and indian agriculture: A state wise analysis. *Economic and Political Weekly, 44*(52), 34–44.

Census of India 1951.

Chand, R., & Kumar, P. (2004). Determinants of capital formation and agriculture growth: Some new explorations. *Economic and Political Weekly, 39*(52), 5611–5616.

De Roy, S. (2017). Economic reforms and agricultural growth in India. *Economic and Political Weekly, 52*(9), 67–72.

Government of India (GoI), Department of Agriculture, Cooperation & Farmers Welfare. (2016). *Pocket book of agricultural statistics*. New Delhi.

Government of India (GoI), Department of Agriculture, Cooperation & Farmers Welfare. (2017). *Pocket book of agricultural statistics.* New Delhi.

https://www.macrotrends.net/2534/wheat-prices-historical-chart-data (accessed on 27/11/18).

https://www.macrotrends.net/2531/soyabean-prices-historical-chart-data (accessed on 27/11/18).

Islam, N., & Valdes, A. (Eds.). (1990). *The GATT agriculture and developing countries*. Washington DC: International Food Policy Research Institute.

Johnson, D. G. (1973). *World agriculture in disarray*. UK: Fontana Press.

Johnson, D. G. (1991). *World agriculture in disarray* (2nd ed.). New York: St. Martin's Press.

Nadkarni, M. V. (2018). *Crisis in Indian agriculture can it be overcome? Economic and Political Weekly, 53*(17), 28–34.

Patnaik, P. (undated). *WTO and agricultural subsidies.* https://peoplesdemocracy.in/content/wto-and-agricultural-subsidy (accessed on 15.09.2018).

Population Reference Bureau 2014, accessed on 26/11/18.

Rao, C. H. (2001). WTO and viability of Indian agriculture. *Economic and Political Weekly, 36*(36), 3453–3457.

Rakshit, M. (2000, March). *Post-Uruguay round negotiations: A developing country perspective*, Artha Vijnana.

Sharma, S. K., & Das, A. (2017). Food sovereignty under WTO unfulfilled promise at Buenos Aires. *Economic and Political Weekly,* 52(52), 16–20.

www.stat.go.jp/data/cpi/historic.htm; also available at http://nbakki.hatenablog.com/entry/Changes_in_Rice_Price (accessed on 23/11/18).

Tyers, R., & Anderson, K. (1992). *Disarray in world food markets: A quantitative assessment.* Cambridge, New York: Cambridge University Press.

United States, Department of Agriculture, Data as of September 7, 2018.

WTO Annual Report 2003.

WTO Annual Report 2015.

Chapter 5
Agriculture and State Policies: Some Critical Issues

Shrabani Mukherjee and Debdulal Thakur

Abstract The chapter analyses the performance of the agricultural sector in India after reforms and associates it with pre-reforms situations. An organized systematic data description is presented to comprehend the factors of poor agricultural performance with reference to agricultural policies and state role during liberalization and post-liberalization period. It has been identified that in the period post the economic reforms there has been structural shift in pattern of cropping—be it food grains or non-food grains. The slowdown in the productivity of agriculture is caused due to other pertinent factors such as withdrawal of state support, poor implementation of policies, lack of infrastructure, technological lock-in, overburden of imports.

5.1 Introduction

Agriculture has a lot of significance in many respects in the Indian economy. Over 58% of the rural households depend directly or indirectly on agriculture for their livelihood (GoI 2018). The primary sector contributed roughly 20% of the gross value added (GVA) during 2016–17. As revealed in Agricultural Statistics at a Glance (2012), India is the world's largest producer of many food and non-food grains (like pulses, major spices, milk, many fresh fruits and vegetables, select fresh meats, select fibrous crops such as jute, etc.). Further, the same report states that India is also one of the largest producers of wheat and rice, cereals, rapeseed, tobacco, eggs, etc. The World Trade Statistical Review (2017)[1] reports that India is the 9th leading exporters of agricultural products, the largest producer of milk and the second largest fruit producer in the world. Agricultural export constitutes roughly 10% of the country's total exports.

[1] For details refer to https://www.wto.org/english/res_e/statis_e/wts2017_e/wts2017_e.pdf.

S. Mukherjee (✉) · D. Thakur
Symbiosis School of Economics, Symbiosis International (Deemed University), Pune, India
e-mail: shrabani.mukherjee@sse.ac.in

D. Thakur
e-mail: debdulal.thakur@sse.ac.in

P. K. Biswas and P. Das (eds.), *Indian Economy: Reforms and Development*, India Studies in Business and Economics, https://doi.org/10.1007/978-981-13-8269-7_5

Against this backdrop, this chapter analyses the major problems and prospects, and the implications of neoliberal policy reforms on Indian agriculture. The study evaluates whether reform measures undertaken by the Indian Government can actually address the problems associated with the slowdown of this sector and farmers' distress associated with crop failure. Traditionally, in India, crop production has accounted for over four-fifths of the total agricultural output; however, over the last two decades, the situation has changed significantly. Also, employment in agriculture has been falling, and presently, it accounts for around 52% of the country's total labour force. India, still a predominantly agriculture-based economy, a faster and sustainable growth in this sector, remains crucial for not only creation of jobs but also for enhancing incomes and ensuring food security. Agricultural production depends on capacity utilization of the potential or productive efficiency and technical efficiency of the farms, given the supply of inputs. These factors are influenced by the changes in the input prices, output prices and available infrastructure. Input prices and output prices of agricultural products, in India, depend primarily on agricultural policies adopted by state government and central government from time to time and the context in which they were adopted.

Agricultural policy has been one of the prime agenda of the national and subnational government in India since independence. Oskam et al. (2011) aptly remark that to achieve certain public goals the agricultural policies should represent a set of mandatory regulations. In the Indian context, it is more sensible because agriculture policy formulation is very complex because larger part of it is within the state domain. Thus, it is important to understand the dynamics in the policy formulation to evaluate progress of agriculture in India.

5.2 Agricultural Policies

There is a need to upsurge productivity by leveraging technology particularly for high yielding and resistant variety seeds. Further, adaptation to info-tech services is needed to increase the price benefits to the farmer by providing market information by reducing the prevalent information asymmetry. Thus, there is a dire need for more investment and technological upgradation in the agriculture sector. However, a close look into the discourse would reveal that while most of the problems originate from the lack of proper public expenditure and laxity in government intervention in a systematic manner in the entire chain right from sowing seeds to selling the product, these are hardly mentioned. Moreover, the huge void in adapting technologies (as for example, high yielding varieties of seeds, drip irrigation, etc.) for an expected efficient production is a perennial problem. But, unless we understand the root cause, boldly debate and address them, the fundamental problems would still persist and no matter whatever good intentions the government may have, it would not lead to potential, visible and sustainable outcomes. Finally, all these taken together will eventually lead to loss of welfare, more so for India being a primarily agriculture-based economy.

In India, the primary concern rests with the fact that still an ample mass of the population is dependent on agriculture to earn their livelihoods. Thus, the dire need for reforms in primary sector to ensure growth with development, agricultural policy became an integral part of developmental policy agenda since 1947, of course through the five-year plans. Table 5.8 (in Appendix) provides a comprehensive list of several policies and projects introduced by the Government of India from 1943 onwards. As seen in Table 5.8, after the High Powered Committee (1990) the next serious attempt to formulate a comprehensive agricultural document was initiated in 1999. However, due to instable government, this policy document could never make it to the parliamentary discussions. Only in the year 2000, the first ever inclusive National Agricultural Policy (NAP) was introduced in the parliament and subsequently, got its approval. The basic objectives of NAP were many folds. For example, it focused to strengthen the rural infrastructure, endorsed value addition, intended to quicken the growth of agro-based business, create employment opportunities in rural areas, secure a reasonable standard of living for the farmers, agricultural workers and their families, etc. Other important goals that NAP intended to achieve were to discourage migration from rural areas to urban areas and face the new genre of challenges arising due to economic liberalization and globalization. Further, NAP was also quite hopeful to create a shield against the evils arising from economic liberalization and globalization by demand-driven growth. As a tool, NAP intended to cater to the domestic markets and thereby, maximize agricultural exports. It also focused to promote ecologically, technologically and also economically sustainable growth path for Indian agriculture sector. But, the irony of NAP was that it was merely an intelligent collation of the then existing literatures related to the improvement of agriculture, customized in the Indian context. Naturally, it grossly lacked any effort to design or propose properly directed programme in a phased manner. As rightly observed by Deshpande et al. (2017), India's experience in drafting its own policy documents related to agriculture is nothing less than pathetic. They clearly pointed out that from the time of independence, India had drafted few policy documents that could at best be labelled as endeavours towards the shaping up of a robust policy; however, immediately after these documents were made public, the thrust was entirely lost. Therefore, to them, the policy documents were always drafted as a reply to meet the ensuing crisis and therefore, could be called as a 'riverine experience'. Critically examining different phases of agriculture in the era of neoliberal economy, Jha and Acharya (2011) classified three distinct phases in the growth path of Indian agriculture.[2] It is beyond debate that in India, largely the policy-related statements for the sectors mostly emerged from the five-year plans. Therefore, based on the classification of Jha and Acharya (2011), we attempt to track the origin and progression by reviewing the plan documents.

[2]For further details refer to http://ras.org.in/expenditure_on_the_rural_economy_in_indias_budgets_since_the_1950s.

5.2.1 Phase I (Early 1940s to Late 1960s)

The first phase can be tracked from the early 1940s to late 1960s. In this period, there was considerable effort to position the agricultural sector on its desired trajectory post the immense damage the sector had experienced throughout the colonial rule by the British. The strategic components of this first phase included policies of land reform. It also included institutional innovations in the form of Community Development Programme (CDP), allocating substantial expenditure by both the union and the state governments on essentials like power and irrigation projects. Added to this was direct public expenditure on agriculture. The First Five-Year Plan gave a predominant importance to the development of agriculture and irrigation, where, out of a total actual investment of Rs. 1960 crores made in the first plan, Rs. 601 crores was allocated to this sector, which is perhaps the highest allocation (30.66%) to agriculture till date. This plan primarily focused on increasing food production, given the severe food shortage in India. Further, it also categorically focused on doing away with the zamindari system, initiating the community development programmes, pave the way for the '*Grow More Food*' drive and development in other interrelated fields like animal husbandry, fisheries, soil conservation and marketing. The efforts resulted in the increment of the production of food grains from 54 million tons in 1950–51 to around 65.8 million tones by the end of the said plan period. The focus thereafter shifted towards industry during the Second Five-Year Plan period (1956–61). The plan expenditure, during this period, for the primary sector was around 20%. For food production through the fixed target was set at 80.5 million tons; however, the actual production was less by 0.80 million tons. A shortage in production except sugarcane was observed. Food grains were, therefore, imported to meet this shortage. The deceleration of the agriculture perhaps started during this era, knowingly or otherwise. The Third Five-Year Plan (1961–66) intended to attain self-reliance in food grains. This was mainly to lift up agricultural production for meeting the necessities of industry and export. Accordingly, higher priority was bestowed to agriculture sector and irrigation compared to industry development. Targetted programmes like the Intensive Agricultural District Programme (IADP) were announced, and High Yielding Variety (HYV) Programs promoted the HYV of wheat and rice. These HYV varieties were developed in Mexico (wheat) and Philippines (rice). Having done all these, the achievements were disappointing as the production only increased by 10% (target being 30%) due to drought condition in 1965–66. In the aforementioned experience during the third plan, the planning commission, therefore, assigned even greater priority towards agriculture in the subsequent plans.

These dialogues to prioritize agriculture must have the best intentions; however, there were major voids, and as a result, the policies thus formulated could not deliver the intended result, be it institutional or technical. As an obvious consequence, even though there was a significant rise in the growth rate of agricultural sector in the first two decades after independence, compared to the phase of the colonial rule, the sector performed way below its potential. In fact, the period from mid-1960s to late 1960s is seen as a phase of a genuine agrarian crisis, which was partly because

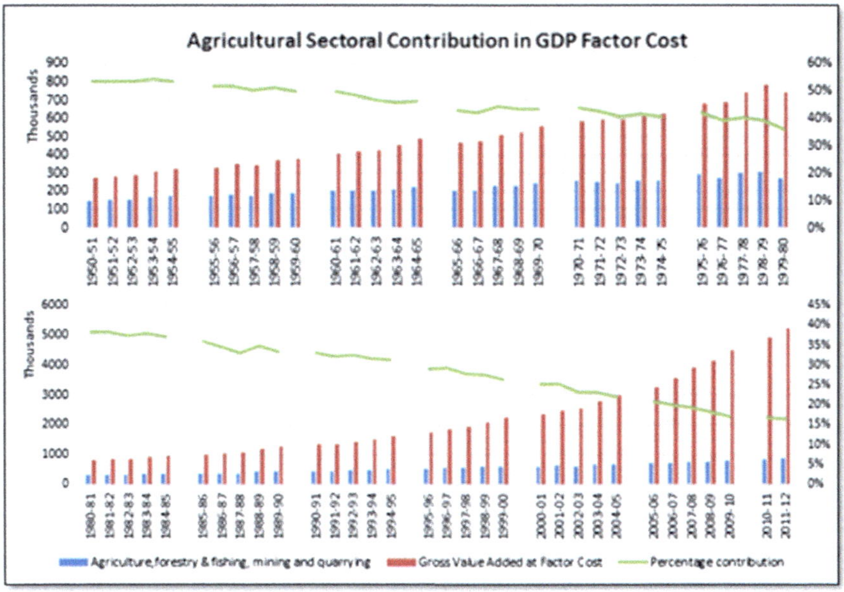

Fig. 5.1 Sectoral contribution of agriculture in GDP at factors cost (various years). *Source* Authors' calculation based on data compiled from Statistical Yearbook, India, various years

of major setback due to the monsoon setbacks for two consecutive years during the mid-1960s and partly because of routine policy failures starting from the early 1950s.

As evident from Fig. 5.1, the contribution of agriculture in the gross domestic product was quite sustained right from the 1950s. However, it only became striking with an accelerated falling tone after late 1980s. From a high of around 40% contribution to GDP during the 1980s, it steadily fell to around 25% during the 1990s and reached a low of around 15% during 2011–12.

5.2.2 *Phase II (Early 1970s to Late 1980s)*

With the realization of the then planning commission, quite obviously the successive initiatives focused to lift up agriculture, more so through a big push. This was thought to be done by adopting packages of seed–fertilizer and water technology, a package linked with the so-called green revolution. During the Fourth Five-Year Plan (1969–74), therefore, two focussed objectives related to this sector were set up: firstly, by providing the settings that are necessary for a continued rise in production of food grains (by about 5% per year) over the period of 1969–78 and secondly, by enabling a major chunk of population in rural India (comprising of the small farmers in the arid areas and the agricultural labourers) to join in the course of agricultural development and thereby share get benefitted. These definitely emphasized the necessity to create conducive economic conditions to promote agriculture and also reflected organized efforts to spread the application of scientific and technological know-how for improving agricultural practices. In tune with the said objective, the share of agriculture was around 23% of the total plan expenditure, but still, the target production was never achieved. This period was followed by a severe economic crisis, and the Fifth Five-Year Plan (1974–79) was announced to realize the twin objectives—eradication of poverty and attaining self-reliance. The way forward to achieve this twofold objective was through raising the growth rate, reducing income inequality and significantly stepping up the domestic rate of saving. For the same, to develop agriculture and irrigation Rs. 8080 crores (which is approximately 21% of the then total plan expenditure) was assigned. This move mainly gave priority to the spread of HYV cultivation, efficient use of fertilizers, pesticides and insecticides to gear up agricultural production. The focus was clearly on small and marginal farmers, dry farming techniques, developing HYV seeds for different crops and also to bring back the fertility of the then arid lands. Nonetheless, at the end of fourth year of the said Fifth Five-Year Plan, in March 1978, it was terminated. This was followed by two Sixth Five-Year Plans (SFYP). The first SFYP was under the regime of the Janata Party during 1978–83. SFYP in its second term (1980–85) was under the Congress regime. During this phase, new stimulus was accorded to agriculture. This time 24% of the budget allocation was meant for the development of agriculture. The sector saw a growth at a yearly rate of 4.3%; 152 metric tons of food grains was produced, and thus, this phase started to be known as the phase of second 'green revolution'. The effect was quite prominent in eastern and central parts of India. This includes states like West Bengal, Bihar, Orissa, Madhya Pradesh and eastern Uttar Pradesh (Kumar et al. 2012). Therefore, during the Seventh Five-Year Plan (1985–90), weightage was given on policies and programmes that would transform into rapid growth in food grains production. Rs. 10.52 crores was allocated as plan expenditure for agriculture in the Seventh Plan, but given the immense importance of the sector, actual spending was more by Rs. 2.27 crores. Emphasis was given on specific projects. For example, Special Rice Production scheme in the Eastern Region, National Watershed Programme for stimulating Rain Fed Agriculture, National Oilseeds Development Project, Social Forestry, etc. The Seventh Five-Year Plan got an extension for two years, and thus, Eighth Five-Year Plan was announced in 1992. It is needless to mention that considerable public expenditure was incurred during this phase in order to promote the package of 'green revolution' which was, till then, limited to only a few regions of the country and only to few crops in the 1970s. In order to enable the farmers to adopt newer production techniques and thus efficient outcomes, two-policy decision of the government played crucial role—firstly, in 1969 the banks were nationalized and secondly the subsequent provisioning of priority sector lending in agriculture. Further, to disseminate and deepen the green revolution fertilizer and other inputs were subsidized, substantial government expenditure was made for research and innovations. The overall conducive government policy regime also played equally vital role. The focus of lifting up of food grain production was gradually achieved. In the 1970s, the annual average growth of agricultural GDP in terms of both crop and geographical coverage was 104%. This now became 4.7% in the 1980s. This marked the beginning of the third phase in the domain of Indian agriculture.

5.2.3 *Phase III (Early 1990s and Onwards)*

The third phase starting from the early 1990s till date echoes the dominance and rule of neoliberal economic policy. If we observe the Indian economy minutely, it would reveal as an irrefutable inference that a major part of this period only witnessed a severe agrarian crisis—if not the worst, since independence. To begin with, it is beyond doubt that in the context of agriculture, capital formation is a major driver of agriculture productivity and growth. In developing countries like India, the concept of capital in agriculture has been broadened to include fixed capital investment, livestock and tree stock. In agriculture, there are two major sources of capital formation, private and public sources. The private sources consist of individuals/households and private corporate sector. The public sources obviously include the public agencies, mainly the government. In the next sections, we shall make an attempt to substantiate the happenings during this third phase and understand the growth of agriculture in India.

5.3 Trends in Investment and Production in Agriculture

There was a steady rise in the share of capital formation. The rise was from public institutions since the mid-1960s, and the average share of public sources was at its high (41.7%) during the 1980s. However, the falling trend was quite notable from 1991 to 1992 and became more striking from 2008 2009 onwards. Capital formation from private sources was around 85% of total capital formation in the sector in 2014–15. From 1991 till 2007, the share of public sources was on an average 21%, whereas from 2008 to 2009 onwards till 2014–15 the average share of public sources in capital formation reduced to 15% (Fig. 5.2).

Further, examining the plan expenditure on agriculture and allied activities, it is seen that issues related to agriculture and allied sectors had a prolonged history to remain as a matter of concern for the country (Table 5.1). It is true that a tenfold rise was seen in plan expenditure on agriculture and allied activities between the Seventh FYP (1985–90) and Eleventh FYP (2007–12) both in absolute terms and also at current prices had happened. However, an investigation of the data as shown in Table 5.1 reflects that the sector suffered due to lack of needed attention even in the pre-reforms period. During the period immediately after independence, there was a push in terms of its share, at least for the first two decades post-1947. However, after the late 1970s, there was a deceleration. The share of agriculture and allied activities declined by 2 percentage points (16.7–14.7%) during the annual plans (average for 1966–69) and Fourth FYP (1969–74), respectively. The same share declined to 3.9%

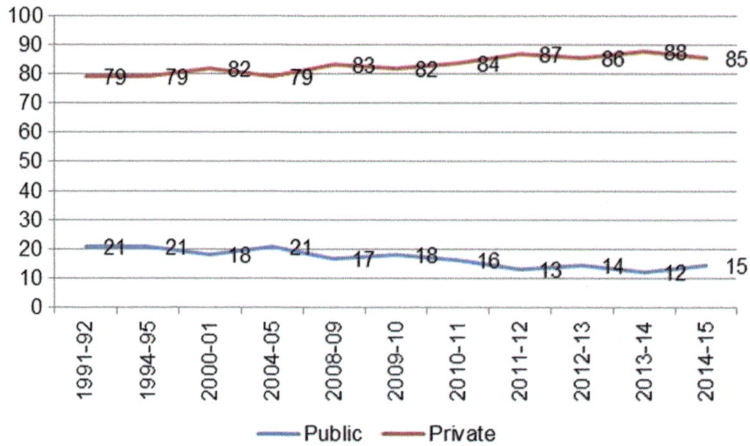

Fig. 5.2 Share of gross capital formation in agriculture (GCFA), various years (in per cent). *Source* CSO, various years

in the Tenth FYP (2002–07) and further to 3.7% during the Eleventh Five-Year Plan (2007–12); it further shrunk to 3.7%. However, the Twelfth FYP projection (at current prices) showed a marginal increase from 3.7% during the Eleventh FYP to 4.7% during the Twelfth FYP.

It has been claimed that private investments resulted in the increase in production of crops—both food grains and non-food grains over the years. During 1950–51, the total crop production was 133.87 million tons, of which food grain production was 50.82 million tons and non-food grains production was 83.05 million tons. This increased to 334.22 million tons during 1980–81 to 506.59 during 1990–91 and further to 647.59 million tons during 2016–17 (Fig. 5.3). The growth rates of these production trends show the other side of the story (Table 5.2).

The slack in the growth rates as shown in Table 5.2 may be attributed to growing slackness in agricultural public investment. Further, one must also note that there have been changes in cropping patterns in Indian agriculture during the aforementioned phases. During Phase II, data suggest that there was an absolute fall in the area cultivated with food grains and coarse cereals. On top of that, during the early periods of Phase III, there was further reduction in the area cultivated with pulses and the area cultivated with oilseeds also declined sharply.

5.4 Agricultural Credit

The insufficiency of fund for agricultural sector had been fetching the attention of the Reserve Bank of India (RBI) even before independence. The Agricultural Refinance Corporation (ARC) and Rural Credit Review Committee were set up in 1963 and

Table 5.1 Share of agriculture and allied services in plan expenditure in Rs. crore, at current prices[a]

Plan period	Agriculture and allied activities
Third FYP (1961–1966)	1088.90
Percentage of total plan expenditure	12.7
Annual plans (1966–1969)	1107.10
Percentage of total plan expenditure	16.7
Fourth FYP (1969–1974)	2320.40
Percentage of total plan expenditure	14.7
Fifth FYP (1974–1979)	4864.90
Percentage of total plan expenditure	12.3
Annual plan (1979–80)	1996.50
Percentage of total plan expenditure	16.4
Sixth FYP (1980–1985)	6623.50
Percentage of total plan expenditure	6.1
Seventh FYP (1985–1990)	12,792.60
Percentage of total plan expenditure	5.8
Annual plan (1990–91)	3405.40
Percentage of total plan expenditure	5.8
Annual plan (1991–92)	3850.50
Percentage of total plan expenditure	5.9
Eighth FYP (1992–1997)	22,467.20
Percentage of total plan expenditure	5.2
Ninth FYP (1997–2002)	42,462
Percentage of total plan expenditure	4.9
Tenth FYP (2002–2007)	58,933
Percentage of total plan expenditure	3.9
Eleventh FYP (2007–2012)	136,381
Percentage of total plan expenditure	3.7
[b]Twelfth FYP (2012–2017)	363,273
Percentage of total plan expenditure	4.7

[a]For centre only, as figures for states and UTs are not yet available
[b]12th plan projections (at current prices)
Source Compiled by authors from the base data given in the Economic Survey, various years, Government of India

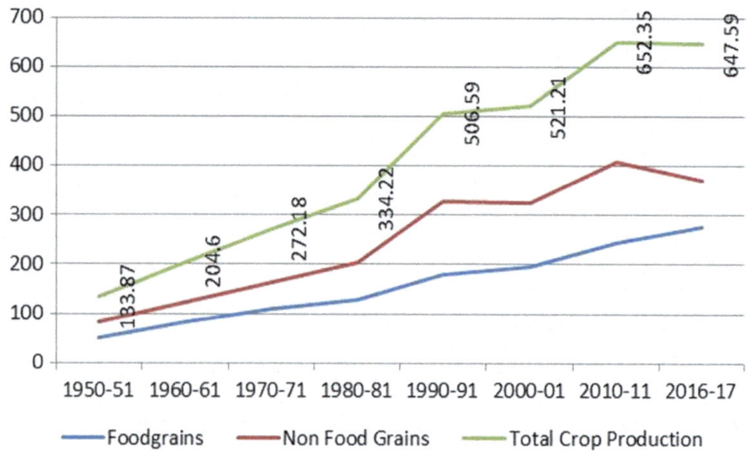

Fig. 5.3 Production of major crops (million tons). *Note* Food grains include—rice, wheat, coarse cereals, pulses; non-food grains include—sugarcane, cotton (m.bls), nine oilseeds, milk, fish. *Source* RBI, Handbook of Statistics on Indian Economy, various years

Table 5.2 CAGR of food and non-food production in India (various years)

Year	Compound growth rates of major crop production (in per cent)	
	Production of food grains	Production of non-food grains
1950–51 to 1960–61	4.90	3.97
1960–61 to 1970–71	2.83	2.94
1970–71 to 1980–81	1.80	2.25
1980–81 to 1990–91	3.13	4.81
1990–91 to 2000–01	1.10	−0.09
2000–01 to 2010–11	2.29	2.32
2010–11 to 2016–17	2.02	−1.53

Source Authors calculation based on data from *Pocket Book of Agricultural Statistics 2017*, Directorate of Economics and Statistics, Ministry of Agriculture and Farmers Welfare, Government of India, New Delhi

in 1966 by the RBI to provide necessary resources by way of refinance and also to monitor the flow of rural credit. Realizing the importance of subsidized credit for agricultural production and to extend rural credit, the Rural Credit Review Committee categorically recommended that commercial banks ought to play a complementary role, parallelly with cooperatives. Moreover, the developmental plans through social control and the subsequent nationalization of major commercial banks in 1969 brought extra momentum to the efforts of leveraging the system for supplying agricultural credit. During the same period, a special reference of priority sector highlighted the agricultural sector further. Mohan (2004) rightly pointed that on one hand policies were not tuned to the needs and requirements of the small and marginal farmers, while the co-operatives, on the other hand, lacked resources to meet the expected demand. Therefore, lead Bank Scheme was set up as part of decentralized credit planning. In 1975, by the Narasimham Working Group (Narasimham 1992), Regional Rural Banks (RRBs) were set up. Following the recommendations of the committee, in 1982 the National Bank for Agriculture and Rural Development (NABARD) was set up. NABARD's objective was to review the measures taken to promote formal credits for agriculture and rural development. In the second phase, the central theme of the structural reforms initiated during 1991 was to call for reform in the financial sector. Various measures have been considered in the domain of agricultural credit. For example, deregulation of interest rates of cooperatives and Regional Rural Banks (RRBs) deregulates the lending rates (for credits above Rs. 2 lakh) of the commercial banks and recapitalization of select RRBs. Further, measures like increasing refinance provision from Reserve Bank of India (RBI) and capital contribution to NABARD, inclusion of prudential accounting norms and provisioning requirements for all rural credit agencies were also taken.

In the areas of rural credit, NABARD has played a significant role in providing financial assistance to the rural mass. Its main role was to facilitate institutional development and encourage promotional efforts. NABARD also administered the Rural Infrastructure Development Fund (RIDF). Formed in steps like introducing the Kisan Credit Card (KCC) scheme and stipulation of interest rate not exceeding 9% for crop loans up to Rs. 50,000 extended by the government sector banks were included as well. The multi-agency credit delivery system comprising cooperative banks, scheduled commercial banks and RRBs has made steady growth in terms of putting in place a wide institutional delivery of short-term and long-term loans, particularly in the aftermath of financial reforms as shown in Tables 5.3 and 5.4.

Another major accomplishment of the financial reforms has been the declining share of non-institutional sources to the agricultural sector. The relative share of borrowing of cultivators' households from nonformal sources reflected a significant reduction from around 93% in 1951 to about 30% during 1991. However, a steady reverse swing recorded during post-reforms period which questions the credit delivery mechanism (Table 5.5).

Furthermore, the rising trend of direct finance to agriculture and allied activities saw a drop in the 1990s (12% of total finance to agriculture) compared to the 1980s (14%) and 1970s (around 16%). This only reflects the fact that the average share of long-term credit in the total direct finance has not only been much lower but has also slowed. Moreover, the disaggregated picture as per size-wise distribution of credit reveals that the growth of direct finance to small and marginal farmers compared to large-scale farmers witnessed a marked deceleration during the 1990s (Fig. 5.4).

Despite huge initiative taken by the government, the amount of financial support to agriculture remains inadequate. In agricultural sector, direct finance to the sector is not the only major constraint to achieve the productivity, but along with it the acceptance of new technological know-how, land improvements and setting up of irrigation and marketing infrastructure and alike factors are causing underutilization of investment capital in farm sector. Farmers had to borrow more short-term credit for meeting the current fixed cost and variable cost to maintain continuity instead of building up of long-term capital formation.

Table 5.3 Direct institutional credit for agriculture and allied activities—short-term (₹ billion)

Year	Loans issued				Loans outstanding at the end of the year			
	Cooperatives	SCBs	RRBs	Total	Cooperatives	SCBs	RRBs	Total
1980–81	13.86	5.17	–	20.47	19.08	11.62	–	32.50
1990–91	34.48	20.48	1.25	59.79	51.78	42.35	5.90	100.02
2000–01	185.56	107.04	30.95	323.55	181.68	154.42	36.92	373.02
2010–11	690.38	1460.63	385.60	2536.61	496.45	1932.62	406.63	2835.70
2011–12	818.29	2178.97	470.11	3467.37	445.17	2690.30	465.80	3601.27
2012–13	1025.92	–	577.57	–	766.22	3534.25	552.55	–
2013–14	1135.74	–	706.46	–	1807.64	3335.72	682.67	–
2014–15	1998.72	–	846.86	–	1893.99	4649.20	826.20	–
2015–16	2275.71	–	981.50	–	2031.90	5203.95	967.02	–
2016–17	2178.97	–	–	–	–	–	–	–

Source Handbook of Statistics on Indian Economy, various years, RBI

Notes 1. Data up to 1990–91 pertain to the period July–June and April–March thereafter. In case of SCBs, data for all the years pertain to July–June period. 2. RRBs came into existence in 1975–76. 3. Data for cooperatives cover only PACS as short-term loans are being provided by them. 4. Data on total loans issued include loans issued by the state governments

Table 5.4 Direct institutional credit for agriculture and allied activities—long-term (₹ billion)

Year	Loans issued				Loans outstanding at the end of the year			
	Cooperatives	SCBs	RRBs	Total	Cooperatives	SCBs	RRBs	Total
1980–81	6.43	7.46	–	13.89	24.07	18.82	2.86	42.89
1990–91	13.72	26.28	2.10	42.09	53.53	127.97	11.63	193.13
2000–01	87.39	57.36	8.71	153.46	279.67	228.28	35.57	543.52
2010–11	90.83	767.29	54.05	912.17	270.29	1643.22	144.04	2057.55
2011–12	61.34	949.80	60.48	1071.62	280.28	1742.68	172.44	2195.40
2012–13	86.11	–	68.92	–	275.79	1690.53	194.06	–
2013–14	63.90	–	77.28	–	339.70	1699.60	220.27	–
2014–15	81.19	–	131.51	–	327.63	2190.49	277.42	–
2015–16	94.92	–	203.84	–	265.87	2944.46	361.10	–
2016–17	108.78	–	–	–	–	–	–	–

Source Handbook of Statistics on Indian Economy, various years, RBI

Table 5.5 Relative share of borrowing of cultivator households from different sources

Sources	1951	1961	1971	1981	1991	2002	2010
Non-institutional	92.7	91.3	68.3	36.8	30.6	38.9	29.7
Of which money lenders	69.7	49.2	36.1	16.1	17.5	26.8	21.9
Institutional	7.3	18.7	31.7	63.2	66.3	61.3	68.8
Of which							
Cooperatives	3.3	2.6	22	29.8	23.6	30.2	24.9
Commercial banks	0.9	0.6	2.4	28.8	35.2	26.3	25.1
Unspecified	–	–	–	–	3.1	–	1.5
Total	100	100	100	100	100	100	100

Source All India Debt and Investment Survey and NSSO

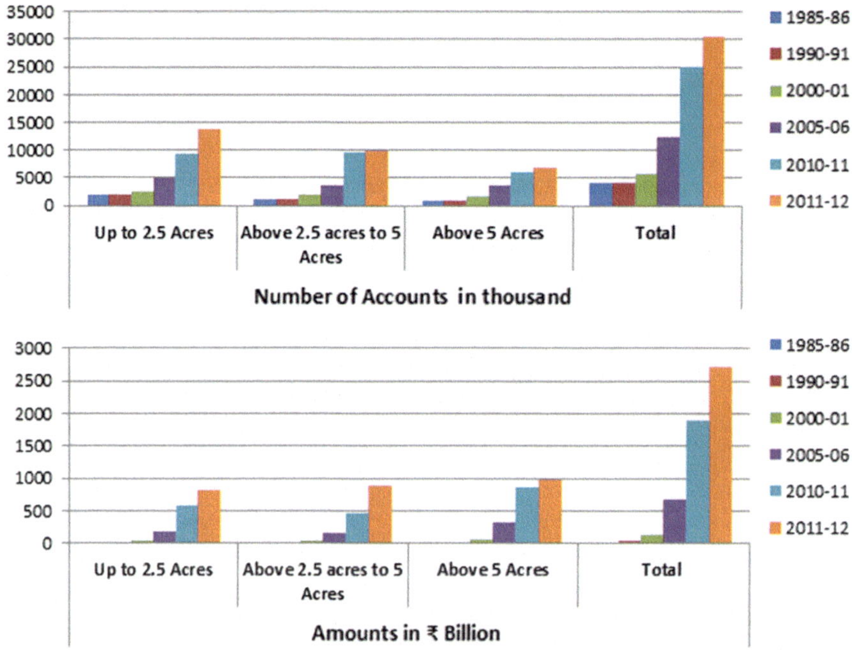

Fig. 5.4 Scheduled commercial banks' direct finance to farmers. *Source* Handbook of Statistics on Indian Economy, RBI, various years

5.5 Input Use Pattern and Potential Loss of Productivity

Table 5.6 shows the pattern of land use and select inputs for agricultural production at different time points during 1950–51 to 2015–16. The gross cropped area increased from 131.89 million hectares in 1950–51 to 200.86 million hectares in 2013–14, whereas the net sown area increased from 118.75 million hectares to 141.86 million hectares during this period. The movements of gross cropped area and net sown area

Table 5.6 Pattern of land use and select inputs for agricultural production (various years)

Year	Net sown area (in million hectares)	Gross cropped area (in million hectares)	Net irrigated area (in million hectares)	Gross cropped area irrigated (in million hectares)	Consumption of fertilizers (lakh tons)	Consumption of pesticides (technical grade materials) ('000 tons)
1950–51	118.75	131.89	20.85	22.56	0.69	2.35
1951–52	119.40	133.23	21.05	23.18	0.66	–
1960–61	133.20	152.77	24.66	27.98	2.92	8.62
1970–71	140.27	165.79	31.10	38.20	21.77	24.32
1980–81	140.00	172.63	38.72	49.78	55.16	45.00
1990–91	143.00	185.74	48.02	63.20	125.46	75.00
2000–01	141.36	185.34	55.13	76.19	167.02	43.58
2010–11	141.56	197.56	63.66	88.93	281.22	55.54
2011–12	140.98	195.69	65.70	91.78	277.90	52.98
2012–13	139.94	194.14	66.27	92.25	255.36	45.62
2013–14	141.43	200.86	68.10	95.77	244.82	60.28
2014–15	–	–	–	–	255.76	56.12
2015–16	–	–	–	–	267.52	50.41

Source Compiled from http://agricoop.nic.in/

suggest the increasing incidence of multiple cropping in Indian agriculture. Further, rapid rise in the use of fertilizers and thereby the pesticides triggered the productivity per hectare during these years. Thus, the shrinking area along with high productivity, massive use of fertilizers, pesticides and water wherever available (as it is one of the other integral inputs for agricultural production) especially during the post-green revolution period, only added to ecological stress High yielding variety seeds are irrigation as well as fertilizer responsive. The use of fertilizers and pesticides in improper dose may have created ecological problem during the post-green revolution period. The input use pattern under green revolution has led to loss of soil nutrients and declining water availability and contributed directly to potential yield loss. There has, however, been lack of initiatives, both by the government and by the private, to compensate this potential loss of land productivity which may cause the future fall in agricultural productivity (Vaidyanathan 2007).

5.6 Changing Pattern of Farm Size

The large and medium holdings together owned around 54% of the total land in 1971. This share dropped to around 25% in 2013 (Table 5.7). The proportion of households

Table 5.7 Size distribution of operational land holdings

Category of household ownership holdings (land size in hectares)	1971	1982	1992	2003	2013
	Percentage distribution of households				
Landless (≤0.002)	9.64	11.33	11.25	10.04	7.41
Marginal (0.002–1.000)	52.98	55.31	60.63	69.63	75.41
Small (1.000–2.000)	15.49	14.7	13.42	10.81	10
Semi-medium (2.000–4.000)	11.89	10.78	9.28	6.03	5.01
Medium (4.000–10.000)	7.88	6.45	4.54	2.96	1.93
Large (>10.000)	2.12	1.43	0.88	0.53	0.24
Total	100	100	100	100	100
	Percentage distribution of area owned				
Landless (≤0.002)	0	0	0	0.01	0.01
Marginal (0.002–1.000)	9.76	12.22	16.93	23.01	29.75
Small (1.000–2.000)	14.68	16.49	18.59	20.38	23.53
Semi-medium (2.000–4.000)	21.92	23.38	24.58	21.97	22.07
Medium (4.000–10.000)	30.73	29.9	26.07	23.08	18.83
Large (>10.000)	22.91	18.01	13.83	11.55	5.81
Total	100	100	100	100	100

Source Household Ownership and Operational Holdings in India, Statement no 4.2, NSS 70th Round (2013), Ministry of Statistics and Programme Implementation, Government of India

with medium and large holdings declined from 10% to around 2% during this period. Thus, by now, the bulk of farms are placed in the category referred to as 'semi-medium' or even smaller. As an outcome of these happenings, the smaller farms started predominating. Further, for them given the near fixity of cultivated land, they accounted for the greater part of the area operated. All this resulted in a downscaling of production. Precisely, cultivation started taking place on progressively smaller-sized farms. Now, such arrangements perhaps started discouraging to allow more labour inputs to work on these small-sized farms, and the members of the family are therefore forced to look for income opportunities outside the farm to supplement their income. This, in turn, forced to neglect production management, thus slowing growth (Sen and Bhatia 2004). In this context, Balakrishnan et al. (2004) pointed out that it is very difficult for most of the Indian farms to access and adapt to new technologies and thus move towards even better and efficient modes of production. This further reduced the farmer's capacity to leverage credit, due to their meagre or falling asset base. Secondly, an upgradation of the farm relative prices could do little to arrest the agricultural decline, especially, when the operational factors that govern production, such as farm size, turn adverse and once and for all.

5.7 Subsidies in Agriculture Under Reforms

The WTO, one of the foremost proponents of the neoliberal agenda, treats agricultural subsidies as 'bad subsidies' or 'market distorting subsidies'. To fulfil the neoliberal agenda, the Government of India has reduced subsidy on essential inputs for agriculture (like fertilizer, irrigation and electricity) by $6.3 billion (from $29.1 billion in 2011 to $22.8 billion in 2014) in recent past. During the same period, the so-called green box subsidies that are the non-market distorting subsidies were also reduced by $6.2 billion (from $24.5 billion in 2011 to $18.3 billion in 2014). Further, the subsidy on fertilizers was Rs. 4967 crores less during 2016–17 compared to its level during 2014–15. Further, as it happened in India, there was a substantial lag between the time of enactment of food subsidy bill (2014–15) and the time of its practical implementation (2015–16). Naturally, the cost meant for this account had risen during this period. Surprisingly, rather than allocating fresh resources to support the food subsidy programme, the government decided to reallocate a large amount (Rs. 45,000 crores), meant to be provided as subsidy, to Indian Food Corporation as debt. Thus, over time, as the targeted subsidies get converted into debt and finally take the form of free-market cash transfers, with more of market and less of government, this will only create a spiral of rising prices and costs.

The neoliberal reform does not allow the system to extend important stimulants like formal safeguard to agriculture, formal credit, affordable technology through public sector, disaster management and so on with the terms of trade gradually getting directed against the poor and the disadvantaged farmers. The minimum support price set by the government does not cover even the cost of cultivation. Thus, the farming may be sustainable if the market price is more than the minimum support price. The farmers who wish to sell their produce at the mandis have to pay a 'market fee' making their products costly. In addition, there are some additional costs related to transportation and payments for several intermediaries. As a result, farmers receive substantial lesser amount as compared to the price at which his produce is sold to the retailer.

5.8 Concluding Remarks

One of the outcomes of neoliberal reforms has been the capitalist mode of development continued along with displacement and destitution. As discussed in this study, there is a growing trend of small and marginal farmers which eventually is giving birth to self-exploiting subsistence petty producers in a booming capitalist structure. It would not be an exaggeration to say that, perhaps, this is a paradox, which would remain unresolved for a long time. The Indian economy is apparently growing at exceptional rates; the petty production sector including peasant agriculture is getting drastically squeezed. The consequence of which is the suicide of more than three lakh peasants over the past two decades. A close introspection of the entire paradigm would reveal that it is not really true that the neoliberal regime calls for a withdrawal of the state per se and only propagates free-market reforms. Rather, it very carefully uses the state to perform and safeguard the interests of the capitalist economy at all spheres. Therefore, the state's withdrawal does happen, but in the form of its role of sustaining and welfare generation of the mass. This study shows with data and evidences that though conformist perception traces the spot of neoliberal policies from 1990 onwards, it had actually started to predominate Indian agriculture much before 1990. In that way, '1990' is just symbolic. Indeed, reforms did happen, and lot of policies was adopted by the state, but mostly without a clear directive.

Appendix

Table 5.8.

Table 5.8 A major agriculture-related policies and projects in India from 1943 till 2017

Year	Major policy	Brief note on the agenda
1943	Food Grains Policy Committee	The first ever committee constituted under the chairmanship of Theodore Gregory. Gregory recommended measures to secure more equitable distribution of what was available. This essentially meant the extension of rationing and the basic plan idea of the central government. The plan was to maintain controlled supplies of food grains from surplus to deficit areas according to fixed quota. This was mainly to control issues like food availability, food supplies and food distribution and also to control price. Price control was needed because of poor food availability situation in India caused due to the World War II
1947	The Food Grains Policy Committee	Purshottamdas Thakurdas chaired this committee. This was formed to study the aspects of food distribution in India. It recommended to gradually decontrol food. The committee quite emphatically recommended the removal of control and restrictions of movements of food grains in a phased manner. Maitra Committee (1950), Mehta Committee (1957), Venkatappaiah Committee (1966): All these three important committees had significant footprint in the formulation of the agricultural policy in India. Most importantly, these committees had a common tune of equating food production as a core to agricultural development

(continued)

Table 5.8 (continued)

Year	Major policy	Brief note on the agenda
1960	Intensive Agriculture District Programme (IADP)	The IADP programme envisioned the choice of favourable areas with maximum irrigation facilities. Added to this, it also preferred areas with low natural hazards, facilities like the provisioning of all the necessary elements of production (such as adequate supply of fertilizers, credit). It aims at a holistic and intensified approach to address the problem of agricultural production, especially in areas that are more receptive to such production efforts
1963	Agricultural Refinance Corporation (ARC)	ARC was started as a refinancing agency. It aimed at providing medium-term and long-term agricultural credit in order to support investment credit needs for the development of the agricultural sector
1964	Intensive Agriculture Area Program (IAAP)	To develop the provision of special harvest
1965	The Commission for Agricultural Costs and Prices	The commission was established to recommend Minimum Support Prices (MSPs). The intention was to motivate cultivators and farmers to adopt the latest available technology. This was expected to optimize the use of resources and raise productivity
1965	The Food Corporation of India	The FCI was set up to implement the major objectives of National Food Policy such as: • Effective price support operations • Distribution of food grains throughout the country for Public Distribution System • Maintaining satisfactory level of operational and buffer stocks of food grains to ensure National Food Security • Regulate market price to provide food grains to consumers at a reasonable price
1964–1965	Intensive Agriculture Area Programme (IAAP)	IAAP was targeted to the development of scientific and progressive agriculture in an intensive manner. It was meant for the areas which have high production potentials. The primary idea was to cover at least 20% of the cultivated area. The emphasis was on important crops such as wheat, rice, millets, cotton. Also paved the way for green revolution
1966–1969	New Agriculture Strategy (Green Revolution)	Increased use of fertilizers, improved water supplies and better agricultural practices. With it are also associated increasing mechanization of agricultural operations and measures of plant protection from pests and diseases
1966–1967	High Yielding Variety Programme (HYVP)	Introduction of new high yielding varieties of improved seeds and enhanced application of the fertilizers and extended use of pesticides were its main features
1969	Nationalization of 14 Commercial Banks	To promote credit to priority sector such as agriculture

(continued)

Table 5.8 (continued)

Year	Major policy	Brief note on the agenda
1973	Marginal Farmer and Agriculture Labor Agency (MFALA)	MFALA was set up for technical and financial assistance to marginal and small farmer and agricultural labour
1974	Minikit Programme for Rice, Wheat and Coarse Cereals	To increase the productivity by popularizing the use of newly released hybrid/high yielding varieties and spread the area coverage under location-specific high yielding varieties/hybrids
1974	Small Farmer Development Agency (SFDA)	To investigate and identify the problems of small farmers and ensure that various services reach to them
1975	Agriculture Refinance and Development Corporation (ARDC)	For technical and financial assistance to small farmers
1981	Coconut Development Board	To increase production and productivity of coconut To bring additional area under coconut in potential non-traditional areas
1982	National Bank for Agriculture and Rural Development (NABARD)	Lay emphasize on developmental and promotional role, besides refinancing activities—successor to ARC of 1963
1983	Farmer Agriculture Service Centres (FASC)	Bank has been entrusted with 'matters concerning policy, planning and operations in the field of credit for agriculture and other economic activities in rural areas in India'
1984	National Oilseeds and Vegetable Oils Development Board (NOVOD)	NOVOD Board covers the entire gamut of activities associated with the oilseeds and vegetable oil industry. These includes—production, marketing, trade, storage, processing, research and development, financing and advisory role to the formulation of integrated policy and programme of development of oilseeds and vegetable oil
1985	Comprehensive Crop Insurance Scheme	To popularize the use of improved agricultural instruments and tool kits
1986	National Pulses Development Project (NPDP)	The main function of NPDP was to increase the production of pulses in the country to achieve self-sufficiency

(continued)

Table 5.8 (continued)

Year	Major policy	Brief note on the agenda
1990	High Power Committee	The first comprehensive policy document that covered all major aspects of the agri-economy in India. This was chaired by Bhanu Pratap Singh and gave 'a great deal of thought' and pointed out the core issues that were expected to influence the food security system in the country. The committee for the first time recommended the personal involvement of the farmers. It mentioned that the farmers are the primary producers and act as the market makers who in turn influence the consumers. Therefore, there is a dire need to protect the farmer and the consumer against the whims of production and the market forces to enhance agricultural productivity and thus ensure fair prices. It also emphasized on the storage, transportation and distribution system and strongly argued in favour of reducing the cost of food grain procurement. The committee further pointed out that there should be in place an efficient delivery system. This would ensure that those in genuine need of subsidies and support are properly targeted and given sufficient access to food grains. The government should also have enough interventionary powers so that in times of need, the government can come forward to protect the interests of producers or consumers as the case may be. Above all, the most notable recommendation, of the High Powered Committee (1990), was perhaps the pulling out of all controls, except quality controls, on movement, processing, marketing and export of farm products except in years of scarcity
1990	Agricultural and Rural Debt Relief Scheme (ARDRS)	The primary objective of the scheme was to provide relief to the farmers, artisans and weavers who are caught in the vicious circle of indebtedness and poverty. Fresh loans would be given to the borrowers for whom the loan was waived off. A debt relief of up to Rs. 10,000 including overdue interest to all the borrowers engaged in agriculture and allied activities, cottage and village industries, weaving and other rural crafts subject to certain eligibility conditions was proposed
1992	Oil Palm Development Programme (OPDP)	To promote oil palm cultivation in the country
1995	Accelerated Maize Development Programme (AMDP)	A 100% centrally sponsored scheme meant for the SC, ST and OBCs. The major programme components covered under the AMDP were related to input demonstration for maize, field school integrated pest management demonstration, incentive for improvement of farm implements, farmers training programme, publicity through electronic media

(continued)

Table 5.8 (continued)

Year	Major policy	Brief note on the agenda
1998	Kisan Credit Card (KCC)	The National Bank for Agriculture and Rural Development (NABARD) proposed this model to provide short-term credit limits for crops, and term loans for agricultural needs
2000	Intensive Cotton Development Programme (ICDP)	ICDP—a centrally sponsored scheme of Technology Mission on Cotton (TMC). This was implemented through its four Mini Missions (MM) for achieving its objectives. The objective of ICDP under MM-II of TMC was mainly to increase cotton production, productivity and improvement of cotton quality. The purpose was to meet domestic and export demands of the country. This was expected to help in the reduction in the cost of cultivation and pesticide consumption for enhancing competitiveness in the international market
2000	National Agriculture Policy	The primary objective of the said National Agricultural Policy was to raise the productivity of inputs, protecting the interest of underprivileged agriculturalists, modernizing agricultural sector, enhancing yield of major commodities, checking environmental degradation, promote agricultural research training
2003	Agricultural Produce Market Regulation Act (Development and Regulation)	The APRA (D&R) wanted to portray the vast unexploited growth potential of Indian agriculture. It also intended to strengthen rural infrastructure in order to support faster agricultural development, to promote value addition. The scheme also focussed to accelerate the growth of agro-business and create employment in rural areas
2007	National Food Security Mission (NFSM)	The primary objective of NFSM was to increase production and productivity of items like *wheat, rice and pulses* and that too on a sustainable basis. This is expected to ensure food security of the country
2007	Warehousing (Development and Regulation) Act 2007	The main focus of this project was to seek authorization for direct procurement from farmers. It also aims the promotion of grading and quality control services, introduction of single-point reasonable market fee within the state and alike
2014	Rashtriya Krishi Vikas Yojana	Incentivize states to help increase and attract private investment in agriculture and allied sectors
2016	Pradhan Mantri Fasal Bima Yojana	This is a crop insurance policy with relaxed premium rates on the principal sum insured for farmers. Implemented with a budget of Rs. 17,600 crores, this scheme will provide financial support to farmers and cover for their losses

(continued)

Table 5.8 (continued)

Year	Major policy	Brief note on the agenda
2016	e Nam (National Agricultural Market)	National Agriculture Market (NAM) is a pan-India electronic trading portal. This networks the existing APMC mandis to create a unified national market for agricultural commodities
2017	Model Agricultural Produce and Livestock Marketing (Promotion and Facilitation) Act, 2017	It is being claimed as a major agriculture marketing reform to enable the farmers directly connect with the different buyers and enable them to discover optimum price for their commodities
2017	Green Revolution—Krishonnati Yojana	Promotion of commercial organic production through certified organic farming. The produce will be pesticide residue free and will contribute to improve the health of consumer

Source Compiled from various documents

References

Agricultural Statistics. (Various Years). Government of India.

All-India Debt and Investment Survey (AIDIS, Various Rounds). *Government of India, Ministry of Statistics—and Programme Implementation*. New Delhi: National Sample Survey Office.

Balakrishnan, P., Golait, R., & Kumar, P. (2004). *Agricultural growth in India since 1991* (Study Number 21). Mumbai: Development Research Group, DEAP, Reserve Bank of India.

Deshpande, R. S., Prachitha, J., Shah, K. (2017). *Making of state agricultural policy: A demonstration* (Monograph No. 90). Karnataka, India: Centre for Multi-Disciplinary Development Research (CMDR).

Economic Survey. (Various Years). Ministry of Finance, Government of India

Five Year Plan. (Various Years). *Planning Commission, Government of India*. Refer to http://planningcommission.nic.in/plans/planrel/fiveyr/welcome.html.

Government of India. (2013). *Household ownership and operational holdings in India*. Statement no 4.2, NSS 70th Round (2013). New Delhi: Ministry of Statistics and Programme Implementation, Government of India.

Government of India. (2018). *Demonetization and GST reforms led to an expansion of the formal economy and brought about increased tax compliance*. Addresses during Confederation of Indian Industry's Partnership Summit 2018, Press Information Bureau, Government of India, Vice President's Secretariat, New Delhi, February 24, 2018.

Handbook of Statistics on Indian Economy. (Various Years). RBI.

Jha, P., & Acharya, N. (2011). Expenditure on the rural economy in India's budgets since the 1950s: An assessment, review of Agrarian studies. *Journal of the Foundation for Agrarian Studies, 1*(2). http://www.ras.org.in/expenditure_on_the_rural_economy_in_indias_budgets_since_the_1950s.

Kumar, A., Bantilan, M. C. S., Kumar, P., Kumar, S., & Jee, Shiv. (2012). Food security in India: Trends, patterns and determinants. *Indian Journal of Agricultural Economics, 67*(3), 445–463.

Ministry of Agriculture & Farmers Welfare, Department of Agriculture, Cooperation & Farmers Welfare, Directorate of Economics & Statistics, New Delhi. Refer to http://agricoop.nic.in/.

Mohan, R. (2004). Agricultural credit in India—Status, issues and future agenda. *Reserve Bank of India Bulletin* 2004. Refer to Lecture http://www.rakeshmohan.com/docs/AgricreditBulletin.pdf.

NABARD. (Various Years). *Annual reports*. Mumbai.

Narasimham, M. (1992). *Committee on the financial system (Narasimham committee report on the financial system)*. Standard Book Company. Retrieved February 23, 2011.

Oskam, A., Meester, G., & Silvis, H. (2011). *EU policy for agriculture, food and rural areas*. Wageningen: Wageningen Academic Publishers.

Sen, A., & Bhatia, M. S. (2004). *Cost of cultivation and farm income*. India: Academic Press.

Statistical year book India. (Various Years). New Delhi: Ministry of Statistics and Programme Implementation, Government of India.

Vaidyanathan, A. (2007). *Water policy in India: A brief overview* (Occasional Paper Number 6). Bangalore: Centre for Public Policy, Indian Institute of Management.

World Bank. (Various Years). *Data bank, world development indicators, various years*. For details refer to http://databank.worldbank.org/data/indicator/NE.EXP.GNFS.ZS/1ff4a498/Popular-Indicators#.

Part III
Manufacturing Sector

Chapter 6
A Study of the Formal Manufacturing Sector in India: Performance of Significant Industries and Spatial Influence

Debashree Chatterjee Sanyal and Debarshi Sanyal

Abstract This chapter looks into the performance of the organised manufacturing sector by analysing technical efficiency (TE) at the firm level, in particular to test the impact of locational concentration of firms. A key objective of the study is to determine if such spatial concentration of firms within a state has any influence on the performance of those firms. The microeconometric analysis is duly controlled using expected determinants of TE including a wide array of state-specific infrastructure parameters. It covers all significant manufacturing industries that together contribute over 80% of the total value added of the formal manufacturing sector. The study observes, quite expectedly, that the size of firms has a significant positive contribution to TE for all of the major industries analysed. Government-owned firms are seen to be less efficient compared to their privately owned counterparts. The interesting aspect of the findings is in the variance observed in the impact of spatial concentration on efficiency. In general, firms located in the urban districts are more efficient. Locational concentration of firms is found to have a positive contribution on performance for sectors like automobiles, coke oven products and machinery and equipment. However, surprisingly, a high degree of spatial concentration is seen to have a negative effect on efficiency for some key sectors like basic metals, food products and beverages, the chemical sector and pharmaceuticals. We attribute this finding to the diseconomies emanating from congestion, higher prices and higher wages as undesirable effects of high industrial concentration, which practically outweigh the positive economies expected from greater access to infrastructure, technology, skill base and knowledge spillovers in the industrialised states.

Portions of the chapter is drawn from a paper presented by the authors at the IEA World Congress, Jordan, 2014. Comments from the session participants are gratefully acknowledged.

D. Chatterjee Sanyal (✉)
Deloitte, Melbourne, Australia
e-mail: debashree.sanyal@gmail.com

D. Sanyal
ANZ Banking Group, Melbourne, Australia
e-mail: dsanyal@gmail.com

P. K. Biswas and P. Das (eds.), *Indian Economy: Reforms and Development*, India Studies in Business and Economics, https://doi.org/10.1007/978-981-13-8269-7_6

6.1 Introduction

India's economic liberalisation programme since the 1990s orchestrated a thorough delicensing of industries making it significantly more efficient for organisations to add industrial plants, change locations or expand. The process of delicensing continued through the 1990s and by the turn of the millennium the process was virtually complete. The economic liberalisation included trade liberalisation that removed several restrictions including formal tariff barriers and non-tariff barriers which had restrictive consequences on foreign investment, adoption of new technology and access to the global markets in the earlier phase. In addition to the strategic transformation since the early 1990s, with economic liberalisation, state-specific infrastructure development, specific incentives to attract industries and the ability of the state to create a favourable environment for industries to thrive have played an important role in the manufacturing sector's growth. The manufacturing sector in India has experienced a high growth phase since the turn of the new millennium. In terms of net value added (NVA) in real terms, the manufacturing sector grew at about 7% compound annual rate during 2000–01 to 2015–16. The growth has not been consistent across states over this period and is likely due to the differences in the quality and scale of infrastructure development and state-specific policies.

This chapter delves into the performance of the manufacturing industries by analysing technical efficiency (TE) at the firm level, controlling for known or expected determinants of technical efficiency and in particular testing the influence of a wide array of state-specific infrastructure parameters. In addition, a key objective of the study is to determine if spatial concentration of firms within a state has any influence on the technical efficiency of those firms. The microeconometric analysis covers all significant manufacturing industries that together contribute over 80% of the total value added of the formal[1] manufacturing sector.

The analysis builds upon a volume of work explaining the performance trends of the manufacturing industries in India. Several studies in recent times have attempted to analyse the performance of manufacturing industries and state-specific factors behind the differences in performance. Gupta et al. (2009) attempts to explain performance of value added of the organised manufacturing industries, pre- and post-liberalisation, with 'delicensing' as a key driver to determine any evidence of performance differences. While this study analysed the performance of manufacturing industries with their contribution in value added, our analysis utilises technical efficiency as the key criteria of firm-level performance. Studies have also explored whether strict labour laws have hindered growth of the sector, especially for labour-intensive industries (Panagariya 2008). Banerjee and Duflo (2014), on the other hand, find that many firms are credit constrained by analysing the access to a targeted lending programme. Studies have also indicated the possibility of regulatory and administrative bottlenecks at the state level as a possible factor behind differences in industrial performance (OECD 2007).

[1]The term 'formal' and 'organised' are used interchangeably in the context of the manufacturing industries.

There has also been notable interest in the spatial dimension of firm performance. Variations in performance have been examined in the context of spatial or locational concentration of firms in these studies. The results demonstrate that location concentration has a role in economic performance of firms and regions (Moomaw 1981, 1988; Henderson 1986; Beeson 1987; Feser 2001). In theory, spatial concentration of firms could be associated with cost-saving externalities. Such economies of scale due to agglomeration can occur within the same industry (localisation economies) or across all industries within a region (urbanisation economies) (Nakamura 1985; Henderson 1986; Moomaw 1988; Feser 2001). In simple terms, firms of an industry group that are dependent on natural resources are likely to benefit by locating near the source of this input, due to the reduction in transportation costs. Similarly, firms relying on a specialised labour force are likely to locate in regions with abundance of skilled workforce. There could, however, be negative externalities of regional agglomerations by way of excessive congestion, pollution, competition and other urban issues. Firms in the industry will enjoy higher efficiency to the extent the economies of concentration outweigh these associated diseconomies. Findings in Lall and Chakravorty (2005) suggest material differences in the pattern of location selection of private and government owned firms in India. While private firms were found to choose the plant location based on availability of physical infrastructure, the same cannot be said for the location decisions of public firms. They further noted that private investments were seen to favour existing industrial clusters or industrially advanced regions.

There has been a volume of studies on the question of the ‘turnaround’ of productivity growth in the context of the Indian organised manufacturing sector in the post-reform period. A number of studies provided evidence of a decline in total factor productivity (TFP) growth rate in the 1990s relative to that of the 1980s (Goldar 2000; Goldar and Kumari 2003; Raj and Mahapatra 2009). Other studies have reported improvement in TFP in the post-reform period (Ahluwalia 2000; Ray 2002; Mitra 1999; Unel 2003; Dholakia and Dholakia 1994; Topalova 2004; Tata Services Limited 2003). Studies analysing the differences in TFP growth in the spatial context and at the disaggregated level are, however, limited. Studies by Trivedi (2004), Veeramani and Goldar (2005), Aghion et al. (2008), Mitra et al. (2002) and Ray (2002) have all dealt with state-level productivity estimates. While output expansion based on increased use of resources is theoretically feasible, it has not been proven to be sustainable. Scarcity of resources, which includes physical, financial and human resources, has been recognised as a limiting factor on the process of economic growth. Therefore, efficiency or productivity of resources becomes a critical factor behind growth.

The growth of TFP may be induced from more efficient utilisation of resources and/or by technical change (Färe et al. 1994). Therefore, in numerous studies, researchers have tried to investigate which of these components have contributed to the observed pattern of TFP growth. Level of technical efficiency is indicative of the degree of successful utilisation of productive resources and thus considered to be an important determinant of productivity growth and international competitiveness in any economy. There is a group of studies that examined the impact of reform on the performance of the manufacturing industries in terms of technical efficiency. Majority of the studies estimated an average production function to evaluate productive efficiency. Some other studies estimate a frontier production function and measure the distance between the efficient frontier and the position of the individual firms as a direct measure of efficiency. There are differences in results regarding the trend of average efficiency reported by the extant studies. Studying the trend of average technical efficiency in the post-reform period Driffield and Kambhampati (2003) found a positive trend in five out of six sectors that they have analysed. They also found that market concentration in general decreases efficiency in the manufacturing sector which is contrary to the findings of Mahambare and Balasubramanyam (2005) and Patibandla (2001). Mitra (1999) measured the state-wise estimates of the technical efficiency of the manufacturing industries for the period 1976–77 to 1992–93 for 17 two-digit Indian industry groups for the 15 major states using a time-variant technical efficiency model. The study indicates an increase in technical efficiency which further gave boost to the TFP growth in most of the states.

Geographical concentration of industries has been prevalent in India much before independence. Port cities and regions with historical industrial specialisations have witnessed industrial growth and concentration at the expense of acutely unindustrialised areas within the country. While specific policies were adopted to achieve industrial dispersal across regions since the planning era, not much success was seen. The protectionist policies existed till the early 1990s, in effect, resulted in a slow, high-cost manufacturing sector which also had regional imbalance in its growth. The historical condition of the manufacturing sector in India has been characterised as sluggish and 'dynamically inefficient' in Bhagwati and Desai (1970) and Bhagwati and Srinivasan (1975). Studies show that geographical concentration of industries determines the pattern of regional development in the longer run. Empirical evidence also corroborates the significant role played by the location of production units in determining productivity growth at the industry level (Aghion and Burgess 2003; Lall and Rodrigo 2001; Mitra 1999). It is important to note that in a more recent study Amirapu et al. (2018) found that the average levels of industrial concentration have in fact fallen significantly between 1998 and 2013.

What effects do these regional concentration patterns of manufacturing industries have on firms' efficiency? Can economies of localisation offset the associated diseconomies in the context of the Indian organised manufacturing sector? Are differences in infrastructure development across states, a driver of efficiency divergences across firms of the same industry group located in different states? Against this setting, the plausible explanation for these questions requires a systematic analysis involving firm-level assessment of technical efficiency and its key determinants across different industry groups. The chapter is hereafter organised as follows. The next section presents recent growth trends in the formal manufacturing sector. We then explain the analytical approach and data used for the econometric analysis to evaluate the performance of the major manufacturing industries. This is followed by a discussion of the main results. Conclusions from the study are summarised in the last section.

6.2 Recent Trends in the Formal Manufacturing Sector in India

Using aggregate data from the Annual Survey of Industries (ASI) published by the Central Statistical Office (CSO), Ministry of Statistics and Programme Implementation (MOSPI), Government of India (GoI), trends in NVA of major formal manufacturing industries at the two-digit classification level (NIC 08) have been analysed. Five rounds of the ASI aggregate data have been used for this analysis covering the period of 2000–01 to 2015–16. Through this study period, NVA in real terms (at 2010 prices) at an annualised rate grew at double digits for some of the largest manufacturing industries. NVA of the coke and petroleum sector in real terms grew at a compound annual rate of 15% through this period followed by the motor vehicle industry which grew at 12%. However, these growth rates have not been consistent over the time period. The petroleum sector, for example, grew massively at a rate of over 20% till 2007–08, driven by increasing global petroleum prices, but fell sharply thereafter at a rate of negative 14% from 2007–08 to 2011–12, again followed by a growth rate of 20% between 2011–12 and 2015–16. This fluctuation is likely to be associated with the volatility of the global crude oil prices through this period. In a similar trend, the basic metal industry also experienced extremely high growth rates of NVA in real terms, in excess of 20% (annualised) from 2000–01 to 2007–08, driven by the global commodities boom. This sector experienced a significant crash (negative 24%) in terms of real net value added between 2011–12 and 2015–16. The motor vehicle industry in India, on the other hand, has experienced a remarkable and consistent growth during the study period. The only major industry that has experienced lacklustre growth through this period is textiles (compound annual growth rate of real NVA at 2%). The compound annual growth rates of NVA in real terms for the major industries are presented in Fig. 6.1.

There has been a significant divergence in the growth patterns across states. While the organised manufacturing sector in the major industrial states of Maharashtra and Gujarat grew at 6 and 10%, respectively (compound annual growth of NVA in real terms from 2000–01 to 2015–16), states like Madhya Pradesh and West Bengal grew only at 3 and 2%, respectively (Fig. 6.2). Key industrialised states like Tamil Nadu, Andhra Pradesh[2] and Karnataka all experienced notable growth rates in the manufacturing sector in terms of NVA during the same period. Most remarkably states like Uttarakhand and Himachal Pradesh demonstrated exceptional growth rates in manufacturing: 23 and 15%, respectively, on an annualised basis through the study period. The stellar performance of Uttarakhand and the puzzling underperformance of certain states like West Bengal in terms of industrial growth in the same period can be explained by a multitude of factors. The drivers could include state-specific infrastructure development, state policies to actively promote organised manufacturing industries as seen in Uttarakhand, ease of doing business and also spatial concentration effects. Khanna and Sharma (2018) demonstrate that

[2]Figures for undivided Andhra Pradesh (Andhra Pradesh and Telangana combined) have been used in 2011–12 and 2015–16 for comparability.

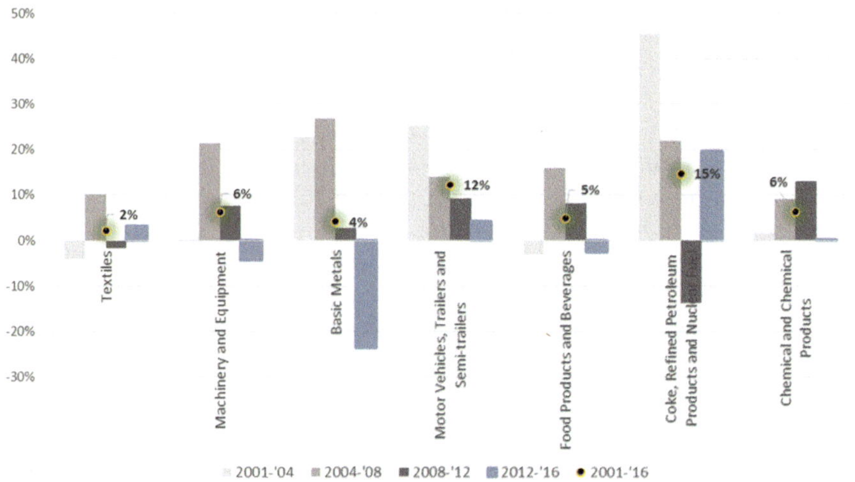

Fig. 6.1 Compound annual growth rate of net value added in real terms: Key industries. *Notes* (1) Estimated from ASI aggregate data. (2) Net value added in real terms (2010 = 100). (3) For 2011–12 and 2015–16 data, NVA is calculated considering NIC 2-digit level concordance with prior rounds. (4) Annualised growth rate across the study period (2000–01 to 2015–16) shown in dots. (5) The Chemical and Chemical Products industry includes Pharmaceuticals, which in the revised industry classification in 2008 has been separated out as an independent 2-digit industry due to its size. For the purpose of this comparative study across the time periods, Pharmaceuticals NVA has been included within the Chemical and Chemical Products for 2011–12 and 2015–16 data
Source As for Fig. 6.1

disparity in governance factors in Indian states impact manufacturing productivity. They further suggest that regional growth inequality could be addressed through reforms to improve the quality of institutions, regulation and governance in the lagging states.

6.3 Data, Econometric Framework and Construction of Variables

The study uses microdata at the plant (factory) level from the Annual Survey of Industries (ASI) for the sample years 2000–01, 2003–04, 2007–08 and 2011–12. It first calculates the TE scores at the plant level for all manufacturing industries (at NIC two-digit level) across states. The ASI data in this study period are based on three different NIC classifications (i.e. NIC 98 for the period 2000–01 and 2003–04, NIC 04 for the period 2007–08 and NIC 08 for 2011–12). Accordingly, an assessment of concordance has been carried out at the two-digit level between the NIC codes used in the input data. It is found that at the two-digit level in both NIC 98 and NIC 04, all relevant industry codes have the same scope. However, appropriate mapping

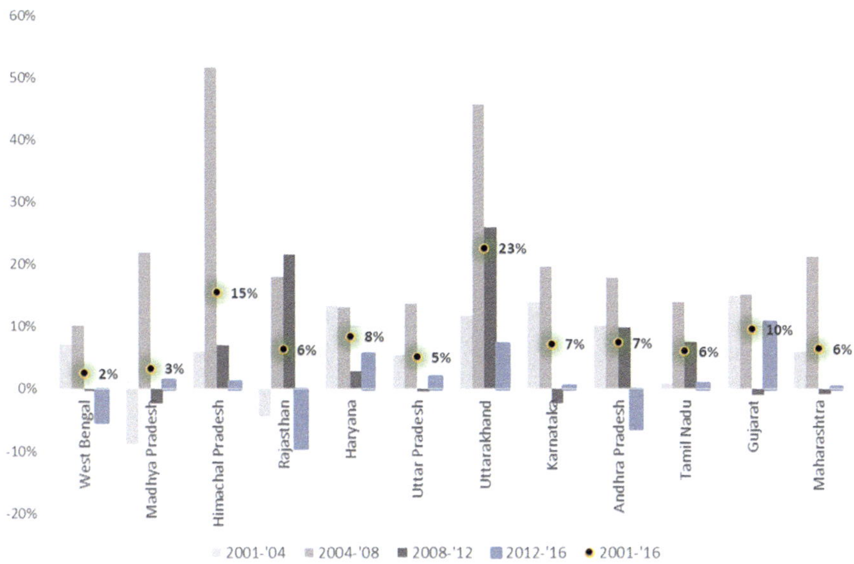

Fig. 6.2 Compound annual growth rate of net value added in real terms: Major states *Notes* (1) Estimated from ASI aggregate data. (2) Net value added in real terms (2010 = 100). (3) For 2011–12 and 2015–16 data, NVA is calculated considering NIC 2-digit level concordance with prior rounds. (4) Annualised growth rate across the study period (2000–01 to 2015–16) shown in dots. (5) Figures for undivided Andhra Pradesh (Andhra Pradesh and Telengana combined) have been used in 2011–12 and 2015–16 for comparability
Source As for Fig. 6.1

between industry codes at the two-digit level was required for NIC 04 and NIC 08.[3] Variance in state-level infrastructure development has been analysed using state-level infrastructure variables (surfaced to total road, teledensity, electrification density and credit-deposit ratio of the state) for each study period. The infrastructure data were collected from different publications of the CSO. The ASI data used in this study do not provide a unique identification number for the plants, which can be tracked over the years thus making construction of a panel data at the factory level difficult. The analysis strategies have been adopted keeping these limitations in mind. Consistent with the objectives of the study, a pooled regression analysis has been performed using the computed TE scores as the dependent variable using the four study periods (2000–01, 2003–04, 2007–08 and 2011–12).

As a first step of the empirical analysis, a stochastic production frontier has been used to estimate the firm-level TE scores of all manufacturing industries at the NIC two-digit level. A translog production function is applied using cross-sectional data and assuming a truncated normal distribution. As standard, labour and capital constitute the inputs into the production function. We have computed gross value added (GVA) for the unit during the production year as a measure of output. We have taken

[3]See Appendix for the concordance mapping.

total man-days worked instead of number of employees as the labour input and gross fixed capital stock at the beginning of accounting year as a measure of capital. We have used a translog (TL) production function as the underlying form of production structure with a distributional assumption on the inefficiency term:

$$\ln(Q_i) = \beta_0 + \beta_1 \ln(K_i) + \beta_2 \ln(L_i) + \beta_3(\ln K_i)^2 + \beta_4(\ln L_i)^2 + \beta_5 \ln(L_i)\ln(K_i) + (V_i - U_i), \quad i = 1, 2, \ldots, N \tag{6.1}$$

where Q_i, K_i and L_i are output, capital and labour, respectively. Aigner et al. (1977) assumed that the V_is were independent and identically distributed (i.i.d) random variables with mean zero and constant variance, σ_v^2, independent of the u_is; i.e., it follows N (0, σ_v^2). U_is are nonnegative random variables which are assumed to account for technical inefficiency in production and are assumed to be independently distributed N (μ, σ_u^2). We utilise the parameterisation of Battese and Corra (1977) who replaced σ_u^2 and σ_v^2 with $\sigma^2 = \sigma_v^2 + \sigma_u^2$ and suggested the parameterisation of $\gamma = \sigma_u^2/\left(\sigma_v^2 + \sigma_u^2\right)$ instead of $\lambda = \sigma_u/\sigma_v$. The maximum likelihood estimates of β, σ^2 and γ are obtained by finding the maximum of the loglikelihood function. The TE of the ith firm is defined as

$$\text{TE}_i = \frac{y_i}{\exp\left(x_i'\beta\right)} = \frac{\exp\left(x_i'\beta - u_i\right)}{\exp\left(x_i'\beta\right)} = \exp(-u_i) \tag{6.2}$$

However, this involves a technical inefficiency effect, u_i, which is unobservable. Even if the true value of the parameter vector, β, in the stochastic frontier model was known, only the difference, $e_i = v_i - u_i$, could be observed. An operational predictor of u_i involves replacing the unknown parameters with the ML estimator. We have used Battese and Coelli (1988) specification of the ML estimator.

After the estimation of TE, we turn to assessing the impact of the locational and other factors, on the industries' productive performance. The pooled regression framework uses data of cross sections over a time series; however, the observations in each cross section do not necessarily refer to the same unit. A pooled array of data are one that combines cross-sectional data on N spatial units and T time periods to produce a data set of $N \times T$ observations which increase the power of statistical analyses by increasing both the sample size and the degrees of freedom. This in turn increases the reliability of parameter estimates. Regression functions are estimated using the ordinary least square method. Normalisation of the explanatory nominal variables is necessary while pooling the data due to the time variances in these variables. To address this, normalised dummies have been used for all relevant explanatory characteristic used in the study.

Consider the model of the general form:

$$\text{TE}_i = \alpha + \beta_1 \,\text{Size\_High}\, D_i + \beta_2 \,\text{Size\_Low}\, D_i + \beta_3 \,\text{Govt\_}D_i + \beta_4 \,\text{Urban\_}D_i + \beta_5 \,\text{OwnIndConcentration\_}D_i + \beta_6 \,\text{Age\_}D_i + \beta_7 \,\text{Year04\_}D_i$$

$$+ \beta_8 \text{ Year08\_}D_i + \beta_9 \text{ Year12\_}D_i + \beta_{10} \text{ InfraIndex\_}D_i + \cdots + e_i \quad (6.3)$$

Two alternate specifications of the empirical model are estimated to analyse the variance of TE across firms and the time series. The first specification deals with a very high level of concentration of the same industry as it is calculated through the 'own industry concentration ratio', and the second specification estimates the effect of moderately high concentration of the same industry. The specifications allow us to measure the impact of the extent of localisation on firm performance.

Accordingly, the model to test the effect of high concentration of firms (specification 1) is indicated as:

$$\begin{aligned} \text{TE}_i &= \alpha + \beta_1 \text{ Size\_High } D_i + \beta_2 \text{ Size\_Low } D_i + \beta_3 \text{ Govt\_}D_i + \beta_4 \text{ Urban\_}D_i \\ &+ \beta_5 \text{ Very High Concentration\_}D_i + \beta_6 \text{ Age\_}D_i + \beta_7 \text{ Year04\_}D_i \\ &+ \beta_8 \text{ Year08\_}D_i + \beta_9 \text{ Year12\_}D_i + \beta_{10} \text{ InfraIndex\_}D_i + \cdots + e_i \end{aligned} \quad (6.4)$$

The following model tests the impact of moderate concentration on firm performance:

$$\begin{aligned} \text{TE}_i &= \alpha + \beta_1 \text{ Size\_High } D_i + \beta_2 \text{ Size\_Low } D_i + \beta_3 \text{ Govt\_}D_i + \beta_4 \text{ Urban\_}D_i \\ &+ \beta_5 \text{ Moderately High Concentration\_}D_i + \beta_6 \text{ Age\_}D_i + \beta_7 \text{ Year04\_}D_i \\ &+ \beta_8 \text{ Year08\_}D_i + \beta_9 \text{ Year12\_}D_i + \beta_{10} \text{ InfraIndex\_}D_i + \cdots + e_i \end{aligned} \quad (6.5)$$

As described earlier, the dummy variables used in the study are computed using distributions of underlying characteristics for the sample year and are therefore normalised. The year dummy used in the equations is to control for the time effect.

Own industry concentration has been computed at the state level and captures the share of the particular state in industry's total employment.

$$\text{OwnIndConc.} = \sum E_{\text{SI}} / \sum E_{\text{I}} \quad (6.6)$$

E_{SI} denotes the share of employment within a state for a particular industry
E_{I} denotes total employment of a particular industry in the country

As the scale of an industry in a region increases relative to the country, significant localisation economies are expected, through the increase in externalities generated within the firms in the same or interrelated industries. The study attempts to capture the varying degree of agglomeration among the same industry group. While doing so, several novelties from the empirical standpoint have been introduced. We have created two dummy variables of 'own industry concentration' to indicate a very high and moderately high level of concentration within the same industry. The very high concentration dummy (High_concD) is based on the top quartile (75th–100th percentile) of the concentration variable (OwnIndConc). The moderately high concentration dummy (AM_concD) is derived based on the 50th–75th percentile of the variable in the own industry group. This dummy indicates a degree of concentration that is above the median (but not in the top quartile) level of concentration for that particular industry group. The dummies constructed in this way are separately used in two different specifications to capture the effect of different levels of agglomeration on TE of the firms.

To capture the effect of firm size on the level of TE of the firm, two dummy variables have been created. Gross sale value of firms has been used to divide them into large and small buckets. The large firm size dummy (Size_HighD) takes the value one when the sale value of the firm is in the top quartile in its industry group for the particular year at the two-digit NIC level. Similarly, for the firms whose sale value falls in the bottom quartile of that particular industry and for the particular year, the small firm dummy (Size_LowD) takes the value of one. Thus, the size of the firm is completely industry and time specific.

A dummy variable has been constructed to distinguish between government-owned firms from private organisations. The government dummy includes the following: (a) wholly central government, (b) wholly state and/or local government and (c) central government and state and/or local government jointly. A government dummy (Govt_D) for a firm takes the value of one if a government institution owns it.

The age of firms as a contributing factor of firm performance has been controlled for by using age dummies. Two specific dummies are constructed. An 'old firm' dummy has been used which takes the value one when the age of the firm is in the highest quartile of all industries in the sample year. The 'new firm' dummy (Age_LowD) takes the value one when the age of the firm is in the first quartile of the age distribution.

ASI data provide an indicator of whether the plant is located in an urban area or in a rural location, which corresponds to the urban or rural areas at a district level. We have used this indicator to derive a dummy for urban location (Urban_D). This dummy is expected to capture the effect of urban location on the firm-level performance.

A higher degree of physical infrastructure reduces the cost of production, facilitates wider diffusion of information and technology and therefore impacts the efficiency of firms. Physical infrastructure is a composite term including facilities like access to quality roads, railway network, telecommunication facility, access to capital, electrification and so on. We specifically focus on the role surfaced roads, telephone density, electricity density and access to credit on the firm-level performance of Indian organised manufacturing industries. The indicators of infrastructure are correlated with each other and cannot be used in a single regression specification due to multicollinearity. While these characteristics could be used alone in regression specifications, none of them in isolation captures the overall availability of infrastructure adequately. Accordingly, the analytical strategy of the study involves the introduction of a single index of infrastructure (InfraIndex) using principal component analysis (PCA) capturing the variance or information contained in different infrastructure variables. This methodology will avoid the issue of multicollinearity and will allow the usage of different dimensions of infrastructure within a single regression specification. The principal components are calculated after standardising each variable with their mean and variance and separately for all four study periods. This composite indicator (InfraIndex) is then used as an independent variable in our pooled regressions.[4]

While ordinary least squares (OLS) is widely used for pooled data regressions, our preliminary analysis indicates the existence of heteroscedasticity in the data.[5] White's (1980) covariance matrix estimator has been therefore used to obtain heteroscedasticity corrected *t* values for all parameter estimates of the regression. White's correction uses an asymptotic covariance matrix to recompute the standard errors of coefficients, and therefore, the *t* statistics and *p* values of the parameter estimates are revised for robustness. Autocorrelation has not been found to be a problem in these regressions, since the pooling is limited to four time periods with a gap of four years each.

6.4 Empirical Findings

This section details with empirical findings regarding the determinants of TE variances across firms within the same industry throughout the study period. First, the distribution of TE across the major manufacturing industries and over time has been analysed. Figure 6.3a, b demonstrate that generally for all industries median TE has increased within the study period from 2000–01 to 2011–12, excepting for an interesting small decline across the board from 2007–08 levels to 2011–12. The variability of TE for all industries has also reduced over time as demonstrated by the smaller size of the 'box' as well as shorter 'whiskers' on either side, i.e. both the first quartile and the fourth quartile. It can also be seen that the variability for certain industries like motor vehicles and machinery and equipment is materially lower than that of the other industries in this figure.

We now present key findings from the pooled regression analysis of TE for major industrial groups including key two-digit industries and a select few major industries at the four-digit level. OLS estimates of the regression equation are presented in Table 6.1a–c. Estimated coefficients for all the industries are found to be statistically significant (*F* test satisfied at the 95% level for all specifications). The notable findings are:

1. Scale effect: In all specifications and across all industries, the size of the firm (derived from gross sales) has a significant and positive contribution to TE. In almost all cases, the high size dummy (firms in top quartile) has a significant positive coefficient estimate, whereas the low size dummy (firms in the bottom quartile) have a negative and significant parameter estimate in all cases.
2. Government ownership: The government dummy has been consistently found to be negative and significant for most of the industry groups. While the liberalisation programme brought about heavy privatisation, the residual government-owned firms are found to be less efficient in most industries.

[4]See Appendix for further details on the PCA results.

[5]Breusch and Pagan (1979) statistic is used to check for heteroscedasticity.

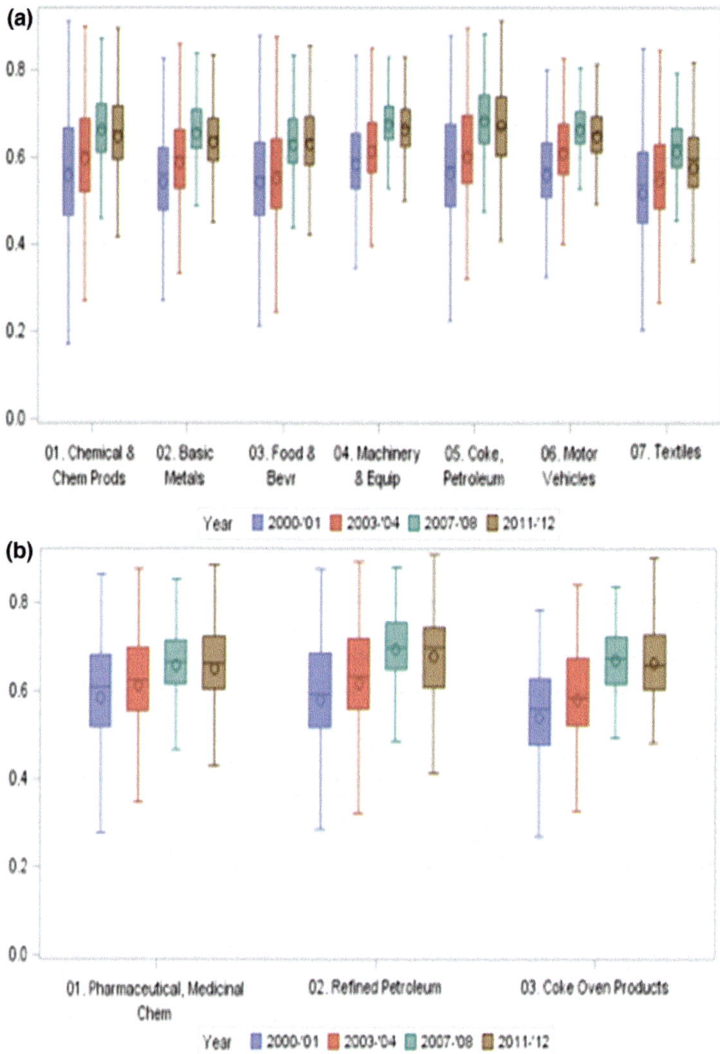

Fig. 6.3 **a** Box plot for TE of key (two-digit) industries, **b** box plot for TE of key (four-digit) industries. *Notes* **a** (1) Estimated from ASI firm-level data. (2) The chemical and chemical products industry includes pharmaceuticals, which in the revised industry classification in 2008 has been separated out as an independent 2-digit industry due to its size. For the purpose of this comparative study across the time periods, pharmaceuticals has been included within the chemical and chemical products for 2011–12 data. See Appendix. (3) Box-plot explained: the length of the box represents the 25th percentile to the 75th percentile of TE, with the median indicated at the middle of the box. The lower whisker represents the first quartile and the upper whisker represents the fourth quartile. **b** (1) Estimated from ASI firm-level data. (2) Pharmaceuticals has been separated out in the revised industry classification in 2008 as an independent 2-digit industry due to its size. Prior to this, it was part of the chemical and chemical products industry. The Pharmaceuticals industry has been separately analysed in this figure and also the pooled regression analysis. See Appendix
Source Authors' estimation with ASI unit level data

Table 6.1 Determinants of TE of key manufacturing industries

(a)								
Industry (NIC—two-digit)								
	Food products and beverages		Textiles		Coke, refined petroleum products and nuclear fuel		Chemical and chemical products	
Intercept	0.5291 (<0.0001)*	0.5288 (<0.0001)*	0.5123 (<0.0001)*	0.5131 (<0.0001)*	0.5611 (<0.0001)*	0.5653 (<0.0001)*	0.5504 (<0.0001)*	0.5415 (<0.0001)*
Size_HighD	0.0276 (<0.0001)*	0.0286 (<0.0001)*	0.0035 (0.2037)	0.0035 (0.2062)	0.0484 (<0.0001)*	0.0493 (<0.0001)*	0.0587 (<0.0001)*	0.0606 (<0.0001)*
Size_LowD	−0.0283 (<0.0001)*	−0.0285 (<0.0001)*	−0.0187 (<0.0001)*	−0.0188 (<0.0001)*	−0.0586 (<0.0001)*	−0.0588 (<0.0001)*	−0.0508 (<0.0001)*	−0.0542 (<0.0001)*
Govt_D	−0.0081 (0.1177)	−0.0080 (0.1205)	−0.1330 (<0.0001)*	−0.1332 (<0.0001)*	0.0070 (0.5801)	0.0074 (0.5587)	−0.0355 (0.0006)*	−0.0344 (0.0008)*
Urban_D	0.0378 (<0.0001)*	0.0376 (<0.0001)*	0.0377 (<0.0001)*	0.0375 (<0.0001)*	0.0118 (0.1208)	0.0114 (0.1327)	0.0254 (<0.0001)*	0.0286 (<0.0001)*
AM_concD	−0.0068 (0.0051)*		0.0002 (0.9510)		0.0098 (0.3443)		−0.0305 (<0.0001)*	
High_concD		−0.0070 (0.0010)*		−0.0020 (0.4821)		−0.0072 (0.4035)		0.0037 (0.1278)
Age_LowD	−0.0023 (0.2421)	−0.0021 (0.2865)	0.0148 (<0.0001)*	0.0147 (<0.0001)*	−0.0137 (0.0905)	−0.0145 (0.0727)	0.0100 (0.0001)*	0.0136 (<0.0001)*
Yr04D	0.0008 (0.7692)	0.0026 (0.3681)	0.0271 (<0.0001)*	0.0269 (<0.0001)*	0.0332 (0.0106)*	0.0336 (0.0094)*	0.0447 (<0.0001)*	0.0442 (<0.0001)*
Yr08D	0.0821 (<0.0001)*	0.0836 (<0.0001)*	0.0911 (<0.0001)*	0.0908 (<0.0001)*	0.1205 (<0.0001)*	0.1209 (<0.0001)*	0.1068 (<0.0001)*	0.1072 (<0.0001)*

(continued)

Table 6.1 (continued)

(a)

Industry (NIC—two-digit)								
	Food products and beverages		Textiles		Coke, refined petroleum products and nuclear fuel		Chemical and chemical products	
Yr12D	0.0828 (<0.0001)*	0.0899 (<0.0001)*	0.0547 (<0.0001)*	0.0558 (<0.0001)*	0.1080 (<0.0001)*	0.1106 (<0.0001)*	0.1038 (<0.0001)*	0.0912 (<0.0001)*
InfraIndex	0.0049 (<0.0001)*	0.0049 (<0.0001)*	−0.0059 (<0.0001)*	−0.0057 (<0.0001)*	0.0020 (0.4504)	0.0018 (0.5116)	−0.0067 (<0.0001)*	−0.0090 (<0.0001)*
N	20,647	20,647	10,772	10,772	4058	4058	12,037	12,037
R^2	0.15	0.15	0.15	0.15	0.09	0.11	0.22	0.21
F statistic	374.15	374.63	190.93	190.98	40.47	51.12	332.18	312.84
F statistic p value	(<0.0001)*	(<0.0001)*	(<0.0001)*	(<0.0001)*	(<0.0001)*	(<0.0001)*	(<0.0001)*	(<0.0001)*

(b)

Industry (NIC—two-digit)								
	Basic metals		Machinery and equipment		Motor vehicles, trailers and semi-trailers		Other transport equipment	
Intercept	0.5381 (<0.0001)*	0.53958 (<0.0001)*	0.5751 (<0.0001)*	0.5724 (<0.0001)*	0.5472 (<0.0001)*	0.5449 (<0.0001)*	0.5739 (<0.0001)*	0.5764 (<0.0001)*
Size_HighD	0.01295 (<0.0001)*	0.01309 (<0.0001)*	0.0391 (<0.0001)*	0.0383 (<0.0001)*	0.0302 (<0.0001)*	0.0305 (<0.0001)*	0.0267 (<0.0001)*	0.0270 (<0.0001)*
Size_LowD	−0.01658 (<0.0001)*	−0.01771 (<0.0001)*	−0.0347 (<0.0001)*	−0.0344 (<0.0001)*	−0.0251 (<0.0001)*	−0.0254 (<0.0001)*	−0.0216 (<0.0001)*	−0.0228 (<0.0001)*
Govt_D	−0.03669 (0.0200)*	−0.03516 (0.0256)*	−0.0208 (0.0786)	−0.0192 (0.1066)	−0.0456 (0.0503)	−0.0444 (0.0510)	−0.0517 (0.0021)*	−0.0539 (0.0013)*

(continued)

Table 6.1 (continued)

(b)								
Industry (NIC—two-digit)								
	Basic metals		Machinery and equipment		Motor vehicles, trailers and semi-trailers		Other transport equipment	
Urban_D	0.01239 (<0.0001)*	0.01187 (<0.0001)*	0.0085 (0.0005)*	0.0091 (0.0002)*	0.0108 (0.0026)*	0.0129 (0.0003)*	−0.0019 (0.6916)	−0.0003 (0.9488)
AM_concD	−0.01065 (0.0032)*		−0.0017 (0.5486)		0.0118 (0.0068)*		0.0002 (0.9716)	
High_concD		−0.00874 (0.0073)*		0.0081 (0.0011)*		0.0116 (0.0070)*		−0.0135 (0.0047)*
Age_LowD	−0.00965 (0.0004)*	−0.00933 (0.0007)*	−0.0060 (0.0295)*	−0.0056 (0.0421)*	−0.0125 (0.0016)*	−0.0119 (0.0027)*	−0.0096 (0.0924)	−0.0097 (0.0879)
Yr04D	0.03975 (<0.0001)*	0.04028 (<0.0001)*	0.0292 (<0.0001)*	0.0294 (<0.0001)*	0.0487 (<0.0001)*	0.0496 (<0.0001)*	0.0284 (<0.0001)*	0.0274 (<0.0001)*
Yr08D	0.11468 (<0.0001)*	0.11402 (<0.0001)*	0.0914 (<0.0001)*	0.0916 (<0.0001)*	0.1039 (<0.0001)*	0.1047 (<0.0001)*	0.0793 (<0.0001)*	0.0804 (<0.0001)*
Yr12D	0.08849 (<0.0001)*	0.09617 (<0.0001)*	0.0765 (<0.0001)*	0.0714 (<0.0001)*	0.0917 (<0.0001)*	0.0818 (<0.0001)*	0.0693 (<0.0001)*	0.0777 (<0.0001)*
InfraIndex	0.00439 (<0.0001)*	0.00413 (<0.0001)*	0.0024 (0.0072)*	0.0015 (0.0910)	0.0017 (0.2966)	0.0007 (0.6741)	0.0017 (0.3478)	0.0032 (0.0842)
N	7708	7708	9448	9448	3871	3871	2389	2389
R^2	0.15	0.15	0.19	0.19	0.17	0.17	0.13	0.13
F statistic	131	131	218.21	219.55	79.72	79.81	35.57	36.45
F statistic p value	(<0.0001)*	(<0.0001)*	(<0.0001)*	(<0.0001)*	(<0.0001)*	(<0.0001)*	(<0.0001)*	(<0.0001)*

(continued)

Table 6.1 (continued)

(c)

Industry (NIC—four-digit)

	Coke oven products		Refined petroleum products		Pharmaceutical, medicinal chemical and botanical products	
Intercept	0.5498 (<0.0001)*	0.5609 (<0.0001)*	0.5806 (<0.0001)*	0.5754 (<0.0001)*	0.5713 (<0.0001)*	0.5669 (<0.0001)*
Size_HighD	0.0419 (0.0066)*	0.0479 (0.0020)*	0.0416 (0.0026)*	0.0405 (0.0032)*	0.0693 (<0.0001)*	0.0686 (<0.0001)*
Size_LowD	−0.0583 (<0.0001)*	−0.0607 (<0.0001)*	−0.0588 (<0.0001)*	−0.0588 (<0.0001)*	−0.0493 (<0.0001)*	−0.0498 (<0.0001)*
Govt_D	0.0017 (0.9550)	−0.0008 (0.9773)	0.0091 (0.5203)	0.0086 (0.5481)	−0.0537 (0.0192)*	−0.0522 (0.0228)*
Urban_D	0.0004 (0.9717)	−0.0022 (0.8583)	0.0112 (0.2797)	0.0106 (0.3105)	0.0244 (<0.0001)*	0.0256 (<0.0001)*
AM_concD	0.0475 (0.0043)*		−0.0099 (0.4884)		−0.0237 (0.0001)*	
High_concD		−0.0202 (0.0710)		0.0111 (0.3612)		0.0029 (0.6057)
Age_LowD	−0.0186 (0.1089)	−0.0184 (0.1157)	−0.0175 (0.1338)	−0.0158 (0.1693)	0.0046 (0.3430)	0.0033 (0.4893)
Yr04D	0.0317 (0.0687)	0.0338 (0.0494)*	0.0388 (0.0311)*	0.0392 (0.0296)*	0.0328 (<0.0001)*	0.0319 (<0.0001)*
Yr08D	0.1216 (<0.0001)*	0.1265 (<0.0001)*	0.1191 (<0.0001)*	0.1190 (<0.0001)*	0.0791 (<0.0001)*	0.0768 (<0.0001)*
Yr12D	0.1279 (<0.0001)*	0.1338 (<0.0001)*	0.0968 (<0.0001)*	0.0924 (<0.0001)*	0.0627 (<0.0001)*	0.0651 (<0.0001)*

(continued)

Table 6.1 (continued)

(c)						
Industry (NIC—four-digit)						
	Coke oven products		Refined petroleum products		Pharmaceutical, medicinal chemical and botanical products	
InfraIndex	0.0043 (0.2543)	0.0024 (0.5363)	−0.0005 (0.8846)	−0.0008 (0.8331)	−0.0053 (0.0017)*	−0.0063 (0.0003)*
N	542	542	613	613	3563	3563
R^2	0.27	0.26	0.19	0.19	0.16	0.16
F statistic	19.61	18.99	13.87	13.91	67.64	65.69
F statistic p value	(<0.0001)*	(<0.0001)*	(<0.0001)*	(<0.0001)*	(<0.0001)*	(<0.0001)*

Source As for Fig. 6.3a
Note Figures in parenthesis are p values. *Indicates significance at 95% confidence level. Heteroscedasticity-adjusted robust p values are reported for the explanatory variables

3. Age factor: The age of firms has different effects across the industries. Newer firms are seen to be more efficient in certain sectors including textiles and the chemical and chemical product industry. However, in the cases of petroleum and coke, machinery and equipment, automobiles and other transport sectors, the coefficient of the low age dummy is negative and significant.
4. Time effect: As noticed in the box plots, TE has increased over time through the study period, which is also validated by the positive and significant coefficient estimates of the time dummies for all regression specifications and across all industries. This is contrary to a volume of earlier works that have argued that industrial development has been lacklustre in the post-reform period. We find quite the opposite in the manufacturing sector since the turn of the millennium.
5. Quality of infrastructure: The differences in infrastructure development across states are expected to influence the efficiency of firms across states. This has been found for a few major industry groups including food and beverages, basic metals, machinery and equipment and other transport equipment sectors. Surprisingly, the infrastructure index has a negative and significant association with TE for industries like textiles, chemical and chemical products and also pharmaceuticals as a separate industry. This possibly indicates that the infrastructure index computed using physical infrastructure parameters and credit offtake are not the only factors driving localisation of industries within the states. Pharmaceuticals, for example, has been a rapidly growing sector, and nearly one-third of the sector's output is generated in the state of Gujarat. This localisation is clearly a function of the incentives rolled out by the state and specific private and public infrastructure initiatives that are not captured within the index we have computed.
6. Urban location: The parameter estimates of the urban dummy variable indicate that there is a significant positive effect of urbanisation on the TE of the firm which has been observed at the district level within the ASI microdata. Our construction of the urban dummy is made to capture any benefits accrued by locating in an urban district or otherwise. We find that this region-specific location effect is quite useful in explaining efficiency variations. In general, we have found that the industries benefit from being located in a diversified urban region. The estimates are significant and positive for most of the industries analysed. The result is indicative of the fact that benefit from urbanisation arising from factors such as access to specialised financial and professional services often offset the high congestion costs of locating in dense urban areas.
7. Spatial concentration effect: In a surprising finding, we notice that the very high concentration dummy has a negative coefficient with statistical significance for certain industries. We find such negative association for the above-median dummy as well. The result from the spatial concentration analysis is presented in Table 6.2.

The negative effect of high concentration of industries on the efficiency of the firms may be due to the locational diseconomies emanating from higher congestion cost or the higher competitive input prices, or higher wages and rent as a result of

Table 6.2 Regression results for the spatial concentration analysis

	Negative coefficient estimate, statistically significant at 95% confidence level	Positive coefficient estimate, statistically significant at 95% confidence level
High concentration dummy	Food prod and beverage Basic metals Other transport equipment	Machinery and equipment Motor vehicles Coke oven products (four-digit level)
Above-median concentration dummy	Food prod and beverage Chemical and chemical products Basic metals Pharmaceuticals (NIC four-digit before 2008, separate two-digit industry since 2008)	Motor vehicles Coke oven products (four-digit level)

Source As for Fig. 6.3a

very high concentration. Thus, the overall impact of locational concentration of same industry group has not been found to be favourable for the firms. The theoretically expected positive relationship between agglomeration and TE is, however, found to be corroborated in case of two major two-digit industries, namely machinery and equipment and motor vehicles. This is also seen in the coke oven products (four-digit level) industry. We have found significant heterogeneity as regards the effect of localisation on firm's efficiency across different industrial sectors that makes it difficult to generalise the effects of localisation economies on firm's efficiency.

6.5 Conclusion

Contrary to the findings of lacklustre performance of the Indian organised manufacturing industries in the post-reform period, this study finds a significant growth in the sector during the study period commencing in 2000–01 for the next twelve years covered in the study. The industrial sectors tightly linked with global price fluctuations, especially after liberalisation, namely petrochemicals and basic metals, have experienced unprecedented growth during the rapid increase of commodity prices till about 2008 and a fall in net value added thereafter also related to the crash in the commodity prices post-2008. Still both of these industries experienced a double-digit annualised growth rate of NVA in real terms during the study period.

The economic liberalisation programme which included delicensing of manufacturing industries, significant liberalisation in trade and foreign exchange meant the manufacturing industries now have wider access for inputs and access to the world markets for their output. The only sector which has not experienced rapid growth in our study is the textile sector. Sectors such as motor vehicles have experienced a

15% annualised growth rate of real NVA during the study period. While the chemical and chemical product sector has grown at an 8% annualised rate, the pharmaceuticals sector which had been a part of this two-digit industry till 2008 has become a dominant player and was separated out as an independent two-digit industry since then. The NVA of the pharmaceuticals industry accounts for 40% of the combined chemical and pharmaceuticals industries in 2011–12. These findings are in contrast to earlier studies like Gupta et al. (2009) which reported a lacklustre performance of the manufacturing industries post-reform. Empirical assessment in Goldar and Parida (2017) corroborates a stronger growth in real value added in the post-reform period for Indian manufacturing. We also find significant state-level differences in the performance of the manufacturing sector. Maharashtra, Gujarat and Tamil Nadu have consistently maintained their top three positions, respectively, throughout the study period. States like West Bengal and Madhya Pradesh have been underperformers. States like Uttarakhand and Himachal Pradesh experienced annualised growth rates of 29 and 21%, respectively, clearly indicating strong focus of these states in industrial development and incentive programmes.

We then attempt to analyse the performance of the manufacturing industries with respect to their TE. We note that across industry groups, TE has increased over time. This is also seen in the pooled regression analysis of TE where time dummies have a statistically significant and positive coefficient estimate. We also find that the dispersion of TE has reduced through the study period, indicating a relatively lower variance of efficiency across firms of the same industry group in more recent times. These are encouraging findings for the Indian manufacturing industries, especially with the context that the sector has been in a decline in many of the major developed and industrialised countries in the world.

We find that the size of the firm has a significant positive contribution to TE for all of the major industries analysed. Government-owned firms, as expected, are seen to be less efficient compared to their privately owned counterparts in the regression analysis. The age of firms has a different impact on efficiency across industry groups. Younger firms are seen to be more efficient in sectors including textiles and the chemical industry which includes pharmaceuticals. However, in the cases of petroleum and coke, machinery and equipment, automobiles and other transport sectors younger firms are seen to be less efficient, likely due to the longer span required to break-even in these sectors.

We also analyse the effects of spatial concentration of firms of an industry group within a location. It is seen that firms located in the urban districts are more efficient, indicating that greater access to the urban infrastructure and information spillovers has beneficial impact on efficiency, outweighing the negative effects of congestion and higher prices. This is contrary to the findings reported in Lall et al. (2004). We constructed a composite index of infrastructure using road density, teledensity, electrification in urban and rural areas and credit offtake to analyse effects of state infrastructure on efficiency. For some major industries, we find a significant and positive association, namely food and beverages, basic metals, machinery and equipment and other transport equipment sectors. We recognise that this index does not fully capture all aspects of infrastructure that the state provides. Specific incentive programmes adopted by the states, special economic zones dedicated to the manufacturing sector and the general environment they provide for industries to thrive are not adequately captured by this infrastructure index. In a surprising finding, we notice that very high concentration of firms of an industry group within a state has a negative effect on the efficiency of these firms for many major manufacturing industries. However, in the era of globalisation, knowledge is no more confined to a location and it gets disseminated relatively faster.

Thus, localisation economies through the benefits of knowledge spillovers may not act as a determinant of firms' location decision. Rather firms located in less industrialised states or less agglomerated regions can have greater access to resources due to less concentration, which could favourably impact their efficiency. This perhaps explains the results we obtained for major industries like food and beverages, basic metals, chemical and chemical products, pharmaceuticals (separated out of the chemical product industry). However, positive effects of location concentration have been seen in the motor vehicles and the machinery and equipment sectors. The benefits of localisation such as greater access to resources and knowledge spillovers outweigh the agglomeration diseconomies for these industry groups including congestion, higher prices and pollution. The empirical findings in this study provide a new understanding of spatial effects on the firm-level performance of major formal manufacturing industries in India.

Appendix

Concordance Table of Industries

The study period includes ASI data sets which are based on three different industry classifications, i.e. NIC 98 used for the ASI microdata for 2000–01 and 2003–04, NIC 04 used for the period 2007–08 and NIC 08 used for 2011–12. Accordingly, an assessment of concordance has been carried out at the two-digit level between the NIC codes used in the input data. At the two-digit level, all the relevant industry codes have the same scope in both NIC 98 and NIC 04. But mapping between industry classifications at the two-digit level was required for NIC 04 and NIC 08 to make the 2011–12 file usable. Concordance and related mapping are presented below (Table 6.3).

Construction of the Infrastructure Index Using Principal Component Analysis

There are several dimensions of physical infrastructure development which are often correlated in the spatial context. In isolation, the key indicators of physical

Table 6.3 Industry mapping between NIC 04 and NIC 08 for comparability over time-series

NIC two-digit in 2008	NIC two-digit in 2004	Industry description	Adjustments to achieve comparability
10	15	Food products and beverages	
12	16	Tobacco products	
13	17	Textiles	
19	23	Coke, refined petroleum products and nuclear fuel	From 2007 to 2008 exclude NIC four-digit 1010 and 1020
20 + 21	24	Chemical and chemical products (includes pharmaceuticals NIC 21 in 2008)	Added NIC 21 to NIC 20 to get the combined chemical and chemical product sector which included pharmaceuticals in prior rounds
24	27	Basic metals	
28	29	Machinery and equipment	
29	34	Motor vehicles, trailers and semi-trailers	
30	35	Other transport equipment	
NIC four-digit in 2008	NIC four-digit in 2004	Industry description	Adjustments to achieve comparability
1910	2310	Coke oven products	
1920	2320	Refined petroleum products	For comparability, NIC five-digit 19204 is excluded
NIC two-digit in 2008	NIC four-digit in 2004	Industry description	Adjustments to achieve comparability
21	2423	Pharmaceutical, medicinal chemical and botanical products	

infrastructure may provide insights into firm performance. However, when the key indicators of infrastructure are used collectively, the analysis will undoubtedly be more robust. Using a large number of disaggregated indicators of infrastructure in the regression analysis is also constrained by the problem of multicollinearity. It is in this context that the statistical technique of PCA is applied in constructing a single index that captures the variance or information contained in several infrastructure variables and thus overcoming the problem of multicollinearity. The multivariate statistical technique of PCA finds linear combinations of the original variables to construct the principal components with a variance greater than any single original variable. In this study, we have used four major components of infrastructure of the Indian states, viz. (i) *road*: proportion of surfaced to total road in each state, (ii) *telecommunication*: state-wise density of telephone (per 100 population), (iii) *credit-deposit ratio*: state-wise distribution of credit and deposit by scheduled commercial banks of India (as a ratio), (iv) *electrification—urban* and *electrification—rural*: state-wise distribution of urban and rural households having electricity (in percentage).

While the first and second principal components are used for the regression analysis, the second component was later dropped due to strong correlations with the first component. The first component explaining roughly 50% of the variability has been used as an index of infrastructure within the pooled regression analysis (Table 6.4).

Table 6.4 Eigenvalues and cumulative proportions by principle component

Principal	2000–01			2003–04			2007–08			2011–12		
compo-nents	Eigenvalue	Proportion	Cumulative	Eigenvalue	Proportion	Cumulative	Eigenvalue	Proportion	Cumulative	Eigenvalue	Proportion	Cumulative
1	2.55	0.51	0.51	2.56	0.51	0.51	2.21	0.44	0.44	2.28	0.46	0.46
2	1.38	0.28	0.79	1.09	0.22	0.73	1.24	0.25	0.69	1.41	0.28	0.74
3	0.56	0.11	0.90	0.75	0.15	0.88	0.69	0.14	0.83	0.81	0.16	0.90
4	0.38	0.08	0.98	0.39	0.08	0.96	0.54	0.11	0.94	0.32	0.06	0.96
5	0.19	0.02	1.00	0.20	0.04	1.00	0.32	0.06	1.00	0.18	0.04	1.00

References

Aghion, P., & Burgess, R. (2003). *Liberalization and industrial performance: Evidence from India and the UK*. Mimeo, London School of Economics, http://www.ycsg.yale.edu/activities/files/Aghion-Burgesspercent20Paper.pdf.

Aghion, P., Burgess, R., Redding, S. J., & Zilibotti, F. (2008). The Unequal Effects of Liberalisation: Evidence from Dismantling the License Raj in India. *American Economic Review, 98*(4), 1397-1412.

Ahluwalia, M. S. (2000). Economic performance of states in post-reforms period. *Economic and Political Weekly, 35*(19), 1637–1648.

Aigner, D., Lovell, C.A.K., & Schmidt, P. (1977). Formulation and estimation of stochastic frontier production function models. *Journal of Econometrics, 6*(1):21-37

Amirapu, A., Hasan, R., Jiang, Y., & Klein, A. (2018). Geographic concentration in Indian manufacturing and service industries: Evidence from 1998 to 2013. *Asian Economic Policy Review, 14*(1).

Banerjee, A., & Duflo, E. (2014). Do firms want to borrow more? Testing credit constraints using a directed lending program. *The Review of Economic Studies, 81*(2), 572–607.

Battese, G.E. & Corra G.S., (1977) Estimation of a production frontier model: with application to the pastoral zone of eastern Australia. *Australian Journal of Agricultural Economics, 21*(3):169–179.

Battese, G. E., & Coelli, T. J. (1988). Prediction of firm-level technical efficiencies with a generalized frontier production function and panel data. *Journal of Econometrics, 38*, 387–399.

Beeson, P. (1987). Total factor productivity growth and agglomeration economies in manufacturing, 1959–73. *Journal of Regional Science, 27*, 183–199.

Bhagwati, J. N., & Desai, P. (1970). *India: Planning for industrialization*. Oxford: Oxford University.

Bhagwati, J., & Srinivasan, T. N. (1975). *Foreign trade regimes and economic development: India*. New York: Columbia University Press.

Breusch, T. S., & Pagan, A. R. (1979). A simple test for heteroscedasticity and random coefficient variation. *Econometrica, 47*, 1287–1294.

Dholakia, B. H., & Dholakia, R. H. (1994). Total factor productivity growth in Indian manufacturing. *Economic and Political Weekly, 30*, 3342–3344.

Driffield, N. L., & Kambhampati, U. S. (2003). Trade liberalization and the efficiency of firms in Indian manufacturing. *Review of Development Economics, 7*(3), 419–430.

Färe, R., Grosskopf, S., & Lovell, C. A. K. (1994). *Production frontiers*. Cambridge Books, Cambridge University Press, number 9780521072069, December.

Feser, E. (2001). A flexible test for agglomeration economies in two US manufacturing industries. *Regional Science and Urban Economics, 31*, 1–19.

Goldar, B. (2000). Employment growth in organised manufacturing in India. *Economic and Political Weekly, 35*(14), 1191–1195.

Goldar, B., & Kumari, A. (2003). Import liberalization and productivity growth in the Indian manufacturing industries in the 1990s. *Developing Economies, 41*(4), 436–460.

Goldar, B., & Parida, Y. (2017). Sustaining India's manufacturing growth in the face of increasing competition from Chinese imports. In P. Agrawal (Ed.), *Sustaining high growth in India*. Cambridge University Press, India.

Gupta, P., Hasan, R., & Kumar, U. (2009). What constrains Indian manufacturing? In B. Eichengreen, P. Gupta, & R. Kumar (Eds.), *Emerging giants: China and India in the world economy*. USA: Oxford University Press.

Henderson, J. V. (1986). Efficiency of resource usage and city size. *Journal of Urban Economics, 19*(1), 47–70.

Khanna, R., & Sharma, C. (2018). Do infrastructure and quality of governance matter for manufacturing productivity? Empirical evidence from the Indian states. *Journal of Economic Studies, 45*(4), 829–854.

Lall, S. V., & Chakravorty, S. (2005). Industrial location and spatial inequality: Theory and evidence from India. *Review of Development Economics, 9*(1), 47–68.
Lall, S. V., & Rodrigo, C. G. (2001). Perspectives on the sources of heterogeneity in Indian industry. *World Development, 29*(12), 2127–2143.
Lall, S. V., Shalizi, Z., & Deichmann, U. (2004). Agglomeration economies and productivity in Indian industry. *Journal of Development Economics, 73*(2), 643–673.
Mahambare, V., & Balasubramanyam, V. N. (2005). *Trade liberalisation and India's manufacturing sector*. Econ WPA in its series Development and Comp Systems with number 0505010. Accessed at http://129.3.20.41/eps/dev/papers/0505/0505010.pdf.
Mitra, A. (1999). Agglomeration economies as manifested in technical efficiency at the firm level. *Journal of Urban Economics, 45*(3), 490–500.
Mitra, A., Varoudakis, A., & Véganzonès-Varoudakis, M.-A. (2002). Productivity and technical efficiency in Indian states' manufacturing: The role of infrastructure. *Economic Development and Cultural Change, 50*(2), 395–496.
Moomaw, R. L. (1981). Productivity and city size: A critique of the evidence. *The Quarterly Journal of Economics, 96*(4), 675–688.
Moomaw, R. L. (1988). Agglomeration economies: Localisation or urbanisation? *Urban Studies, 25,* 50–161.
Nakamura, R. (1985). Agglomeration economies in manufacturing: A case study of Japanese cities. *Journal of Urban Economics, 17*(1), 108–124.
OECD. (2007). *OECD economic surveys: India.*
Panagariya, A. (2008). *India an emerging giant.* Oxford University Press.
Patibandla, M., & Phani, B. V. (2001). Market reforms and industrial productivity. *Economic and Political Weekly, 37*(1), 59–64. http://www.jstor.org/stable/4411569.
Raj, R. S. N., & Mahapatra, M. K. (2009). On measuring productivity growth in Indian industry: Analysis of organised and unorganised sector in selected major states. In *Productivity, efficiency, and economic growth in the Asia-Pacific region, contributions to economics.* Physica-Verlag HD. http://www.springerlink.com/content/978-3-7908-2071-3.
Ray, S. C. (2002). Did India's economic reform improve efficiency and productivity? A nonparametric analysis of the initial evidence from manufacturing. *Indian Economic Review, 37*, 23–57.
Tata Services Limited. (2003). *Total factor productivity of Tata companies vis-a-vis other manufacturing firms and manufacturing sector*. Mumbai: Tata Services Limited.
Topalova, P. (2004). *Trade liberalisation and firm productivity: The case of India.* IMF Working Paper, No. WP/04/28.
Trivedi, P. (2004). An inter-state perspective on manufacturing productivity in India: 1980–81 to 2000–01. *Indian Economic Review, 39*(1), 203–237.
Unel, B. (2003). *Productivity trends in India's manufacturing sectors in the last two decades*. IMF Working Paper, No. WP/03/22.
Veeramani, C., & Goldar, B. (2005). Manufacturing productivity in Indian states: Does investment climate matter? *Economic and Political Weekly, 40*(24), 2413–2420.
White, H. (1980). A heteroscedastic-consistent covariance matrix estimator and a direct test of heteroscedasticity. *Econometrica, 48,* 817–838.

Data Sources

Annual Survey of Industries (ASI), factory sector, various years. Available at http://mospi.nic.in/Mospi_New/upload/asi/ASI_main.htm?status=1&menu_id=88.
Annual Survey of Industries (ASI), firm-level data, various years. Available at ICSSR Data Service: Social Science Data Repository.
Central Statistical Office (CSO), National accounts statistics 2000–01, 2003–04, 2007–08.

Central Statistical Office (CSO), Annual statistical abstract of India (New Delhi: Government of India, various issues).

Central Statistical Office (CSO), India statistics. Available at http://mospi.nic.in/Mospi_New/site/India_Statistics.aspx?status=1&menu_id=43.

Central Statistical Office (CSO), Annual survey of industries—Summary results for factory sector-various years.

Economic and Political Weekly Research Foundation, Annual Survey of Industries—A data base on industrial sector in India. Annual Survey of Industries (ASI) 1973–74 to 2003–04, Vol. II. Available at http://www.epwrf.res.in/displaycategory.aspx?id=6.

Central Statistical Office (CSO), Government of India, Ministry of Statistics and Programme Implementation (MOSPI), Time-series data on annual survey of industries (1998–99 to 2007–08). Available at http://mospi.nic.in/Mospi_New/upload/asi/ASI_main.htm?status=1&menu_id=88.

National Sample Survey Office (NSSO), Government of India, Ministry of Statistics and Programme Implementation (MOSPI), various rounds. Available at http://mospi.nic.in/Mospi_New/Site/inner.aspx?status=3&menu_id=31.

Planning Commission, Govt. of India, http://planningcommission.nic.in/data/central/index.php?data=centab.

Planning Commission, Govt. of India, Data for use of Deputy Chairman, Planning Commission, April, 2012. Available at http://planningcommission.nic.in/data/datatable/0904/comp_data0904.pdf.

Ministry of Finance, Government of India, Union Budget and Economic Survey, various years. Available at http://indiabudget.nic.in/survey.asp.

Reserve Bank of India (RBI) Data Warehouse, Database on Indian Economy, various years. Available at http://dbie.rbi.org.in/DBIE/dbie.rbi?site=statistics.

Reserve Bank of India (RBI), RBI Bulletin, various years. Available at http://www.rbi.org.in/scripts/BS_ViewBulletin.aspx.

Reserve Bank of India (RBI), Annual statistical tables on Indian banks (New Delhi: Government of India, various issues).

Chapter 7
Productivity Dispersion and Firm Size: An Inquiry with Indian Manufacturing Firms

Debarati Chatterjee Ray

Abstract This study focusses on the prevalence of productivity differential among firms with different scales of production across manufacturing industries in India. We hypothesize that manufacturing firms are heterogeneous in technology and their structure even within a narrowly defined sector; but, they are expected to be homogeneous within a particular firm size (If a firm enters into a market with new technology and competes with other firms using conventional technology, the incumbents will fail to survive and exit from the market through the process of creative destruction as used the concept by Schumpeter (Capitalism, socialism, and democracy. Harper Torchbooks, New York, 1942). In this process, only successful firms can survive, and resources are transferred from less productive firms to more productive firms. This turnover of the firms also expected to facilitate certain amount of uniformity of the performance among existing firms within a narrowly defined sector.). To analyse the existence of productivity dispersion across different firm sizes for the manufacturing sector, this study uses factory-level data from the Annual Survey of Industries (ASI), the primary data source for registered manufacturing in India, for the period 2009–2012. We have grouped the factory units of similar industries by their firm size into four categories (micro, small, medium and large) at the two-digit level of NIC (2008) by following the definitions as provided in MSME Act 2006. The study found that the productivity dispersion is a deep-rooted problem as total factor productivity of the firms is widespread not only within an industry but even within a firm size of a specific industry.

7.1 Introduction

The slow rate of technological progress in the manufacturing sectors, perhaps, is one of the major indicators of economic backwardness in India. The low level of total factor productivity (TFP) coupled with productivity differential pose the real deterrence of achieving desired performance for manufacturing sector. Productivity

---

D. C. Ray (✉)
Department of Economics, University of Calcutta, Kolkata, India
e-mail: chatterjeedebarati1@gmail.com

P. K. Biswas and P. Das (eds.), *Indian Economy: Reforms and Development*, India Studies in Business and Economics, https://doi.org/10.1007/978-981-13-8269-7_7

differential persists not only between industry groups but also between firms within a particular industry. In India, the predominance of smaller firm size is considered traditionally as one of reasons for low productivity in the manufacturing sector. However, technical efficiency of small firms may be higher as a result of their being exposed to more competition than larger firms. On the contrary, many researchers argued that the larger firms are more efficient than the smaller ones. Jovanovic (1982) concluded that higher efficiency of larger firms is the result of a selection process where efficient firms grow and survive, while inefficient firms stagnate or exit the industry.

There are many studies on the prevalence of productivity dispersion within a narrowly defined industry (Bartelsman and Doms 2000; Ito and Lechevalier 2009; Martin 2008; Orr 2018). The persistence of productivity differential indicates that technology or knowledge is not being diffused across different firms coexisting in the same sector. Baily et al. (1992) showed that productivity level in an industry may change because of the changes in market shares of firms with different productivity levels even when individual firms' productivity level remains unchanged. Most of the studies on productivity differential at firm level focused on technological explanations, such as R&D expenditure as a reason for these differences but Syverson (2004) argued by proposing that demand-side features also play a role in creating the observed productivity variation. He argued that in a relatively dense cluster, competitive market consumers can switch between producers more easily and as a result relatively inefficient producers find it more difficult to operate profitably. As inefficient firms leave, the minimum level of productivity as well as average level of productivity increases and thus resulting in the changes in productivity distribution of that sector. The degree of competition in a particular sector has a greater implication on the productivity dispersion.

Most of these studies on productivity dispersion, on both Indian economy and other economies, treat firms within a manufacturing sector as homogeneous one. But a closer look reveals the significant heterogeneity even within an industry group. The same products are being produced by different sized firms using related but different technologies which ultimately affecting the TFP dispersion within a sector. Thus, each scale of production of the same industry shows unique set of industrial dynamics within itself. Given this argument of segregation of firm sizes within an industry, one may expect certain amount of homogeneity within a particular firm size of a sector. As pointed out by Schumpeter (1942), a firm enters a market with new technology and competes with incumbents that use conventional technology. If the new innovator firm can cope with the competition, the entrants will be able to replace the incumbents. If not, they will fail to survive and exit from the market. In the process of creative destruction, only successful firms can survive in the market, and resources are transferred from less productive firms to more productive firms. This turnover of the firms also expected to facilitate certain amount of uniformity of the performance among existing firms within a narrowly defined sector. Following this argument for a scale-defined industrial sector, one may expect fairly homogeneous distribution of TFP within a firm size.

Given the relatively small size of many manufacturing firms, India is reaping far smaller gains from scale economies than many other countries (Dougherty et al. 2009). But many researchers advocated promotion of small-scale industries mainly from the equality and welfare aspects. It is argued that greater presence of small-scale industries could counter the unemployment problems as they are expected to use more labour-intensive techniques. Apart from addressing the unemployment issue, an expansion of the small-firm segment reduces unequal income distribution and more efficient resource allocation. In addition to these arguments, this process takes time which further ensures larger firms experience learning-by-doing effects that make firms more efficient as a result of their growing stock of experience (Malerba 1992).

Again in India, the definition of Small Scale units (SSI) has undergone multiple changes over time. In 1955 for the first time, the official criterion has been set to identify the SSI units having investment of Rs. 5 lakh and employing less than 50 persons when not using power. Over the year, this investment limits as well as employment and energy usage criteria have changed, and finally in 2006, Government of India introduced a comprehensive Act (MSME Act 2006)[1] to set the limits for different sizes of units.

In India, a large number of researches have been carried out to study the changes and attributes of productivity, more specifically manufacturing productivity. But a very few studies look into the productivity differential even within a particular industry group by taking into account the scale of production or firm size. The objective of this chapter is to examine the prevalent dispersion of TFP for different sized firms for Indian manufacturing sector. High level of productivity dispersion within a narrowly defined sector is a sign that knowledge or technology is not being diffused across different firms coexisting and competing in a relatively same environment.

7.2 Data and Construction of Variables

To study the existence of productivity dispersion across different firm sizes for Indian manufacturing sector, we have taken firm-level data provided by the Central Statistical Office (CSO) in the form of Annual Survey of Industries (ASI) for the period 2009–2012. Using the firm-level pooled data, we have calculated total factor productivity for each firm by taking real gross value added (GVA) by the factory unit. Although double deflation method is more accurate one, real GVA is calculated following single deflation method as in ASI data details of the inputs required to apply a double deflation method, are not provided.

The firm-level data set includes descriptive data and firm-specific characteristics, such as state, output produced, input usage, number of workers and industry. The data set only considers the period between 2009 and 2012 that the time span starts immediately after the beginning of the financial and economic crisis of 2008. For our

[1]See Appendix for details.

study, the cleaning of data was an important step as improper data set could impact the result of the model significantly. Apart from considering all working firms, we pursuit some specific data cleaning in order to exclude outliers and firms whose values for several variables were not correctly plotted.

Although firms with less than ten numbers of employees are not required to register in India, still around 16–20% of the registered firms in ASI data set for different years are found to having less than equal to ten numbers of employees.[2] For our study, we excluded firms that are reported to be closed but retained firms in that have fewer than ten employees. The ASI provides multipliers for each firm, indicating the inverse sampling probability. We estimated aggregate and average numbers for the population of firms and GVA by weighting firm-level observations by inverse sampling multipliers.

To look into the disparity among firms producing similar products, we have grouped the firms following classification of NIC two-digit classification (2008). By using the concordance table provided by the CSO, we matched industries at NIC three-digit classification for other years. Once we classify industries as per NIC 2 digit of 2008, we grouped firms of similar industries according to firm size. Four sizes of firms have been considered following MSME Act 2006—micro, small, medium and large firms. The arguments for grouping similar firms according to firm size are based on the fact that technology used by similar firms largely depends on the firm size of operation. A small-sized firm follows a set of technology which differs from the set of technology used by a large firm, producing similar or related products. Again the legal, financial and other related environment for carrying out the production process is highly different for different sized firms in India.[3] Therefore, it seems logical and necessary to categorize the firms according to firm sizes to get a true insight into existence of productivity dispersion among Indian manufacturing industries.

7.3 Measurement of Productivity

The LevPet algorithm (LP) developed in Levinsohn and Petrin (2003)[4] is used to calculate total factor productivity (TFP) at the firm level. In the LP method, production technology follows the Cobb–Douglas production function:

---

[2]Many closed firms still appear in the list of registered firms, and as pointed out by Bedi and Banerjee (2007), the reason for their appearance in the ASI data set is that many registered firms may have decreased their employment below the ten-employee mark.

[3]a. Singh (2016).

b. Hasan and Jandoc (2010).

c. Beck, Kunt and Maksimovic; 'Financial and legal constraints to growth: does firm size matter?' World Bank resources; 2003.

[4]Many alternative techniques are there in the available literatures: within-group fixed effects (WG), least squares models, Harris (2005); GMM system model (Blundell and Bond 1998); frontier models and semi-parametric models like Olley and Pakes (1996) are also broadly used.

$$Y_{it} = A_{it} K_{it}^{\beta_K} L_{it}^{\beta_L} M_{it}^{\beta_M} \tag{7.1}$$

where
Y_{it} = physical output of the ith firm in period t.
K_{it} = capital input measured by total fixed assets of firm i in period t.
L_{it} = labour input measured by manufacturing mandays
M_{it} = material and energy used as input.
A_{it} = Hicks-neutral production technology.

Taking log of Eq. (7.1), we get

$$y_{it} = \beta_0 + \beta_K k_{it} + \beta_L l_{it} + \beta_M m_{it} + \varepsilon_{it} \tag{7.2}$$

Here $\log(A_{it}) = \beta_0 + \varepsilon_{it}$, where β_0 is mean productivity irrespective of inputs used and ε_{it} is the random error measuring deviation from that mean.

The error term is decomposed into two parts:

$$\varepsilon_{it} = \omega_{it} + \gamma_{it} \tag{7.3}$$

Here, ω_{it} represents transmitted productivity component which is related to firm's input choice decision, whereas γ_{it} is independent of input use. Now given this statement regarding ω_{it}, it seems leading to the simultaneity problem. Thus, ignoring the correlation between inputs and this ω_{it} will give inconsistent results. To overcome this problem, the LP model assumes that intermediate input demand function, i.e.

$$M_{it} = M_{it}(\omega_{it}, K_{it}) \tag{7.4}$$

is monotonically increasing in ω_{it}, thus allowing inversion of intermediate demand function. Hence we can write

$$\omega_{it} = \omega_t(M_{it}, K_{it}) \tag{7.5}$$

Therefore, unobservable productivity ω_{it} is now solely determined by two sets of observed inputs M_t and K_t. Following the identification problem as mentioned by Olley and Pakes (1996), LP also assumed that the productivity is governed by a first-order Markov process.

$$\omega_t = E\left[\omega_t/\omega_{t-1}\right] + \xi_t \tag{7.6}$$

where ξ_t is an innovation to productivity that is uncorrelated to K_t but not necessarily with L_t. In this study, total factor productivity (TFP) has been used to ascertain the performance of the manufacturing sector of different unit sizes.[5]

[5]Here 'unit' size is defined following the MSME Act 2006.

Table 7.1 Percentage distribution of firms by firm size

Year	Share of manufacturing units			
	Micro	Small	Medium	Large
2009–2010	57.54	32.33	3.83	6.30
2010–2011	55.19	33.90	3.86	7.05
2011–2012	53.52	34.88	4.11	7.50
2012–2013	50.97	36.25	4.60	8.17

Source Author's calculation with ASI unit-level data for 2009, 2010, 2011, 2012

7.4 Some Stylized Facts

Indian manufacturing industries have been dominated by the micro-units (Table 7.1). But, the share of micro-units declined while the shares of small-, medium- and large-scale units showed rising trend during the period 2009–2012. The share of large-scale units increased at a higher rate than the shares of medium- and small-scale units during this period. The micro-sector is more volatile in nature as long as entry and exit of firms are concerned. Apart from frequent entry and exit, the micro-sector firms are also susceptible to temporary closure due to various reasons. These characteristics of micro-sector could be the possible reasons for showing an unclear trend in the numbers of functioning firms for the period under considerations.

Table 7.2 shows the average gross value added, manufacturing mandays and total fixed capital by different firm-sized units between 2009 and 2012. Apart from micro-units, all three firm sizes show a dip in the GVA particularly after 2010 and the more consistently in total mandays all through the period. On the contrary, we find a rising level of fixed capital for all four sizes of firms for the same period of time. We observe a sharp decline in the average gross value added by the medium- as well as large-scale units from 2011 to 2012. At the same time, average mandays worked per unit for these two scales have also declined considerably. But for the same period, we noticed an increase in the average GVA per unit for micro-industries and also a marginal increase in the average mandays for the same. The average fixed capital per unit increased significantly for micro-units as well as for medium-scale units between 2010 and 2011. The average level of fixed capital has increased for all four subsections of the manufacturing industries but for micro –units, this witnessed an increase of more than 50%, whereas for large-scale units the increment stood at around 20% for the same time period. The increase in the average level of fixed capital is the lowest, around 2.5% for the medium-scale industries, whereas for small-scale industries it is just at 9% during the period between 2009 and 2012.

Table 7.3 presents the changes of structural ratios in terms of labour productivity, capital output ratio and outstanding loan-to-asset ratio. We define labour productivity as GVA per unit mandays. Labour productivity in Indian manufacturing increased with firm size. The contribution of labour in terms of labour productivity exhibited a rising trend for all industries irrespective of their firm size. The movement of

Table 7.2 Changes of average GVA, mandays and fixed capital for different sized firms (2009–2012)

Firm size	Year	GVA[a]	Mandays[b]	Fixed capital[c]
Micro	2009–2010	36.44	8	13.05
	2010–2011	37.9	7.52	13.26
	2011–2012	40.84	6.99	20.45
	2012–2013	42.9	7.2	20.63
Small	2009–2010	234	19.47	188
	2010–2011	239	19.63	190
	2011–2012	236	18	201
	2012–2013	233	17	206
Medium	2009–2010	774	51.89	936
	2010–2011	860	52.58	911
	2011–2012	822	49.01	953
	2012–2013	756	45.84	960
Large	2009–2010	5680	172.08	11,200
	2010–2011	5660	164.28	12,300
	2011–2012	5620	158.79	12,500
	2012–2013	5160	147.06	13,500

Note All values are calculated in real term (in 2004–2005 prices in two digits following NIC-08)
[a]GVA is measured in lakh
[b]Total mandays are measured in thousands
[c]Fixed capital is measured in value (lakh)
Source As for Table 7.1

capital intensity, measured by fixed capital per mandays, shows the similar pattern as for labour productivity across firm size as well as over time. Another interesting factor to look at for these different firm sizes of manufacturing units is loan-to-asset ratio which is measured by taking ratio of outstanding loan to total fixed capital. This particular ratio is highest for the micro-units, although it is declining steadily for the period under consideration for almost all subsections of industries. But most importantly, the loan-to-asset ratio is declining with the unit size itself with the figure standing at less than one for two larger scales of industries. This may indicate failure of smaller-sized firms to use loans into asset creation.

7.5 Empirical Findings

Partial factor productivity approach fails to capture the contribution of other inputs in the production process. A rapid growth in a partial factor productivity could be due to significant increase in the other inputs or factors (Diewert and Nakamura

Table 7.3 Labour productivity, capital intensity and loan-to-asset ratio for four different sized firms (2009–2012)

Firm size	Year	Labour productivity	Capital intensity	Loan-to-asset ratio
Micro	2009–2010	597.35	297.84	657.4
	2010–2011	637.17	369.89	765.81
	2011–2012	707.84	461.2	478.41
	2012–2013	726.28	590.91	487.57
Small	2009–2010	1493.77	1882.32	1.3
	2010–2011	1591.58	2133.8	1.36
	2011–2012	1637.87	2253.16	1.36
	2012–2013	1721.51	2472.47	1.47
Medium	2009–2010	2016.34	4021.11	0.83
	2010–2011	2242	5783.91	0.83
	2011–2012	2499.09	6515.31	0.78
	2012–2013	2434.38	6496.23	0.75
Large	2009–2010	2985.14	9777.94	0.67
	2010–2011	3204.47	8735.3	0.63
	2011–2012	3238.13	10,693.68	0.7
	2012–2013	3108.65	12,703.59	0.65

Source As for Table 7.1

2003). Therefore, the understanding of the differences in the inherent structure of four different firm sizes of Indian manufacturing could remain incomplete without discussing TFP separately for all four sectors. The TFP not only gives an insight into the impact of technical progress but also of enhanced skill of existing labour, learning-by-doing and better utilization of existing capacity (Ahluwalia 1991).

In this study, we have estimated TFP using a production function approach following LP method of estimation for different sized firms for Indian registered manufacturing sector for a cross-sectional data of four years (2009–2012). The production function analysis also provides estimates of output elasticity of labour and capital. Table 7.4 shows that the estimated elasticity of labour and capital is significantly different from zero for all four firm sizes of industries.

The estimated production function shows that elasticity of labour is significantly higher than elasticity of capital for micro- and small-scale industries. But, for medium and large scales, elasticity of capital becomes higher than that of labour. This result implies higher role of labour in the lower firm sizes of production. The role of capital is more important than role of labour for medium-scale industries as well as large-scale units. This, however, corroborates our previous finding of lower capital intensity in lower firm sizes. The relatively lesser role played by labour in the production process in the higher firm sizes could be a cause of concern as these firm sizes have larger mandays as compared to smaller firm sizes.

Table 7.4 Output elasticity of inputs

Firm size	Labour	Capital
Micro	0.71 (0.010)	0.20 (0.014)
Small	0.55 (0.011)	0.33 (0.019)
Medium	0.45 (0.027)	0.55 (0.067)
Large	0.44 (0.026)	0.47 (0.041)

Note All values are statistically significant at 5% level. Figures in the parenthesis are standard errors
Source As for Table 7.1

In the next step of LP method, we estimated the productivity (ω) for 23 two-digit industries separately for four different firm sizes. Table 7.5 shows the variation of estimated productivity achieved by four different firm sizes for 23 two-digit industries (NIC-08) by firm size. There exists significant difference in productivity of the same product produced in different firm sizes. Smaller firm sizes seem to attain higher productivity mainly in the traditional sectors such as food, beverages, leather, wood and paper products. The mean productivity is around 172% of the average productivity of the sector for small-scale units for manufacturing of furniture also. For rubber and related products, this figure stands around average industry productivity for small-scale units. Mean productivity for micro-units too is in or around industry average for traditional sectors like tobacco, textiles, leather, wood and paper. The mean productivity for both micro- and small-scale units is much less than the industry average for most of the modern sectors. Medium-scale units seem more productive for particularly two sectors—manufacture of coke and refined petroleum products and manufacture of pharmaceuticals. Apart from these two-printing, chemical products, basic metal and apparel are the sectors where medium-scale units performed well in terms of attaining average industry productivity. Manufacturing of wearing apparels is the only sector where three different firm sizes attained above average industry productivity. Large-scale units are more productive in most industries except few such as printing, pharmaceuticals, coke and petroleum products, etc., for manufacture of chemicals and chemical products, rubber and plastics products, electrical equipment and machinery and equipment—large-scale units have attained more than double of the industry average, while triple for other non-metallic mineral products and fabricated metal products.

The TFP for different firm sizes is significantly different for most of the industries. But even within a firm size, the TFP is not uniform for most of the industry sectors. To assess productivity dispersion at the aggregate level, we first consider the analysis of variance for each manufacturing sector. Figure 7.1 shows the decomposition of TFP dispersion between the four firm sizes and within firm sizes. For almost all the industries, the major source of dispersion is the dispersion within a particular scale than the dispersion between scales. Except few industries such as 17, 19 20 and 23, for all other industries the dispersion between scales is less than 20%.

Now for individual industries, the coefficient of variation is significantly high for all major industries except 31 (Fig. 7.2). For industry 33, the coefficient of variation

Table 7.5 Percentage of average productivity (mean productivity) achieved by four different scale sizes for 23 two-digit industries (2009–2012)

Industries	Micro	Small	Medium	Large
Manufacture of food products	56.9	90.8	42.9	150.6
Manufacture of beverages	15.6	220.3	18.6	145.4
Manufacture of tobacco products	161.5	36.4	58.6	143.6
Manufacture of textiles	167.6	29.2	10.8	192.4
Manufacture of wearing apparels	115.3	17.9	110.6	156.2
Manufacture of leather and related products	97.7	127.5	90.9	84.0
Manufacture of wood products	85.7	146.9	72.4	94.9
Manufacture of paper and paper products	82.2	111.4	80.1	126.3
Printing and reproduction of recorded media	31.1	212.9	116.8	39.2
Manufacture of coke and refined petroleum products	2.8	96.3	276.0	24.8
Manufacture of chemicals and chemical products	10.3	16.8	125.0	247.9
Manufacture of pharmaceuticals	NA[a]	16.3	241.9	41.8
Manufacture of rubber and plastics products	37.4	99.5	52.4	210.6
Manufacture of other non-metallic mineral products	7.4	13.0	23.0	356.6
Manufacture of basic metals	49.6	52.6	157.4	140.4
Manufacture of fabricated metal products	11.4	27.3	13.8	347.5
Manufacture of computer, electronic, etc.	19.4	68.2	31.7	280.7
Manufacture of electrical equipment	NA[a]	8.8	38.3	252.9
Manufacture of machinery and equipment	61.2	34.4	60.9	243.5
Manufacture of other transport equipment	59.5	199.6	55.4	85.5
Manufacture of furniture	44.4	172.8	96.0	86.8
Other manufacturing	143.9	24.3	205.1	26.7
Repair and installation of machinery and equipment	47.8	163.3	69.0	119.9

[a]Numbers of units are negligible for these firm sizes. 'Manufacturing of motor vehicles' is not included as most of units mainly come under large-scale units only

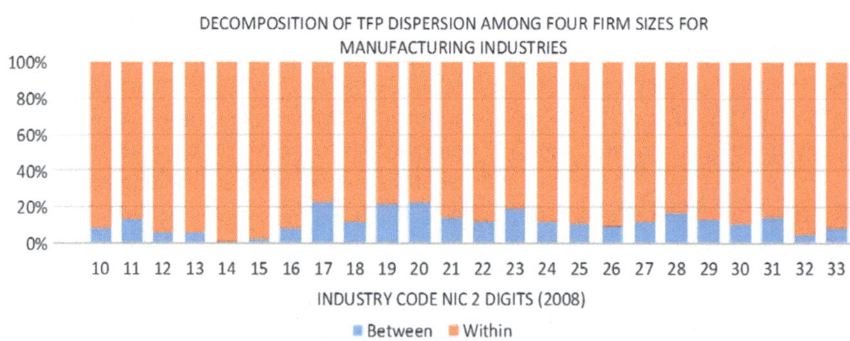

Fig. 7.1 Decomposition of TFP dispersion among four firm sizes for manufacturing industries. *See appendix for detailed list of two digits industries (NIC_08)

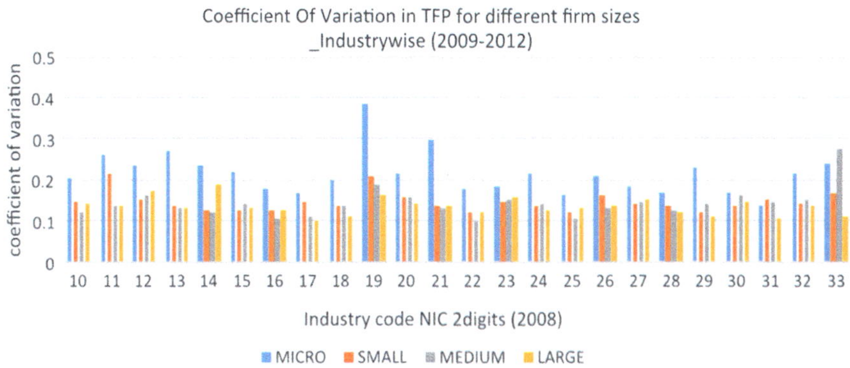

Fig. 7.2 Coefficient of variation in TFP for different firm sizes. *Source* As for Table 7.1

is highest for medium-scale units. Not only the micro-units of production, but for small-scale units too, 'the coefficient of variation' is much greater than higher scales of production except few occasions. The prevalence of high degree of variation in the total factor productivity among particularly tiny units is more apparent for traditional sectors.

But, we observe a completely opposite picture when we consider the log difference between 90th and 10th percentiles (Fig. 7.3). The dispersion is more pronounced for large-scale units compared to smaller units. This observation on larger units is more prominent for firms operating in modern sector. Now when we look into the details of productivity dispersion, we find for the performance of the 10th percentile is very similar to the performance of the median particularly for modern sectors and thus the greater dispersion of larger-scale units is essentially due to the good performance of the 90th percentile.

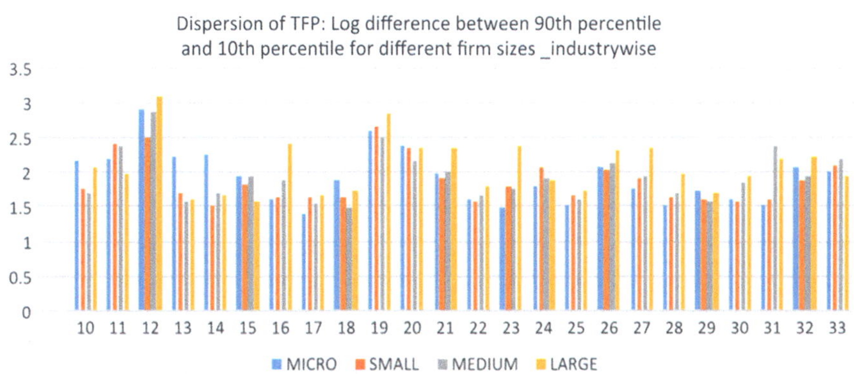

Fig. 7.3 Log difference (in TFP) between 90th and 10th percentiles for different firm sizes industry-wise. *Source* As for Table 7.1

7.6 Conclusions

This study analysed the productivity performance of different firm size of the Indian manufacturing sector for a cross-sectional period (2009–2012). In doing so, the study also examined the differences in the productivity for 23 two-digit industry sector. Both partial and total factor productivity were employed to compute productivity levels of respective firm sizes. Labour productivity is the partial factor productivity measure used in the study, while a Cobb–Douglas production function following the LP method is employed to estimate TFP. To correct the endogeneity bias associated with the production function estimation, we employed the LP method of productivity estimation. Our analysis reveals that although labour productivity and capital intensity for all firm sizes increase for the period under consideration, the gap among firm sizes for the same remained statistically significant. The study also found the declining role of labour as one move to higher firm sizes. This finding is interesting one as each unit of larger firm size is providing more mandays on average. The sector-wise analysis of productivity reveals that performance of different firm size is not uniform across industries with respect to mean productivity, while smaller-sized firms are performing better than their larger counterpart in some traditional sectors and larger firm sizes in both traditional and modern sectors but more prominently in modern sectors.

Regarding the dispersion of TFP among different firm sizes, TFP dispersion is greater for firms in the lower end of the size distribution of firms if one observes the coefficient of variation. But the log difference of 90th and 10th percentiles is largest for the ‘large-scale’ firms in modern sectors as well as few traditional sectors. In the absence of this linear relationship, we would expect that differential patterns of TFP growth could explain divergence, too. Productivity dispersion within narrowly defined sectors is a sign that technology or knowledge is not being diffused across different firms coexisting in the same country. This could be a result of the difficulties of transferring knowledge, intensified with poor labour mobility or lack of competition.

Appendix I

MSME Act 2006 (source: https://msme.gov.in/know-about-msme):

Definitions of micro, small and medium enterprises. In accordance with the provision of Micro, Small and Medium Enterprises Development (MSMED) Act, 2006, the micro, small and medium enterprises (MSME) are classified in two classes:

1. Manufacturing enterprises: The enterprises engaged in the manufacture or production of goods pertaining to any industry specified in the first schedule to the industries (Development and Regulation Act, 1951) or employing plant and machinery in the process of value addition to the final product having a

distinct name or character or use. The manufacturing enterprises are defined in terms of investment in plant and machinery.

2. Service enterprises: The enterprises engaged in providing or rendering of services and are defined in terms of investment in equipment.
   1. Manufacturing Sector

Enterprises	Investment in plant and machinery
Micro enterprises	Does not exceed twenty-five lakh rupees
Small enterprises	More than twenty-five lakh rupees but does not exceed five crore rupees
Medium enterprises	More than five crore rupees but does not exceed ten crore rupees.

   2. Service Sector

Enterprises	Investment in equipment
Micro enterprises	Does not exceed ten lakh rupees
Small enterprises	More than ten lakh rupees but does not exceed two crore rupees
Medium enterprises	More than two crore rupees but does not exceed five crore rupees

Appendix II

NIC_2008 (two-digit industry code):

Industries	(NIC_2008_two-digit industry code)
Manufacture of food products	10
Manufacture of beverages	11
Manufacture of tobacco products	12
Manufacture of textiles	13
Manufacture of wearing apparels	14
Manufacture of leather and related products	15
Manufacture of wood products	16
Manufacture of paper and paper products	17
Printing and reproduction of recorded media	18
Manufacture of coke and refined petroleum products	19
Manufacture of chemicals and chemical products	20
Manufacture of pharmaceuticals	21
Manufacture of rubber and plastic products	22
Manufacture of other non-metallic mineral products	23
Manufacture of basic metals	24

(continued)

(continued)

Industries	(NIC_2008_two-digit industry code)
Manufacture of fabricated metal products	25
Manufacture of computer, electronic, etc.	26
Manufacture of electrical equipment	27
Manufacture of machinery and equipment	28
Manufacture of motor vehicles	29
Manufacture of other transport equipment	30
Manufacture of furniture	31
Other manufacturing	32
Repair and installation of machinery and equipment	33

References

Ahluwalia, I. J. (1991). *Productivity and growth in indian manufacturing*. New Delhi: Oxford University Press.

Baily, M. N., Hulten, C., & Campbell, D. (1992). Productivity dynamics in manufacturing plants. *Brookings Papers on Economic Activity, 23*(1992), 187–267.

Bartelsman, E. J., & Doms, M. (2000). Understanding productivity: Lessons from longitudinal microdata. *Journal of Economic Literature, 38*(3), 569–594.

Beck, T., Kunt, A., & Maksimovic, V. (2005). Financial and legal constraints to growth: Does firm size matter? *The Journal of Finance, 60*(1), 137–177.

Bedi, J. S., & Banerjee, P. K. (2007). Discrepancies and validation of Indian manufacturing data. *Economic and Political Weekly, 42*(10), 883–891.

Blundell, R., & Bond, S. (1998). Initial conditions and moment restrictions in dynamic panel data models. *Journal of Econometrics, 87*(1998), 115–143.

Diewert, W. E., & Nakamura, A. O. (2003). Index number concepts, measures and decomposition of productivity growth. *Journal of Productivity Analysis, 19,* 127–159.

Dougherty, S., Herd, Richard, & Chalaux, Thomas. (2009). What is holding back productivity growth in India? Recent micro evidence. *OECD Economic Studies, 45*(1), 59–80.

Harris, P. M., Milton, M., Smith, I. M., Brown, A. S., & Goody, B. A. (2006). Implementation of a generalized least-squares method for determining calibration curves from data with general uncertainty structures. *Metrologia, 43*(2006), S291–S298.

Hasan, R., & Jandoc, K. L. (2010). The distribution of firm size in India: What can survey data tell us? *ADB Economics Working Paper Series* (213).

Ito, K., & Lechevalier, S. (2009). The evolution of the productivity dispersion of firms: A reevaluation of its determinants in the case of Japan. *Review of World Economics, 145*(3), 405–429.

Jovanovic, B. (1982). Selection and evolution of Industry. *Econometrica, 50*(3), 649–670.

Levinsohn, J., & Petrin, A. (2003). Estimating production functions using inputs to control for unobservables. *The Review of Economic Studies, 70*(2), 317–341.

Malerba, F. (1992). Learning by firms and incremental technical change. *Economic Journal, 102*(413), 845–859.

Martin, R. (2008). *Productivity dispersion, competition and productivity measurement* (CEP discussion paper 0692). Retrieved from URL http://cep.lse.ac.uk/pubs/download/dp0692.pdf.

Olley, G. S., & Pakes, A. (1996). The dynamics of productivity in the telecommunications equipment industry. *Econometrica, 64*(6), 1263–1297.

Orr, S. (2018). *Productivity dispersion, import competition, and specialization in multi-product plants* (working paper). University of Toronto. Retrieved from URL faculty.chicagobooth.edu/workshops/appliedecon/pdf/SCOTT_ORR_JMP-1.pdf.
Schumpeter, J. (1942). *Capitalism, socialism, and democracy*. New York: Harper Torchbooks.
Singh, C. (2016). *Finance for micro, small, and medium-sized enterprises in India: Sources and challenge* (IIMB-WP N0. 525).
Syverson, C. (2004). Market structure and productivity: A concrete example. *Journal of Political Economy, 112*(6), 1181–1222. University of Chicago Press.

Part IV
Service Sector

Chapter 8
Causes and Consequences of Service Sector Growth: Perceptions and Realities

Nitya Nanda

Abstract While the service sector has shown impressive performance at the aggregate level, there is very little to show that there has been any transformative change, except in cases of telecommunication and information technology services. The service sector has been showing better performance compared to agriculture and industry all along since the late 1960s. While it was premised that post-reform access to services will improve along with quality, the performance in most sectors did not meet the expectations. Even in some sub-sectors where improvement has been observed, it is difficult to attribute the same to the policy reforms. Rather they might have been due to technological changes that are exogenous to the reforms process. Moreover, the business process reengineering also meant that several activities that were done in the manufacturing sector is now being outsourced to external agencies which might have shown in terms of better performance of the service sector. Given this, it is not only difficult to claim that India had service-led growth, maintaining overall growth with excessive reliance on the service sector can become difficult in the future.

8.1 Introduction

When India embarked on economic reforms in 1991, the dominant narrative was that the process will help India change its development strategy and it will shift from an import-substituting growth path to an export-led growth path which will accelerate economic growth rate in the country. While the country was able to maintain the growth momentum that started in the early 1980s, and to some extent accelerated it in later years, it was not an export-led growth as observed in East Asian or South-East Asian countries in the sense that they could achieve higher exports of industrial or

Senior Fellow and Associate Director, Resource Efficiency and Governance; and Editor, Journal of Resources, Energy and Development (JREaD).

N. Nanda (✉)
The Energy and Resources Institute (TERI), New Delhi, India
e-mail: nitya@teri.res.in

P. K. Biswas and P. Das (eds.), *Indian Economy: Reforms and Development*, India Studies in Business and Economics, https://doi.org/10.1007/978-981-13-8269-7_8

manufactured goods. However, it was pointed out that India was possibly experiencing an export-led growth but in a different sense (Banga 2006).

Historically, economic development has been accompanied by a structural change in the economy with a rapid increase in the share of industry which has been attributed to higher economies of scale, higher income elasticity of demand for industrial goods and potential for higher productivity growth (Kaldor 1967; Chenery et al. 1986; Ocampo et al. 2009). Industrial sector, however, starts losing its dominance after a point gradually and concedes the dominant share to the services sector. While faster growth of services at a later stage has often been attributed to fast-growing-business-related services (Franke and Kalmbach 2005), it has also been argued that the share of services grows due to lower productivity and associated price increase in the services sector (Baumol 1967). Baumol's Cost Disease Hypothesis indicates that service sector occupying the dominant role is not good for an economy as an economy's growth rate and productivity gains are likely to decline along with the increase in the share of services.

While Baumol's Cost Disease Hypothesis is essentially a developed world phenomenon, it does not necessarily mean that in developing countries, the service sector growth is due to growth in business-related services. Moreover, in a developing country context, an absence of productivity growth is unlikely to enhance the share of the service sector as there is no shortage of labour. This can also give credence to the claim that India's service sector growth can be a manifestation of export-led growth in the service sector as services have become tradeable now. Export-led growth for the industrial sector was considered to be not applicable for services as services were not tradeable. It is also important to note, however, that higher share of service could also be due to an increase in disguised unemployment in the sector. While disguised unemployment is generally associated with agriculture, there has been an increasing incidence of it in urban areas also due to migration of labour from countryside who pick up casual jobs and petty trading (Lewis 1954; Ray 1998). This can lead to higher output in the service sector as people are willing to work at very low wage and the urban middle-class people hire them to do things that they might have been doing themselves earlier. Often they are hired by people who themselves are also migrants and they now pay higher rates than they paid such people at their place of origin.

Indeed India achieved among the highest growth rates in services exports ever achieved by countries all over the world. Hence, India's growth was possibly service-export-led economic growth. It was also observed that the share of the service sector in GDP was also growing. Hence, it was also believed that India was possibly leapfrogging and the growth of manufacturing that could be observed in most developed countries in their initial stage of development will not be observed and India is directly getting into a service-dominated economy bypassing the industrial sector growth contradicting the growth experience as observed in most developed countries (Ghani and Kharas 2010).

Ironically, India's share of manufacturing increased steadily during 1950–1980, but it experienced stagnation or slow growth thereafter and even decline in recent years. It might have been partly due to business process reengineering in which some activities that were an integral part of a manufacturing firm are now outsourced and hence accounted in the service sector. While the policymakers have emphasised the need for growth in manufacturing but it was due to the concern that service sector was not generating enough quality jobs, particularly for low-skilled labour (though some jobs like street vending have also been generated in the services sector) and not that the hypothesis of a service-led growth was questioned. While it was also pointed out that if premature deindustrialization could be a concern, the services sector could provide an additional engine of growth and could help India leapfrog in technology to catch up with advanced economies (Dasgupta and Singh 2006).

What is now well understood is that despite high growth of export of services, India's growth in the service sector is largely due to increased domestic demand rather than export (Ghosh 2014). In fact, India's exports of services have been largely concentrated in the information technology sector. For all other types of services, India's export record is quite poor. In fact, in terms of overall exports of services, China is far ahead of India. It is only in IT-related services, India is ahead of China. A new research has shown that manufacturing and intermediate services tend to collocate (Kuan 2017).

Given this, question may be raised if Indian service sector might find it difficult to sustain its growth in the absence of adequate growth in manufacturing. It is quite possible that India's service sector growth has largely been driven by growth in final services rather than intermediate services. The quagmire in the energy sector is probably an indication of this as the sector is experiencing substantial excess capacity leading to huge non-performing assets, which in turn led to poor health of the banking sector. However, it is not an easy question to answer because just like industrial goods, several services are used both for final consumption as well as intermediate inputs.

Given this backdrop, Sect. 8.2 gives a snapshot of the reforms in the services sectors in India. Section 8.3 analyses the service sector growth performance over long term, while Sect. 8.4 looks at the structure of growth performance in India. Section 8.5 discusses the trade dimensions of the service sector, while Sect. 8.6 examines the issues of quality of growth in the service sector. Section 8.7 concludes the chapter.

8.2 Service Sector Reforms in India

This section briefly discusses the nature of reforms undertaken for the Indian services sector since 1991. The structure and dynamics of the services sector are much more complex than those in the manufacturing or industrial sector. Hence, it is not easy to describe what can be termed as the reforms in the services sectors. In the manufacturing sectors, broadly, there have been three types of liberalisation: delicensing, privatisation or opening up of a sector to private entities and opening up of the sector to foreign players. While liberalisation in the sense of delicensing was an important component of reforms in the manufacturing sector, in services, the licensing arrangements were more or less retained due to the very nature of it which is highly prone to market failures. However, the other two components, namely opening up of the sector to private players and progressive opening up for the foreign players, were important parts of service sector reforms. Since services are relatively non-tradable, opening up for the foreign players generally meant progressive opening up for foreign direct investment. An important part of the reforms in the sector included the creation of regulatory institutions to address the market failure issues.

As can be seen from Table 8.1, telecommunications, banking and finance and airlines are the sectors that have gone through major reforms as these sectors were the exclusive domain of the public sector. In other sectors, private players played a major role even before the reforms were initiated. However, these sectors had restrictions as far as foreign investors are concerned. Over the last couple of decades, these sectors have been made wide open to foreign investors. In sectors like education and health, public sector refused to expand capacity in the face of growing demand creating space for the growth of private players.

8.3 The Service Sector Growth Performance

The popular narrative is that India became a service-led economy since 1991 when it introduced some deep economic reforms. However, a closer look at the growth rates would reveal this is far from the truth. Figure 8.1 provides the Hodrick–Prescott trends of growth rates of GDP and different sectors of the economy. Since growth rates show substantial fluctuations, Hodrick–Prescott trends were fitted to smoothen the series and understand the trend better. Now if we look at the growth rates of different sectors during the post-Independence period, it is observed that till the late 1960s, growth rate of industrial sector was higher than that of the services sector. The trend reversed thereafter. This happened not because the service sector growth rate picked up fast, but because of a sharp decline in the growth rate of the industrial sector. In fact, the service sector also experienced deceleration in its growth rate.

However, once the service sector growth rate became higher than the growth rate of the industry, the gap between the growth rates of these two sectors continued to rise. During the period 1950–65, Indian industrial sector posted an average growth rate of 6.6% per annum, a level of performance it could never repeat, though the industrial growth rate could surpass this only for a short period of 5–6 years starting around 2002–03 (Table 8.2). It is also noteworthy that the service sector showed relatively consistent growth performance, compared to the growth performance of the industrial sector which has been subject to higher fluctuations.

However, the service growth rate was always higher than the growth rate of GDP during almost the entire period of post-Independence history. Nevertheless, the industrial growth rate also continued to remain higher than the GDP growth rate, and they converged around the turn of the century. They continued hand in hand for some years, and then, the GDP growth rate became higher than the growth rate of the industrial sector around 2008–2009. Hence, in a strict sense, Indian economy became service-led only around the year 2008–09. However, if the service sector is considered to be

Table 8.1 Key reforms in select sectors

Sector	Entry of domestic players	Entry of foreign players	Regulatory reforms
Telecommunications	1997—Opening up for basic services on duopoly basis 2000—Long distance service open to private players 2001—Unlimited entry for basic and mobile services 2002—International long distance opened up	1997—Foreign equity participation in both basic and cellular mobile services was permitted up to 49%. 2005—Foreign holding limit increased to 74%. FDI permitted up to 100% in value-added services such as email, voice mail, electronic data interchange 2014—100% FDI	National Telecom Policy 1994 Telecom regulatory authority of India 1997 NTP 1999 2001—The licence regime migrated from fixed fee to revenue sharing
Banking/finance/insurance	1993—Entry of private sector banks 2000—Entry of private insurance companies 1993–97: Phase-out of privileged access by development finance institutions	2001—FDI limit increased to 49% 2004—FDI limit up to 74% and foreign banks able to operate through subsidiaries (earlier only branches) 2000—Insurance FDI up to 26% 2014—Insurance FDI up to 49%	1992—Securities and Exchange Board of India (SEBI) given statutory power 1994—Board for Financial Supervision (BFS) within RBI 1996—Guidelines issued for setting up new private local area banks 1999—Insurance Regulatory and Development Authority of India
Higher education	A university can be established only through legislation at centre or states. But private colleges and institutes have been there all along. 1995—First private university (Sikkim Manipal University) 1993—Manipal Academy of Higher Research, first institute to receive deemed university status by UGC. No new deemed university since 2010 Currently 280 + private universities in India	Foreign equity participation up to 100% for entry through franchises, twinning arrangements, study centres and programme collaboration, and up to 49% for research and teaching activities	1987—AICTE (All India Council for Technical Education) given statutory status National Assessment and Accreditation Council established by UGC in 1994
Retail services	Has been in private hands all along	51% FDI in single-brand retailing since 2006 2012—100% FDI in single-brand retailing with sourcing restriction and 51% FDI in multi-brand retail	No specific regulation

(continued)

Table 8.1 (continued)

Sector	Entry of domestic players	Entry of foreign players	Regulatory reforms
Construction services	Has always been open for private players except in some specific areas	2001—100% FDI through approval route 2005—100% FDI with some restrictions 2014—100% FDI under automatic route (not for real estate business)	The Real Estate (Regulation and Development) Act 2016, established Real Estate Regulatory Authority (RERA) in each state
Health care (hospitals and diagnostics)	About 80% of the hospitals are in private sector	2000—100% FDI through automatic route	State government/authority regulates private medical establishment (state specific). They have been there for long, but many of them went through major changes
Hotels and restaurants	Has always been open for private players except in some specific areas	1980—Partial liberalisation 1995—51% FDI under automatic approval 2002—100% FDI with prior approval 2003—100% under automatic route	No specific regulation except on food safety by local authorities
Airlines/airports	Open Sky Policy 1990	2018—100% FDI in private airlines (automatic) and 49% FDI in Air India	Directorate General of Civil Aviation 2008—Airport Economic Regulatory Authority of India
Shipping	Shipping services have always been open to private players 1993—Private participation in ports	1996—100% in ports with approval 1998 ports—100% automatic approval 2000—100% FDI in shipping	Directorate General of Shipping (Several amendments to relevant Act and Rules) 1997—Tariff Authority for Major Ports

Source Author's compilation from different sources

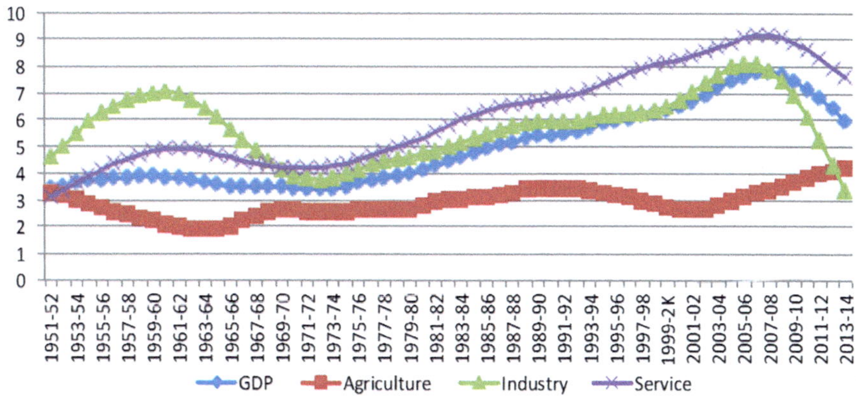

Fig. 8.1 Hodrick–Prescott trends of growth rates (per cent)

Table 8.2 Growth rates of GDP and different sectors

Period	1950–2014	1950–1965	1965–1980	1965–2014	1980–1991	1991–2014	1950–1991	1980–2014
Agriculture	2.90	2.92	1.42	2.90	4.37	3.16	2.75	3.55
Industry	5.76	6.61	3.91	5.52	6.10	6.30	5.46	6.23
Service	6.12	4.58	4.23	6.56	6.48	8.12	4.97	7.59
GDP	4.96	4.09	2.94	5.21	5.56	6.52	4.06	6.21

Sources National Accounts Statistics of India, Central Statistical Organisation

the engine of growth just because its growth rate is higher than the other two sectors, namely agriculture and industry, then it happened way back in the late 1960s.

Overall economic decline started in India in the mid-1960s that can be attributed to several factors including successive wars and droughts, political instability and oil price shock (Nanda 2008). However, when the economy picked up again, it was the service sector rather than the industrial sector that accelerated faster despite the fact that in the mid-1960s, the industrial sector had a sharper fall. This was not the time when outsourcing started happening. So this was not due to some activities that could have been classified as industry earlier, were classified as services now. Service sector is less prone to fluctuations, but this could not explain the inability of the industrial sector to recover either.

A general argument is that as real income rises, the consumer demand for services rises more than proportionately, i.e. the income elasticity of demand for services is greater than one (Eichengreen and Gupta 2009). However, this cannot be an adequate explanation as there was not much growth in real income around that time. It was also not a case when pent-up demand being served due to the liberalisation of services which could be a reason for the acceleration of services during the post-1991 period. Das and Saha (2011) argued that differences in returns to scale between the two sectors and employment frictions in manufacturing underlie how the growth rate of the services sector may be higher. However, though this could be a factor of the service sector showing improved performance in general, it could not also explain the situation prevailing in the 1970s and 1980s.

It is also important to note that it was not just a case of service sector picking up, but it was also a case of industrial sector falling sharply but not recovering adequately. Performance of development finance institutions as a supply-side factor might partly explain this. Nayyar (2015) observed that the development finance intuitions experienced a marked decline in India since the mid-1960s. Naseemullah (2016) argued that with the decline of development finance institutions in India, the government lost its capability to divert financial resources available in the country into the sectors that it favours. It was well known that before 1965, the government favoured the industrial sector over other sectors of the economy and hence directed financial resources towards it which was not happening in the 1970s.

Some important events of the early 2000s could have made the industrial sector less attractive to investors. In 2002, India had to remove its quantitative restrictions on trade. India also had to remove indigenization and performance requirements after it lost a dispute at the WTO. However, what was possibly more important, and had far-reaching consequences is that, in December 2001, China became a member of the WTO. India also continued to reduce its import duties on industrial goods. These might have made the tradable sectors highly competitive even though tariff cuts were more drastic during the decade of the 1990s. When the competition was getting tougher in tradable sectors, investors could have given more attention to non-tradable sectors.

Despite service sector growth in India, there has been a sharp decline in the share of Indian ships in the carriage of India's overseas trade from about 40% in the late 1980s to 7% in 2015–16, a survey tabled in Parliament said. Since 2000, 100% FDI is allowed in shipping as well as in ports. More importantly, the sector has always been open for private investment. In fact, the Shipping Corporation of India Limited was established by the Government in 1963 as the private sector did not show much enthusiasm in this sector. This shows how India performed when India had to compete globally in providing services. Investors did not show much interest in this sector as this sector is tradable.

8.4 Structure of Growth Performance

According to Eichengreen and Gupta (2011), over 1991–2007, a big chunk of services growth has come from traditional services which account for about 60% of the services sector. Broadly, services could be disaggregated into three categories: (i) trade, hotels, transport and storage and communication; (ii) finance, insurance, real estate and business services; and (iii) community, social and personal services. The first category of services is largely traditional except communication services. This type of services is used both by business and households and its growth will depend on the growth of other sectors as well growth in incomes. Trade, transport and storage are primarily used as intermediate inputs in manufacturing and trade itself.

Table 8.3 Growth rates in different sub-sectors of services

	Trade, hotels, transport and communication	Finance, Insurance, real estate and business services	Community, social and personal services
1950–2014	6.56	6.45	5.29
1950–1965	5.45	3.08	4.36
1965–1980	4.64	3.90	4.32
1965–2014	6.89	7.48	5.57
1980–1991	5.58	9.25	5.62
1991–2014	8.97	8.96	6.35
1950–1991	5.19	5.04	4.69
1980–2014	7.88	9.05	6.12

Source National Accounts Statistics of India, Central Statistical Organisation

The second type of services uses ICT, but they are consumed largely by business, and hence, its growth will depend largely on the growth of other sectors unless there are substantial exports. With the development of ICT, this sector can export to foreign countries. The third category of services is largely consumed by households. The consumption of this category of services including education, health, community services, etc. is quite closely aligned with income levels. So is the case for hotels and restaurants. They have limited tradability as well.

As can be seen from Table 8.3, the first category has seen the highest growth during the period 1950–2014. The second category of services although witnessed high growth during the 1980–1991 period, moderated a bit to give the highest rate tag to the first category of services during the post-1991 period. What is interesting is the fact that the IT and IT-enabled services belonged to this category which has seen substantial exports in the post-1991 period. Absent such export performance, this category of services could have performed much worse. This category is expected to increase its share with growth in GDP, and hence, subdued performance in spite of high exports could be a cause of concern.

As Table 8.4 shows, trade, hotels and restaurant remained the mainstay till the time estimates were made at factor cost. While financing, insurance, real estate and business services improved its share, it remained below that of trade, hotel and restaurants. Communication is often considered the success story of India's service sector, but its share remained less than 2% and actually fell below even 1% in 2011–12. After the methodology of estimating GDP changed (from factor cost based to market price based), the share of trade, hotels and restaurant fell substantially and that of financing, insurance, real estate and business services increased to that extent.

Table 8.4 Share of India's services sector and its sub-sectors (at factor cost for 2000–12, market prices for 2015–16) (per cent)

	2000–01	2005–06	2006–07	2007–08	2008–09	2009–10	2010–11	2011–12	2015–16
Trade, hotels and restaurants	*14.6*	*16.7*	*17.1*	*17.1*	*16.9*	*16.5*	*17.2*	*18*	*11.4*
Trade	13.3	15.1	15.4	15.4	15.3	15.1	15.7	16.6	10.4
Hotels and restaurants	1.3	1.6	1.7	1.7	1.5	1.4	1.5	1.5	1
Transport, storage and communication	*7.6*	*8.2*	*8.2*	*8*	*7.8*	*7.7*	*7.3*	*7.1*	*7*
Railways	1.1	0.9	0.9	1	0.9	0.9	0.8	0.7	0.8
Transport by other means	5	5.7	5.7	5.6	5.5	5.3	5.3	5.4	3.4
Storage	0.1	0.1	0.1	0.1	0.1	0.1	0.1	0.1	
Communication	1.5	1.6	1.5	1.4	1.4	1.4	1.1	0.9	
Financing, insurance, real estate and business services	*13.8*	*14.5*	*14.8*	*15.1*	*15.9*	*15.8*	*16*	*16.6*	*20.1*
Banking and insurance	5.4	5.4	5.5	5.5	5.6	5.4	5.6	5.7	5.8
Real estate, ownership of dwellings and business services	8.7	9.1	9.3	9.6	10.3	10.4	10.4	10.8	15.3
Community, social and personal services	*14.8*	*13.5*	*12.8*	*12.5*	*13.3*	*14.5*	*14*	*14*	*13.4*
Public administration and defence	6.6	5.6	5.2	5.1	5.8	6.6	6.1	6.1	
Other services	8.2	7.9	7.6	7.4	7.5	7.8	7.9	7.9	
Construction	*6*	*7.9*	*8.2*	*8.5*	*8.5*	*8.2*	*8.2*	*8.2*	*8.1*
Total Services	*50.8*	*53.1*	*52.9*	*52.7*	*53.9*	*54.5*	*54.4*	*55.7*	*52.9*
Total Services (incl. Construction)	*56.8*	*61*	*61*	*61.2*	*62.4*	*62.7*	*62.6*	*63.9*	*61*
Total GDP	*100*	*100*	*100*	*100*	*100*	*100*	*100*	*100*	*100*

8.5 Trade Dimension of Services Sector in India

During the Uruguay Round of trade negotiations, developing countries were against the inclusion of services as they considered it will work only in favour of developed countries. However, during the last couple of decades or so, some developing countries, including India, have been able to increase their share in the global trade in services. This is often attributed to the GATS, and it is argued that developing countries have actually benefited from it. Hence, it is often believed that developing countries will benefit from further liberalisation of trade in services. However, it could be problematic to take this in its face value. The types or mode of services that have been helping the developing countries increase their share, particularly in the context of India, have largely been possible due to the emergence of new technologies, and the role of GATS is limited. So the linking of better performance of India in trade in services with GATS is not appropriate.

When GATS was being negotiated during the Uruguay Round, Mode 1 (cross-border supply) was yet to emerge as an important mode of service export. In any case, this is not a mode where developed countries have a substantial advantage. The GATS agenda was primarily set by the developed countries and developing countries hardly had any understanding of how they could benefit through trade in services. As a result Mode 3 (commercial presence) and Mode 4 (movement of natural persons) received relatively more attention, and hence, these are the modes in which countries made greater market access commitments (Nanda 2008). It may be noted that Mode 4 is about intra-company transfer which was mainly to facilitate Mode 3 only.

India's exports of services have mostly been in IT and IT-enabled services. This is also the sector where India enjoys substantial surplus. India also enjoys small surplus in travel services, but it has deficit in all other services (Table 8.5). In the IT and ITES segment, India essentially started with Mode 1, but in recent years it has also established commercial presence in importing countries and hence has been able to take advantage of Mode 4 as well. Nevertheless, even now, almost two-thirds of India's software exports occur through Mode 1 (Table 8.6). Since India's exports in other segments are relatively much less and it also imports more, Mode 1 is the most important mode for India. However, as countries liberalised least in Mode 1, India's benefit from GATS is largely limited to its recent exports through Mode 3 and Mode 4. India received substantial remittances from its workers abroad but it has nothing to do with Mode 4 or GATS.

8.6 Quality of Service Sector Growth

While it is often argued that a service-led growth as against an industry-led growth is not appropriate for India due to employment generation consideration, there are other reasons also. This is due to the special nature of this sector, especially in developing countries. What is noteworthy here is that not all of the growth of services comes

Table 8.5 Trade performance in service sector (major sub-sectors)

	Value (US $ Billion)	Share (%)	Growth (%)	
	2016–17	2016–17	2015–16	2016–17
Services exports	*163.1*	*100*	*−2.4*	*5.7*
Travel	23.2	14.2	4.6	9.3
Transportation	15.9	9.7	−19.9	13.2
Software services	73.7	45.2	1.4	−0.7
Business services	32.9	20.2	2	13.6
Financial services	5.1	3.1	−12.7	3.1
Services imports	*95.7*	*100*	*3.7*	*13.0*
Travel	16.4	17.2	−3.4	11.1
Transportation	14.1	14.8	−6.8	−6.3
Software services	3.6	3.7	−0.3	32.9
Business services	32.3	33.7	12.5	3.7
Financial services	5.9	6.1	−12.4	86.7
Net services exports	*67.5*	*100*	*−9.0*	*−3.2*

Economic Survey 2017–2018

Table 8.6 Software services exports by different modes

Type of mode	2009–10	2010–11	2011–12	2012–13	2013–14	2014–15	2015–16	2016–17
Mode 1 (cross-border supply)	64.6	67.4	69.0	74.7	69.0	68.4	64.8	66.5
Mode 2 (consumption abroad)	0.0	0.1	0.5	1.6	0.1	0.1	0.2	0.2
Mode 3 (commercial presence)	17.6	14.8	15.4	9.4	13.7	14.4	18.9	19.4
Mode 4 (movement of natural persons)	17.8	17.7	15.1	14.3	17.1	17.1	17.1	13.9

Source Reserve Bank of India: Survey on Computer Software and Information Technology Enabled Services Exports from "value added" services such as information technology. Part of the growth of the service sector since 1997 was "spurious" as it reflects revaluation of the value added in the "administrative and defence" that was simply caused by pay hikes in the government sector. Acharya (2001), for example, observed that if this erroneous growth estimate is accounted for, the GDP growth rate will drop by at least 0.5% points. In a sense, every Pay Commission that raised the salaries and other benefits of government employees led to expansion in Public Administration and Defence but not because they generated more services but they were paid more for delivering the same quantity of services.

Public Administration and Defence is not the only sub-sector that could bring spurious growth in the sense that work is done by somebody else without changing the quantity of services generated in the economy, and non-economic service gets converted to economic service. This happens when the same work is done by somebody else. If a family decides to dine outside instead of cooking at home, additional income is generated though the quantity of goods and services produced in the economy remains the same. A family member is not paid for cooking but if somebody else cooks, then that person is paid for it. Similar logic applies to a situation when people decide to hire a driver or domestic servants instead of doing the jobs themselves. In other words, when some non-marketed services enter the domain of the market, previously unaccounted services get accounted. There can, of course, be situations when people can hire services of others to do something else themselves which will generate additional income.

In addition, the growth of services may also be brought about in part by the growth of unproductive services. For example, the production of unproductive services occurs when criminal activity increases and people are forced to hiring security services. This applies to both private and government security services. Increased inefficiency or lack of competition may also increase income resulting from, for example, transportation and trading of the same quantity of goods and services may bring much higher income if market distortions increase. In some cases, additional employment may occur along with the increase in income, but in other cases, it might involve redistribution of income only, which may even lead to an increase in inequality (Nanda 2009). This is of course not to suggest that the entire growth in the service sector is spurious. However, the fact that a change in methodology in national accounting (from factor cost to market prices based) led to substantial reduction in the share of services as well as substantial changes in the composition of sub-sectors within service amply shows how unreliable the growth story of service sector could be.

With the changes in technology and the way production is organised in manufacturing, a part of the service sector includes activities that were earlier considered as manufacturing. This is because manufacturing companies outsource several activities now which were considered integral parts of their own activities earlier (Banga and Goldar 2004). According to Eichengreen and Gupta (2011), over 1991–2007, about a quarter of services growth is due to outsourcing by industry. This also means that now the services sector is more closely linked to the manufacturing sector and hence the growth in services may not be sustainable in the long run unless there is concomitant growth in the manufacturing sector as well.

Report of the Committee for Evolution of the New Education Policy (The TSR Subramanian Committee) in its report submitted in 2016 observed that uncontrolled privatisation of higher education has resulted in the proliferation of private institutions for higher education most of which are nothing more than shops selling degrees. Gross enrolment ratio in higher education remains low compared to other major developing countries. While several studies have found poor employability of Indian graduates, one study has found that nearly half of the students in private sector went to a private facility because they could not secure admission in a public sector institute (Panigrahi and Singh 2016). This means that the money spent by people to buy services, though generate income, does not produce "real services" with expected quality.

A systematic review of health sector performance in developing countries (Basu et al. 2012) finds the private sector to be more expensive, resulting in part from perverse private sector incentives for unnecessary testing and treatment including surgical procedures. It also finds private sector providers more frequently violated medical standards of practice and had poorer patient outcomes. Irrational drug prescribing, kickbacks for referrals and unnecessary investigations and surgical procedures are common in India (Gadre 2015; Gadre and Shukla 2016). Another study concludes that unethical revenue targets that the private hospitals thrust upon their doctors result in unnecessary tests and surgery that not only pose unnecessary financial burden but also harm the patients (Kay 2015).

India accounts for over half of the estimated 100 million people pushed into extreme poverty worldwide every year due to out-of-pocket expenses on health care as 17.3% of India's population spends over 10% of household income every month to meet health care expense (World Bank 2017). This clearly indicates that health care is moving away from the reach of the people in general and the poor in particular.

Despite high economic growth and substantial privatisation and growth of health care and educational services, India continues to rank low in human development index. When income is generated through unnecessary and harmful medical tests and treatment, it is simply rent-seeking rather than the generation of genuine income. When people spend money to receive a poor quality education that has no value, the income generated through this is simply spurious.

It is well recognised that the share of unorganised sector is quite low in the service sector. While the estimated size of the unorganized sector for services depends upon definitions, unorganised employment in services ranged from 74 to 90% of services employment in 2006. According to another NSS survey, in 2015, outside agricultural and construction services, service sectors accounted for more than two-thirds of unorganized employment, and trade alone employed more than one-third of total unorganized employment (outside agriculture and construction). Hence, the possibility of disguised unemployment in the service sector is also quite high. It is well recognised that if agriculture is the sector that somehow absorbs excess labour through disguised unemployment in rural areas, in urban areas, it is the service sector that plays a similar role, and a large number of people might be engaged with marginal productivity much lower than the market wage rate making the output of the sector higher than what it could be in the absence of such disguised unemployment. In this context, it is important to note that, according to an NSSO survey of service firms, 650 largest firms accounted for 38% of service output but employed only 2% of service sector workforce in 2006–07. In other words, 98% of the workforce in the service sector produced just 62% of the output. It is unlikely that the situation has changed much by now.

8.7 Conclusion

Whether or not we describe the Indian growth experience as a case of service-led growth, there is no denying the fact that service sector has shown better performance compared to other sectors, particularly in the last one decade or so. There have been several factors that determined such outcome. While economic reforms on the internal front in the form of delicensing and freeing up of sectors that were earlier reserved for public sector made it easier to invest in service sectors, reforms on the external front made it difficult to do business in the manufacturing sector forcing investors to move towards non-tradable sector like services. Business process reengineering in the form of outsourcing also contributed to the process.

While in the 1980s and 1990s service sector growth has been largely due to freeing up of pent-up demand, since the 1990s it has also been due to IT exports. But this has largely been due to advent of new technology rather than economic reforms or market opening in foreign countries. The developments in the field of information and communication technology (IT) in recent years have expanded the range of services that can be traded internationally. Many of the services that were considered non-tradable till recently are now actively being traded though much of this started picking up since the mid-1990s. However, India's service exports are highly vulnerable as it is concentrated virtually in one sector and to one destination (USA) where recent political developments are not encouraging. Indian exports of services are already seeing stress in the US market.

As of now the share of service is quite high in India compared to its level of income. The existence of higher share service sector has been a phenomenon of high-income countries. If the service sector occupies very high share in a relatively poorer country, it could be both a cause and effect of higher inequality and poverty. However, beyond a point it might be difficult to sustain high growth in services with high inequality and poverty. While the growth of services sector increased demand for manufactured goods, the same has been met largely by imports.

While telecommunications and airlines are talked about as the great success stories of the service sector in India, they contribute hardly 1.0 and 0.2%, respectively, to GDP. Telecommunication success story is more of technology story that brought even more network advantage as mobile phone became possible. In this technology, once the basic infrastructure is in place, giving an additional connection or making an additional call is almost zero. Such an advantage is not possible in most other sectors. Costs of services have not come down, or quality has not gone up in services like health and education, for example. A large number of people remain without electricity despite India having a huge surplus generation capacity. Hence, if there has been an element of service-led growth, it is largely due to technology rather than economic reforms in India.

References

Acharya, S. (2001). India's macroeconomic performance in the nineties. *SANEI Distinguished Lecture*, November 9, Colombo, Sri Lanka.

Banga, R. (2006). Critical issues in India's services-led growth. *INRM Policy Brief No. 2*. Manila: Asian Development Bank.

Banga, R., & Goldar, B. (2004). *Contribution of services to output growth and productivity in Indian manufacturing: Pre and post reforms* (ICRIER Working Paper 139). New Delhi: ICRIER.

Basu, S., Andrews, J., Kishore, S., Panjabi, R., & Stuckler, D. (2012). Comparative performance of private and public healthcare systems in low- and middle-income countries: A systematic review. *PLoS Medicine*, *9*(6). https://doi.org/10.1371/journal.pmed.1001244.

Das, S. P., & Saha, A. (2011). *On the growth of the services sector*. Indian Statistical Institute—Delhi Centre.

Baumol, W. J. (1967). Macroeconomics of unbalanced growth: The anatomy of urban crisis. *The American Economic Review*, *57*(3), 415–426.

Chenery, H. B., Robinson, S., & Syrquin, M. (1986). Structural transformation. In H. B. Chenery, S. Robinson, & M. Syrquin (Eds.), *Industrialization and growth: A comparative study* (pp. 11–12). Oxford: Oxford University Press.

Dasgupta, S., & Singh, A. (2006). *Manufacturing, services and premature deindustrialization in developing countries: A kaldorian analysis* (Research Paper No. 2006/49). Helsinki: UNU-WIDER, World Institute of Development Economics Research.

Eichengreen, B., & Gupta, P. (2009). *The two waves of service sector growth* (Working Paper No. 14968). NBER.

Eichengreen, B., & Gupta, P. (2011). *The service sector as India's road to economic growth* (Working Paper No. 16757). NBER.

Franke, R., & Kalmbach, P. (2005). Structural change in the manufacturing sector and its impact on business-related services: An input-output study for Germany. *Structural Change and Economic Dynamics, 16*(4), 467–488.

Gadre, A. (2015). India's private healthcare sector treats patients as revenue generators. BMJ 2015: 350, https://doi.org/10.1136/bmj.h826. February 24, 2015.

Gadre, A., & Shukla, A. (2016). *Dissenting diagnosis*. New Delhi: Random House/Vintage.

Ghani, E., & Kharas, H. (2010). Service led growth in South Asia: An overview. In E. Ghani (Ed.), *The service revolution in South Asia*. India: Oxford University Press.

Ghosh, A. K. (2014). *India's services-led growth* (Working Paper 01/2014). New Delhi: Institute of Human Development.

Kaldor, N. (1967). *Strategic factors in economic development*. Ithaca, NY: Cornell University.

Kay, M. (2015). The unethical revenue targets that India's corporate hospitals set their doctors. *BMJ, 2015,* 351. https://doi.org/10.1136/bmj.h4312. September 03, 2015.

Kuan, M. L. (2017). Does manufacturing collocate with intermediate services? Analyzing the world input-output database. In A. Noman & J. Stiglitz (Eds.), *Efficiency, finance, and varieties of industrial policy: Guiding resources, learning, and technology for sustained growth*. New York: Columbia University Press.

Lewis, W. A. (1954). Economic development with unlimited supplies of labour. *Manchester School, 22*(2), 139–191.

Nanda, N. (2008). *Expanding frontiers of global trade rules: The political economy dynamics of the international trading system*. London: Routledge.

Nanda, N. (2009). The Indian growth story: Myths and realities. *Journal of Asian and African Studies, 44*(6), 74–765.

Naseemullah, A. (2016). *Development after statism: Industrial firms and the political economy of South Asia*. Cambridge: Cambridge University Press.

Nayyar, D. (2015). Birth, life and death of development finance institutions in India. *Economic and Political Weekly, 50*(33), 51–60.

Ocampo, J. A., Rada, C., & Taylor, L. (2009). Economic structure, policy, and growth. In J. A. Ocampo, C. Rada, & L. Taylor (Eds.), *Growth and policy in developing countries: A structuralist approach* (pp. 1–24). New York: Columbia University Press.

Panigrahi, S., & Singh, J. (2016). Private higher education is burgeoning in India—But millions can't afford it. (https://scroll.in/article/823743/) pmed.1001244.

Devraj, R. (1998). *Development economics*. Princeton: Princeton University Press.

World Bank. (2017). *Tracking universal health coverage: 2017 global monitoring report*. Washington, D.C.: World Bank Group.

Part V
Unorganised Sector, Employment and Inequality

Chapter 9
Growth Characteristics of the Unorganized Sector in India in the Post-reform Era

Pradip Kumar Biswas

Abstract It traces the pattern of growth of the unorganized sector at disaggregated levels identifying the factors responsible for the growth and the associated changes in productivity after reforms. Liberalization affects the unorganized sector through exposing the hitherto protected producers to cut-throat competition in the market leading to decline of a sizeable section of them. However, many competent producers may locate markets beyond their neighbourhood and grow quickly. Further, the corporate develops subcontracting relationships with the small producers and also contracts out non-core activities like housekeeping or security to the unorganized sector enterprises in an effort to minimize costs and avoid labour laws. Moreover, distress-driven growth of the own account enterprises is no less important in the context of liberalization. The sector started with moderate growth of employment and number of enterprises in the 1990s, then to high growth during 2000s, and thereafter in the first half of 2010s it considerably slowed down. Labour productivity growth was however found to be faster when employment growth was slow and vice versa. Since efforts were made to improve the quality of employment, not just growth of employment, the latter is studied together with changes in productivity and other conditions. Size-class-wise estimates reveal that relatively larger sized enterprises like directory establishments could benefit more than the OAEs, both in terms of share of employment and number of enterprises.

9.1 Introduction

Non-agricultural unorganized sector is a highly heterogeneous group covering wide varieties of economic activities related to manufacturing, trade and services and the technology used in these activities ranges from traditional and archaic to the modern and sophisticated ones. Production organization also varies from tiny self-employed or own account enterprises to the ones employing several hired workers. Not all are operating for profit maximization as many poor people after failing to get wage

P. K. Biswas (✉)
CVS, Delhi University, New Delhi, India
e-mail: pkbiswas1963@gmail.com

P. K. Biswas and P. Das (eds.), *Indian Economy: Reforms and Development*, India Studies in Business and Economics, https://doi.org/10.1007/978-981-13-8269-7_9

employment start OAEs for self-employment, even for a short period or for a particular season, in order to survive (Biswas 2001). Further, a majority of the unorganized sector enterprises serve local markets while several others cater to national and international markets. There exists a kind of internal competition among enterprises within unorganized sector. However, the sector is not insulated from the competition from the organized sector or from imports from foreign countries. Small retailers including pop-and-mom stores are affected by the corporate retailers (Biswas 2016). It is obvious that different sections of the unorganized sector in India would be affected differently by the liberalizing reforms implemented in the beginning of the 1990s depending on the ability of the enterprises to withstand competition, often unequal, in the market and to exploit new economic opportunities. For an understanding of the overall impacts of the reforms on the unorganized sector, we need to look into the effects on different sub-sectors identifying the beneficiaries and the losers. The two major problems in measuring the overall effects are (i) the lack of an objective definition of 'unorganized sector' and (ii) non-availability of comprehensive data for some pre- and post-reform years, although the concept of the unorganized sector, variously termed as informal sector, decentralized sector, is evolving over the years and also efforts are made to collect more and more comprehensive data through agencies like NSSO. This is further complicated due to the fact that the starting or closing of self-employed enterprises follows stochastic process and their numbers fluctuate widely depending on immediate local economic conditions which make it difficult to ascertain long-term trend based on data collected at five/ten years' intervals as done by NSSO and Economic Census or MSME Census.

Although reforms facilitated introduction and promotion of new economic activities and created growth opportunities for many entrepreneurs, several traditional activities become redundant and many small, self-employed or own account entrepreneurs engaged in manufacturing, trade and services are forced out of the market not only due to output market competition but also due to constraints in infrastructure, finance, technology, inputs or lack of access to information. However, the existing database does not record these losers. So, it becomes difficult not only to have an estimate of the persons displaced from their non-agricultural activities, but also to find whether these displaced persons are able make a living or how they are surviving. Only broad aggregates of the existing enterprises on certain parameters can be obtained from the available database, which are used in the present exercise.

Unorganized sector has been identified as a residual category of economic activities, which are operated informally, and therefore, their operations need not follow many of the government rules and regulations, and at the same time, they are deprived of several benefits, such as cheap finances from formal lending institutions.[1] One however cannot say that the enterprises running these activities are not-organized, or disorganized, as a large majority of them operate quite systematically following

[1]The vast majority of workers in India are in informal jobs. As observed by ILO (2016): Although there has been a shift out of agriculture, construction has absorbed more workers than other sectors in recent years … most of the new jobs being created in the formal sector are actually informal because the workers do not have access to employment benefits or social security (p. 1; ILO 2016, *India Labour Market Update*, July).

varying conditions of the markets for outputs and inputs and availability of family labour and skills. A sizeable section of them often ties up with other enterprises horizontally or vertically for developing common facilities or infrastructure, collective procurement or marketing, access to finance, long-distance market, technology, latest design and so on. In the case of several traditional crafts, services and repairing activities, the unorganized enterprises have helped evolve highly effective apprenticeship system for skill formation, which not only sustained and improved the traditional crafts but also facilitated servicing and maintenance of latest high-tech consumer goods like mobile phone, computer, refrigerator, air conditioner, automobile, etc (Biswas and Raj 1996; Biswas 2010).

9.1.1 Evolution of the Concept of Unorganized Sector in India

Formally, 'unorganized sector' is associated with manufacturing where a factory unit employing 10 or more workers and using power, or simply employing 20 or more workers, is required to be registered under the Factory Act 1948. The remaining factories or manufacturing units that employ less than 20 workers without using power, or simply employing less than 10 workers, are not required to be registered under the Act and thus categorized as belonging to the 'unorganized sector'. This concept and definition of 'unorganized sector' are, however, not applicable to the enterprises involved in non-manufacturing activities, such as trade and services, where there is no mandatory requirement to make formal registration of the enterprises under any act, based on size of employment or any other criteria. It is left to the individual enterprises whether they would go for formally incorporating and registering the business entities with the Registrar of Companies in particular state. Those enterprises that do not register are clubbed as belonging to unorganized sector. This would make the estimate of the unorganized sector arbitrary depending on the decisions of the enterprises to register.

Central Statistical Organization (CSO) and The National Commission for Enterprises in the Unorganized Sector (NCEUS) came out with different working definitions for organized sector (and thereby unorganized sector, as a residual) in the case of trade and services. According to the NCEUS (2007) if a private or proprietary enterprise employs 10 or more workers or providing social benefits, the enterprise is considered as belonging to organized sector. According to CSO, if a private or proprietary enterprise is registered under some act such as Factory Act, Sales Tax Act, individual state's Shops and Establishment Act, it is considered as belonging to organized sector.[2] On the other hand, according to NSSO, which is the major source

[2]This is a gross under-estimation of the unorganized sector as may be seen in *NSS Report no. 528* (NSSO 2009a; p. 39) which notes that as much as 37% of the service sector OAEs are registered with at least one authority or under at least one Act, whereas it was 66% in the case of establishments, who would be categorized as organized under this definition. According to the report, around 85%

of data on unorganized sector, '*The* unorganized sector comprised the following types of enterprises: *(i) All the enterprises except units registered under Section 2m(i) and 2m(ii) of Factories Act, 1948 and Bidi and Cigar Workers (condition of employment) Act 1966. (ii) All enterprises except those run by Government (Central Government, State Governments, Local bodies)/Public Sector Enterprises*' (NSSO 2003, p. 12). This definition would highly overestimate the unorganized sector as it would include large private corporate enterprises involved in trading and services. While analyzing NSSO data on unorganized service sector enterprises, Dahejia and Panagariya (2013) commented, 'Most private sector service enterprises, whether small or large, are officially in the unorganized sector. For instance, large private sector banks such as the ICICI bank or HDFC bank and software export giants such as the Infosys, Wipro and Satyam are officially in the unorganized sector' (p. 97). Thus, for a clear and more realistic picture of the unorganized non-agricultural sector an unbiased definition is required.

The NCEUS has adopted a labourist approach of informality, used among others by ILO, which takes consideration of the conditions of employment or work in both the cases of establishments as well as OAEs. It would provide a better approximation of the scenario of the unorganized sector. Under this informal approach, work conditions of a worker are not clearly laid down following labour laws; employment benefits (paid annual or sick leave, etc.) are denied; working hours and timing of work are also not defined. Work conditions of a self-employed entrepreneur are no different in respect of working hour, timing of work, employment benefit like leave, retirement benefits. Thus, both the informal establishments and the OAEs together constitute the informal sector, which is quite close to the definition of unorganized sector. NSSO 55th round survey of the non-agricultural enterprises in the informal sector makes a comprehensive survey of the unorganized manufacturing, trade and service activities (with the exception of construction). Similar comprehensive survey is undertaken by the NSSO during 67th round and 73rd round but with slight change in the category of the enterprises surveyed—instead of informal sector enterprises it included unincorporated enterprises, which are also informal in nature but easily identifiable. In fact, these two terms—informal and unorganized—despite having distinct roots are now used alternately, which we will follow here. There are also several other NSSO rounds when only one of the three segments, viz. manufacturing, trade and services, of the unorganized sector has been surveyed and are good source of data.

The notion of the informal sector is an offshoot of the Lewisian two-sector model of development—when the workers do not find jobs in the formal sector for some time after migrating from the rural areas, stay in the urban periphery and engage in low remunerative and low productive activities ranging from shoe shining to small-scale peddling or petty trades, rickshaw pulling and artisanal crafts that are informal in nature. As the developing countries have tried to expand more of their industries

---

of the service enterprises are OAEs, run by self-employed persons who do not employ any hired labour on a regular basis. Therefore, calling 37% of these OAEs organised simply because they are registered with some agency would underestimate the size of the unorganized sector.

and the formal sector activities in the urban areas, migration occurs at much faster rates than the rate of formal job creation leading to proliferation of the informal sector in the urban areas (Harris and Todaro 1970; Fields 1975). It has been soon realized that the job creation ability of the formal sector is too limited relative to the arrival of migrants (Bangasser 2000, p. 4) and that the growth of the informal sector, an integral part of the development process, is not a transitory one which calls for special measures to improve the work conditions of the informal sector workers.[3] It has been further realized that the informal sector, rather than being a problem representing poor work and living conditions, can be used as a dynamic sector of job creation in the face of growing unemployment problem in the developing countries.

The concept of 'informal sector' was first applied to urban small-scale non-agricultural activities in African countries in the early 1970s [ILO (1972) on Kenya and Hart (1973) on Ghana] and then gained prominence in the development/employment policy literature as well as its scope extended to include rural non-farm activities (Bangasser 2000; ILO 1991; Amin 2002), possibly, in view of the limitation of the urban infrastructure to accommodate ever-expanding informal sector. As it is noted in the ILO (1991) report, 'there can be no question of the ILO helping to 'promote' or 'develop' an informal sector as a convenient, low-cost way of creating employment unless there is at the same time an equal determination to eliminate progressively the worst aspects of exploitation and inhuman working conditions in the sector' (p. 58). Several ILO studies have focused on employment generation through the informal sector and searched the possibility of raising the quality of work and applying international labour standards where there is virtually no laws to provide protection to workers and self-employed persons (Sethuraman 1981; Amin 2002). The concern for low-cost way of employment generation would extend the domain of informal sector from urban areas to rural areas, thus making the notion of informal sector similar to unorganized sector.

In India, there exists long tradition of arts and crafts in both the rural and urban areas that were partially destroyed with the advent of modern factories and imports of Western factory-made goods which led to severe criticism of the colonial government and the nationalist leaders insisted on the protection and revival of these traditional rural industries and artisanal crafts. Later on, after independence, the Government of India, besides developing the large-scale modern industries, made special efforts through successive five-year plans to develop these small and decentralized industries under Khadi and Village Industries, handloom, handicraft, small-scale and ancillary industries, etc., that are jointly called unorganized sector industries.[4] Indian planners and policymakers were well aware that the large-scale industrialization was essential, but they also knew that it would not be able to create adequate employment

[3]ILO (1991) report clearly states "Contrary to earlier beliefs, the informal sector is not going to disappear spontaneously with economic growth. It is, on the contrary, likely to grow in the years to come, and with it the problems of urban poverty and congestion will also grow" (p. 63).

[4]In fact, both the industrial policy resolutions of 1948 and 1956 assigned vital role to the cottage and small industries. Further, off-farm employment need not be created in the urban areas only, and therefore, promotion of rural industries has been emphasized from the very beginning of the plan periods.

opportunities for the growing number of population of the country. Thereby, special emphasis was laid on employment generation through the growth of these unorganized sector industries—a large number of products were reserved for exclusive manufacturing by the unorganized sector. As a result, both the production and employment generation grew quite fast keeping pace with the growth of other sectors like agriculture, large industries, exports and imports that are linked to this sector, generating demand for its products and/or supplying inputs. It was however only after 1991 with economic liberalization and globalization that the reservation was withdrawn for a large number of products exposing the unorganized sector to vigorous market competition both from domestic products of the large manufacturers as well as from imports of cheap goods from countries like China.

9.1.2 Reforms and the Challenges to Unorganized Sector

Failure to cope with the competition as well as rapid change in market conditions would lead a sizeable section of the small producers to exit the scene. Further, introduction of improved or new products by large manufacturers and importers would make the products of traditional small producers obsolete. It would be difficult to rehabilitate these small producers through reskilling them in new trade that are on demand. A large section of the small producers who started acting as subcontractors to large producers would gradually become subservient to the latter and find their product prices to be very low barely covering wages for their self-employment. Further, this subcontracting system would substantially reduce the cost of production for the large firms and raise their profits (Breman 2013). A slower process of economic transformation would have given these displaced producers opportunity to adjust such as through reskilling or finding alternative sources of livelihood over a period of time. Quick economic transformation would render the weak and poor more vulnerable, helpless and marginalized.

It is quite obvious that under liberalization, small producers would face unequal competition from the large producers who would also try to expand market and thus invest in the development of technology and products. Some of the small producers would now act as subcontractors to the large firms and benefit from the improved technology and products, and this arrangement would help large firms to cut down costs or raise profits. Opening up of the home market and export market would not only benefit the large producers but also the small producers, especially the efficient ones, who would expand their production and take the opportunity. Overall growth of the economy would also raise demand for unorganized sector products, although the latter growth rate being lower than the former growth rate.

Prior to economic reforms, policies to promote unorganized sector were more or less confined to the manufacturing activities ignoring the trade and service activities. With the introduction of reforms focus of development has been extended from small industries to small and medium enterprises (SMEs) and later micro and small enterprises (MSEs), which along with manufacturing include trade as well as service activities. Liberalization would also have effects on the unorganized trade and service sectors. In general, liberalization would lead to innovation of many new activities and products and many smaller entrepreneurs would definitely take advantage of this development. At the same time, small entrepreneurs would face competition from the corporate world, including from the multinationals. Further, liberalization would enable the corporate to transfer part of their non-core activities, such as housekeeping, securities, production, procurement, legal service, R&D, data processing, marketing or advertisement, depending on their core competence, to the small enterprises belonging to the unorganized sector so as to minimize cost. Finally, growth of the unorganized sector need not necessarily imply development due to the creation of profitable avenues of investment for the SMEs—it may reflect distress-driven phenomena when a mass of unemployed people, driven out of agriculture or lost formal sector jobs due to liberalization, in order to survive or to supplement family income start OAEs with a little capital and very low productivity (Biswas 2001). Thus, together with growth, one needs to see the aspects of the conditions of work and productivity.

Given these diverse effects of reforms on the unorganized sector, the present chapter looks into the pattern of growth of the sector, particularly in terms of employment, value added per worker or productivity, as well as the conditions of the enterprises and workers, in the post-reform period. Section 9.2 tries to find out if there is any change in the overall growth of employment and the number of enterprises in the unorganized manufacturing, trade and service sectors in the post-reform period over the pre-reform decade. In Sect. 9.3, an analysis of the growth of productivity across production organizations or size classes of enterprises has been made. It then makes disaggregated analysis of the employment and productivity growth across two-digit sectors of manufacturing, trade and services during the reform periods. Section 9.4 looks into the major problems faced by the enterprises and the changes in organization structure during reform periods. Finally, Sect. 9.5 presents concluding observations.

9.2 Growth of the Number of Enterprises and Employment in Unorganized Manufacturing, Trade and Services in the Pre- and Post-reform Decades

9.2.1 Manufacturing Sector Growth

NSSO data on unorganized sector for the pre-reform decade and the decade after reform are available only for the manufacturing sector and trading sector. Relevant data for the service sector are conspicuously missing. In the case of unorganized manufacturing 33rd round (1978–79) NSS data do not include DMEs. For an understanding of the pre-reform trend, only OAMEs and NDMEs are considered. Between 1978–79 and 1984–85, there was a spectacular growth of the unorganized manufacturing sector—number of enterprises and employment grew at 15.44 and 14.38%, respectively (Table 9.1). The first half of the 1980s was marked by steady agricultural growth throughout the country (GoI 2004; Biswas 2008; Sanyal et al. 1998), which must have contributed to the rapid progress of the unorganized manufacturing through forward and backward linkages, and creating demand through raising income of the poor. However, validity of such a rapid growth of the unorganized manufacturing was doubted even by the NSSO (1989, p. 22) itself. Possibly, there was either some overestimation for the year 1984–85 or underestimation for the year 1978–79. The next five years witnessed substantial decline in the unorganized manufacturing, although there was no apparent reason for the same. During this period, the agricultural growth was quite broad-based and diverse maintaining the growth momentum of the first half of the decade (GoI 2004). It was only since the beginning of the 1990s that agricultural growth started decelerating in different parts of the country (Biswas 2008), which might have restrained the recovery of the unorganized manufacturing activities.

After 1989–90, three more rounds of survey on unorganized manufacturing were conducted, which are 51st round (reference year 1994–95), 56th round (reference year 2000–01) and 62nd round (reference year 2005–06). All these rounds, including 45th round, have covered the three main types of organizational forms such as OAEs, NDEs and DEs, of the unorganized manufacturing sector. It may be noted in Table 9.1 that the pre-reform declining trend of the sector continued well into the first five years of the reform periods, although with reduced rate, and then in the next five years not only the negative trend was reversed, but it also achieved fast growth. The negative growth in the first half of the 1990s cannot be attributed to economic reforms that removed various protections against competition, particularly exclusive manufacturing rights enjoyed by the unorganized sector enterprises. The growth of the second half of the 1990s was quite consistent with the high overall growth of the economy and particularly of the manufacturing industries. This upswing however could not be sustained as there was a marginal decline in employment in 2005–06 as compared to that in 2000–01. The decline is however counter-intuitive in the sense that this period represents one of the very high growth phases of the economy, which involved substantial growth of manufacturing. Since there was no further NSS round on unorganized manufacturing, links of the growth of the manufacturing sector and of the overall economy with the growth of unorganized manufacturing sector cannot be ascertained.

However, since 1999–2000 NSSO started periodically collecting data on informal sector, which includes manufacturing, trade and other services. There is a small difference between informal manufacturing and unorganized manufacturing where the former considers only unincorporated proprietary and partnership enterprises representing a smaller set of enterprises than the latter. Informal sector data also cover own account enterprises, non-directory establishments and directory establishments. Till date, informal sector data are collected at three time points, the first one in 1999–2000 (55th round), the second one in 2010–11 (67th round) and the third one in 2015–16 (73rd round). These three rounds of NSSO data would provide a comprehensive view of the unorganized manufacturing sector over a fairly long period.

Table 9.1 Growth of number of enterprises and employment in unorganized manufacturing sector

Year/period	Estimates of enterprises		Estimates of employment	
	Total number (in lakh)	Share of OAMEs (%)	Total number (in lakh)	Share of OAMEs (%)
1979–1990	*Includes OAMEs and NDMEs of unorganized sector*			
1978–79 [1]	81.3	88.3	144.0	80.7
1984–85 [2]	192.5 (15.44)[a]	88.8	322.5 (14.38)	84.4
1989–90 [3]	157.3 (−3.95)	89.7	290.2 (−2.09)	84.3
1990–2006	*Includes OAMEs, NDMEs and DMEs of unorganized sector*			
1989–90 [4]	160.7	84.7	349.8	69.9
1994–95 [5]	145.1 (−2.02)	84.5	332.1 (−1.03)	69.0
2000–01 [6]	170.2 (2.69)	86.1	370.8 (1.85)	66.3
2005–06 [7]	170.7 (0.06)	85.6	364.4 (−0.35)	64.0
2000–2016	*Includes OAMEs, NDMEs and DMEs of informal sector* [11]			
1999–2000 [8]	142.5	86.6	296.5	68.9
2010–11 [9]	172.0 (1.73)	83.9	348.9 (1.49)	59.7
2015–16 [10]	196.7 (2.71)	85.5	360.4 (0.65)	62.9

[1] NSS 33rd round; DMEs are not included in the survey
[2] NSS 40th round, report number, 363, pp. 21–22. It is stated in the NSS report number 363 that 'the estimate of the number of enterprises … has more than doubled between 33rd and 40th rounds. Though causes for this are not evident, a sizeable real increase seems to be in consonance with tempo of general development activity in the country'
[3] NSS 45th round report no 396/1, pp. 7–8
[4] Report No. 433(51/2.2/1)
[5] Report No. 433(51/2.2/1), NSS 51st round
[6] NSS 56th round
[7] NSS 62nd round
[8] NSS 55th round, report no. 456; since this year informal sector enterprises are surveyed and it also includes DMEs that are not formally incorporated
[9] NSS 67th round, report number 549
[10] NSS 73rd round NSS KI (73/2.34)
[11] Informal sector covers all unincorporated enterprises in the non-agricultural sector which operated on either proprietary or partnership basis
[a]Parentheses indicate compound annual percentage change over previous round

Employment in the informal manufacturing sector has increased at a rate of one and a half percent per year over eleven year between 1999–2000 and 2010–11, and the corresponding growth of number enterprises is 1.73% per annum. According to NSS 56th and 62nd rounds data, unorganized manufacturing employment declined at 0.35% per annum in the first half of the 2000s, which implies that in the second half the rate of employment growth exceeded 3% per annum. The employment growth rate during the first half of 2010s slowed down to 0.65% per annum although the number of enterprises increased at a high rate of 2.71% per annum.

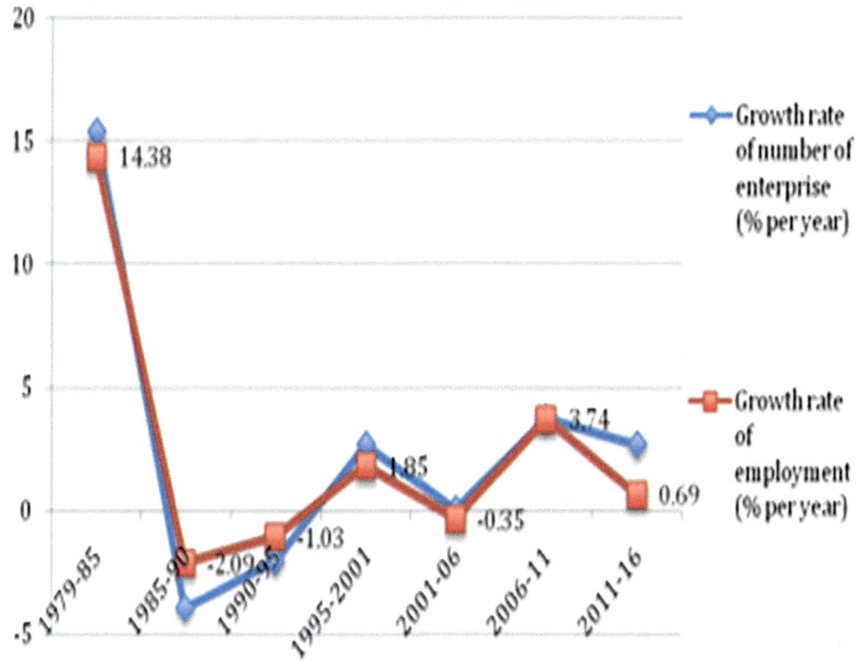

Graph 9.1 Cyclical growth pattern of unorganized manufacturing

Growth of employment in the unorganized manufacturing sector follows a cyclical pattern—period of high growth is followed by a decline or very low growth and vice versa, although it maintains a rising long-term trend (Graph 9.1). As regards impact of reforms, although causality cannot be established, one may notice that after the initiation of reforms the intensity of decline of employment in this sector was first reduced and the declining trend was then reversed to fast growth one which however continued for 5 years before entering the slowdown or stagnation phase of the cycle. It however needs to be mentioned that the estimates should be read with caution and trend would be misleading, as there could be wide occupational swings resulting from short-term fluctuations in local economic conditions in different NSS rounds.

9.2.2 Growth of Unorganized Trade

NSSO conducted several rounds of survey on different types of trading organizations although emphasis shifted over the years. Four rounds of survey, namely 34th round (1979–80), 41st round (1985–86), 46th round (1990–91) and 53rd round (1997), are conducted on small trading organizations covering own account enterprises and non-directory establishments of wholesale, retail and other types of trading, such as commission agents. Thereafter as a part of informal sector survey, conducted in 55th round (1999–2000), 67th round (2010–11) and 73rd round (2015–16), it covered all kinds of informal trading organizations. It may be mentioned that informal trading sector covers all unincorporated proprietary and partnership enterprises. It may be noted that, quite similar to unorganized manufacturing, the number of enterprises and the number of employment in small trading increased at rapid rate during the first half of 1980s (Table 9.2). Their growth momentum, unlike unorganized manufacturing, continued to the second half of the 1980s, although employment growth rate substantially reduced from 10.03 to 6.56%. The first decade of liberalization witnessed stagnation of the small trading sector as both the number of enterprises and employment increased at very low rates of 0.65 and 0.16%, respectively, between 1990–91 and 1997. Within small trade, retailing appears to be the most important for employment generation and is also growing steadily.

Informal sector data however reveal that the number of trading enterprises as well as employment generated by them continued to increase at fairly high rates over one and a half decades since 2000. Both retail and wholesale trade are the primary contributors to the growth. It appears that the first decade of reform was not very conducive to the growth of small trade. In the long term, once the reform measures are implemented and the required institutional changes are taken place, the informal sector trade revived its growth momentum. However, the growth of employment in retail trade may be predominated by the growth of OAEs for self-employment in the absence of gainful employment opportunity elsewhere. It may reflect desperate attempt to survive or supplement family income through petty trading even on a seasonal or part-time basis. It needs to see whether the growth of employment in unorganized trade is associated with productivity growth.

9.2.3 Growth of Unorganized Services

Comprehensive survey on unorganized service sector has been conducted by the NSSO in 57th round (2001–02) and 63rd round (2006–07) covering all the non-governmental service sector enterprises that are not registered under the Factory Act. As already discussed, unorganized service sector covers OAEs as well as all kinds of private sector establishments, including large corporate, involved in service activities. Prior to this only in 34th round (1979–80), NSSO collected data only on OAEs of the service sector. Three rounds of NSSO surveys on informal sector enterprises also cover service sector enterprises that are unregulated and operating informally for the reference years 1999–2000, 2010–11 and 2015–16. Therefore, no comprehensive data on the service sector enterprises that are small or unregulated or operating informally are available for the decade before and after reforms.

It may be seen in Table 9.3 that between 2001–02 and 2006–07, the number of unorganized service sector enterprises increased at a very slow rate but the number of persons employed increased at much higher rate. The number of OAEs increased at less than 1%, but their employment growth rate exceeded 6% per annum whereas in

Table 9.2 Growth of enterprises and employment in unorganized trade (in lakh)

	Whole-sale trade	Retail trade	Others	All trade unorganized	Annual growth rate of all trade over previous round (%)
Number of small trading enterprises (OAEs and NDEs)					
34th round (1979–80)	1.18	57.09	1.08	59.35	–
41st round (1985–86)	5.16	89.41	3.70	98.27	8.77
46th round (1990–91)	5.50	105.96	27.62	139.08	7.19
53rd round (1997)	8.02	119.4	17.62	145.04	0.65
Number of employment in small trading units (OAEs and NDEs)					
34th round (1979–80)	1.95	86.26	1.73	89.94	–
41st round (1985–86)	11.49	143.37	4.72	159.58	10.03
46th round (1990–91)	11.78	162.86	44.66	219.30	6.56
53rd round (1997)	15.12	176.48	29.92	221.52	0.16
Number of enterprises in informal trade (OAEs, NDEs and DEs)					
55th round (1999–2000)	10.10	141.46	2.24	153.79	
67th round (2010–11)	13.85	190.73	2.42	207.00	2.74
73rd round (2015–16)	16.28	211.98	1.66	229.91	2.12
Number of employment in informal trade (OAEs, NDEs and DEs)					
55th round (1999–2000)	24.93	222.29	4.25	251.46	
67th round (2010–11)	32.96	302.36	5.01	340.33	2.79
73rd round (2015–16)	39.03	344.26	3.12	386.41	2.57

Note Data pertain to small trading units covering OAEs and non-directory establishments only
Source 1. Figures for years 1979–80, 1985–86, 1990–91 and 1997 are compiled in NSSO (1998), *Statement 3a: Comparable statement showing the number of enterprises and number of persons employed in unorganised trade over NSS rounds*, Report No. 444 (53/2.41.2/1), p. 13
2. Figures for the years 1999–2000, 2010–11 and 2015–16 are computed from the NSSO unit level data of 55th, 67th and 73rd round

Table 9.3 Growth of enterprises and employment in unorganized service sector (in lakh)

	Own account enterprises	Establishments	All
Number of enterprises in unorganized service sector (in lakh)			
34th round 1979–80	24.95	–	–
57th round 2001–02 [1]	120.85	23.88	144.73
63rd round 2006–07 [2]	126.84 (0.97)[a]	23.14 (−0.63)	149.98 (0.72)
Employment in unorganized service sector (in lakh)			
34th round 1979–80	29.66	–	–
57th round 2001–02 [1]	158.37	107.19	265.56
63rd round 2006–07 [2]	212.58 (6.06)	122.58 (2.72)	335.16 (4.77)
Number of enterprises in informal service sector (in lakh)			
55th round (1999–2000)	89.34	16	109
67th round (2010–11)	165.56 (5.77)	31.56 (6.38)	197 (5.53)
73rd round (2015–16)	170.72 (0.62)	36.16 (2.76)	207 (1.00)
Employment in informal service sector (in lakh)			
55th round (1999–2000)	124.4	65.8	190
67th round (2010–11)	244.14 (6.32)	145.47 (7.48)	390 (6.72)
73rd round (2015–16)	195.00 (−4.34)	169.85 (3.15)	365 (−1.30)

[1] and [2] Data pertain to unorganized service sector which includes OAEs and all establishments except those run by government (central, state, local bodies)/public sector enterprises and financial intermediaries

[a]Parentheses indicate annual percentage change over previous round

Source NSSO (1987) Number 327; NSSO (2003) Report No. 482(57/2.345/1) and NSSO (2009b) Report No. 529 (63/2.345/2); NSSO 55th, 67th and 73rd rounds

unorganized manufacturing the number of OAEs stagnated and that of employment declined indicating possibility of job switching from the latter to the former. However, informal sector data indicate that, between 1999–2000 and 2010–11, both the number of enterprises involved in services and employment generated by them increased at fast rate keeping with the overall high growth of the economy. In the next five years, the sector stagnated—the number of enterprises grew by one per cent per annum while employment declined at a rate of 1.3%. It appears that after fast growth, there was some kind of consolidation—establishments substantially raised both number of enterprises and employment while OAEs marginally raised the number of enterprises but witnessed substantial decline in employment.

In brief, immediately after liberalization of the early 1990s both the unorganized manufacturing and trade, for which data are available, witnessed decline. For manufacturing, this declining trend started in the second half of 1980s, much before liberalization. This sector recovered and started growing fast in the second half of the 1990s, and thereafter, it followed a cyclical pattern of high and low growth. In the case of small trade, it had high growth in the 1980s, but a deceleration started in the middle of the decade. Thereafter almost throughout the 1990s, it stagnated and the liberal-

Table 9.4 Sectoral distribution of unorganized sector enterprises and employment

Year	All sectors (in lakh)	Share of manufacture (%)	Share of trade (%)	Share of services (%)	Share of OAEs (%)	Growth rate of All sectors aggregate over previous round (%)
Number of enterprises						
1999–2000	443.5	33.53	40.82	25.65	87.35	
2010–11	576.8	29.84	35.98	34.18	84.63	2.42
2015–16	633.9	31.02	36.34	32.64	84.17	1.91
Number of employment						
1999–2000	797.1	38.46	36.83	24.70	70.49	
2010–11	1079.8	32.31	31.61	36.08	64.61	2.80
2015–16	1112.7	32.39	34.82	32.79	62.09	0.60

Note It covers unincorporated non-agricultural enterprises
Source Estimated from NSS 55th, 67th and 73rd rounds' unit level data

ization was of little help if not counterproductive. By the turn of the century, the unorganized trade sector however gathered growth momentum. On the unorganized service sector, no data are available for the 1980s and 1990s. Therefore, an aggregate picture of the unorganized sector cannot be constructed during the 1980s and 1990s.

A comparative analysis of the performance of the three sectors, viz. manufacturing, trade and services, would be possible based on informal sector data since 1999–2000 when the reform measures are fully in operation after implementation over a decade. Data sets of the three rounds of informal sector survey would also provide an aggregate picture of the unorganized sector for a fairly long period.

The present size of the unorganized non-farm sector is huge employing 11.23 crore persons in 6.34 crore enterprises in the year 2015–16 (Table 9.4). The number of unorganized sector enterprises and the persons employed by them increased at sizeable rates of 2.42 and 2.80% per year, respectively, over the 11 years period between 1999–2000 and 2010–11 which corresponds to one of the fastest growing phases in India's post-reform era. In the next five years, respective growth rates declined to 1.91 and 0.60% per annum, which corroborate the popular perception of jobless growth.

One salient feature of the unorganized sector's growth is that over the years, the self-employed OAEs are losing their share in both the number of enterprises as well as in total employment, although the loss is much more in the latter (Table 9.4). It implies some sort of consolidation is slowly taking place within unorganized sector where proportionately more establishments are being set up and the average size of the establishments is also rising. This long-term trend is possibly the effect of reforms and the resultant competitive environment, which makes it more difficult for the OAEs and tiny enterprises to survive as against relatively bigger establishments.

Notwithstanding this overall trend of employment growth in unorganized sector, manufacturing sector's relative position vis-a-vis trade and services declined. In 1999–2000, manufacturing had the highest employment share of 38.46%, followed by trade with 36.83% share and services with the lowest share of 24.7%. As regards the number of enterprises, the distribution is however slightly more in favour of trade followed by manufacturing and services in that order. During the high growth phase of the economy, between 1999–2000 and 2010–11, employment growth was fastest in the service sector (6.72% p.a.), slowest in manufacturing (1.49% p.a.) and in-between trade (2.79% p.a.) leading to the service sector becoming the largest employment-generating sector. Pattern of sectoral growth of the number of enterprises was quite similar to that of employment. As a result, service sector's share substantially increased and that of manufacturing and trade declined. This trend is quite consistent with the service sector led growth of the economy during its high growth phase.

In the next five years between 2010–11 and 2015–16, the overall economic growth slowed down. For the unorganized sector, this is reflected in terms of slow down of the growth of employment as well as number of enterprises. This time employment growth of the unorganized sector, although quite slow, is led by trade with growth rate of 2.57% p.a., while manufacturing attained a modest growth rate of 0.65% p.a. and the services witnessed significant decline (−1.30% p.a.). The decline in the service sector was however confined to OAEs, which were competed out by the fast-growing establishments. The latter are generally larger in size, have greater access to resources and are supposed to be more efficient than OAEs. This consolidation process thus rendered many petty producers jobless. Apparently, many of them moved to petty trading and a few in manufacturing. In any case, this inter-sectoral movement of petty producers led the distribution of employment to be more or less uniform among the three sectors with slight edge in favour of trade. The sectoral distribution of the number of enterprises is a bit more skewed with 36% share for trade, 33% for services and 31% for manufacturing.

9.3 Liberalization and Growth of Employment and Productivity

9.3.1 Productivity Growth Across Production Organizations (Size Classes of Enterprises)

Systematic and comparable data on value added per labour for different size classes of enterprises covering the immediate pre-reform decade and the post-reform decade are available only for the unorganized manufacturing sector. For the unorganized trade and service sectors, no such comparable data sets covering the 1980s and

1990s are available. However, for all the three sectors systematic and comparable labour productivity data are available for the years 1999–2000, 2010–11 and 2015–16 under informal sector survey. Therefore, discussion on labour productivity trends in the 1980s and 1990s would be based on manufacturing sector only, and for the next one and a half decades, it would cover all the sectors.

Prior to reform, productivity growth of the unorganized manufacturing sector follows the similar trend of the industry growth, particularly of its employment growth. High employment growth rate of the first half of 1980s was associated with high growth of labour productivity, whereas decline of employment in the second half was associated with near stagnation of labour productivity; in fact, it declined for NDMEs (Table 9.5). During the first half of the 1990s, coinciding with the initial years of reforms, there was decline of employment, but this was accompanied by a significant rise in labour productivity, which was much higher for DMEs. During the second half of the 1990s, the unorganized manufacturing witnessed high growth of both employment and labour productivity. Further, the productivity growth was faster for larger sized enterprises. During 2001–05, employment declined in absolute terms but the average labour productivity, measured as the ratio between manufacturing valued added to manufacturing employment, maintained a fairly high growth. But this masks the fact that the persons engaged in OAEs, which account for 66.3% of the unorganized manufacturing employment in 2000–01, experienced decline in productivity and many left the industry. The NDMEs and DMEs however witnessed substantial increase in labour productivity and, further, between the two size classes the growth was faster in DMEs. The trend across size classes therefore suggests that there is some kind of differentiation and consolidation going on within unorganized manufacturing induced by reforms that enabled relatively larger enterprises to take advantages of access to better technology, lucrative markets or other business information. The tiny enterprises, particularly OAEs, who are generally starved of capital and other resources, find it hard to survive in the changed market condition where they have to compete often with the domestic and foreign big producers.

A comparison of labour productivity across sectors is made in Table 9.6. It may be noted that the value added per worker is generally lower in manufacturing as compared to trade or services. The disparity is particularly striking for OAEs. The productivity differences between trade and services are not very high although the former generally maintains higher values. As regards growth of labour productivity over the successive rounds, the following observations may be made:

i. Unorganized sector labour productivity growth rate was found to be much higher in the second period (2011–16) when employment growth rate was very low, as compared to the first period (2000–11), which was characterized by higher growth of overall GDP, employment as well as number of enterprises. The difference in labour productivity growth between the two periods is found to be sizeable for all the three size classes, namely OAEs, NDEs and DEs.
ii. Among the three sectors, manufacturing had the highest growth rate of labour productivity and the trade had the lowest growth rate during the first period. However, in the second period all the three sectors witnessed increase in the rate

Table 9.5 Value added per worker in unorganized manufacturing (in Rs.)

Year/period	Value added per worker at current prices (Rs.)			Value added per worker at 1999–2000 prices (Rs.) [7]		
	OAEs	NDEs	All	OAEs	NDEs	All
1978–79 [1]	1032	2213	1260	6416	13,762	7834
1984–85 [2]	2189	6498	2860	7522	22,329	9828
1989–90 [3]	3373	9421	4411	7851	21,930	10,268
1994–95 [4]	6081	15,675	8297	8558	22,060	11,676
2000–01 [5]	10,154	27,079	16,233	9834	26,225	15,721
2005–06 [6]	11,846	36,543	24,034	9441	29,125	19,155
CAGR during the period (%)						
1979–1985	13.35	19.66	14.64	2.69	8.40	3.85
1985–1990	9.03	7.71	9.05	0.86	−0.36	0.88
1990–1995	12.51	10.72	13.47	1.74	0.12	2.60
1995–2001	8.92	9.54	11.84	2.34	2.92	5.08
2001–2006	2.60	5.12	6.76	−0.68	1.76	3.35

[1] NSS 33rd round data compiled in NSSO (1989), report number 363, pp. 21–22
[2] NSS 40th round data compiled in NSSO (1989), pp. 21–22
[3] NSS 45th round report no 396/1, pp. 7–8
[4] NSS 51st round, report number 433(51/2.2/1)
[5] NSS 56th round, Report No. 477(56/2.2/1)
[6] NSS 62nd round, Report No. 526(62/2.2/3)
[7] GDP deflator has been used to estimate value added per worker at constant price of 1999–2000

of growth of labour productivity. But the manufacturing maintained its lead in the productivity growth.

iii. If we compare Tables 9.5 and 9.6, there is a clear decelerating trend of labour productivity in the unorganized manufacturing sector that started in 2001 and continued till the end of the decade. During the next five years, very slow growth of manufacturing employment was accompanied by fast growth of productivity. As the size class increases from OAEs to DMEs, productivity growth rate decreased in the first period but increased in the second period indicating occurrence of some sort of consolidation within unorganized manufacturing sector in the latter period.

iv. Decline in employment in the service sector during the second period was confined to OAEs who also experienced higher productivity growth as compared to NDEs and DEs.

v. Among the trading enterprises, OAEs had much higher productivity growth rate than NDEs and DEs during the first period. OAEs' productivity growth rate further increased in the next period.

Table 9.6 Value added per labour and its growth in unorganized non-agricultural sector

Period/year	At current prices				At constant 2015–16 prices			
	OAEs	NDEs	DEs	All	OAEs	NDEs	DEs	All
Value added per labour in manufacturing (Rs.)								
1999–2000	10,666	34,542	34,693	17,395	24,989	80,926	81,280	40,752
2010–11	28,287	70,782	64,152	42,148	36,910	92,360	83,709	54,996
2015–16	49,341	129,721	153,836	76,514	49,341	129,721	153,836	76,514
Value added per labour in trade (Rs.)								
1999–2000	24,272	63,360	110,863	31,601	56,865	148,441	259,729	74,034
2010–11	55,326	122,909	213,371	69,583	72,192	160,377	278,416	90,795
2015–16	95,486	216,937	224,869	117,859	95,486	216,937	224,869	117,859
Value added per labour in services (Rs.)								
1999–2000	21,246	32,814	37,333	24,692	49,775	76,876	87,463	57,850
2010–11	48,756	96,006	85,452	57,855	63,620	125,273	111,501	75,492
2015–16	93,586	138,008	151,373	100,713	93,586	138,008	151,373	100,713
Value added per labour in unorganized non-agricultural sector (Rs.)								
1999–2000	17,007	42,119	44,343	24,242	39,844	98,677	103,887	56,794
2010–11	41,498	91,831	87,071	58,193	54,148	119,825	113,614	75,933
2015–16	73,951	155,033	162,194	103,744	73,951	155,033	162,194	103,744
CAGR of value added per labour in manufacturing (%)								
2000–2011	9.27	6.74	5.75	8.38	3.61	1.21	0.27	2.76
2011–2016	11.77	12.88	19.12	12.67	5.98	7.03	12.94	6.83
CAGR of value added per labour in trade (%)								
2000–2011	7.78	6.21	6.13	7.44	2.19	0.71	0.63	1.87
2011–2016	11.53	12.03	1.06	11.11	5.75	6.23	−4.18	5.36
CAGR of value added per labour in services (%)								
2000–2011	7.84	10.25	7.82	8.05	2.26	4.54	2.23	2.45
2011–2016	13.93	7.53	12.12	11.72	8.02	1.96	6.30	5.93
CAGR of value added per labour in unorganized sector (%)								
2000–2011	8.45	7.34	6.33	8.29	2.83	1.78	0.82	2.68
2011–2016	12.25	11.04	13.25	12.26	6.43	5.29	7.38	6.44

Note GDP deflator has been used to estimate value added per worker at constant price of 2015–16
Sources Estimated from NSSO 55th, 67th and 73rd rounds' unit level data

9.3.2 Growth of Employment and Productivity at Disaggregated Levels of Industries

Among the manufacturing industries, food and beverage, tobacco products, textiles, apparel, wood and cork, other non-metallic minerals, fabricated metals, furniture and other manufacturing not elsewhere classified are most important for employment generation (Table 9.7). Out of these eight industry groups, only in four employments could grow in both the periods, and in the other four, it declined in at least one period. Excepting paper, all the nineteen industry groups experienced rise in labour productivity in both the periods irrespective of employment growth. However, there are several industries that witnessed substantial growth in productivity together with decline in employment. The latter indicates emergence of a process of technological up-gradation or innovations, or even organizational innovations. However, all this happens in several industries without commensurate increase in market demand for their products, which results in very slow growth of employment. It may be seen in the same table that the proportion of part-time workers in total number of persons employed in manufacturing declined in most of the industry groups in both periods. These changes suggest emergence of work continuity and thus development of skill, which are necessary for adoption and use of innovated technology in the face of competition in the market.

In trade, which is predominated by retailing, there was substantial growth of labour productivity in both the periods and it rapidly accelerated, like in the manufacturing, in the second period. But in the second period, unlike in the manufacturing where employment growth decelerated, trade witnessed substantial increase in employment growth rate. However, both the trade and industry sectors observed secular decline in the proportion of part-time workers.

One of the long-term effects of reforms is the steady growth of labour productivity in the unorganized sector. This is in line with the arguments put forward by the proponents of reforms which argue that unconstrained movement of resources would ensure utilization of resources in most productive manner, and as a corollary, labour productivity continued to increase. Obviously, the inefficient and low-skilled ones would be the losers. A large number of the poor including landless labourers, marginal farmers and housewives used to be engaged in off-farm activities on part-time basis either as workers or as self-employed in order to supplement family income (Biswas 2001). With the rise of professionalism, technological innovations and adoption of labour displacing technologies under reforms the scope for part-time employment would shrink affecting the livelihood of poor households. So long as economy grew at high rate and the labour demand continued to grow at fairly high rate during 2000–11, the poor could get supplementary income through part-time work. However, as soon as economic growth slows down and the labour demand stagnates, many of these unskilled part-time workers became redundant. In several small enterprises, women and elderly persons of the family and neighbour work on part-time basis after fulfilling domestic works with very low income in order to supplement the family income. As these enterprises face more competition, for survival

Table 9.7 Sector-wise growth of employment, productivity, share of part-time workers

Items	CAGR of value added per worker (%)*		CAGR of employment (%)		Workers ('000)	Share of part-timers in total employment (%)		
	2000–11	2011–16	2000–11	2011–16	2016	2000	2011	2016
Food and beverage	3.55	5.80	1.48	1.30	5090	18.66	11.33	10.25
Tobacco products	1.04	6.13	0.46	5.06	3944	11.39	13.14	14.76
Textiles	2.53	4.21	2.82	−3.21	4969	16.07	11.72	8.99
Apparel	1.66	5.81	5.89	3.78	7839	11.89	10.9	7.40
Leather	2.43	6.78	−1.03	7.21	458	10.55	13.79	3.32
Wood and cork	4.48	4.42	−2.34	−5.03	2182	23.99	11.45	8.00
Paper	−3.13	−1.42	7.59	−6.58	242	18.88	8.96	6.05
Printing	3.63	4.78	−0.76	−0.91	505	6.41	4.00	1.74
Coke and petroleum	6.88	5.56	−6.34	3.68	12	16.86	16.49	3.94
Chemicals	3.18	1.95	1.06	−4.74	393	11.82	16.3	13.95
Plastics	0.20	7.38	6.80	−5.59	417	9.09	4.97	5.19
Other non-metal minerals	4.62	6.92	5.22	−0.24	2784	17.81	11.04	6.44
Basic metals	1.72	10.43	−3.32	6.54	176	3.04	3.51	0.93
Fabricated metals	4.39	7.69	3.71	2.06	2012	8.40	3.80	3.82
Machinery and equip.	6.83	12.54	−3.40	12.65	546	8.23	1.38	0.75
Comp, electr. and opt. pdt.	5.73	9.75	2.23	−10.79	36	5.86	3.32	1.31
Electrical machinery	2.49	7.56	−5.17	6.68	179	4.44	2.83	0.39
Motor vehicles	4.47	1.01	7.74	0.08	95	0.29	2.16	1.09
Furniture, othr. manuf.	3.94	8.04	4.85	−0.07	3510	18.36	8.49	5.76
All manufacturing	**2.76**	**6.83**	1.48	**0.66**	***35,917***	**15.64**	**10.66**	**8.43**

(continued)

Table 9.7 (continued)

Items	CAGR of value added per worker (%)*		CAGR of employment (%)		Workers ('000)	Share of part-timers in total employment (%)		
	2000–11	2011–16	2000–11	2011–16	2016	2000	2011	2016
All trade	**1.87**	**5.36**	1.69	**2.57**	***38,641***	***10.22***	***7.85***	***5.32***
Hotel and restaurant	2.42	8.26	5.16	2.45	7435	9.60	7.78	6.48
Land transport	2.79	6.09	4.57	0.57	6571	4.00	2.93	2.1
Auxlr. transp. trav. agency	−2.65	9.38	4.34	−4.19	174	8.93	7.72	7.39
Post and telecom.	−1.80	26.83	1.68	−11.32	364	14.26	5.35	3.18
Financial intermedi-aries	−18.55	49.26	35.21	−44.58	299	7.12	5.89	10.53
Insurance and pension	15.16	12.85	4.97	−1.43	57	8.24	6.56	1.65
Auxlr. financial actv.	0.85	0.27	20.76	20.10	1025	8.57	8.88	14.07
Real estate actv.	1.64	2.16	19.25	1.28	617	8.08	1.75	1.88
Renting mach. and equip.	2.59	6.32	8.16	6.20	1337	16.97	12.39	8.71
Comp. and related activities	1.66	2.21	9.45	7.38	258	5.83	43.27	2.93
Other business activities	5.70	0.21	7.45	1.93	1897	7.92	3.01	4.39
Education	7.48	7.14	10.63	5.03	5965	10.76	5.57	3.34
Health and social work	3.89	6.58	5.73	3.42	2323	3.35	5.47	3.72
Acti. of mem. orgn., sport	1.63	7.06	8.41	−1.13	1277	22.16	14.54	9.46
Personal and other services	6.97	7.03	3.47	−1.39	4467	12.45	6.98	6.34

(continued)

Table 9.7 (continued)

Items	CAGR of value added per worker (%)*		CAGR of employment (%)		Workers ('000)	Share of part-timers in total employment (%)		
	2000–11	2011–16	2000–11	2011–16	2016	2000	2011	2016
Repair comp. and hh. goods		8.06		−25.36	676		4.31	3.09
All Services	2.45	5.93	***6.40***	***−1.30***	***36,193***	9.04	***10.3***	***6.12***
All	2.68	6.44	2.8	0.60	***111,270***	***11.95***	***10.24***	***6.75***

Note Manufacturing does not include construction;
*CAGR implies compound annual growth rate
bold indicates aggregates

they need to innovate or change the way of doing businesses such as changing products, processes or skills, tying up with other enterprises for accessing inputs, markets, technology or information, finances. Those who failed to do so are competed out of the business. Growth of corporate or organized retailing put the traditional retailers in a challenging position forcing the latter to upgrade storage, cold-storage or preservation facilities, store display, transport and communication systems wherever applicable. All this contributes to growth of labour productivity.

9.4 Major Problems Faced by the Enterprises and Their Adjustments to Overcome These Problems

Informal sector enterprises in India usually face different types of problems like non-availability of raw materials, erratic power supply, shortage of raw materials, shrinkage of demand, non-availability and high cost of credit, non-recovery of financial dues, non-availability of skilled labour. Intensity of these problems however varies over time and across industry sectors as may be evident from the NSS estimates. While conducting NSSO surveys, enterprises were asked if they face any problem in their operation, and if the answer was in the affirmative, they were asked to mention two most important problems with first problem being most severe. The proportion of enterprises reported facing one or more of these problems was not only high but also increased between 2011 and 2016 in all the three groups, viz. manufacturing, trading and services. As much as 40% of the unorganized sector enterprises are reported to be facing some or other problems in 2016 which was 6% points higher than the figure for 2011. Among the three industry groups, trading was more affected in 2016 when close to 43% of the enterprises reported to have faced problems. Despite these rising problems, trade sector could attain high growth of employment. Although significantly lower proportion of the service sector enterprises used to face problems, the sector witnessed decline in number of person employment in the second period and substantial rise in the first period. Probably, the intensity of the problems that the service sector enterprises are now facing is much severe. According to NSS estimates for the year 2010–11, manufacturing had the highest proportion of enterprises facing problems, which further increased in the second period.

The most important problems that the entrepreneurs of these three sectors are now commonly facing include shrinkage of demand, non-availability or high costs of credit and non-recovery of financial dues (Table 9.8). Additionally, a sizeable proportion of manufacturing sector enterprises faces problems of raw materials' shortage. The three most common problems mentioned above are however inter-related, although shrinkage of demand appears to be the main determining factor. Because of demand shrinkage goods are not being sold, investment and employment are reduced, and therefore, households cannot pay for the goods and services purchased on credit to the retailers. As a result, the suppliers and manufactures would also fail to recover their dues. It is obvious that under these circumstances, lenders, particularly the institutional lenders, would be more reluctant to lend money to these producers.

The increase in the incidence of problems faced by the unorganized enterprises is reflected in terms of deterioration of their growth performance. Based on NSS data, it is estimated that in 2015–16, 29.76% of the enterprises are expanding, 45.56% stagnant, 11.77% contracting, over the last three years. The same in 2010–11 were 31.85, 43.03 and 8.37%, respectively. It is further estimated that start-ups constitute 12.90% of the enterprises in 2016 and 16.75% in 2011 indicating reduced business opportunities. In general, these estimates reflect worsening of the overall business environment for the unorganized sector enterprises.

As regards problem of finance, the most striking feature is the least involvement of the commercial banking institutions in catering the needs of the unorganized sector enterprises. According to NSSO estimates, about 2.8% of the enterprises have loan outstanding with the commercial banks in 2011 and the corresponding figures for 2000 and 2016 are 2.4 and 2.6%. Even the central and state level term lending institutions (responsible for providing term loans needed for fixed capital formation), governments and other institutional sources have negligible financial contribution to these capital starved enterprises. Similarly, cooperatives catered to as low as 1% of these enterprises. All the institutional sources together served 4.3% of the entrepreneurs in 2000, which barely rose to 5% in 2011 and remained around that level till 2016. It therefore suggests that close to 95% of the unorganized sector entrepreneurs are deprived of financial assistance from the institutional sources of finance. For these entrepreneurs, the non-institutional sources of finance like friends and relatives, moneylenders, business partners, suppliers/contractors continue to be very important as they served another 4.5% of the entrepreneurs in 2011 which further rose to around 8% in 2016 (Table 9.9). Most important among the non-institutional sources are moneylenders and friends and relatives. However, both formal and informal sources together could cater to even less than 10% of the entrepreneurs in 2011, which slightly exceeded 12% in 2016 and the remaining entrepreneurs would rely on self raised fund.

Table 9.8 Problems faced by the entrepreneurs, 2016

	Manufacturing		Trade		Services	
Percentage of enterprises reported faced problem	41.10 (37.6% in 2011)		42.70 (34.8% in 2011)		35.60 (30% in 2011)	
Distribution of two major problems (reported by the entrepreneurs who faced problems)						
	Problem 1	Problem 2	Problem 1	Problem 2	Problem 1	Problem 2
Erratic power supply/cuts	11	8.1	5.6	5.9	8.5	5.7
Shortage of raw materials	8.6	7.1	2.6	1.9	0.7	1.2
Shrinkage/fall of demand	37.1	19	35.8	17	40.3	17.3
Non-availability/high cost of credit	11.3	18	18.1	22.3	13.8	22.1
Non-recovery of financial dues	9.6	20.5	22.4	33.5	14.1	23.5
Non-availability of labour as and when needed	1.8	3.7	1.1	1.7	1.8	3.7
Non-availability of skilled labour as and when needed	2.2	4.4	0.6	1.3	2.2	5.7
labour disputes and related problems	0.1	0.3	0.1	0.1	0.3	0.3
Others	18.3	18.9	13.9	16.3	18.4	20.5

Note Problem 1 means first problem, and Problem 2 means second problem

Table 9.9 Percentage of enterprises borrowed from different sources, 2016

Sources	All enterprises	Manufacturing	Trade	Services
All	12.20 (9.48)	7.98	15.57	11.67
Commercial banks	0.18 (2.77)	0.11	0.23	0.16
All institutional	5.05 (5.02)	3.31	5.28	6.12
Moneylender	2.71 (2.21)	1.94	3.32	2.57
All non-institutional	7.70 (4.46)	4.98	11.01	6.1

Note Parentheses indicate figures for 2011

One of the long-term effects of liberalization and emergence of competitive market is the growth of the contracting system to overcome uncertainties in the markets for output, raw materials as well as to access latest information about designs, products, processes, technology, finances and the like. According to NSS estimates in 2011, 6.30% of the enterprises (36.2 lakh) operated under contract with other, possibly larger, enterprises. Out of these 36.2 lakh contracting enterprises, 62.5% supply to single unit and 24.52% are covered with post-agreement input price escalation. In 2016, around 10.24% of the enterprises (i.e. 63.6 lakh) are estimated to be operating on contract basis. It is further noted that around 23% of the cases of contracting the contractors supplied equipment to the producers, and in 94% of the cases, the former supplied raw materials to the latter. Most importantly, 89% of the cases contractors specified designs to the producers.

Thus faced with various problems under competitive pressure, a large mass of capital-starved micro and small enterprises need to mobilize resources to upgrade technology and raise their skill, competence and productivity. However, they often fail to do so on their own. Although a section of them borrowing from the formal and informal sources and directly dealing in the marker for sale or purchase of raw materials, designs, other inputs, finished products, many informal enterprises have established long-term relationship with other, often larger, enterprises forming a kind of network. These enterprises regularly transact with the network members. They regularly receive contracts, product designs, raw materials, and finances and after production deliver the goods to the contractor. This would not only help to improve technology, skills and productivity but also enable to access preferred market for product, raw materials as well as technological information. However, there can be many forms of agreements, often informal, among the network members as regards work order, design specification, input provision, advances, payment, etc. Notwithstanding these innovations in organizing production and exchange by the unorganized sector enterprises in order to overcome several problems does not guarantee that they will be better off or will not be exploited by the contractor. But certainly, it would help them survive, and if it is a kind of long-term relationship, they are more likely to be better off (Biswas 2011). Of course, state interventions in terms of arranging finance, ensuring payments within a fixed time period after delivery of goods or services, provision of required infrastructure, adequate power supply, critical inputs and organizing training for skill development would definitely help these unorganized sector enterprises.

9.5 Concluding Observations

Unorganized sector has been assigned the task of job creation in non-agricultural activities. The sector has traditionally been acting as a refuse to those who moved away from farming activities but failed to get job in the formal or organized sector. Importance of this sector is rapidly growing in this country over the past few decades due to three main reasons: (i) continued high population growth and resultant high growth of workforce; (ii) agriculture's capacity to absorb workforce has been saturated and, in fact, workers are moving out of agriculture to find jobs in off-farm activities; and (iii) in the organized sector, employment growth is very slow despite high growth of production, and it is evident that the sector is unlikely to absorb the new addition of workers in the labour market and those moving out of agriculture. Once it is realized that the unorganized sector is not a stop gap-arrangement for the newly arrived workers but where the workers are going to stay for a longer period, the attitude of the policy makers towards the sector is changed. Along with job creation, the quality of jobs has also become a concern—not only new jobs would be created at fast rate but also the conditions of work of the self-employed or hired workers should be improved and decent. Being informal in nature, Government does not have much control over the unorganized sector enterprises to regulate employment contracts of hired workers or work conditions of self-employed persons. Government however could assist the enterprises in improving the work conditions through various means like arranging loans, machinery, tools and equipment, organizing training for skill development related to technology and management, provide information related to products, markets, technologies and also create necessary infrastructure, including IT services and so on. This would drastically raise productivity and earnings of the workers in the long term. Higher skill and productivity of workers would raise their mobility and reduce the chances of being coerced to work on adverse conditions. Further, government has to ensure that these enterprises are not being exploited while transacting with the larger enterprises, such as through delaying payments after delivery, renegotiations, imposing retrospective discounts. This has become all the more important in the present context of liberalization when unorganized sector producers are increasingly tying up with the larger enterprises for regular businesses in view of severe competitions, uncertainties in the markets for products and inputs and non-availability of institutional finances.

There is no doubt that the government has been quite active in promoting the unorganized sector enterprises and protecting their interests through various means even after liberalization. Excepting late 1980s and early 1990s, the sector maintained reasonably high employment grow and picked up momentum in 2000s when reform measures were already fully effective. Periods of high employment growth were usually accompanied by low growth of labour productivity excepting in the 2000s when both employment and productivity increased at fast rate. The decade 2000s are characterized by high growth of the overall economy which has direct influence on the growth of the unorganized sector. However in the first half of the 2010s, the employment growth drastically slowed down along with the overall slowdown of the economy, but the labour productivity increased quite significantly. The liberalization induced competition however adversely affected OAEs who were compelled to reduce costs, adopt improved and capital-intensive technology and consequently witnessed slower growth of employment and fast growth of productivity. Moreover, within unorganized sector relatively large enterprises, having access to finance and other renounces could take advantages of liberalization and perform better in term of both employment growth as well as productivity.

Finally, there is a rising tendency of the unorganized sector enterprises towards tying up with larger enterprises and become a part of their business networks. This would help them overcome the problem of shortage of capital or non-availability of credit/institutional loans as well as various uncertainties in the market. The informal enterprises through joining networks also benefit in the form of availing updated technology and design, market access, raw materials and regular work opportunities. State may channelize various assistances, including new technology, organizing training for skill development through these networks for their effective use. The commercial banks generally refuse to lend money directly to the unorganized sector enterprises due to the lack of collateral and the absence of formal records of financial transactions can now channelize their credit through these networks.

References

Amin, N. (2002). *The informal sector in Asia from the decent work perspective*. Geneva.

Bangasser, P. E. (2000). *The ILO and the informal sector: An institutional history*. Geneva: ILO.

Biswas, P. K. (2001). Surplus yield and production structure: The case of small-scale rural industries in West Bengal. *Journal of Peasant Studies, 28*(2).

Biswas, P. K. (2008). Nutrient mismanagement and degradation of soil: Some implications on deceleration of foodgrain production in India. In M. S. Bhatt, S. Ashraf, & A. Illiyan (Eds.), *Problems and prospects of environment policy: An Indian perspective*. New Delhi: Aakar Publishers.

Biswas, P. K. (2010). Systems of education, training and skill formation: How relevant for small enterprises? In Keshab Das (Ed.), *Micro and small enterprises in India: The era of reforms*. India and UK: Routledge.

Biswas, P. K. (2011). Networks of small enterprises, architecture of governance and incentive alignment: Some cases from India. *AI & Society, 26*(4).

Biswas, P. K. (2016). Corporate retailing in the advanced countries: Some salient features. In M. Das, S. Kar, & N. Nawn (Eds.), *Economic challenges for the contemporary world: Essays in honour of Prabhat Patnaik*. New Delhi: Sage Publications.

Biswas, P. K., & Raj, A. (1996). Skill formation in the indigenous institutions: Cases from India. In P. Banerjee & Y. Sato (Eds.), *Skill and technological change: Society and institutions in international perspective*. New Delhi: Har-Anand Publications.

Breman, J. (2013). *At work in the informal economy of India: A perspective from the bottom up*. Delhi: Oxford University Press.

Dahejia, R., & Paragariya, A. (2013). Services growth in India: A look Inside the black box. In J. Bhagwati & A. Panagariya (Eds.), *Reforms and economic transformation in India*. New York: Oxford University Press.

Fields, G. S. (1975). Rural-urban migration, urban unemployment and underemployment and job search activity in LDC's. *Journal of Development Economics, 2*(2), 165–188.

GoI (Government of India), Ministry of Agriculture and Cooperation. (2004). *Agricultural statistics at a glance*, New Delhi, August, 2004.

Harris, J. R., & Todaro, M. P. (1970). Migration, unemployment and development: A two sector analysis. *American Economic Review, 60*(1), 126–142.

Hart, Keith. (1973). Informal income opportunities and urban employment in Ghana. *Journal of Modern African Studies, 11*(1), 61–89.

ILO. (1972). *Employment, incomes and equality—A strategy for increasing productive employment in Kenya*. Geneva.

ILO. (1991). *The dilemma of the informal sector.* Report of the Director-General, International Labour Conference, 78th Session, Geneva.

ILO. (2016). *India labour market update*. July.

NCEUS. (2007). *Report on conditions of work and promotion of livelihood in the unorganised sector*. National Commission for Enterprises in the Unorganised Sector, Government of India, New Delhi.

NSSO. (1987). *Number 327: Tables with notes on own account enterprises in service sector.* Department of Statistics, New Delhi, March.

NSSO. (1989). *Tables with notes on survey of unorganized manufacturing*. NSS Report No. 363/1, 40th Round (July 1984–June 1985).

NSSO. (1998). *Small trading units in India and their basic characteristics: 1997 (Volume II)*. Report No. 444 (53/2.41.2/1).

NSSO. (2003). *Unorganised service sector in India 2001–02: Salient features*. Report No. 482(57/2.345/1), NSS 57th Round (July 2001–June 2002).

NSSO. (2009a). *Service sector in India (2006–07): Operational characteristics of enterprises*. Report No. 528 (63/2.345/1), NSS 63rd Round (July 2006–June 2007).

NSSO. (2009b). *Service sector in India (2006–07): Economic characteristics of enterprises*. Report No. 529 (63/2.345/2), NSS 63rd Round (July 2006–June 2007).

Sanyal, M. K., Biswas, P. K., & Bardhan, S. (1998). Institutional change and output growth in West Bengal agriculture. *Economic and Political Weekly* (Special Issue on West Bengal Economy), *33*(47 & 48), 2979–2986.

Sethuraman, S. V. (1981). *The urban informal sector in developing countries: Employment, poverty and environment*. Geneva: ILO.

Chapter 10
Structural Transformation of Employment and Wage Inequality in the High Growth Regime: A Study with Micro-Level Data in India

Panchanan Das

Abstract This study explores how inequality in wage income is associated with workers' human capital and employment status during the high growth regime that started in the early 1980s in India, with household and personal-level information from employment and unemployment survey. The study observes that 'within' group inequality declined very slowly, but the 'between' group inequality increased markedly during this period. Conditional wage earnings at different quantiles have been estimated to locate the possible effects of human capital, particularly education and employment characteristics. The study observes that the wage gap between workers at different percentiles increased over time during the high growth regime, and at a higher rate at the upper end of the wage distribution. The workers' schooling has favourable effect on wage income as expected. Wage income is increased with higher level of education at a higher proportional rate at higher percentiles in the wage distribution. As returns to education have significant impact on wage income, the wage distribution became more unequal because of the difference in access to education.

10.1 Introduction

The development experience of Asian developing countries is different from what was observed in the developed countries during the golden era of capitalist development.[1] In the OECD countries, the share of agriculture in total output and employment

[1] The process of development of the OECD countries has been experienced with increasing inequality in the initial stages and declining it in the latter stages with the transfer of labour from low-productive agricultural activities to relatively high-productive manufacturing (Kuznets 1955). Inequality increases in the first stage of growth, especially when it involves gradual migration from the rural areas to the urbanised sectors where differential access to finance, education and job opportunities is associated with greater inequality. But, after decades of growth, the wages in low-income rural sector would increase possibly because of the adaption of better technologies in farming, leading to the fall in inequality.

P. Das (✉)
Department of Economics, University of Calcutta, Kolkata, India
e-mail: p.das.wbes@gmail.com

P. K. Biswas and P. Das (eds.), *Indian Economy: Reforms and Development*, India Studies in Business and Economics, https://doi.org/10.1007/978-981-13-8269-7_10

declined with growing importance of industries and then services. While structural change appears in GDP in the Asian economies by following roughly the similar pattern as observed in the OECD countries, there has been no significant structural transformation in employment matching with the change in output share in many Asian countries. In India, for example, the fall in output share of agriculture has not been accompanied by the proportionate fall in employment share implying that income per capita in agriculture has been declining. In services, on the other hand, there has been no significant growth of employment despite its higher proportional output growth indicating increasing per capita income in the services sector. No significant transference of labour from land-based activities to manufacturing or services has been observed in the Indian economy (Das 2007a). The failure of manufacturing to absorb the growing labour force has likely consequences in the distribution of labour income in the Asian economy. The inherent differences in the changes in structural characteristics of employment between the Asian developing nations and the post-war Western European countries may lead to different distributional outcomes in labour income between these two groups of economies.

In the context of this type of structural changes in employment and output in India, this chapter analyses the distribution of wage income over the new growth regime in India that started in the early 1980s. The structural break in economic growth appeared in the Indian economy in 1983, much before the 1991 reforms (Wallack 2003; Das 2007b). The early 1980s also marked the turning point for the dynamics of income inequality in India and indeed across the world. While average income grew faster since the mid-1980s than it had in the planning period,[2] inequality increased rapidly primarily because of an enormous increase in incomes at the top, particularly incomes at the very top (Basole 2014). The top 1% in income distribution owned roughly 9% of the national income in India in the late 1990s (Banerjee and Piketty 2005; Chancel and Piketty 2017).

The new economy of the 1980s and 1990s exhibited higher proportional rates of growth of income at the top percentiles than the growth rates at the bottom level ensuring increasing inequality during the high growth regime. In the early 1990s, the economy of the country opened its doors to the world. Subsequently, people with accumulated or inherited wealth benefited the most from the openness of this kind. The pro-business policies made more wealth for the upper end while the lower end dropped down further increasing the "between" group inequality enormously. Skill-biased technological change has been an important driving force of rising inequality experienced by the developing countries after the opening of their domestic market to the global one (Johnson 1997). Technological change of this type has enhanced the employment and wages of skilled workers while depressing the employment opportunities and earnings of the less-skilled. Increasing trade openness in India is associated with increasing labour productivity and also wage inequality between

[2]The first three decades of planning (1950s–1970s) were associated with a marked decrease in inequality that had prevailed during the colonial period in India. In particular, the growth rates of real income of the rich, the super-rich, and the ultra-rich, as defined in Banerjee and Piketty (2005), declined significantly, even as average income grew slowly.

skilled and unskilled workers in the organised manufacturing sector (Galbraith et al. 2004; Dutta 2005; Das 2007c).

Accumulation of skill through education and training enables workers to get job in the high-skilled high-productive sector for higher wage. It is well documented that better-educated persons are able to earn higher wages, experience less unemployment, and work in more high-status occupations than their less-educated counterparts (Cohn and Addison 1997). The returns to schooling increase with skill-biased technical change demanding more skilled workers. Thus, human capital, particularly education, is very much crucial in explaining inequality in wage income, particularly during the technology-driven new growth phase.

This study estimates the extent of inequality in wage income and examines how it is associated with employment characteristics and workers' human capital by applying quantile regression model using the survey data from India during the period when transformation has been started from planning-based development to market-oriented development through the growing integration of the domestic economy into global trade and financial system.[3] Structural transformation of such type has a far-reaching impact on inequality in wage income. Using the survey data at different time points during the past three decades (1983–2012), this study observes that inequality in wage income increased partly because of inequality in workers' education, and the effect is dissimilar across different workers' group with different employment characteristics at different locations of the wage distribution. The differences in wage income across quantiles are substantially higher for workers with education-level graduate and above than for less-educated workers.

The study is organised into six sections. After some introductory remarks in Sect. 10.1, Sect. 10.2 describes, in short, the data used in this study. Section 10.3 discusses the econometric methodology applied to analyse the disproportional effects of returns to schooling and employment characteristics on conditional wage. Some observed facts about employment structure, workers' education and inequality in wage income are displayed in Sect. 10.4. Section 10.5 discusses and interprets in detail the empirical results obtained by estimating quantile regression equation. Section 10.6 summarises and concludes.

10.2 Data

National Sample Survey Office (NSSO) has been carrying out household-level survey on employment and unemployment situation in India roughly five years' interval

[3]Many countries in Asia, most notably India and China (PRC), are in a transition from planned economies to market-oriented economies. The structural transformation of the Indian economy from a socialistic to a pro-business path was well-underway before the 1991 reforms. China decided to liberalise its economy by the end of 1978 and towards the end of the 1980s, China entered into a new phase of reforms with a massive programme of rapid integration of its economy into the world economy, while India charted out its new course of development based on neo-liberal reforms in the early 1990s.

since the early 1970s (27th round survey). The survey data are available in digital form since 1983 (38th round survey). In this study, we have used this database from 38th, 50th, 61st and 68th round survey for the period 1983, 1993–94, 2004–05 and 2011–12, respectively. We have constructed a pooled sample of unit-level observations by using these four samples drawn independently from the same population at different points of time. The survey on employment and unemployment gathers information about wage income, household consumption, education and demographic characteristics of household members, weekly time disposition, and their main and secondary job activities. The principal job activities are defined for all household members as self-employed, regular salaried worker, casual wage labourer and so on.

Wages are recorded in the survey valued at current prices on weekly basis which are used to analyse wage distribution and employment characteristics. The nominal wages at different survey rounds are converted into real terms by deflating with consumer price index for the corresponding period with the same base (2000–01). We restrict the sample to wage earners aged between 15 and 65, the working age in the Indian labour market. Students and unpaid family workers have been excluded from the sample.

The activity status is classified into 13 groups consisting mainly different forms of self-employment, wage employment and other activities. Self-employed are those who operate their own farm or non-farm enterprises or are engaged independently in a profession or trade. The self-employed are further categorised into own-account workers, employers and unpaid workers in household enterprises. Wage employment is divided into regular wage employment and casual employment. Regular wage workers are those who work in other's farm or non-farm enterprises of household or non-household type and get salary or wages on a regular basis, not on the basis of daily or periodic renewal of work contract. This category not only includes persons getting time wage but also persons receiving piece wage or salary and paid apprentices, both full time and part-time. On the other hand, a person working in other's farm or non-farm enterprises, both household and non-household type, and getting wage according to the terms of the daily or periodic work contract is a casual wage labour. The survey data also provide the nature of job contract as no written job contract, written job contract for 1 year or less, written job contract for more than 1–3 years and written job contract for more than 3 years. By matching with type of job contract, it is observed that regular wage workers have written job contract for longer period while most of the casual workers have no written job contract at all. Thus, regular wage workers with job contract for longer years are treated as permanent workers and casual wage workers with no written job contract or job contract for very short period as temporary workers.

The structure of employment is different in the rural economy from that in the urban sector. In the rural economy, employment structure is classified broadly into farm and non-farm employment. Farm employment is further categorised into self-employment in agriculture (a major part of them are cultivators), agricultural workers and other workers. Rural non-farm employment is classified again into self-employment in non-agriculture, casual workers and other workers. The urban employment, on the other hand, is divided into self-employment, wage employment on regular basis and wage employment on casual basis.

10.3 Econometric Model

This study analyses the distribution of wage income in terms of human capital and employment characteristics of the working-age people by using quantile regression model. The wage equation is estimated at the selected quantiles of the wage distribution. The quantile regression model has been popularised after the publication of Koenker and Bassett (1978, 1982). The literature has been developed further by Machado and Mata (2005), Melly (2005), Firpo et al. (2009), Fortin et al. (2011), Lechmann and Schnabel (2012), Magnani and Zhu (2012), Chi and Li (2014). Quantile regression has been used in many empirical researches in analysing the distributional content of wage income because it has some advantages over the ordinary least square.[4] Quantile regression is more robust to non-normal errors and outliers. It allows to consider the impact of a covariate on the entire distribution of the dependent variable, daily wage in our model, not merely its conditional mean.

The basic model used in this study is described in short as follows:

We estimate the following wage regression equation:

$$lnw_i = \acute{X}_i\beta(\theta) + \varepsilon_i \qquad (10.1)$$

here, w_i is wage earned by worker i, X_i is the vector of covariates including job types, education, experience, gender of worker i and so on, β is the coefficient vector, θ represents quantile of the wage distribution and ε_i is the idiosyncratic error.

The population conditional quantile distribution of (10.1), for all θ given the set of covariates X is

$$Q_\theta(lnw_i|X_i) = \acute{X}_i\beta(\theta), \qquad (10.2)$$

Here, the underlying assumption is $Q_\theta(\varepsilon_i|X_i) = 0$ for all $\theta \in (0, 1)$.

Thus, Eq. (10.1) becomes

$$lnw_i = Q_\theta(lnw_i|X_i) + \varepsilon_i \qquad (10.3)$$

Equation (10.3) states that the unconditional quantile wage is equal to its wage conditional on the vector of explanatory variables at the same quantile plus the random error.

The coefficient vector $\beta(\theta)$ at quantile θ can be estimated by minimising the following objective function (Koenker and Bassett 1978):

[4]For example, Poterba and Rueben (1995) and Mueller (2000) studied public–private wage differentials in the USA and Canada analysed the income and wealth distribution in the UK.

$$\hat{\beta}(\theta) = \underset{\beta}{argmin}\left[\frac{1}{n}\left(\sum_{i=1}^{n}\rho_\theta(lnw_i - X_i\beta)\right)\right] \tag{10.4}$$

Here, $\hat{\beta}(\theta)$ is called θ_{th} regression quantile, for any quantile $\theta \in (0, 1)$.

The objective function denotes the loss associated with the prediction errors. Quantile regression minimises a sum that gives asymmetric penalties $(1-\theta)|\varepsilon|$ for overprediction and $\theta|\varepsilon|$ for under prediction:

$$\rho_\theta(\varepsilon) = \theta\varepsilon, \text{ if } \in > 0$$

$$\rho_\theta(\varepsilon) = (\theta - 1)\varepsilon, \text{ if } \in < 0$$

Thus, the θ_{th} quantile regression estimators, $\hat{\beta}(\theta)$ are chosen by solving the following problem

$$\hat{\beta}^t(\theta) = \underset{\beta}{argmin}\left[\sum_{i\in\{i:lnw_i \geq X_i\beta\}}\theta|lnw_i - X_i\beta| + \sum_{i\in\{i:lnw_i < X_i\beta\}}(1-\theta)|lnw_i - X_i\beta|\right] \tag{10.5}$$

This non-differentiable function could be minimised by applying the simplex method. The median regression, least-absolute-deviations regression, is obtained by minimising

$$\hat{\beta}(0.5) = \sum_i |lnw_i - X_i\beta| \tag{10.6}$$

The median-regression line must pass through the pair of data points with half of the remaining data lying above the regression line and the other half falling below.

We have used bootstrap standard errors in estimating the conditional distribution of wages for given X_i and θ by applying the principle described in (10.4) or, (10.5):

$$\widehat{lnw_i} = \acute{X}_i\hat{\beta}(\theta) \tag{10.7}$$

The estimated coefficient vector measures the rates of return to the corresponding covariates at the selected quantile of the conditional wage distribution. Under some regularity conditions, the estimated conditional quantile function is a consistent estimator of the population conditional quantile function, uniformly in θ (Koenker and Bassett 1982; Hendricks and Koenker 1992).

10.4 Employment Structure and Inequality in Wage Income: Some Observed Facts

The broad structural characteristics together with economic and political institutions have an influence on employment and wage structure in the labour market, which in turn affect the distribution of wage income. The structural transformation in employment occurred in rural India from the farm to the non-farm sector, although very slowly. While agricultural households have been dominating in the rural economy, the share of employment in agriculture, both as self-employed and casual labour declined systematically since the early 1980s (Table 10.1). Increasing share in non-farm employment in the rural economy assumes significance in analysing the changing pattern of distribution in wage income. The scope of getting a job in the non-farm sector in rural India increased with growth and development and the observed statistics support this fact. The share of self-employment in non-agricultural activities increased till 2005 and stagnated thereafter, while casual workers in the non-farm sector increased significantly over the survey rounds.

The urban households are mostly engaged in non-farm employment in the form of self-employment followed by regular wage or salaried workers (Table 10.2). Self-employment in the urban sector is more heterogeneous than in the rural sector. It ranges from street vending to high-skilled professional in finance or information technology. The share of self-employment in urban households increased during 1993–2005, but declined thereafter. While the share of wage earners on regular basis declined during the early phase of new growth regime, it remained stagnant, and the share of casual workers increased during 2005–2012. Thus, the casualisation of employment increased in the non-farm sector both among the rural and urban households. The expansion of employment on permanent basis is restricted mainly for a very few well-endowed groups of workers keeping a large proportion remained in low-productive informal employment on casual basis. It results in widening wage gap between farm and non-farm sectors, and even between different segments within the non-farm sector in the economy.

Table 10.1 Changes in employment structure in rural India

Employment type	Employment share			
	1983	1993–94	2004–05	2011–12
Self-employed in agriculture	55	47	44	41
Self-employed in non-agriculture	10	13	17	17
Regular wage earning				9
Casual labour in agriculture	25	24	22	17
Casual labour in non-agriculture	5	7	10	13
Others	5	9	8	3

Source Author's calculation with data from 38th, 50th, 61st and 68th rounds of NSSO

Table 10.2 Changes in employment structure in urban India

Employment type	Employment share			
	1983*	1993–94	2004–05	2011–12
Self-employed	45	43	48	46
Regular wage earning	0	41	37	37
Casual labour	0	12	11	13
Others	55	4	3	4

Note *In 38th round survey household types are categorised into self-employment and other workers
Source As for Table 10.1

Around 30% of rural workers and 50% of urban workers were in wage employment, regular and casual basis taken together, in 2011–12 (Tables 10.1 and 10.2). Before estimating how returns to schooling affect the wage income at different locations of the wage distribution we have looked at how wage workers are distributed by their levels of education at each survey round and the estimated figures are shown in Table 10.3. The distributional pattern of wage workers in terms of their education has been changed in favour of the share of workers with higher education during the high growth regime in India. The share of workers in lower strata in terms of their education level declined while the share of those with higher levels of education increased significantly over time. The share of graduate and postgraduate workers increased spectacularly in 2011–12 as compared to the respective share in 1983. In 2011–12, around one-fourth of the wage earners were educated at secondary or higher secondary level while one-fifth of wage workers were illiterate and just above 17% had education-level graduate and above.

In 2011–12, majority of the rural working people with no education or schooling up to primary education were absorbed as casual workers in non-farm activities followed by self-employment in farming (Table 10.4). A significant part of the persons with schooling up to primary level, however, were engaged in self-employment in the non-farm sector. Rural people who have education at middle school or secondary level were mostly engaged in self-employment group either in the farm or non-farm

Table 10.3 Distribution of wage workers by levels of education in India (rural and urban)

Education level	1983	1993–94	2004–05	2011–12
Not literate	49.2	36.8	28.0	20.6
Below primary	23.0	11.1	9.8	8.2
Primary	12.2	12.1	12.7	11.2
Middle	10.8	13.5	16.9	17.1
Secondary	0.3	17.0[a]	19.3[a]	25.3[a]
Graduate and above	4.5	9.5	13.4	17.6

Note [a]Includes both secondary and higher secondary levels
Source As for Table 10.1

sector. While the majority of the working-age people in the rural economy with higher level of education (higher secondary, diploma, graduate, postgraduate and above) absorbed as wage or salaried workers on regular basis in the non-farm sector, a notable share of them engaged as self-employed or family workers.

On the other hand, majority of the urban working people with no education or schooling up to primary education or middle school education were absorbed as own-account workers in informal activities like small trading or street vending (Table 10.5). More than one-fourth of the working people without any formal or informal education worked very indecent activities including begging as indicated by the category *other workers*. In the urban economy, roughly one-fifth of the working population were absorbed in wage employment on casual basis in the private sector activities. A significant part of the persons with schooling up to middle school level were either regular wage worker or casual wage worker of the private sector. The share of regular wage employment increased with the level of education. Nearly three-fourths of the urban working people who have education at postgraduation or above were mostly engaged in wage employment on regular basis. The shares of this type of employment for graduate workers and workers with diploma holders were just above 60 and 70%, respectively. However, a significant part of the workers with higher level of education (higher secondary, diploma, graduate, postgraduate and above) were self-employed as own-account worker.

Therefore, accumulation of human capital through education is no longer a guarantee of getting better job with higher earning. Many socio-economic and cultural factors actually restrict the vulnerable people to enter into higher hierarchy employment. Moreover, in recent years, the nature of jobs has changed dramatically because of pro-business market openness and deregulation of labour market in transitional economies. Labour market flexibility enhances the peripheral segment of the labour market by reducing the core segment of it. The distribution of workers as shown in Tables 10.4 and 10.5 for rural and urban areas respectively support indirectly these facts.

We have looked into the observed inequality in wage income keeping in mind the distribution of wage workers by their education and employment characteristics. Unequal access to education is one of the major causes of earning inequality. To understand how the incidence of inequality in wage income changes over time with levels of education we have estimated Gini index[5] of wage among workers by

[5]The Gini index for subgroup j is given by

$$G_{jj} = \frac{\sum_{i=1}^{n_j}\sum_{r=1}^{n_j}(y_{ij}-y_{rj})}{2n_j^2\bar{y}_j}$$

The within-group inequality index is the sum of Gini indices for all subgroups weighted by the product of population shares and wage shares of the subgroups:

$$G_w = \sum_{j=1}^{k} G_{jj}p_j s_j$$

If the population share and wage share in sub group j are $p_j = \frac{n_j}{n}$ and $s_j = \frac{p_j\bar{y}_j}{\bar{y}}$, respectively, the contribution to total inequality attributable to the differences between the k population subgroups is

Table 10.4 Distribution of educated working-age people by types of employment in rural India: 2011–12

Employment status	Education level									
	Not literate	Below primary	Primary	Middle	Secondary	Higher secondary	Diploma course	Graduate	Postgraduate and above	All
Farm sector										*39.1*
Self-employed	27.2	51.4	23.6	22.9	22.1	18.4	8.4	12.4	8.5	22.7
Family worker	17.8	25.0	15.2	15.6	16.6	17.1	7.3	10.3	5.7	15.4
Regular wage worker	0.1	0.4	0.2	0.3	0.3	0.5	0.6	0.4	0.1	0.2
Casual wage worker	1.0	1.9	1.0	0.9	0.4	0.2	0.2	0.2	0.0	0.7
Non-farm sector										*60.9*
Self-employed	14.7	41.7	21.7	22.1	22.8	19.3	17.4	17.4	12.7	19.4
Family worker	4.2	7.7	4.9	5.8	5.5	5.9	2.9	4.2	2.0	4.8
Regular wage worker	4.4	14.7	9.0	12.8	19.8	31.5	58.0	52.9	69.9	16.6
Casual wage worker	30.6	54.7	24.5	19.7	12.7	7.0	5.2	2.3	1.1	20.1

Source Author's calculation with 68th round unit level NSSO data

Table 10.5 Distribution of working-age people with different levels of education by employment type in urban India: 2011–12

Employment status	Education level									
	Not literate	Below primary	Primary	Middle	Secondary	Higher secondary	Diploma course	Graduate	Postgraduate and above	All
Own-account worker	27.0	32.7	33.5	35.3	37.7	34.3	18.9	25.1	18.0	30.7
Employer	0.4	0.8	1.1	1.5	2.4	2.5	2.2	3.1	2.3	1.8
Unpaid family worker	7.1	8.3	9.1	10.4	9.1	10.4	3.8	7.4	4.2	8.4
Regular worker	17.5	22.1	29.1	33.2	38.3	46.1	70.1	61.7	74.1	39.3
Casual worker in public sector	0.7	0.6	0.7	0.5	0.2	0.2	0.1	0.0	0.0	0.4
Casual worker in private sectors	20.5	21.3	19.9	14.9	8.5	3.9	3.6	1.3	0.3	11.4
Others	26.8	14.3	6.7	4.2	3.8	2.4	1.2	1.4	1.1	8.0

Source As for Table 10.4

Table 10.6 Gini index of weekly wages by workers' education

Education level	Survey years			
	1983	1993–94	2004–05	2011–12
Not literate	0.83	0.66	0.48	0.45
Below primary	0.83	0.71	0.51	0.48
Primary	0.84	0.71	0.50	0.48
Middle	0.73	0.70	0.48	0.49
Secondary	0.76	0.64	0.46	0.47
Graduate and above	0.83	0.51	0.38	0.40
All workers	**0.84**	**0.73**	**0.53**	**0.51**
Within group	0.21	0.12	0.10	0.10
Between groups	0.35	0.54	0.60	0.56
Overlapping groups	0.44	0.34	0.30	0.33

Note Bold indicates estimate for all workers
Source As for Table 10.1

segregating wage workers by their education level (Table 10.6). Incidence of inequality is different among workers with different education. However, no specific pattern is observed between inequality and education. In 2011–12, wage inequality was the highest among workers with education at middle school level followed by primary or below primary level of education. Inequality in wage income among workers declined over the survey rounds, but the rate of decline over the last two survey rounds (2004–05 and 2011–12) was very slow. The rate of decline of wage inequality was different for different groups of workers by their education level. Inequality in wage income among workers with education-level graduate and above increased during the period between 2004–05 and 2011–12. The decomposition of Gini index suggests that inequality in wage income is driven mainly by 'between' group inequality. While overall inequality declined, 'between' group inequality increased during the high growth regime in the post-reform period. In 2011–12, about 56% of overall

$$G_b = \sum_{j=1}^{k} \sum_{\substack{h=1 \\ j \neq h}}^{k} G_{jh} D_{jh} (p_j s_h + p_h s_j)$$

If subgroups are non-overlapping, total inequality can be expressed as the sum of within-group and between-group indices. The groups are non-overlapping means each individual's wage income in one group is greater or lower than each individual in the other groups. But, if the subgroups are overlapping, Dagum (1997) suggests another component of inequality measuring the contribution of the intensity of transvariation. This component is a part of the between-group disparities issued from the overlap between the two distributions. The contribution of the transvariation between the subpopulations to G:

$$G_t = \sum_{j=1}^{k} \sum_{\substack{h=1 \\ h \neq k}}^{k} G_{jh} (1 - D_{jh}) (p_j s_h + p_h s_j)$$

Thus, Gini index can be decomposed into three components: within-group inequality, between-group inequality and inequality due to group overlapping:

$$G = G_w + G_b + G_t$$

inequality was attributed to 'between' group inequality, where groups are formed by workers' education, while 10% was contributed by 'within-group' inequality.

10.5 Estimating Quantile Regression on Wage Income

To find out how wage income is affected by workers' education and employment status at different time points during the high growth regime, we have estimated conditional wage earnings at quantiles 0.10, 0.25, 0.50, 0.75 and 0.90 denoted, respectively, by Q_{10}, Q_{25}, Q_{50}, Q_{75} and Q_{90}. The sample observations used in estimating quantile regression are obtained by pooling of four independent samples at four different time points (1983, 1993–94, 2004–05 and 2011–12) taken from the same population. We have taken real weekly wage as a response variable (w). The predictors are the variables, both qualitative and quantitative that capture different dimensions of employment characteristics and education. The regression model at quantile θ shown in Eq. (10.1) is specified in expanded form as

$$w_i = \beta_0^\theta + \sum_j \beta_{1j}^\theta D_{i,\text{year}} + \beta_2^\theta D_{i,\text{F}} + \beta_3^\theta D_{i,\text{R}} + \sum_k \beta_{4k}^\theta D_{i,\text{edu}} + \beta_5^\theta D_{i,\text{TE}} + \beta_6^\theta \exp$$

$$+ \beta_7^\theta \exp^2 + \sum_l \beta_{8l}^\theta D_{i,\text{ES}} + \sum_{j,k} \gamma_{jk}^\theta D_{i,\text{year}} D_{i,\text{edu}} + \sum_{j,l} \delta_{jl}^\theta D_{i,\text{year}} D_{i,\text{ES}} + \varepsilon_i^\theta \qquad (10.1')$$

Here, D_{year} is a time dummy measuring the effect over time, D_{F} is a female dummy used for detecting gender gap in wage earnings, D_{R} is a dummy variable for capturing rural–urban differences, D_{ES} is used to capture earnings differences for workers with different employment statuses. Level of education, training and work experience are taken into the model to capture different dimensions of human capital. Education is taken as a categorical variable in terms of dummies (D_{edu}) based on different levels of education: below primary, primary, middle school, secondary, graduate and postgraduate. Work experience (exp) is calculated as workers' age less year of schooling. The squared term of experience is taken as one of the explanatory variables to examine the diminishing effect of experience on wage. The effects of vocational training and technical know-how on wages have been estimated by incorporating appropriate dummies (D_{TE}). We also incorporate interaction dummies to estimate the change in wage earnings over time for different types of workers and different education levels. Here, $0 < \theta < 1$ indicates the proportion of the population having scores below the quantile at θ. The ε^θ is independently and identically distributed random error.

The estimated results are shown in Table 10.7. The quantile regression parameter estimates the change in a specified quantile of the response variable produced by a one unit change in the predictor variable. It allows comparing how some quantiles of the wage may be more affected by education and employment structure than other quantiles. The intercept term shows the real weekly wages at different percentiles of the sample in 1993–94 in the absence of effect of any predictor incorporated in the model. The real wage income at 90th percentile is more than 2.5 times the median wage income and more than 8.5 times the wage at the 10th percentile implying significant gap in wage income in the Indian labour market in the early 1990s. The three time dummies used in the model measure the time effect of wage income. The year 1993–94, just after the initiation of liberalising policy, is used as a reference period. The coefficients of the time dummies suggest that real wages increased after 1993–94 and relatively at higher rates at the upper percentiles. Thus, the wage gap between workers at different percentiles increased over time during the post-reforms period, and at a higher rate at the upper end of the wage distribution.

The workers' schooling has favourable effect on wage income as expected. To estimate how workers' education has had impact on wage income, we have taken workers without any formal education as a reference group and compared wage earnings across workers with different levels of education by incorporating education dummies. The estimated results suggest that higher the level of education, higher is the wage earned by the workers supporting the hypotheses put forward in the human capital theory. As shown in Table 10.7, wage income is increased with higher level of education at a higher proportional rate at higher percentiles in the wage distribution. For example, the conditional weekly wages for workers with education-level graduate and above was higher by Rs. 1359.15 than the wage for illiterate workers at 90th percentile, while the wage gap between the similar workers group was only Rs. 151.63 at 10th percentile. The returns to education at every level increase as we move from lower to upper end of wage the distribution implying that education has positive impact on inequality. As returns to education have significant impact on wage income, the wage distribution became more unequal because of the difference in access to education. Gap in wage income across quantiles is relatively low at the below primary level and remarkably high at the graduate or postgraduate level of workers education. The coefficients of interaction dummies for time and education at graduate and above demonstrate that the dis-equalising effect of higher education escalated over time. The effect of education at secondary or higher secondary level on wage reduced at 25th percentile but increased significantly at the upper percentiles over the period between 1993–94 and 2011–12. Thus, earnings inequality between different groups of workers even at the same level of education increased over time during the high growth regime.

Work experience has significant positive effect on wage at every percentile, but at higher proportional rate up to 75th percentile. The rural–urban earnings differential and gender gap in wage earnings are also high at the upper end of the wage distribution. A significant wage premium is observed for workers with technical education at every location of the wage distribution. The wage gap among workers because of the differences in technical know-how may be because of skill-biased technological change during the high growth phase in India.

To estimate the wage gap between workers in different employment statuses, we have taken *other* workers' group as the reference group. The estimated coefficients (β_8) suggest that workers in wage employment on regular basis are better off at every

Table 10.7 Quantile estimates of conditional earnings

Coefficients	Quantile level				
	Q_{10}	Q_{25}	Q_{50}	Q_{75}	Q_{90}
β_0	50.89***	96.79***	173.67***	268.00***	442.55***
$\beta_{1,1983}$	−4.52	−9.35	−28.92	−51.08	−96.65*
$\beta_{1,2004}$	94.72***	154.69***	254.59***	588.66***	1238.74***
$\beta_{1,2011}$	181.75***	289.56***	425.79***	809.44***	1812.05***
β_2	−23.39***	−38.52***	−56.35***	−73.97***	−95.35***
β_3	−33.02***	−58.88***	−103.72***	−171.45***	−246.12***
$\beta_{4,\text{below primary}}$	9.56***	16.78***	31.37***	53.37***	66.56***
$\beta_{4,\text{primary}}$	13.07***	21.31***	43.42***	81.66***	108.41***
$\beta_{4,\text{middle school}}$	25.40***	46.39***	94.44***	193.72***	217.97***
$\beta_{4,\text{secondary}}$	70.61***	162.04***	349.28***	456.38***	521.93***
$\beta_{4,\text{graduate and above}}$	151.63***	530.15***	777.76***	1032.14***	1359.15***
β_5	60.24***	180.00***	330.61***	508.11***	749.15***
β_6	0.57***	1.11***	2.27***	4.53***	5.95***
β_7	−0.0001	−0.00001	−0.0001**	−0.00002*	−0.0001**
$\beta_{8,\text{regular wage}}$	80.85***	146.29***	222.94***	277.10***	299.61***
$\beta_{8,\text{casual wage}}$	40.60***	46.61***	34.01***	5.62	−45.63*
$\gamma_{1983,\text{graduate and above}}$	−105.38***	−480.50***	−553.98***	−588.59***	−734.27***
$\gamma_{2004,\text{graduate and above}}$	61.34***	46.94***	415.22***	636.05***	639.66***
$\gamma_{2011,\text{graduate and above}}$	90.08***	41.21***	689.69***	1151.88***	1024.16***
$\gamma_{1983,\text{secondary}}$	−43.52***	−133.61***	−261.74***	−244.97***	−241.62***
$\gamma_{2004,\text{secondary}}$	8.37*	−10.12	96.15***	382.63***	334.02***
$\gamma_{2011,\text{secondary}}$	17.65***	−28.24***	2.68	550.58***	404.77***
$\delta_{1983,\text{regular wage}}$	−94.29***	−163.48***	−208.40***	−258.57***	−282.29***
$\delta_{2004,\text{regular wage}}$	−78.58***	−153.93***	−276.34***	−493.69***	−825.58***
$\delta_{2011,\text{regular wage}}$	−94.36***	−185.47***	−325.71***	−537.30***	−852.34***
$\delta_{1983,\text{casual wage}}$	−22.80**	−30.78**	−24.19	−7.46	25.60
$\delta_{2004,\text{casual wage}}$	−78.67***	−130.68***	−220.22***	−534.27***	−1152.42***
$\delta_{2011,\text{casual wage}}$	−85.19***	−145.33***	−243.88***	−574.79***	−1489.18***
Pseudo R^2	0.0634	0.1125	0.2025	0.2943	0.3532

Note ***significant at less than 1% level, **significant at 5% level, the rest are statistically insignificant

Source Author's estimation with data from 38th, 50th, 61st and 68th rounds of NSSO by using STATA 15.1

location of the wage distribution and a greater extent at the top of the distribution. While the casual wage workers have got higher wages than the other workers up to 75th percentile level, they have earned lower wage at 90th percentile. Inequality in wage income is observed across different statuses of employment partly because of the differences in human capital. Workers endowed with higher education mainly from the upper social status are engaged in better quality jobs. But, the casual wage workers, the majority of them are vulnerable, earned lower income than other types of working people at 90th percentile level. However, the wage gap between workers in different employment statuses has been declining over time during the high growth regime in India.

10.6 Conclusion

In this study, we have analysed how wage income has been changed with workers' education and employment structure over the new growth regime in India. The structural transformation in employment occurred in rural India from the farm to non-farm sector very slowly, and in the form of informal employment. The scope of getting job in the non-farm sector in rural India increased with growth and development mainly in the form of casual employment. The type of structural transformation of employment widens the wage gap between farm and non-farm sectors, and even between different segments within the non-farm sector in the economy.

The distributional pattern of wage workers in terms of their education has also been changed in favour of share of workers with higher education during the high growth regime in India. In 2011–12, while the majority of the working-age people in the rural economy with higher level of education absorbed as wage workers on regular basis in the non-farm sector, a notable share of them engaged as self-employed or family workers. In the urban economy, roughly one-fifth of the working population were absorbed in wage employment on casual basis in the private sector activities. Nearly, three-fourths of the urban working people who have education at postgraduation or above were mostly engaged in wage employment on a regular basis. Therefore, the accumulation of human capital through education is no longer a guarantee of getting a better job with higher earning.

Incidence of inequality is different among workers with different education. In 2011–12, wage inequality was the highest among workers with education at middle school level followed by primary or below primary level of education. Inequality in wage income among workers declined over the survey rounds, but inequality in wage income among workers with education level graduate and above increased during the period between 2004–05 and 2011–12. While overall inequality declined, 'between' group inequality increased during the high growth regime in India.

To find out how wage income is affected by workers' education and employment status at different time points during the high growth regime, we have estimated conditional wage earnings. The wage gap between workers at different percentiles increased over time during the high growth regime, and at a higher rate at the upper end of the wage distribution. The workers' schooling has a favourable effect on wage income as expected. Wage income is increased with a higher level of education at a higher proportional rate at higher percentiles in the wage distribution. As returns to education have significant impact on wage income, the wage distribution became more unequal because of the difference in access to education. The rural–urban earnings differential and gender gap in wage earnings are also high at the upper end of the wage distribution.

Workers in wage employment on regular basis are better off as compared to other workers at every location of the wage distribution and a greater extent at the top of the distribution. Inequality in wage income is observed across different statuses of employment partly because of the differences in human capital. One can reconcile wage inequality across education with labour market segmentation by types of employment. Labour market in India is segmented between the core (formal) and the periphery (informal) sectors consisting of permanent employment with high wage and contractual employment with low wage, respectively. Working conditions in the core segment are better in terms of wages and social security benefits than those in peripheral employment. The expansion of non-farm employment opportunities is restricted for a very few well-endowed groups of workers keeping a large proportion remained in low-productive informal employment. It results in widening wage gap between farm and non-farm sectors, and even between different segments within the non-farm sector. While higher level of education enables people to increase their chances of having access to employment by enhancing the quality of their job search, there are many socio-economic and other restrictions for the lower strata of the people to enter into higher hierarchy employment.

References

Banerjee, A., & Piketty, T. (2005). Top Indian incomes, 1922–2000. *World Bank Economic Review, 19*(1), 1–20.

Basole, A. (2014). Dynamics of income inequality in India—Insights from World top incomes database. *Economic and Political Weekly, 49*(40), 14–16.

Chancel, L., & Piketty, T. (2017). Indian income inequality, 1922–2014 From British Raj to Billionaire Raj? Online publication: September 5, 2017. Available at http://wid.world/document/chancelpiketty2017widworld/ as on 19-10-2017.

Chi, W., & Li, B. (2014). Trends in china's gender employment and pay gap: Estimating gender pay gaps with employment selection. *Journal of Comparative Economics, 42,* 708–725.

Cohn, E., & Addison, J. T. (1997). *The economic returns to lifelong learning. Working paper B-97-04* (Division of Research, University of South Carolina College of Business Administration).

Dagum, C. (1997). A new decomposition of the gini income inequality ratio. *Empirical Economics, 22,* 515–531.

Das, P. (2007a). Economic reform, output and employment growth in registered manufacturing industries in India: Testing Kaldor's hypotheses. *Economic and Political Weekly, 42*(39), 3978–3985.

Das, P. (2007b). Economic growth and structural break in India: Testing unit root hypothesis. *The Journal of income and wealth, 29*(2), 29–43.

Das, P. (2007c). Wage inequality in manufacturing industries 1979–2002: A case of West Bengal and Gujarat. *Indian Journal of Labour Economics, 50*(2), 303–316.

Dutta, P. (2005). *Accounting for wage inequality in India*. PRUS Working Paper no. 29, Poverty Research Unit at Sussex, Department of Economics, University of Sussex.

Firpo, S., Fortin, N., & Lemieux, T. (2009). Unconditional quantile regressions. *Econometrica, 77,* 953–973.

Fortin, N., Lemieux, T., & Firpo, S. (2011). Decomposition methods in economics. In O. Ashenfelter & D. Card (Eds.), *Handbook of labor economics* (pp. 1–102). Amsterdam: Elsevier.

Galbraith, J., Chowdhury, D. R., & Srivastava, S. (2004). *Pay inequality in the Indian manufacturing sector, 1979–98*. University of Texas Inequality Project Working Paper No. 28.

Hendricks, W., & Koenker, R. (1992). Hierarchical spline models for conditional quantiles and the demand for electricity. *Journal of the American Statistical Association, 87,* 58–68.

Johnson, G. E. (1997). Changes in earnings inequality: The role of demand shifts. *Journal of Economic Perspectives, 11*(2), 41–54.

Koenker, R., & Bassett, G. (1978). Regression quantiles. *Econometrica, 46,* 33–50.

Koenker, R., & Bassett, G. (1982). Robust tests for heteroscedasticity based on regression quantiles. *Econometrica, 50,* 43–61.

Kuznets, S. (1955). Economic growth and income inequality. *American Economic Review, 45*(1), 1–28.

Lechmann, D. S. J., & Schnabel, C. (2012). Why is there a gender earnings gap in self-employment? A decomposition analysis with German data. *IZA Journal of European Labor Studies, 1,* 1–25.

Machado, J., & Mata, J. (2005). Counterfactual decompositions of changes in wage distributions using quantile regression. *Journal of Applied Econometrics, 20*(4), 445–465.

Magnani, E., & Zhu, R. (2012). Gender wage differentials among rural–urban migrants in China. *Regional Science and Urban Economics, 42,* 779–793.

Melly, B. (2005). Decomposition of differences in distribution using quantile regression. *Labour Economics, 12,* 577–590.

Mueller, R. (2000). Public-and private-sector wage differentials in Canada revisited. *Industrial Relations, 39*(3), 375–400.

Poterba, J., & Rueben, K. (1995). *The distribution of public sector wage Premia: New evidence using quantile regression methods*. NBER Working Paper No. 4734.

Wallack, J. S. (2003). Structural breaks in Indian macro economic data. *Economic and Political Weekly, 38*(41), 4312–4315.

Part VI
Banking and Finance

Chapter 11
Post-reform Development of Banking Sector in India

Sadhan Kumar Chattopadhyay

Abstract The study examines several facets of the banking sector development during the post-reform period starting from change in structure of banking sector to efficiency, productivity and soundness. This is done with the help of accounting measures. Indian banking sector has been able to transform itself from a traditional banking set-up to a modern and universal banking system by providing various services without distorting the social banking component. Adoption of new technology facilitated such transformation. It is now following the best international practices as set by the Basel norms. As a result, various efficiency/productivity and soundness parameters have moved towards the best global standard. Significant achievement was observed in case of public sector banks without damaging social obligations. It is now competing with the new private sector and foreign banks which operate in free environment unlike the public-sector banks. The analysis of various accounting measures suggests that there has been a significant improvement in the efficiency and productivity of the commercial banks in the post-reform period, although the degree of improvement varies across the bank groups. It has placed itself into a global standard in many aspects, including new product, service quality and improved payment and settlement system. However, at the same time lot of challenges are also being faced by the banking sector, which needs special attention.

11.1 Introduction

There has been a substantial growth in the banking sector in India since the onset of neoliberal regime in 1990s. Starting from providing plain vanilla services, the banks have now transformed into universal banks by providing various services including social banking. Banks are no more confined to the brick-and-mortar concept in the post-reform period. Now the norm is "anytime anywhere banking". This has been made possible by the introduction of Automated Teller Machine (ATM), Internet banking, mobile banking, etc. Our payment system now is very well comparable

S. K. Chattopadhyay (✉)
Mumbai, India
e-mail: sadhanchattopadhyay@gmail.com

P. K. Biswas and P. Das (eds.), *Indian Economy: Reforms and Development*, India Studies in Business and Economics, https://doi.org/10.1007/978-981-13-8269-7_11

with the developed world's payment system, for which the Reserve Bank of India, the central bank of our country, should be credited.

The nature of banking sector growth may be understood from the fact that during 2017–18, non-cash payment has gone up to 96.8% of the total transaction in terms of value and 95.2% in terms of volume as against 92.5 and 84.2%, respectively, in 2012–13. As per government's objective, the payment through cheques has come down drastically from 16% in 2012–13 to mere 4% in 2016–17 (RBI).

Over the past 28 years since the banking reforms, deposit of the banking sector grew at a compound rate of 16.3% and at 16.4% on an annual average basis. Further, bank credit also had grown at a compound rate of 17.3% during the same period and at 17.5% on annual average basis. On the other hand, while total investment of the banking sector was only Rs. 750.65 billion as at end-March 1991, it went up to Rs. 33,184.54 billion as at end-March 2018. However, the growth in banking is not restricted to urban and metropolitan areas alone. It has percolated to the rural areas as well, especially after the initiatives of the RBI in 2006 and subsequently by the central government. During the period, the Reserve Bank initiated in its flagship programme to bring the rural population, hitherto neglected, under the ambit of the institutional finance, specifically bank finance, which is popularly known as "financial inclusion"—the buzzword now in the banking parlance. The idea is to encourage these people to have banking habits and they are advised to open bank accounts with zero deposits (no-frill accounts) and once they are acquainted with the system they can take the loans from the banks at a much lower rate for productive purpose. Ultimately, by this process it was thought that rural poor including small and marginal farmers, landless labourers, small retailers, etc., would be able to come out of the clutches of the usurious money lenders and they can join with the country's growth process, which is known as "inclusive growth", coined by the then UPA government. Inclusive growth can not only increase growth, but also it can reduce inequality which is the ultimate goal of a nation. Under this backdrop, in this study we try to assess the overall development of banking sector during the post-reform period, focussing mostly on efficiency and productivity with the help of various parameters.

So far as literature is concerned, there is no dearth of studies on banking sector that deals with various aspects. Narain and Ghosh (2001) dealt with the supervisory arrangements for banks. The study questioned the effectiveness of maintaining financial stability by the Central Bank if the supervision is retained by the latter. Rajaraman and Vasistha (2002) examined the determinants of NPLs in public sector banks and observed that there is a significant negative impact of operating efficiency on the asset quality of banks. Ranjan and Dhal (2003) explored how banks' NPAs are influenced by macro-economic and financial factors. Ram Mohan (2017) argued in his study that the large banks are safer during the post-crisis period than a decade ago. Singh et al. (2015) investigate system-wide macro-stress testing for credit risk for the banking sector which has become very important after the global financial crisis. Chavan (2016) argued that although the state of Maharashtra is well-banked, there is a disparity in distribution of credit across districts. Samantaraya (2016) observed that accommodative monetary policy was not effective in increasing the credit growth during the recent period due to huge NPA overhang in the banks. It states that excessive credit growth in the past is mostly responsible for the huge NPA. The study emphasised on counter-cyclical capital buffer, dynamic provisioning, corporate governance, etc. Ram Mohan (2016) argued that India's public-sector banks have served the economy well by improving efficiency and stability during the post-reform period. Goyal (2017) overviewed various issues, viz. non-performing assets of banks, slowdown in credit growth, corporate debt, absence of modern risk-based approaches to management and regulation, the poor record of banks in transmitting monetary policy impulses and their contributions to financial inclusion. Chandrasekhar and Ghosh (2018) opined that neoliberal reform in early 1990 indeed has some positive impact in terms of profitability and reduction of NPAs of the banking industry. However, during the earlier period NPA was shared equally by the priority and non-priority sectors, while more recently NPAs are mostly accounted for by the large corporate, which indicates the failure of neoliberal banking reform. Kochar (2018) examined the effectiveness of India's financial inclusion drive on the savings and other outcomes of rural households. The study finds that the scheme has generated an unprecedented increase in access to financial institutions by using mobile technologies and banking correspondent (BC) models. Gulati et al. (2018) found that both macro-economic and bank-specific factors explain the formation of credit risk in the Indian banking sector. It also argued that greater market concentration, more diversification, higher credit growth and large size of banks increase the probability of defaults in the sector.

As can be observed from the review of literature, almost all the studies focus mostly on a specific issue at the micro-level and as such there is no study available in the literature which provides overall development of the banking sector during the post-reform period. Almost two decades have passed after reform, and various types of measures have been taken to address various issues over time. Therefore, it is high time to analyse these developments from various angles, viz. overall performance, technological development, new products and services, etc. In view of this, we examine the banking sector development touching upon technological development, productivity and profitability of banking sector during the post-reform period. Structure of our study is as the following. We have briefly discussed the structure of banking sector in Sect. 11.2, while Sect. 11.3 deals with the post-reform growth of commercial banks. After the reform, the issues of efficiency, productivity and soundness of the banking sector have received lot of attention. This is discussed in Sect. 11.4. Summary and conclusions are provided in Sect. 11.5.

11.2 Structure of Banking Sector

An efficient and sound banking system plays a very crucial role in promoting economic growth. An efficient functioning of the banking sector leads to efficient allocation of resources by eliminating the in-built asymmetric problem due to which moral hazard behaviour crops up among the borrowers (Report on Currency and Finance,

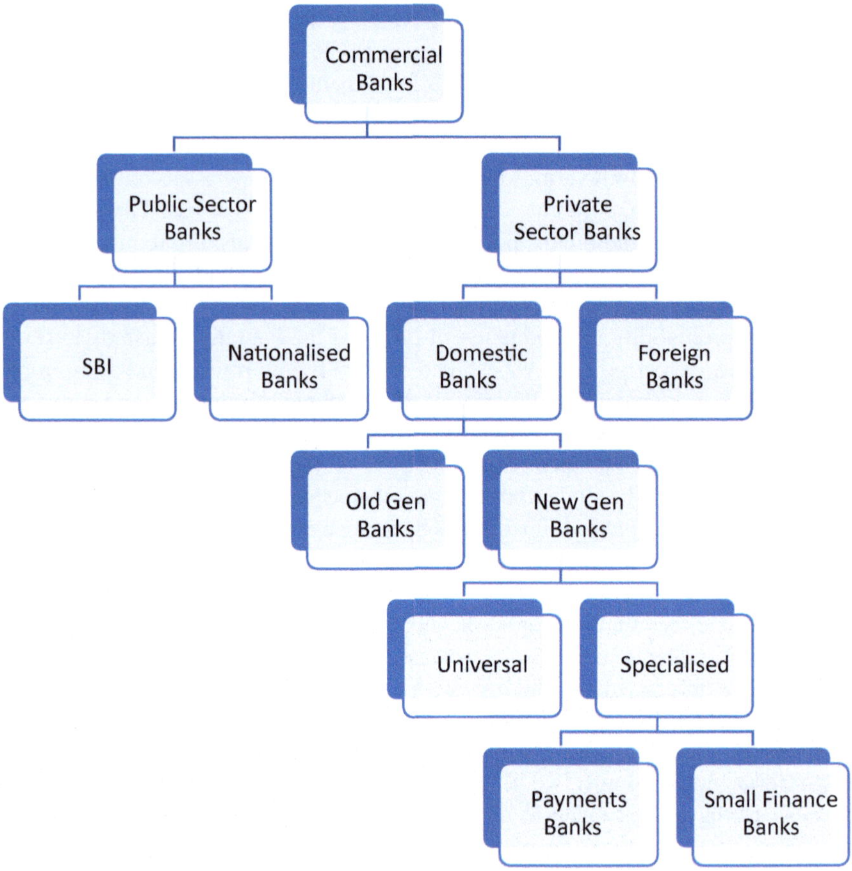

Fig. 11.1 Present structure of Indian commercial banks. *Source* Reserve Bank Staff College (2017)—Reserve Bank of India—Functions and Working

RBI). Even the developed countries like Germany and Japan and also emerging countries like India have been benefitted by the banking developments.

Indian financial system is mostly bank-driven, although the scope of alternative sources of finance is increasing over time. Accordingly, the Indian banking sector is quite diverse with various types of banks catering diverse groups of the society. Based on the ownership structure, it can be broadly divided into two sectors, viz. public sector bank and private sector banks (Fig. 11.1). Private sector banks are of two types—domestic and foreign banks. While public sector banks have been constituted under respective enactment of the Parliament, the private and foreign banks are deemed as the banking companies as defined in the banking regulation Act, 1949. As of now, 84 commercial banks are operating in India, out of which 18 banks are public sector banks and 22 are private sector banks.

11.3 Post-reform Growth of Commercial Banks in India

During the pre-reform period, India's commercial banking system was not performing well due to various problems imbedded in it, including controls of interest rates, large pre-emption of bank resources to finance government deficit through imposition of high statutory liquidity ratio (SLR), etc. Banks were nationalised in two phases, viz. 1969 and 1983, in order to impose social control over the banks so that a developmental thrust can be given. The emphasis was also given to extend this sector to rural areas to bring the people, hitherto untouched, under the ambit of institutional finance. However, the whole banking system suffered from inadequate prudential regulations, non-transparent accounting practices and weak supervision by the regulator.

Under this backdrop, banking sector reforms were brought after the recommendations of the Committee on the Financial System (Narasimham Committee), which submitted its report in December 1991 aiming efficiency in the banking sector. Following the East Asian Crisis in 1997, it became more important that strong banking system was required not just for efficient financial intermediation but also an essential condition for macro-economic stability. In view of this, the government appointed a Committee on banking sector reforms to review the progress of banking sector reforms and to align with the international best practices suggested by the international bodies and adopted by other countries also. Thus, in a way, these two reports set a road map that has guided the principles of banking reforms.

The major recommendations of the Narasimham Committee include lower SLR and CRR, no further nationalisation of banks, no bar on new private sector banks, liberal policy towards foreign banks, abolition of dual controls of banks, RBI to be the controlling authority of the total banking system, phasing out of concessional interest rates, depoliticisation of chief executives' appointment, etc. Thus, the reforms suggested by the Committee had a far-reaching impact in the financial liberalisation and growth of money and capital markets in India. In the meantime, the Basel Committee on Banking Supervision (BCBS), based in Basel (Switzerland), came out with a series of highly influential policy recommendations known as the Basel Accords to set right the banking sectors in terms of resilience. There are not bindings on the part of the national policymakers in order to be enforced, but they have generally formed the basis of banks' capital requirements in countries represented by the Committee. The Basel I standards that were formulated by the Committee of the Bank for International Settlement, popularly known as BIS, aimed at increasing competition to promote greater efficiency. However, the banking sector reforms were more gradualist than many other countries, which was in line with general strategy of the government and due to some urgency amidst crisis. By introducing the reforms in the banking sector, government intended to create a level playing field for all the sectors of the banks, viz. public, private and foreign banks with a healthy competition and thereby raising efficiency. There has been a great deal of progress in implementing the prudential norms as set out in Basel Accords for income recognition, asset classification and capital adequacy in a phased manner. Now the whole banking system in India has been following the best practices for which it has been able to withstand various shocks including the great financial crisis of 2008.

Due to its branch expansion policy and banking penetration policy, Indian banking system has displayed a substantial achievement in branch network. In about five decades after the nationalisation of banks in 1969, the number bank branches increased from 8187 to 142,642 in 2018 (Table 11.1). During the pre-nationalisation period, the share of rural branches was the lowest, while in 2018 it is the highest at 35.6%, followed by semi-urban (27.8%), metropolitan (18.8%) and urban centres (17.8%). In order to spread the banking network, banks were given various incentives in different phases.[1] As a result of branch expansion, population per branch has come down drastically from 65,000 in 1969 to 13,756 in 1990 and further to 9,226 in 2018, which indicates successful penetration. Apart from bank nationalisation, the financial inclusion programme, flagship programme of RBI, has also played a major role in branch expansion and savings habit by opening bank accounts.

11.3.1 Progress of the Banking Sector in India

The Indian banking system has not only made commendable progress in extending its geographical coverage, it has also increased its deposit and credit base over the years. In 1969, bank deposits amounted to 13% of GDP and advances to 10%, and the corresponding figures went up to 38% and 25%, respectively, by 1991. In 2018, the same has gone up to 68% and 51%, respectively, indicating gradual deepening of financial intermediation of the banking system (Fig. 11.2a, b).

Due to increase in deposits and credit of the commercial banks, total banking business also increased significantly during the reform period (Fig. 11.2b). In order to examine if there is any structural break in the banking business, we conducted Bai–Perron test for the period 1962–1918 and we observed that there are two structural breaks in the series. One was found to be in 1976 and another was found to 2007–08. But it is quite obvious from the Fig. 11.2b that there is a substantial increase in banking business after the reform period. As far as CD ratio is concerned, it is observed that there are three phases in the ratio (Fig. 11.3). During the first phase (1962–77), the CD ratio was above 70%. During the second phase (1978–2004), it was hovering between 60 and 70%, and in the third phase (2005–18) it went up to 78%.

During the period from 1980 to 2018, non-food credit (NFC) grew at 17.3% per annum on an annual average basis. Decade-wise, it grew at the highest rate of 23.4% during 2001–10. It may be observed that although there has been a gradual increase in NFC over the years in absolute terms, the growth rate has gone down over the year (Fig. 11.4a). The growth of NFC has gone down to 14.2% during 2010–18 with the slowdown of the economy after the global financial crisis. It may be observed that

[1]In 1977, banks were given the incentive of a licence to open one branch in metropolitan and one in urban areas, and four branches in rural areas (RCF, RBI).

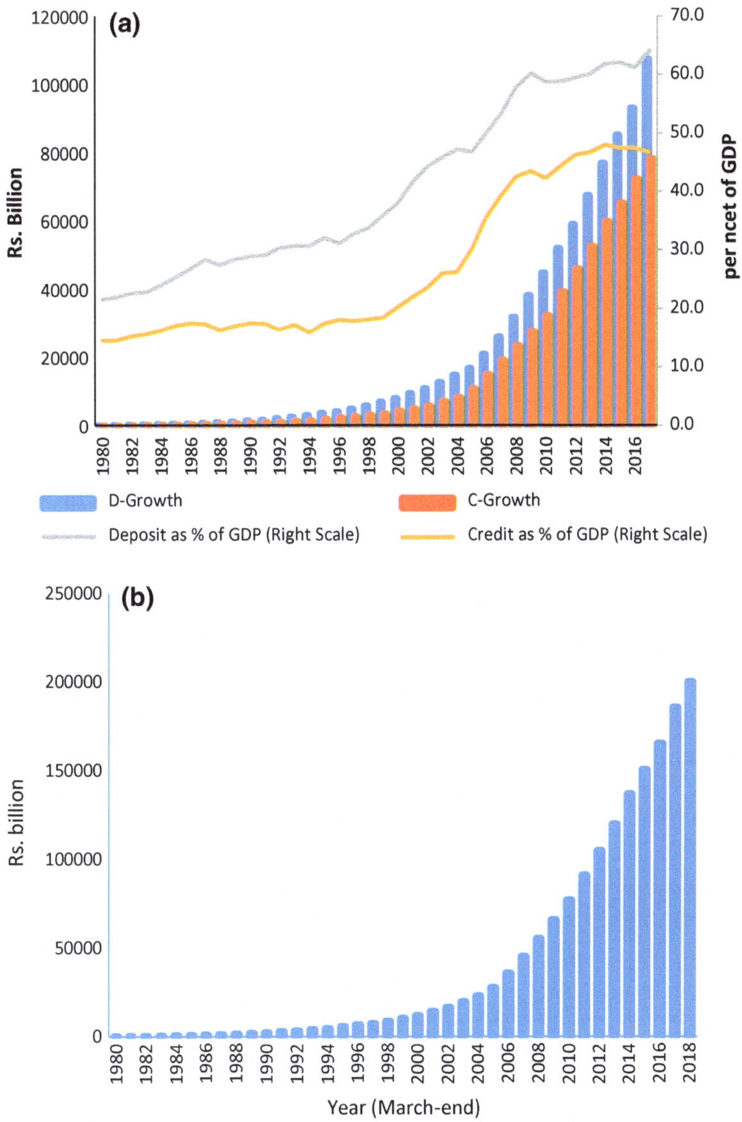

Fig. 11.2 **a** Deposits and credit of all commercial banks in India (1980–2017); **b** banking business in India (1962–2018). *Source* Statistical Tables Relating to Banks in India, RBI (various issues)

Table 11.1 Branch network of commercial banks (number of branches)

Year	In rural centres	In semi-urban centres	In urban centres	In metropolitan centres/port towns	Total	Population per branch
1969	1443	3337	1911	1496	8187	65,000
	(17.6)	(40.8)	(23.3)	(18.3)		
1975	6807	5598	3489	2836	18,730	31,660
	(36.3)	(29.9)	(18.6)	(15.1)		
1980	15,105	8122	5178	4014	32,419	20,481
	(46.6)	(25.1)	(16.0)	(12.4)		
1985	30,185	9816	6578	4806	51,385	14,381
	(58.7)	(19.1)	(12.8)	(9.4)		
1990	34,791	11,324	8042	5595	59,752	13,756
	(58.2)	(19.0)	(13.5)	(9.4)		
1995	33,004	13,341	8868	7154	62,367	14,880
	(52.9)	(21.4)	(14.2)	(11.5)		
2000	32,734	14,407	10,052	8219	65,412	15,578
	(50.0)	(22.0)	(15.4)	(12.6)		
2005	32,082	15,403	11,500	9370	68,355	16,180
	(46.9)	(22.5)	(16.8)	(13.7)		
2010	31,845	21,313	16,621	15,391	85,170	13,925
	(37.4)	(25.0)	(19.5)	(18.1)		
2015	48,140	34,526	23,098	20,879	126,643	10,131
	(38.0)	(27.3)	(18.2)	(16.5)		
2018	50,748	39,695	25,348	26,851	142,642	9226
	(35.6)	(27.8)	(17.8)	(18.8)		

Note Figures in the brackets indicate percentage share in total
Source Banking Statistics 1972 and Handbook of Statistics on the Indian Economy, RBI (various issues)

sector-wise, industrial sector accounted for the highest share of credit throughout this period, although its contribution to GDP remained low. For example, during 2017, while industrial sector contributed 23.5% of GDP, its share of total non-food credit was 35%, much higher than the services sector (Fig. 11.4b).

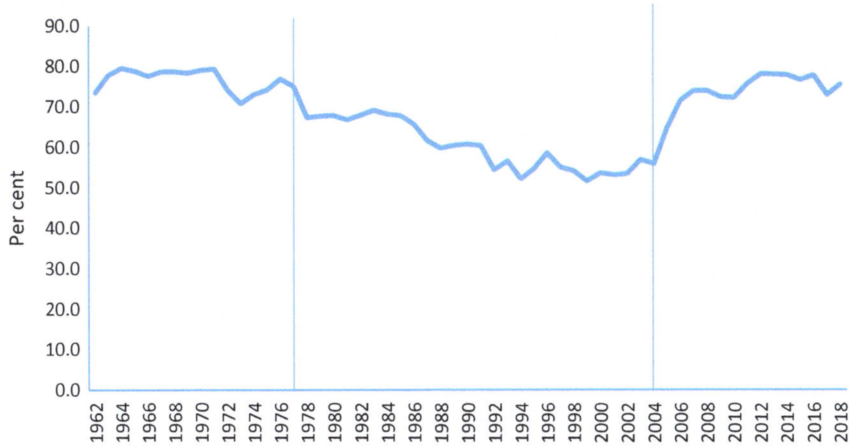

Fig. 11.3 Trends in C-D ratio. *Source* Handbook of Statistics on the Indian Economy, RBI (various issues)

11.3.2 Recent Technological and Other Developments in Banking Sector

Information technology has brought a new age in the Indian banking sector. In fact, it has helped to increase the overall banking business through computerisation of transactions and new delivery channels such as internet banking, phone banking, ATMs, EFT, ECS and EDI. With migration from traditional paper-based funds movements to quicker and efficient electronic mode, payment system has become very easy and efficient. However, usage of electronic mode has a long way to go. This is because, it is still concentrated within the metropolitan and large cities due to lack of financial literacy and awareness. Due to unawareness and cybercrime, people are scared of using the electronic mode of payment. Although Reserve Bank has taken various initiatives including creation of banking ombudsman at the Reserve Bank as also at the individual bank, people are not aware of these developments. Therefore, need of the hour is increasing awareness through financial literacy and campaign.

The most important development through which introduction of advanced technology was made possible is computerisation of the banking sector which was opposed vehemently by the staff unions at the initial stage of development. Entry of new-generation private banks and foreign banks with advanced technology has put more pressure on the public-sector banks to computerise their banking operations. This technological development has helped the banks to adopt the Core Banking Solutions (CBS), which is nothing but services provided by a group of networking bank branches. The CBS systems have facilitated the banking system to improve operations, reduce costs, check frauds in certain areas, etc. With the advancement of technology core systems now has been able to cover more and more functionality providing the bank an integrated solution for most of its operations in different

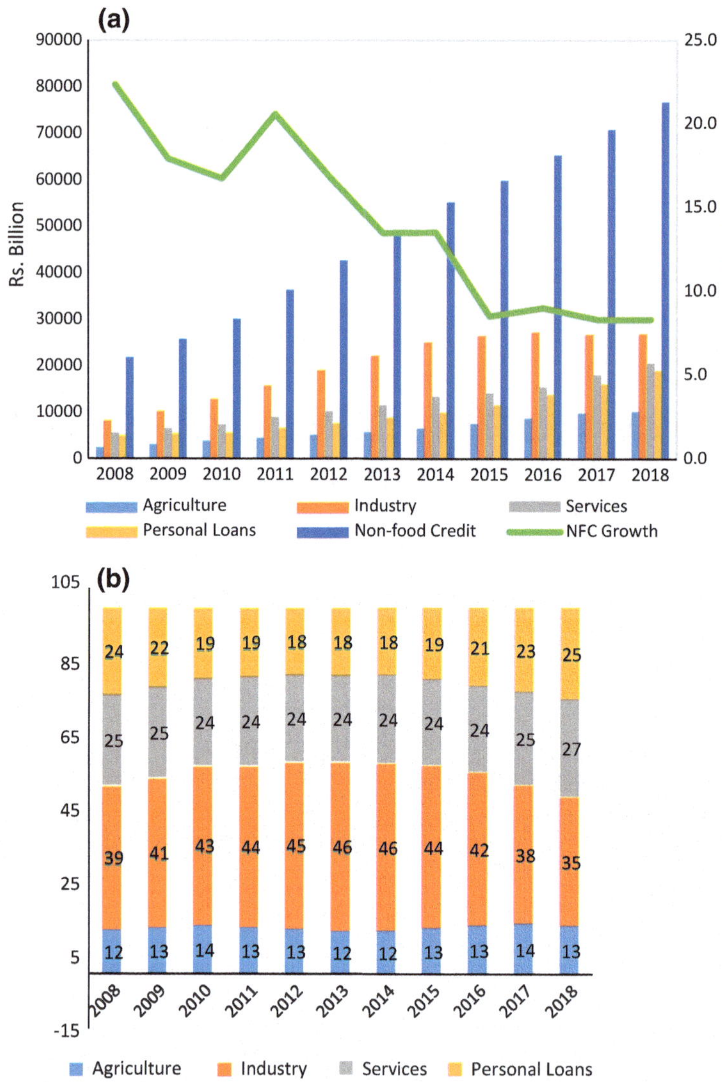

Fig. 11.4 **a** Sector-wise credit and non-food credit growth; **b** share of NFC credit (sector-wise). *Source* Data-base on Indian Economy, RBI

Table 11.2 ATMs of scheduled commercial banks

Sr. No.	Bank group	On-site ATMs	Off-site ATMs	Total number of ATMs	Off-site ATMs as per cent of total ATMs
I	Public sector banks	86,545	62,010	1,48,555	41.7
I.1	Nationalised banks	56,960	32,332	89,292	36.2
I.2	SBI and its associates*	29,585	29,678	59,263	50.1
II	Private sector banks	23,045	35,788	58,833	60.8
III	Foreign banks	219	747	966	77.3
	All SCBs(I + II + III)	1,09,809	98,545	2,08,354	47.3

Source Report on Trends and Progress of Banking in India, Reserve Bank of India, 2017–18
*All the associate bank of SBI have merged with State Bank of India

business lines. Besides, it also provides a centralised database for the customers' asset and liability position facilitating a 360° view of the customer's relationship with the bank, which is one the fundamental conditions for the Customer Relationship Management (CRM) strategy of the bank in modern age.

Another important development, which has revolutionised the delivery and payment channel in the banking sector, has been the introduction of Automated Teller Machines (ATMs). The first bank to introduce ATM concept in India was the Hong Kong and Shanghai Banking Corporation (HSBC) in 1987. Now, almost every commercial bank is providing ATM facilities across the country. There has been steady growth of ATMs after 1987. As of now, more than 2 lakhs ATMs installed across the country which was little over 75,000 in 2010 (Table 11.2).

However, although the number of ATMs has increased substantially over time, the percentage of off-site ATMs to total ATMs witnessed a decline from 55.7% in 2009–10 to 47.3% in 2017–18. More than 71% of total ATMs belonged to the public-sector banks as at end-March 2018. During 2017–18, number of credit cards grew at 22.1% over the previous year, indicating an increase in income from off-balance sheet activities of banks including credit card business (Fig. 11.5). While growth of credit card is the highest at 26.5% in case of private sector banks, that on debit cards is the highest in case of foreign banks. Further during the same period, number of debit cards grew at 16.6% in sync with ATM machine growth, indicating increasing usage of plastic money. Further, the share of private sector banks is highest in case of credit card issuance, while that of debit cards is highest in case of public sector banks (Fig. 11.6, Table 11.3).

In order to make banks more customer-friendly, a number of steps have been taken including setting up of full-fledged customer service department in 2006 by RBI. This helps in enhancing the pace and quality of provision of customer services.

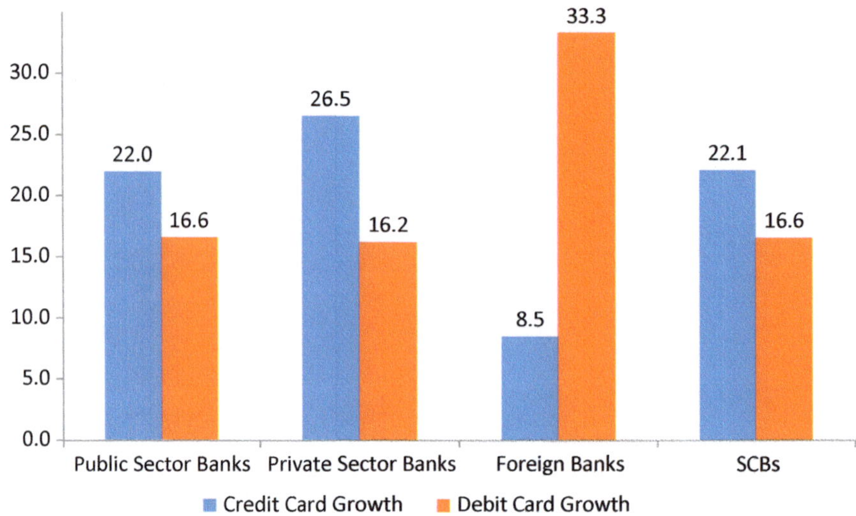

Fig. 11.5 Growth in credit and debit cards in 2017–18 over 2016–17. *Source* Data-base on Indian Economy, RBI

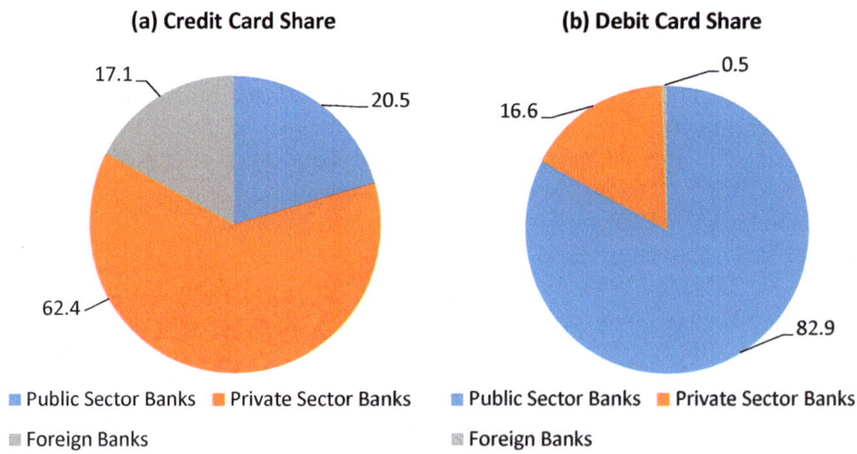

Fig. 11.6 Bank-group-wise share of credit and debit cards in 2017–18. *Source* Data-base on Indian Economy, RBI

Table 11.3 Credit and debit cards issued by scheduled commercial banks (as at end-March 2017) (in millions)

Sr. No	Bank group	Outstanding no. of credit cards		Outstanding no. of debit cards	
		2016	2017	2016	2017
I	Public sector banks	5.0	6.1	548.5	639.5
II	Private sector banks	14.7	18.6	110.3	128.2
III	Foreign banks	4.7	5.1	3.0	4.0
	All SCBs (I + II + III)	24.4	29.8	661.8	771.6

Source Report on Trends and Progress of Banking in India, Reserve Bank of India, 2017–18

This apart, as stated earlier Banking Ombudsman (BO) scheme has been initiated by the RBI in 1995. As of now, there are 22 BO offices operating in the country. Earlier these were located in all the major RBI offices in the country covering all the areas across the country. However, apart from this, RBI created an Internal Ombudsman (IO) in 2015 in each bank with an idea that complaints should be sent to banks at the initial stage. In fact, it is a vetting process of customer's grievances. When a customer raises a complaint in the bank, it may refer the case to their IO, who in turn, will vet the case. It may go in favour of the bank or the customer. If the case goes against the customer and the issue is not resolved, then customer can go to BO at Reserve Bank.[2]

11.3.3 Financial Inclusion

RBI defines financial inclusion as the following:

> Financial inclusion is the process of ensuring access to appropriate financial products and services needed by vulnerable groups such as weaker sections and low-income groups at an affordable cost in a fair and transparent manner by mainstream institutional players.

The genesis of financial inclusion can be traced back to the year 1969 when 14 major banks were nationalised in order to give a social thrust so that people not benefitted from the banking system should get the benefit and come out of the clutches of the moneylenders. However, even after five decades of bank nationalisation, it was observed that still 40% of the people are dependent on non-institutional sources, especially the professional moneylenders (Fig. 11.7).

In view of this, it was decided to bring the people, hitherto neglected, under the ambit of institutional finance. Thus, the Reserve Bank of India in coordination with Government of India and other stakeholders has come up with various policy initiatives to enhance financial inclusion and increase financial literacy in the country

[2]Details may be found in https://rbi.org.in.

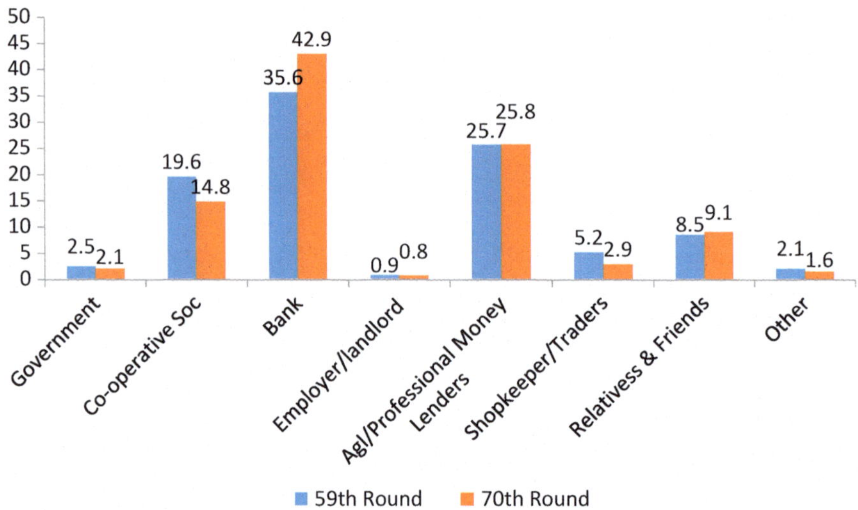

Fig. 11.7 Outstanding loans by sources of loans. *Source* NSSO 59th Round (2003) and 70th Round (2013)

from time to time starting from 2006. The scheme was more intensified in 2010 with the adoption of financial inclusion plans, which are self-set targets in blocks of three years developed by the board of banks to expand the outreach in terms of outlets and product. The new products under the scheme were introduced are opening of "no-frill" accounts,[3] Kisan Credit Cards (KCCs), General Credit Cards (GCCs), etc. Another salient feature of FI is relaxed regulatory requirements like (i) relaxed regulatory dispensation on Know Your Customers (KYC) norms, (ii) simplified branch expansion, (iii) Business Correspondent/Business Facilitator model, (iv) opening of branches in un-banked rural areas, (v) Special Dispensation Scheme for opening of branches in north-east region and financial inclusion plans for banks.

In August 2014, the Government of India launched an ambitious financial inclusion mission—the *Pradhan Mantri Jan Dhan Yojana* (PMJDY)—to ensure basic banking services including remittances, credit, insurance and pension in an affordable manner. As on 6th December 2017, 307 million accounts were opened with a balance of Rs. 698 billion.

11.3.4 Micro-finance

As per the textbook definition "Micro-finance activities revolve around providing very small loans to poor people or nations in order to help start a business or fund

[3]No-frill account is one for which no minimum balance is insisted upon and there is no service charges for non-maintenance of minimum balance, as directed by RBI in 2005.

a social project". These micro-finance activities may include grants, low-interest micro-loans and making credit available. In India, MFIs exist in various forms like joint liability group, self-help group, Grameen bank model and rural co-operatives. Features of these institutions are provided in the following. As can be observed from Table 11.4 that there has been a steady progress in delivery of micro-finance through the SHGs and JLGs. However, SHG bank linkage appears to be dominant with 1.9 million SHGs credit linked with bank financing of Rs. 388 billion during 2016–17. The Grameen bank model adopted in India in the name of RRBs, which was created in the Bangladesh Model pioneered by Nobel laureate Prof. Muhammad Yunus, did not work well due to various problems like recovery problems and non-performing assets that led to failure of these regional banks (Shastri 2009). The success of rural co-operatives was also limited due to its complex monitoring mechanism (Chetty 2017). Besides these, there is another kind of MFIs which comprise NGOs, trusts or societies working on not-for-profit model and even bigger players like Spandana, SKS, Basix, SHARE Microfin in Andhra Pradesh—which work on for-profit model. However, as can be seen from Table 11.5 that although there is a substantial increase in the number of MFIs, the amount disbursed by them is much less.

11.4 Efficiency, Productivity and Soundness of the Banking Sector

One of the main objectives of banking sector reforms in India was to promote flexibility, operational autonomy and infuse competition in the banking system so that the whole banking system rises to the international best practices. In order to do so, several measures were initiated since the early 1990s. These measures along with the technological developments have changed the operating environment of the banking system drastically and transformed the banking system into a modern one from the traditional banking system. They are now exposed to the competition with the foreign banks and new-generation private sector banks with new products and new ideas. All the 18 public-sector banks have accessed the capital market during the post-reform period. This has made them change their capital structure and market disciplined. The administered interest rate, which was a stumbling block for efficiency, was deregulated completely in 2010. Statutory pre-emptions in the form of SLR and CRR have been reduced significantly. Banks are now allowed to get into the non-traditional activities, for which their income from off-balance sheet activities has increased significantly. Banks have been provided with operational flexibility and functional autonomy which has helped them to take their decisions as per the arising situation. Earlier huge amount of non-performing assets was piled up in the banking system and there was no special recovery mechanism. Subsequently, a number of measures have been taken to recover loan from NPAs and deal with wilful defaulters. Various types on institutional and legal arrangements have been put in place in order to arrest NPA.

Table 11.4 Structure of micro-finance in India

	Joint liability group	Self-help group	Grameen bank model	Rural co-operatives
Size	5–10 members	10–20 member group	Starts with only two members per group in a village, eventually increased after the loan is successfully repaid	70–80 member per group
Services	Generally lending only, irrespective of savings amount	Regular savings in deposit accounts with the financial institutions	Savings and deposits to extremely poor sections of the society for business, health and housing	Primarily lending services for agricultural purposes
Model	Members invest loan amount for different purposes, but are guarantors of each other	All individuals of group work together on the same activity	Field Manager visits villages to form groups of five and lends to two. Amount recovered is reinvested in further lending and infrastructure development in villages	Co-operative society consisting of members are formed for a singular purpose; such as real estate, agriculture and infrastructure.
Structure	All members interact with the financial institution individually	More formal with defined positions in each group like treasurer and secretary	Formal structure consisting of Unit Manager, Field Manager, etc., who interact with every family in a village	All members interact with the financial institution jointly

Source Chetty (2017)

Under this milieu, we discuss the efficiency, productivity and soundness issues in the following sections to provide a holistic picture of the banking sector. Productivity and efficiency can be analysed using accounting measures and economic measures. Accounting measures are nothing but the ratio analysis like intermediation cost, interest spread, operating expenditure, cost-to-income ratio, return on assets, return on equity, business per employee, income per employee and business per branch. We discuss the productivity and efficiency with the help of these ratios in the following paragraphs.

Table 11.5 Progress of micro-finance programmes in India (as at end-March)

Item	Self-help groups							
	Number (in millions)				Amount (in billions)			
	2013–14	2014–15	2015–16	2016–17	2013–14	2014–15	2015–16	2016–17
Loans disbursed by banks	1.4 (0.2)	1.6 (0.7)	1.8 (0.9)	1.9 (1.0)	240 (35.0)	276 (114.0)	373 (194.0)	388 (200.0)
Loans outstanding with banks	4.2 (1.3)	4.5 (2.2)	4.7 (2.5)	4.8 (2.8)	429 (102.0)	515 (232.0)	572 (306.0)	616 (341.0)
Savings with banks	7.4 (2.3)	7.7 (3.4)	7.9 (3.9)	8.6 (4.3)	99 (25.0)	111 (55.0)	137 (73.0)	161 (87.0)
	Micro-finance institutions							
	Number				Amount (in billions)			
	2013–14	2014–15	2015–16	2016–17	2013–14	2014–15	2015–16	2016–17
Loans disbursed by banks	545	597	647	2314	103	147	208	193
Loans outstanding with banks	2422	4660	2020	5357	165	219	256	292
	Joint liability group							
	Number (in millions)				Amount (in billions)			
	2013–14	2014–15	2015–16	2016–17	2013–14	2014–15	2015–16	2016–17
Loans disbursed by banks	0.21	0.46	0.57	0.7	22	44	62	95

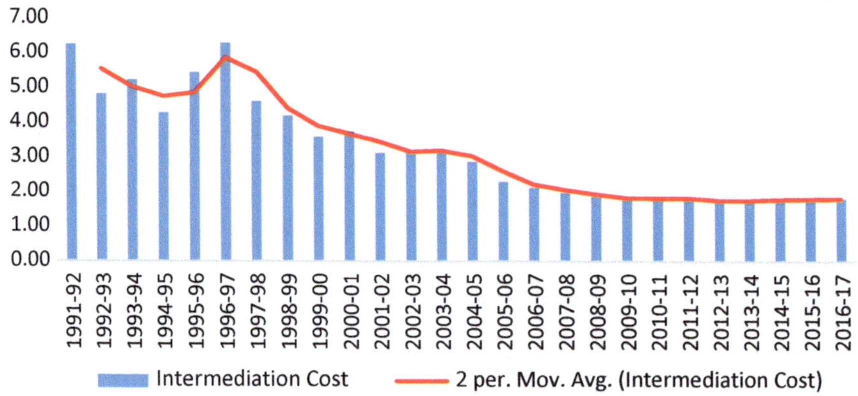

Fig. 11.8 Intermediation cost. *Source* Data-base on Indian Economy, RBI

11.4.1 Intermediation Cost

There is no consensus in the definition of intermediation cost. Different researchers have defined the term in different ways. But normally, it is defined as the spread between the cost of deposits and return on loans assets. Once a bank becomes productive and efficient, it is expected to reduce the transaction costs to mobilise funds and lending to borrowers. After the economic reforms, banking industry has been able to reduce the intermediation cost over the years from 6.24% in 1991–92 to 1.75% in 2012–13, although there was a marginal increase during the following years (Fig. 11.8). However, the intermediation cost is higher in case of private sector banks and foreign banks (Annex Table 11.6).

11.4.2 Operating Cost to Total Assets

Operating costs are expenses associated with the maintenance and administration of a business on a day-to-day basis. The ratio indicates the amount of operating cost per unit of assets. The bank will be considered more efficient if it is in a position to reduce the same cost. That means there is an inverse relationship between this ratio and efficiency—higher the ratio lower is the efficiency. It is observed from Fig. 11.9 that there is a gradual decrease in this ratio during the post-reform period. It declined from 2.93 in 1995–96 to 1.63 in 2012–13, although there was a marginal increase in the following years (Annex Table 11.7). Bank-group-wise, the ratio is lowest at 1.51 for the nationalised banks in 2016–17 followed by State Bank group. This is quite high for private sector banks (2.11) and foreign banks (2.04). This has happened mainly due to outsourcing of activities by many banks, rationalisation of labour force through voluntary retirement scheme (VRS), etc. On the other hand, in

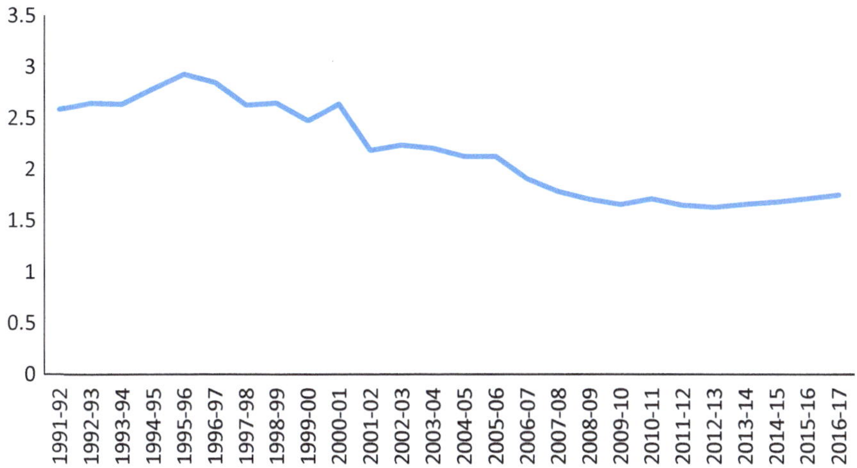

Fig. 11.9 Operating cost to total asset. *Source* Data-base on Indian Economy, RBI

case of foreign banks and private sector banks, the higher ratios are due to increase in technology upgradation, attracting best talents with handsome salaries and perks (Report on Currency Finance, 2006–08). However, it is also important to note that off-balance sheet exposure is very high for private and foreign banks. Thus, while such business entails cost they are not reflected in the balance sheet. Thus, in a way, there is an upward bias in this ratio for these banks and hence it may be somewhat misleading.

11.4.3 Cost-to-Income Ratio

The cost-to-income ratio is one of the most important indicators of efficiency. It is directly linked with profitability of banks. Thus, higher the ratio lower is the efficiency. As per the international best practices norms, the ratio should be at 40%.[4] So, India has long way to go in order to achieve this standard (Fig. 11.10). However, foreign banks operating in India have reached this standard and hence they are in a competitive advantageous position as against the Indian banks (Table 11.8).

[4]Ghosh et al. (2004), "Strategic Models for Repositioning of Public Sector Banks—Creating Global Winners" Bancon 2004.

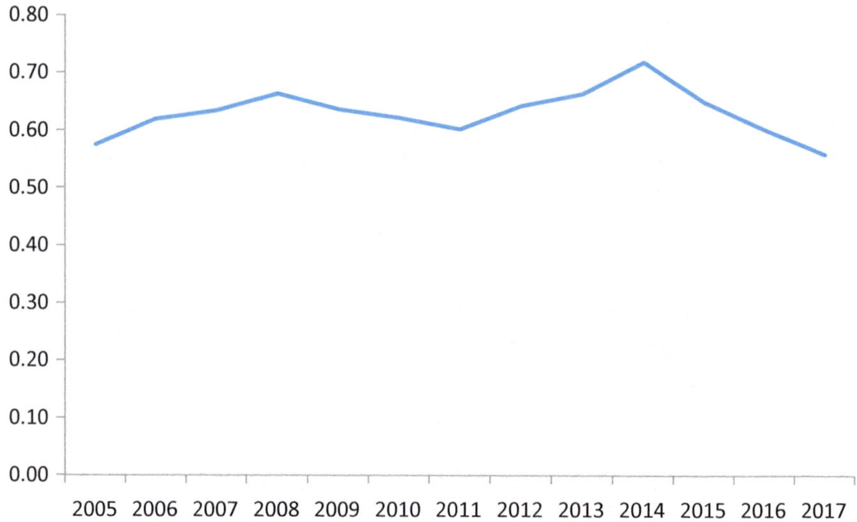

Fig. 11.10 Cost-to-income ratio. *Source* Data-base on Indian Economy, RBI

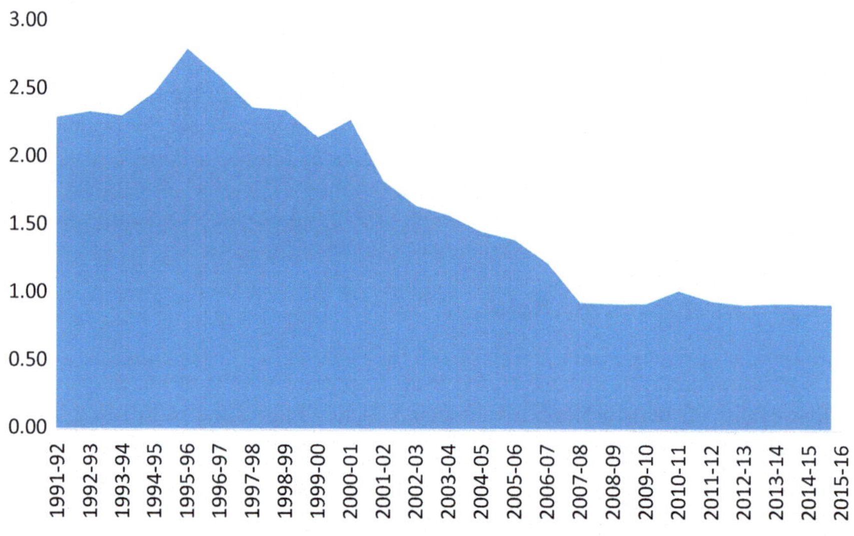

Fig. 11.11 Labour cost per unit of earning assets. *Source* Data-base on Indian Economy, RBI

11.4.4 Labour Cost Per Unit of Earning Assets

Banking industry is human capital dominated industry and also information technology dependent. But they are not perfect substitute of one another. Hence, labour cost is the most important component of operating cost. A bank will be more efficient if it is in a position to generate maximum possible output by using a given number of employees in combination with advanced technology. As can be observed from Fig. 11.11, there has been significant improvement in efficiency during the post-reform period. It has come down drastically from 2.30% in 1991–92 to 0.91% in 2016–17. Although foreign and private sector banks are leading and public sector banks are laggard in this respect, the gap between them is narrowing. Public and foreign banks have been able to reduce labour cost because of their reliance on technology (Table 11.9). On the other hand, public sector banks were able to reduce the same due to rationalisation of workforce by implementation of voluntary retirement scheme.

11.4.5 Non-labour Cost Per Unit of Earning Assets

With the increased dependence on technology to provide efficient services to the varied customers, non-labour costs became an important indicator of profitability and efficiency. As can be seen from the Fig. 11.12, the ratio was high in the early reform period due creation of infrastructure which involved huge costs. However, the ratio started declining from mid-1990s, although it is still high for private and foreign banks (Table 11.10). There are two main reasons for this. First, they spend more for technology upgradation and adoption of new technology as compared with public sector banks. Secondly, since their off-balance sheet exposure is more than the balance sheet exposure and these costs are reflected in the balance sheet, although the earnings from this head is not reflected in the balance sheet. As a result, the ratio becomes very high. Therefore, in a way, it is a biased parameter for them and to an extent it is misleading.

11.4.6 Ratio of Labour Cost to Non-labour Cost

Ratio of labour cost to non-labour cost can be considered as a measurement of labour intensity. Although there is a general trend in reduction of non-labour cost, it is quite interesting to note that there has been a declining trend in the ratio of labour cost to non-labour cost over time. Although it is still very high in public sector banks in comparison to private and foreign banks, it has managed to reduce the labour cost drastically (Table 11.11). This was made possible mainly due to usage of advanced technology and rationalisation of labour force.

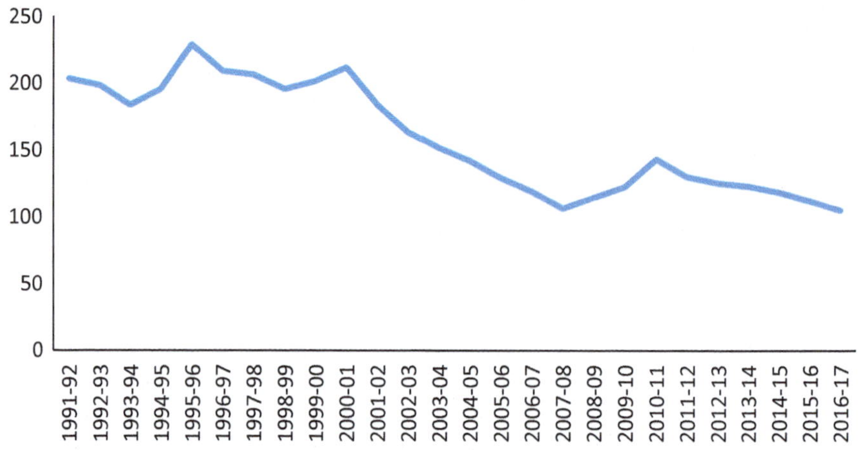

Fig. 11.12 Non-labour cost per unit of earning assets. *Source* Data-base on Indian Economy, RBI

11.4.7 Net Interest Margin

Net interest margin is defined as the difference between total interest earned and total interest expended, normalised by assets. Lower the ratio higher is the efficiency. During 1991–92, the ratio was high at 3.20 and it gradually went down to 2.57 in 2001–02 (Fig. 11.13). Subsequently, it increased marginally due to increase in its economic activity. During the earlier period, NIM was higher mainly due to monopoly market and there was hardly any competition among the banks. However, with the introduction of the reforms and due to competition among the banks, NIM started declining (Table 11.12). Increase in NIM may increase profitability, but we cannot say it is efficient because it increases the cost of intermediation in the economy. Thus, a balanced approach is required with efficiency and profitability in mind. Over the years, decrease in NIM indicates higher efficiency. It can also be stated that due to competition with the new private sector banks and foreign banks in terms of products and service quality rent seeking practice of the banks has gone down. The experience across the world shows that in a competitive environment, NIM tends to decline (Report on Currency and Finance, 2006–08). This is because, banks try to attract depositors by offering higher interest rate and they attract the borrowers by offering attractive (lower) interest rate to expand their business base.

11.4.8 Other Income to Total Income

This ratio indicates off-balance sheet exposure of banks and income from non-traditional sources. This source of income has gained a lot of importance during the recent period with the increase in competition. With the increase in transparency

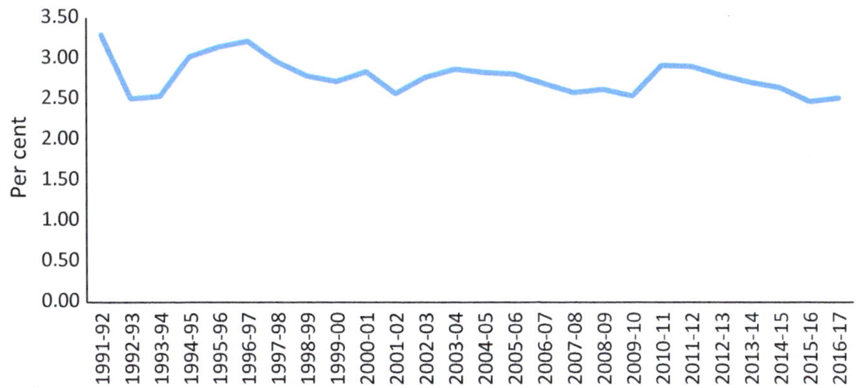

Fig. 11.13 Ratio of NIM to total assets. *Source* Data-base on Indian Economy, RBI

in the money market and improved monetary transmission mechanism, banks facing stiff competition which makes them difficult to set the interest as per their choice. As a result, they are to depend more on non-traditional sources, which is already being followed by the foreign banks and private banks. The share of other income in total income is significantly higher for private and foreign banks than the public-sector banks. This is mainly because the off-balance sheet exposure of the former banks is much higher than the latter banks. In fact, foreign banks' business strategy is entirely different from the domestic banks (Table 11.13). These banks' business is mostly concentrated in the fee-based activities rather than the intermediation activities.

11.4.9 Business Per Employee/Business Per Branch

Business per employee and business per branch are the two most important indicators of labour productivity. Business per employee has increased more than 29 times from 46.66 lakhs in 1991–92 to 1446.47 lakhs in 2016–17 (Fig. 11.14). The rise is observed across all the bank groups. The growth in business per employee is less in the old private banks; the new private sector banks' performance is much higher than public sector banks and almost at par with foreign banks. However, the performance of public sector banks is magnificent since they started with low base (Table 11.14). Further, rationalisation of workforce through VRS during 2000s and outsourcing some jobs by recruiting people on off-role basis has contributed to better performance. Their operations are more broad-based than the foreign and private sector banks. Further, social responsibility performed by these banks is much more than any other types of banks.

However, business per employee is very high in case of foreign banks due to obvious reasons. Most of the foreign banks' business model is entirely different from the domestic banks. First of all, their business is not as broad-based as the public sector

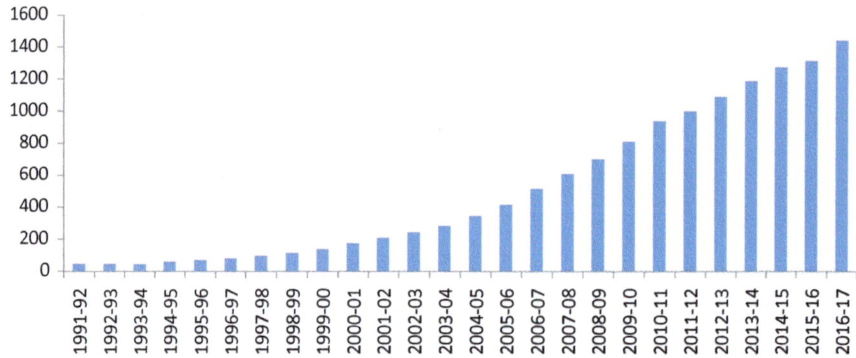

Fig. 11.14 Business per employee of commercial banks. *Source* Data-base on Indian Economy, RBI

banks and they depend less on human resources and more on technology. So, their labour productivity will be much higher. On other hand, public sector banks work in a very complicated situation. On the one hand, they are to compete with the private and foreign banks, and on the other hand, they have their social responsibility in terms of service and employment generation. If there is any shortcoming in recruitment, there will be lot of pressure from the workers' union. Furthermore, if there occurs any lapse in lending they will face huge political pressure. Therefore, even considering all these constraints, public sector banks performed well.

11.4.10 Return on Assets

Return on assets (ROA) is one of the most important indicators of productivity because it indicates how much profit is generated from each unit of asset. Hence, there is a direct positive relationship between ROA and productivity. As per Basel II norms, the ratio should be more than 1%. Although during the early reform period, ROA was very low and even negative during 1992–93 and 1993–94 it exceeded the Basel norm during 2007–8 till 2012–13 (Fig. 11.15). However, the ratio came down drastically in 2013–14 and reached at 0.35 in 2016–17 (Table 11.15). This has happened mainly because of public sector banks whose ROA has become negative in 2015–16 and 2017–18. Foreign and private sector banks have been at a very high level of ROA. In fact, during the recent period, public sector banks have been facing a problem of very high non-performing loans (NPAs), which is crippling the public sector banks.

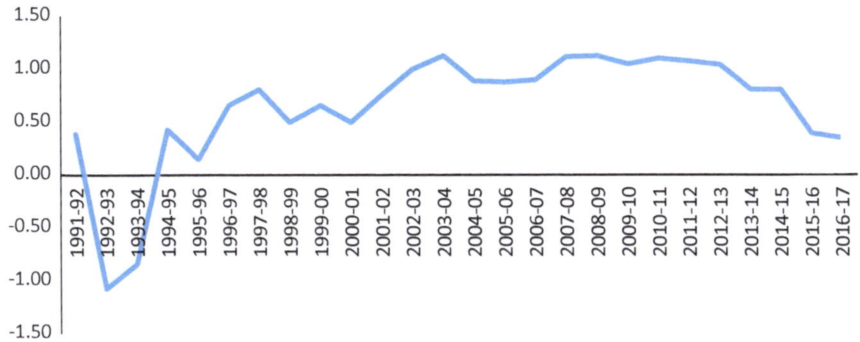

Fig. 11.15 Return on assets. *Source* Data-base on Indian Economy, RBI

11.4.11 Return on Equity

The Return on Equity (ROE) is defined by the amount of profits a business unit is generating per unit of equity. This is mostly used by the investors to take investment decisions. Higher the value higher is the profitability and hence increase in productivity. As can be observed from Fig. 11.16, the trend in ROE is almost similar with the ROA. In case of public sector banks, ROE is negative in the recent period (Table 11.16). This is mainly due to loss incurred by the Indian PSBs during the recent past. The cumulative loss of public sector banks crossed Rs. 87,357 crores in 2017–18. Out of 21 public sector banks, only two banks—Indian Bank and Vijaya Bank—posted profits during the year. Some banks are also reeling under various scams which has dented their earnings. Weak financials due to bad debt pushed 11 PSBs out of 21, under Prompt Corrective Action (PCA) framework of the Reserve Bank of India. However, performance of the private and foreign sector banks is much better than the PSBs as the ROE of private and foreign sector banks is much higher than the PSBs.

11.4.12 Soundness of the Banking Sector

With the increase in competition among the banks and interlinkage with the other financial institutions, banks are exposed to various kinds of risks. Global financial crisis in 2008 became more serious due to contagion effect. Therefore, there is a need for risk mitigation mechanism in the banking sector. The regulator, Reserve Bank of India, is constantly monitoring the soundness indicators and tries to ensure that the banks have systems and procedure in place as per the norms set by RBI following the Basel norms and adequately capitalised to withstand any unanticipated risks either due to own operations or any disruptive market movements. Because of market risks increased due to market integration, Reserve Bank monitors the bank not only at the individual level, but also at the systemic level. It brings out Financial Stability

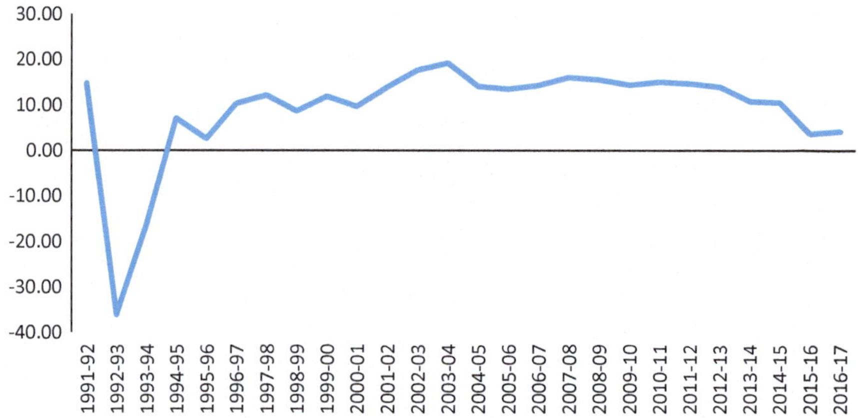

Fig. 11.16 Return on equity. *Source* Data-base on Indian Economy, RBI

Report giving the details of risks in the financial system and also performs the stress tests in order to examine the financial conditions and communicate to the market. Further, the factors such as deregulation, market fluctuations, foreign exchange rate fluctuations and interest rate volatility have given the birth of various derivative instruments like swaps, option, futures, foreign exchange forward as also granting of standby commitments and letter of credit, collectively known as off-balance sheet items. Dr. Raghuram Rajan, Former Governor of the Reserve Bank stated before the crisis, "… the financial market had developed to become more complicated and less safe. He said financial instruments such as derivatives like credit default swaps were risky."[5] Thus, there are inherent risks involved in the derivative products. Under this milieu, it is important to examine the soundness indicators of banks, which is discussed in terms of capital to risk-weighted assets (CRAR) and quality of assets in terms of non-performing assets (NPAs).

11.4.13 Capital to Risk-Weighted Assets (CRAR)

Capital adequacy ratio is one of the most important indicators of soundness. It is defined as the banks available capital expressed as percentage of risk-weighted credit exposure. Higher the ratio greater is the capacity of the bank to absorb unexpected losses. It is a kind of mechanism to protect the depositors' money. The CRAR of all the banks in India has improved over the years. Although it was very low during the initial stages of the reform period, it started improving gradually (Fig. 11.17). From 1999 onwards, it has maintained the minimum stipulated level of 8–9%.[6]

[5]See "When Raghuram Rajan proved giant Alan Greenspan wrong", Economic Times, 15 September 2018.

[6]It was 9% from 31 March 2000.

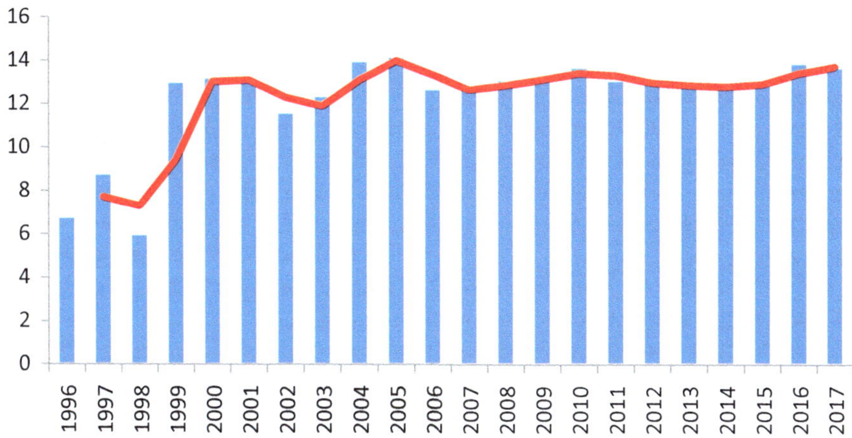

Fig. 11.17 CRAR of commercial banks. *Source* Data-base on Indian Economy, RBI

After the global financial crisis, Basel Committee on Banking Supervision (BCBS) has come out with some other parameters in addition to maintenance of CRAR. These are leverage ratio, liquidity coverage ratio, Net Stable Funding Ratio. "Leverage Ratio defined as the ratio of Tier I capital to total exposure (including on-balance sheet exposures, derivative exposures, securities financing transaction exposures and off-balance sheet items)".[7] This was introduced in India from 1st April 2015. The Reserve Bank set the ratio at 4.5% for the individual bank. The basic idea of introducing this ratio is to restrict the banks from building up leverage to avoid destabilising deleveraging.

Further, Liquidity Coverage Ratio was introduced by the Reserve Bank on 1 January 2015, following Basel III norms. The basic objective of LCR is to promote banks' short-term resilience to potential liquidity shocks. It requires that the banks to have adequate stock of unencumbered high-quality liquid assets (HQLAs) so that they can withstand a 30-calendar day liquidity shock under severe liquidity stress scenario. LCR is more sophisticated tool than the statutory liquidity ratio (SLR) for liquidity risk management (Report on Trend and Progress of banking in India 2016–17).

While LCR is a short-term tool for liquidity risk management, net stable funding ratio (NSFR) is a long-term one as stipulated by the Basel III norms. This norm ensures that the banks are resilient over longer time horizon to fund their activities from a stable source on an ongoing basis. NSFR is defined as "the ratio of available stable funding relative to the amount of required stable funding".[8] However, this is not yet implemented so far in India.

---

[7]Report of Trend and Progress of Banking in India—(2016–17), Reserve Bank of India.

[8]Report of Trend and Progress of Banking in India—(2016–17), Reserve Bank of India.

11.4.14 Non-performing Assets

Quality of asset of a bank is directly related to its performance. If the asset quality is very poor, it has to go for provisioning and write-off, which will have direct impact on its profitability and ultimately erode the capital position. Therefore, mere holding sound capital position is not important, but maintaining high-quality assets is most important. The non-performing assets in India have gone down significantly over the years, although the trend has changed during the recent past. For the banking system, as a whole, gross NPA came down to 2.3% of gross advances in 2003–4 (Fig. 11.18). This was possible mainly due to the public sector banks which were contributing more to the NPA. Otherwise, private and foreign banks maintained their NPA reasonably at a lower level due to their better monitoring mechanism (Table 11.17). Public sector banks were in position to reduce their NPA during that period due to strengthening of income recognition, asset classification and provisioning norms periodically. This apart, several institutional measures such as balance sheet cleansing through compromise settlements, corporate debt restructuring, setting up of debt recovery tribunals enforcement security interest for realising the dues, have helped them improve their asset position. However, the quality of the assets for the public sector banks started deteriorating from 2011 to 12 and gross NPA went up to double-digit level in 2017 due to various reasons. The most important cause which can be held responsible for high NPA growth is the rapid credit growth flowing to a particular "asset class" and specific sectors during good time which turned into bad loans later, bank failures in different forms, write offs, large equity dilutions, bail outs and bankruptcies. Moreover, various types of corruption revealed during the recent period led to the high NPA. As of March 2017, around 56% of the total advances were accounted for by the large borrowers with exposure of Rs. 50 million and more and they accounted for about 87% of all NPAs (Report on Trend and Progess of Banking in India, 2016–17). As per Report on Trend and Progress, more than three-fourths (76.3% of total NPA) of the stressed assets are concentrated in the non-priority sector as of end-March 2017. The industries which had high stressed assets are basic metals and products, vehicle and transport equipment, cement, construction, textiles and engineering. Infrastructure—mainly power and telecommunications—is also badly affected.

11.5 Summary and Conclusion

After the BOP crisis in India in 1991, Indian government brought out several measures in various sectors including banking in order to transform the economy and align with the globalised world. Measures in banking were taken to make it competitive, efficient and sound. Reform is now more than two decades old, and it is useful to assess the performance of this sector. Developments in respect of various parameters like growth, technology, productivity, efficiency and soundness have been dealt with

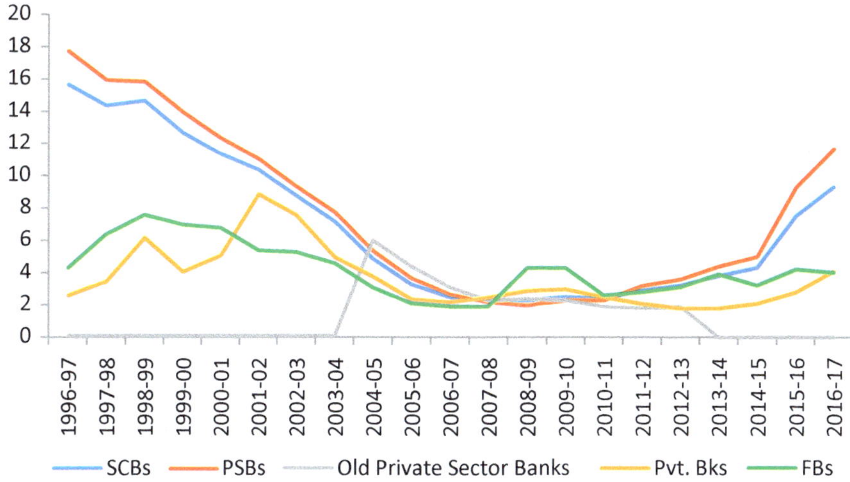

Fig. 11.18 Bank-group-wise gross NPAs as percentage of gross advances. *Source* Data-base on Indian Economy, RBI

for all the sectors of banks, viz. public, private and foreign banks. Our discussion is, however, based only on accounting approach, i.e. ratio analysis.

It is observed that the reforms enabled the Indian banking sector to transform itself from a traditional banking system to modern one. Its operations are no more concentrated within the intermediation activity. It has transformed itself into a modern banking system. It is now following the best international standard as set by the Basel norms. As a result, various efficiency/productivity and soundness parameters of the banking system in India have moved towards global level. Significant achievement was observed in the case of public sector banks without damaging the social responsibility. Rather it has increased its base in respect of social banking. It is now competing with the new private sector and foreign banks, which operate in a relatively free environment unlike the public-sector banks.

The analysis of various accounting measures suggests that there has been a significant improvement in the efficiency and productivity of the banking sector in the post-reform period. However, the degree of performance varies across the bank groups. During the early reform period, the performance of the public-sector banks worsened due to new environment. But with the passage of time, the PSBs started accepting new challenges and almost reached the global standard in respect of many parameters. Although the intermediation cost and net interest margin declined over time, the banking sector managed to make profit. This is not because of mark-up pricing, but due to increase in efficiency and productivity. This reflects competition across banks with innovation of products with new technology and ideas which enabled them to garner profits. Reform process has replaced the narrow banking system by the modern banking system. Due to increase in productivity, business per employee and business per branch have improved also. This has led to improvement in return on assets and return on equity during the post-reform period.

However, in respect of various parameters private and foreign banks are much ahead of the public sector banks. For example, in respect of cost to income ratio, labour productivity, etc., private and foreign banks have performed much better than the public sector banks. However, it needs to be mentioned that the responsibility of public sector banks can never be compared with the private and foreign banks. This is because there are lot of bindings on the part of the public sector banks like social banking, which is almost absent in case of private and foreign banks. Lot of targets are set for these banks which are time bound and banks are accountable if there is any lapse on this. These apart, there are lot of political pressure, labour union pressure which come in the way of their productivity and efficiency.

Because of various factors stated above, public sector banks are lagging in respect of soundness parameters. All the banks showed significant achievement in the capital to risk-weighted assets during the post-reform period. However, the situation started aggravating from 2008 to 09, especially for the public sector banks. NPA of the public sector banks started increasing gradually from 2008 to 09 and reached at the double-digit level in 2017. Reserve Bank has taken various steps to address this issue, and it is hoped that the problem will be resolved soon.

In a nutshell, it may be stated that during the post-reform period the banking system in India has transformed itself from traditional banking system to a modern sophisticated one. It has placed itself into a global standard in many aspects, including new product, service quality and improved payment and settlement system. However, at the same time lot of challenges are also there which need special attention by the authority.

Annexure

See Annex Tables 11.6, 11.7, 11.8, 11.9, 11.10, 11.11, 11.12, 11.13, 11.14, 11.15, 11.16 and 11.17.

Table 11.6 Intermediation cost of commercial banks in India

Year	Public sector banks			Private sector banks	Foreign banks	All commercial banks
	State bank group	Nationalised banks	PSBs			
1991–92	5.92	5.66	5.77	6.13	13.28	6.24
1992–93	4.05	4.26	4.22	5.54	12.81	4.82
1993–94	4.85	4.84	4.85	5.78	9.25	5.22
1994–95	3.54	4.17	3.95	5.06	7.30	4.27
1995–96	4.69	5.58	5.26	5.31	7.03	5.43
1996–97	5.83	6.18	6.06	6.62	7.45	6.28
1997–98	3.68	4.58	4.26	5.17	6.89	4.61
1998–99	3.49	4.23	3.96	4.03	6.32	4.19
1999–00	2.69	3.88	3.45	3.68	4.88	3.59
2000–01	3.09	3.86	3.58	3.48	5.81	3.74
2001–02	2.15	3.14	2.79	4.15	5.12	3.12
2002–03	1.79	3.33	2.78	4.07	5.22	3.17
2003–04	1.82	3.36	2.82	4.18	4.72	3.18
2004–05	2.28	2.28	2.28	2.18	3.05	2.87
2005–06	2.39	2.07	2.18	2.41	3.32	2.30
2006–07	2.13	1.84	1.94	2.33	3.27	2.12
2007–08	1.87	1.63	1.71	2.40	3.24	1.99
2008–09	1.75	1.58	1.64	2.21	3.04	1.87
2009–10	1.88	1.48	1.61	2.10	2.52	1.78
2010–11	1.94	1.60	1.70	2.17	2.71	1.86
2011–12	1.94	1.44	1.59	2.20	2.47	1.77
2012–13	1.94	1.41	1.57	2.20	2.33	1.75
2013–14	2.06	1.43	1.62	2.19	2.21	1.77
2014–15	2.00	1.44	1.60	2.23	2.17	1.80
2015–16	1.87	1.52	1.63	2.22	2.07	1.79
2016–17	1.85	1.54	1.64	2.25	2.06	1.82

Source Report on Currency and Finance, RBI, 2009 and Statistical Tables Relating to Banks in India (various issues), RBI

Intermediation cost = Operating expenses/Average of Total Assets

Average of total assets = Average of current year asset and previous year assets

Table 11.7 Operating cost to total assets of commercial banks in India (Per cent)

Year	Public sector banks			Private sector banks	Foreign banks	All commercial banks
	State bank group	Nationalised banks	PSBs			
1991–92	2.48	2.67	2.60	2.97	2.26	2.59
1992–93	2.64	2.67	2.64	2.71	2.70	2.65
1993–94	2.68	2.64	2.65	2.49	2.65	2.64
1994–95	2.95	2.76	2.83	2.35	2.72	2.79
1995–96	3.09	2.93	2.99	2.47	2.77	2.93
1996–97	2.94	2.85	2.88	2.36	3.04	2.85
1997–98	2.68	2.65	2.66	2.14	2.98	2.63
1998–99	2.70	2.63	2.65	2.04	3.39	2.65
1999–00	2.46	2.58	2.52	1.85	3.11	2.48
2000–01	2.66	2.76	2.72	1.87	3.05	2.64
2001–02	2.11	2.40	2.29	1.45	3.00	2.19
2002–03	2.11	2.33	2.25	1.99	2.78	2.24
2003–04	2.21	2.21	2.21	2.02	2.75	2.21
2004–05	2.14	2.06	2.09	2.03	2.88	2.13
2005–06	2.28	1.93	2.05	2.11	2.94	2.13
2006–07	1.98	1.67	1.77	2.06	2.78	1.91
2007–08	1.68	1.48	1.54	2.16	2.84	1.79
2008–09	1.57	1.42	1.47	2.12	2.76	1.71
2009–10	1.79	1.35	1.49	1.99	2.55	1.66
2010–11	1.82	1.46	1.57	1.97	2.56	1.71
2011–12	1.85	1.35	1.49	2.01	2.27	1.65
2012–13	1.80	1.32	1.46	2.03	2.24	1.63
2013–14	1.95	1.33	1.51	2.06	2.05	1.66
2014–15	1.84	1.39	1.53	2.08	2.16	1.68
2015–16	1.76	1.51	1.59	2.02	1.99	1.72
2016–17	1.75	1.51	1.59	2.11	2.04	1.75

Source Report on Currency and Finance, RBI, 2009 and Statistical Tables Relating to Banks in India (various issues), RBI

Table 11.8 Total cost-to-total income ratio of commercial banks in India (per cent)

Year	Public sector banks			Private sector banks	Foreign banks	All commercial banks
	State bank group	Nationalised banks	PSBs			
1991–92	47.44	67.51	58.41	58.96	30.91	55.30
1992–93	59.19	86.35	73.72	66.75	59.15	71.80
1993–94	64.84	79.09	73.08	57.33	41.22	68.10
1994–95	60.43	72.65	67.57	52.21	40.34	63.51
1995–96	59.53	71.98	66.66	51.53	45.36	63.25
1996–97	57.37	69.33	64.31	51.31	45.54	61.00
1997–98	56.85	66.61	62.72	48.47	43.04	58.88
1998–99	62.41	68.29	65.94	58.96	56.61	64.26
1999–00	58.64	66.25	63.23	48.62	48.35	59.86
2000–01	65.15	68.22	67.01	51.75	49.90	63.37
2001–02	52.11	56.65	54.93	45.61	48.76	53.01
2002–03	48.16	49.97	49.30	45.05	46.35	48.34
2003–04	45.76	45.03	45.30	47.13	42.92	45.38
2004–05	46.74	50.16	48.87	53.03	49.13	49.56
2005–06	51.19	52.69	52.11	55.19	46.79	52.11
2006–07	52.80	49.36	50.58	52.17	44.64	50.15
2007–08	68.53	70.58	69.89	67.10	38.63	66.26
2008–09	66.82	69.61	68.68	63.55	27.71	63.54
2009–10	67.99	67.62	67.75	56.18	23.33	62.07
2010–11	58.20	64.52	62.55	59.22	36.95	60.10
2011–12	60.19	68.18	65.77	65.63	40.89	64.17
2012–13	66.31	69.34	68.43	65.19	45.25	66.25
2013–14	67.48	68.44	68.15	62.26	40.37	66.58
2014–15	64.56	69.75	68.16	60.76	42.22	64.82
2015–16	61.40	63.37	62.74	57.38	41.06	60.09
2016–17	54.81	60.39	58.51	52.88	40.08	55.81

Source Report on Currency and Finance, RBI, 2009 and Statistical Tables Relating to Banks in India (various issues), RBI

Table 11.9 Labour cost per unit of earning assets of commercial banks in India (Per cent)

Year	Public sector banks			Private sector banks	Foreign banks	All commercial banks
	State bank group	Nationalised banks	PSBs			
1991–92	2.41	2.34	2.36	2.86	1.08	2.30
1992–93	2.51	2.40	2.44	2.59	0.96	2.34
1993–94	2.51	2.38	2.43	2.22	1.10	2.31
1994–95	2.86	2.48	2.61	2.05	1.23	2.48
1995–96	3.22	2.89	3.01	1.91	1.37	2.80
1996–97	3.01	2.73	2.83	1.56	1.45	2.60
1997–98	2.75	2.51	2.59	1.38	1.31	2.37
1998–99	2.70	2.52	2.58	1.30	1.37	2.35
1999–00	2.37	2.40	2.39	1.17	1.31	2.15
2000–01	2.55	2.62	2.59	0.99	1.24	2.28
2001–02	1.93	2.11	2.04	0.93	1.33	1.83
2002–03	1.80	1.91	1.87	0.86	1.10	1.65
2003–04	1.78	1.80	1.79	0.84	1.17	1.58
2004–05	1.66	1.62	1.63	0.81	1.15	1.46
2005–06	1.79	1.46	1.57	0.83	1.34	1.40
2006–07	1.51	1.23	1.32	0.84	1.56	1.23
2007–08	1.03	0.93	0.96	0.77	1.16	0.94
2008–09	0.97	0.91	0.93	0.84	1.11	0.93
2009–10	1.12	0.85	0.94	0.83	1.09	0.93
2010–11	1.21	0.98	1.05	0.90	1.11	1.02
2011–12	1.21	0.86	0.96	0.89	0.99	0.95
2012–13	1.14	0.84	0.93	0.88	0.95	0.92
2013–14	1.25	0.84	0.96	0.87	0.84	0.93
2014–15	1.15	0.86	0.94	0.87	0.93	0.93
2015–16	1.06	0.91	0.96	0.83	0.85	0.92
2016–17	1.04	0.90	0.95	0.84	0.83	0.91

Source Report on Currency and Finance, RBI, 2009 and Statistical Tables Relating to Banks in India (various issues), RBI

Table 11.10 Non-labour cost per unit of earning assets of commercial banks in India (per cent)

Year	Public sector banks			Private sector banks	Foreign banks	All commercial banks
	State bank group	Nationalised banks	PSBs			
1991–92	1.02	1.05	1.04	1.17	2.18	1.12
1992–93	0.98	1.05	1.03	1.10	2.89	1.17
1993–94	1.23	1.12	1.16	1.11	2.36	1.25
1994–95	1.09	1.21	1.17	1.05	2.53	1.26
1995–96	1.09	1.07	1.08	1.38	2.53	1.22
1996–97	1.14	1.03	1.07	1.47	2.67	1.24
1997–98	0.92	0.97	0.95	1.41	2.77	1.14
1998–99	1.09	0.91	0.98	1.36	3.27	1.20
1999–00	0.94	0.86	0.89	1.21	2.63	1.06
2000–01	0.94	0.83	0.87	1.36	2.69	1.07
2001–02	0.78	0.79	0.79	1.26	2.68	0.99
2002–03	0.73	0.79	0.77	1.54	2.38	1.00
2003–04	0.80	0.78	0.79	1.58	2.50	1.04
2004–05	0.80	0.75	0.77	1.58	2.58	1.02
2005–06	0.85	0.77	0.80	1.61	2.57	1.08
2006–07	0.79	0.70	0.73	1.60	2.36	1.03
2007–08	0.67	0.57	0.60	1.42	1.72	0.88
2008–09	0.61	0.54	0.56	1.31	1.69	0.81
2009–10	0.69	0.51	0.57	1.19	1.49	0.75
2010–11	0.63	0.49	0.53	1.11	1.48	0.71
2011–12	0.66	0.50	0.55	1.16	1.30	0.72
2012–13	0.68	0.49	0.55	1.19	1.31	0.73
2013–14	0.72	0.51	0.57	1.22	1.22	0.75
2014–15	0.71	0.55	0.60	1.24	1.25	0.78
2015–16	0.72	0.62	0.65	1.22	1.15	0.82
2016–17	0.75	0.64	0.67	1.29	1.22	0.87

Source Report on Currency and Finance, RBI, 2009 and Statistical Tables Relating to Banks in India (various issues), RBI

Table 11.11 Ratio of labour cost to non-labour cost of commercial banks in India (Per cent)

Year	Public sector banks			Private sector banks	Foreign banks	All commercial banks
	State bank group	Nationalised banks	PSBs			
1991–92	236.24	221.98	227.08	245.12	49.36	204.72
1992–93	257.00	227.60	237.99	235.20	33.23	199.59
1993–94	203.81	213.47	209.79	199.84	46.79	184.95
1994–95	262.2	204.24	223.47	194.83	48.68	196.74
1995–96	294.18	269.41	278.48	138.37	54.35	230.20
1996–97	264.38	264.02	264.16	106.44	54.52	210.34
1997–98	299.84	258.05	272.09	98.11	47.20	207.60
1998–99	246.80	276.16	264.51	95.60	41.81	196.81
1999–00	251.97	278.45	268.24	96.72	49.61	202.81
2000–01	270.32	317.40	298.02	72.71	46.28	212.80
2001–02	247.87	266.69	259.7	73.81	49.63	184.85
2002–03	245.97	241.73	243.25	56.03	46.21	164.28
2003–04	221.91	231.26	227.72	53.19	46.70	152.33
2004–05	207.03	215.01	212.07	51.34	44.72	142.73
2005–06	209.33	189.16	196.54	51.20	52.10	129.99
2006–07	189.80	174.46	179.94	52.52	66.12	119.90
2007–08	153.68	162.47	159.20	54.09	67.72	107.04
2008–09	158.98	168.65	165.07	64.33	65.87	115.30
2009–10	162.52	166.11	164.73	70.23	73.57	123.38
2010–11	193.26	197.96	196.30	80.53	75.40	144.04
2011–12	183.58	171.23	175.58	76.58	76.10	130.92
2012–13	168.86	171.45	170.50	73.42	72.67	126.09
2013–14	171.95	163.26	166.45	70.95	69.27	123.77
2014–15	161.14	155.78	157.70	70.27	74.45	119.24
2015–16	148.18	147.28	147.60	68.32	73.85	112.79
2016–17	139.32	140.67	140.16	64.88	68.05	105.57

Source Report on Currency and Finance, RBI, 2009 and Statistical Tables Relating to Banks in India (various issues), RBI

Table 11.12 Ratio of NIM to total assets of commercial banks in India

Year	Public sector banks			Private sector banks	Foreign banks	All commercial banks
	State bank group	Nationalised banks	PSBs			
1991–92	3.80	2.86	3.22	4.01	3.90	3.30
1992–93	3.01	2.02	2.39	2.92	3.57	2.51
1993–94	2.68	2.17	2.36	3.01	4.20	2.54
1994–95	3.27	2.73	2.92	3.07	4.27	3.03
1995–96	3.34	2.95	3.10	3.10	3.75	3.15
1996–97	3.48	2.97	3.16	2.95	4.13	3.22
1997–98	3.14	2.78	2.91	2.46	3.98	2.96
1998–99	2.85	2.78	2.81	2.11	3.52	2.79
1999–00	2.76	2.67	2.70	2.13	3.85	2.72
2000–01	2.76	2.90	2.84	2.33	3.64	2.84
2001–02	2.71	2.74	2.73	1.58	3.25	2.57
2002–03	2.77	2.99	2.91	1.96	3.36	2.77
2003–04	2.83	3.06	2.98	2.21	3.57	2.87
2004–05	3.06	2.82	2.91	2.34	3.34	2.83
2005–06	3.07	2.73	2.85	2.40	3.58	2.81
2006–07	2.79	2.58	2.65	2.45	3.74	2.69
2007–08	2.49	2.28	2.35	2.67	4.33	2.58
2008–09	2.39	2.32	2.35	2.86	4.33	2.62
2009–10	2.36	2.26	2.29	2.90	3.96	2.54
2010–11	2.84	2.74	2.77	3.10	3.86	2.91
2011–12	3.25	2.55	2.76	3.09	3.89	2.90
2012–13	2.98	2.39	2.57	3.22	3.83	2.79
2013–14	2.87	2.28	2.45	3.31	3.54	2.70
2014–15	2.81	2.15	2.35	3.37	3.54	2.64
2015–16	2.60	2.06	2.23	3.41	3.59	2.47
2016–17	2.39	1.99	2.12	3.38	3.38	2.51

Source Report on Currency and Finance, RBI, 2009 and Statistical Tables Relating to Banks in India (various issues), RBI

Table 11.13 Share of other income to total income of commercial banks in India (Per cent)

Year	Public sector banks			Private sector banks	Foreign banks	All commercial banks
	State bank group	Nationalised banks	PSBs			
1991–92	12.31	9.73	10.74	9.62	22.72	11.82
1992–93	12.87	9.88	11.04	10.76	7.88	10.73
1993–94	14.44	11.88	12.83	12.88	18.20	13.34
1994–95	15.40	11.17	12.77	13.85	19.80	13.48
1995–96	16.79	10.85	13.13	14.46	18.31	13.72
1996–97	14.41	10.54	12.01	13.40	18.64	12.79
1997–98	14.72	11.60	12.75	16.59	21.98	14.08
1998–99	14.39	10.44	11.91	12.25	19.35	12.67
1999–00	14.19	11.62	12.59	16.15	20.72	13.75
2000–01	13.60	11.16	12.09	12.65	20.93	12.95
2001–02	13.44	14.50	14.10	20.51	25.20	15.93
2002–03	16.37	16.68	16.56	22.88	25.43	18.34
2003–04	21.05	19.97	20.36	22.88	29.76	21.49
2004–05	17.71	16.17	16.74	19.51	29.65	18.10
2005–06	16.19	12.26	13.71	18.68	30.41	16.02
2006–07	12.16	10.47	11.04	17.86	27.80	14.09
2007–08	14.37	12.82	13.34	19.33	30.25	16.37
2008–09	15.27	12.55	13.46	17.35	32.94	16.22
2009–10	15.81	12.79	13.78	19.78	27.38	16.03
2010–11	14.91	10.08	11.58	17.75	27.87	13.98
2011–12	11.04	8.72	9.42	15.69	23.24	11.64
2012–13	10.76	8.65	9.28	15.18	21.00	11.35
2013–14	10.98	8.87	9.50	15.79	22.76	11.77
2014–15	12.02	9.19	10.06	16.35	22.88	12.34
2015–16	13.46	9.25	10.60	16.68	19.33	12.69
2016–17	16.03	13.47	14.33	18.52	23.52	16.04

Source Report on Currency and Finance, RBI, 2009 and Statistical Tables Relating to Banks in India (various issues), RBI

Table 11.14 Business per employee of commercial banks in India (Rs. Lakhs)

Year	Public sector banks			Private sector banks	Foreign banks	All commercial banks
	State bank group	Nationalised banks	PSBs			
1991–92	42.99	46.37	45.15	33.48	199.47	49.66
1992–93	47.28	48.24	47.91	43.49	233.66	50.32
1993–94	49.65	41.69	44.10	55.26	287.39	47.57
1994–95	56.58	60.10	58.87	73.68	326.96	63.40
1995–96	65.65	67.52	66.86	99.74	393.63	73.42
1996–97	72.51	76.86	75.30	129.76	448.24	84.09
1997–98	84.43	91.91	89.20	165.91	480.99	100.04
1998–99	102.45	107.67	105.78	193.95	504.81	117.72
1999–00	122.11	126.18	124.71	255.23	627.00	140.92
2000–01	158.83	160.18	159.69	296.39	720.19	179.43
2001–02	181.54	197.59	191.57	333.86	773.40	213.97
2002–03	205.09	221.05	215.09	445.68	909.68	247.02
2003–04	232.90	255.74	247.22	527.85	952.50	286.90
2004–05	284.04	318.92	305.96	578.65	966.11	348.27
2005–06	337.79	383.07	366.61	670.67	955.41	419.77
2006–07	435.52	490.21	470.99	694.07	995.09	521.94
2007–08	506.86	574.95	551.25	700.45	1059.86	612.66
2008–09	586.78	705.86	662.14	689.58	1257.87	705.07
2009–10	669.48	840.14	778.63	746.30	1433.31	814.33
2010–11	722.20	1006.16	899.60	886.24	1586.32	942.54
2011–12	834.56	1107.02	1008.56	776.74	1923.41	1003.41
2012–13	922.94	1219.60	1109.85	834.46	2141.24	1094.91
2013–14	1044.94	1305.97	1214.05	883.09	2576.37	1190.98
2014–15	1172.36	1344.61	1286.90	984.22	2826.17	1277.02
2015–16	1311.84	1374.70	1353.84	983.54	3211.75	1319.73
2016–17	1485.35	1467.52	1473.34	1135.54	3164.75	1446.47

Source Report on Currency and Finance, RBI, 2009 and Statistical Tables Relating to Banks in India (various issues), RBI

Table 11.15 Return on assets of commercial banks in India

Year	Public sector banks			Private sector banks	Foreign banks	All commercial banks
	State bank group	Nationalised banks	PSBs			
1991–92	0.21	0.33	0.28	0.57	1.56	0.39
1992–93	0.22	−1.71	−0.99	0.34	−2.70	−1.07
1993–94	0.25	−1.98	−1.15	0.58	1.72	−0.84
1994–95	0.54	0.10	0.25	1.16	1.87	0.43
1995–96	0.42	−0.36	−0.07	1.20	1.59	0.15
1996–97	0.82	0.41	0.56	1.15	1.20	0.66
1997–98	1.04	0.62	0.77	1.04	0.97	0.81
1998–99	0.51	0.37	0.42	0.67	1.01	0.50
1999–00	0.80	0.44	0.57	0.90	1.24	0.66
2000–01	0.55	0.33	0.42	0.71	1.00	0.50
2001–02	0.77	0.69	0.72	0.66	1.35	0.76
2002–03	0.91	0.98	0.96	0.99	1.59	1.00
2003–04	1.02	1.19	1.12	0.95	1.64	1.13
2004–05	0.91	0.85	0.87	0.83	1.29	0.89
2005–06	0.86	0.80	0.82	0.87	1.54	0.88
2006–07	0.82	0.83	0.83	0.87	1.65	0.90
2007–08	0.97	1.01	1.00	1.13	2.09	1.12
2008–09	1.02	1.03	1.03	1.13	1.99	1.13
2009–10	0.91	1.00	0.97	1.28	1.26	1.05
2010–11	0.79	1.03	0.96	1.43	1.75	1.10
2011–12	0.89	0.88	0.88	1.53	1.76	1.08
2012–13	0.93	0.74	0.80	1.63	1.92	1.04
2013–14	0.63	0.45	0.50	1.65	1.54	0.81
2014–15	0.66	0.37	0.46	1.68	1.84	0.81
2015–16	0.42	−0.30	−0.07	1.50	1.45	0.40
2016–17	−0.02	−0.14	−0.10	1.30	1.61	0.35

Source Report on Currency and Finance, RBI, 2009 and Statistical Tables Relating to Banks in India (various issues), RBI

Table 11.16 Return of equity of commercial banks in India

Year	Public sector banks			Private sector banks	Foreign banks	All commercial banks
	State bank group	Nationalised banks	PSBs			
1991–92	12.72	10.45	11.02	26.77	42.26	14.77
1992–93	12.55	−52.44	−36.41	13.62	−47.00	−36.10
1993–94	7.44	−33.14	−22.91	19.04	24.44	−16.55
1994–95	15.23	1.31	4.28	29.76	19.73	7.07
1995–96	11.21	−5.46	−1.31	16.12	15.23	2.53
1996–97	17.02	6.16	9.37	16.88	10.73	10.25
1997–98	20.04	8.93	12.21	15.88	8.58	12.07
1998–99	11.10	6.26	7.78	11.70	10.96	8.59
1999–00	17.25	7.98	11.10	14.73	12.97	11.83
2000–01	12.77	6.44	8.65	13.09	11.53	9.61
2001–02	17.20	12.98	14.45	10.99	14.61	13.81
2002–03	19.50	18.34	18.75	15.86	14.15	17.59
2003–04	20.25	21.22	20.88	15.46	15.30	19.13
2004–05	17.32	14.55	15.46	11.50	10.51	14.02
2005–06	15.82	13.68	14.38	11.38	12.62	13.43
2006–07	15.30	14.65	14.86	12.81	13.86	14.24
2007–08	17.21	17.09	17.13	13.43	16.05	15.98
2008–09	17.74	18.05	17.94	11.38	13.75	15.44
2009–10	15.92	18.30	17.47	11.94	7.34	14.31
2010–11	14.11	18.19	16.90	13.70	10.28	14.96
2011–12	16.00	15.05	15.33	15.25	10.79	14.60
2012–13	15.29	12.34	13.24	16.46	11.53	13.84
2013–14	10.03	7.78	8.48	16.22	9.03	10.69
2014–15	10.56	6.44	7.76	15.74	10.24	10.42
2015–16	6.78	−8.51	−3.47	13.81	8.00	3.58
2016–17	−0.69	−2.81	−2.05	11.87	9.12	4.16

Source Report on Currency and Finance, RBI, 2009 and Statistical Tables Relating to Banks in India (various issues), RBI

Table 11.17 Gross NPA of scheduled commercial banks (bank-group-wise)

	Sch. commercial banks		Public sector banks		Old private sector banks		New private sector banks		Foreign banks In India	
	As percentage of gross advances	As percentage of total assets	As percentage of gross advances	As percentage of total assets	As percentage of gross advances	As percentage of total assets	As percentage of gross advances	As percentage of total assets	As percentage of gross advances	As percentage of total assets
1996–97	15.7	7.0	17.8	7.8	0.1	0.1	2.6	1.3	4.3	2.1
1997–98	14.4	6.4	16.0	7.0	0.1	0.1	3.5	1.5	6.4	3.0
1998–99	14.7	6.2	15.9	6.7	0.1	0.1	6.2	2.3	7.6	3.1
1999–00	12.7	5.5	14.0	6.0	0.1	0.1	4.1	1.6	7.0	3.2
2000–01	11.4	4.9	12.4	5.3	0.1	0.1	5.1	2.1	6.8	3.0
2001–02	10.4	4.6	11.1	4.9	0.1	0.1	8.9	3.9	5.4	2.4
2002–03	8.8	4.1	9.4	4.2	0.1	0.0	7.6	3.8	5.3	2.4
2003–04	7.2	3.3	7.8	3.5	0.1	0.0	5.0	2.4	4.6	2.1
2004–05	4.9	2.4	5.4	2.6	6.0	3.1	3.8	2.0	3.1	1.5
2005–06	3.3	1.9	3.7	2.1	4.4	2.5	2.4	1.3	2.1	1.0
2006–07	2.5	1.5	2.7	1.6	3.1	1.8	2.2	1.2	1.9	0.9
2007–08	2.3	1.3	2.2	1.3	2.3	1.3	2.5	1.4	1.9	0.8
2008–09	2.3	1.3	2.0	1.2	2.4	1.3	2.9	1.6	4.3	1.6
2009–10	2.5	1.4	2.3	1.3	2.3	1.3	3.0	1.5	4.3	1.6
2010–11	2.4	1.3	2.3	1.3	1.9	1.2	2.5	1.3	2.6	1.0
2011–12	2.9	1.6	3.2	1.9	1.8	1.1	2.1	1.1	2.8	1.1
2012–13	3.2	2.0	3.6	2.4	1.9	1.2	1.8	1.0	3.1	1.2
2013–14	3.8	2.4	4.4	2.9	–	–	1.8	1.1	3.9	1.5
2014–15	4.3	2.7	5.0	3.2	–	–	2.1	1.3	3.2	1.4
2015–16	7.5	4.7	9.3	5.9	–	–	2.8	1.8	4.2	1.9
2016–17	9.3	5.6	11.7	7.0	–	–	4.1	2.6	4.0	1.7

Source Handbook of Statistics on Indian Economy, Reserve Bank of India

References

Chandrasekhar, C. P., & Ghosh, J. (2018). The banking conundrum. *Economic and Political Weekly, 53*(13).
Chavan, P. (2016). Regional divide in banking development in Maharashtra. *Economic and Political Weekly, 51*(13), 46–56.
Chetty, P. (2017). Types of microfinance institutions in India. Available at https://www.projectguru.in/publications/types-microfinance-institutions-india/.
Goyal, A. (2017). Indian banking perception and reality. *Economic and Political Weekly, 52*(12).
Gulati, R., Goswami, A., & Kumar, S. (2018). What drives credit risk in the Indian banking industry? An empirical investigation. *Economic Systems*. https://doi.org/10.1016/j.ecosys.2018.08.004.
Kochar, A. (2018). Branchless banking: Evaluating the doorstep delivery of financial services in rural India. *Journal of Development Economics, 135*, 160–175.
Narain, A., & Ghosh, S. (2001). Bank supervisory arrangements: International evidence and Indian perspective. *Economic and Political Weekly, 36*(37).
Rajaraman, I., & Vasishtha, G. (2002). Non-performing loans of PSU banks: Some panel results. *Economic and Political Weekly, 37*(05).
Ram Mohan, T. T. (2016). The changing face of Indian banking—Is banking safer today than before the crisis? *Economic and Political Weekly, 52*(24).
Ram Mohan, T. T. (2017). Is banking safer today than before the crisis? *Economic and Political Weekly, 52*(24).
Ranjan, R., & Dhal, S. C. (2003). Non-performing loans and terms of credit of public sector banks in India: An empirical assessment. *Reserve Bank of India Occasional, 24*(3), 81–121.
Reserve Bank of India, Report on Currency and Finance. (2006–08). Special Edition, Vol. V.
Reserve Bank of India: Report on Trend and Progress of Banking, 2016–17.
Reserve Bank Staff College. (2017). Reserve Bank—functions and working.
Samantaraya, A. (2016). Procyclical credit growth and Bank NPAs in India. *Economic and Political Weekly, 51*(12).
Singh, S., Majumdar, S., & Singh, B. (2015). Macro stress testing of Indian banking system focused on the tails. *Economic and Political Weekly, 50*(17).
Shastri, R. K. (2009). Microfinance institutions and poverty reduction in India (A comparative study with Asian Countries). *African Journal of Business Management, 3*(4), 136–140.

Chapter 12
Does Local Financial Development Matter for Growth? Evidence from Indian Districts

Samaresh Bardhan and Rajesh Sharma

Abstract This chapter investigates finance–growth relationship at district level and attempts to provide policy implications relating to access to financial services, hence, growth in local economy. The districts with higher financial development also experience higher growth rate of per capita gross district domestic product and per capita gross district domestic product (GDDP) during 2004–05 to 2010–11. We found relatively stronger effect of deposit than credit on economic growth that highlights the critical role of branch access in unbanked locations in district economy. Our findings implicate the importance of bottom-up approach of decision-making in which local financial conditions are as significant as financial development at macro-level financial development in the process of growth. Economic reforms played a significant role to this effect through various policy instruments meant for local economy. Banks and financial institutions became instrumental to foster savings and hence investments by providing better financial access to local people. This, in turn, augmented economic growth in local economy. While analysing the role of financial development, we also find positive and significant effect of human capital on growth that may activate alternative channels of growth and production which are less finance-intensive.

Samaresh Bardhan acknowledges invaluable contributions of Prof. Manoj Kumar Sanyal to teaching economics and shaping a better understanding of the subject. The author also acknowledges his unforgettable guidance, support, encouragement and extraordinary kindness.

S. Bardhan (✉)
Department of Humanities and Social Sciences, Indian Institute of Technology, Ropar, Punjab, India
e-mail: samaresh@iitrpr.ac.in

R. Sharma
University School of Management & Entrepreneurship, Delhi Technological University, Vivek Vihar, Phase II, Delhi, India
e-mail: rajesh.sharma@dtu.ac.in

P. K. Biswas and P. Das (eds.), *Indian Economy: Reforms and Development*, India Studies in Business and Economics, https://doi.org/10.1007/978-981-13-8269-7_12

12.1 Introduction

Since last few decades, Indian economy has been able to achieve consistently high growth rate and is considered as one of the fastest growing economies in the world (Dreze and Sen 2013). Process of economic reforms initiated in early 1990s played a significant role in setting India on a path of higher growth, by removing several regulatory restrictions in different market segments (Bhagwati and Panagariya 2013). Despite the record of high economic growth and strong growth potential, Indian economy is thought to suffer a severe setback in recent decades given that there has been growing inequality in income distribution along with few other factors such as lack of social services and underutilisation of resources (Dreze and Sen 2013). Economists and policy makers now agree that growth has been divergent across different dimensions such as regions, states, rural and urban areas (Bardhan 2010). Resulting income disparities in India led to considerable debates and discussions over how benefits of growth in India are percolated across all sections of society. It also led to debates on the role of markets vis-a-vis government in sustenance of growth (Bhagwati and Panagariya 2013; Dreze and Sen 2013). Given this phenomenon of uneven growth in India, more emphasis is given to the issues related to convergence (or divergence) of per capita income. However, majority of studies on growth and convergence focused on interstate differences, and most of these studies showed evidence of divergence (Ghosh 2008; Das 2012; Ghate and Wright 2012; Bandyopadhyay 2012). It is also argued that although Indian states share common institutions and national economic policies, wide diversity in geographic, demographic and economic features such as lack of public infrastructure resulted in unbalanced growth across Indian states (Basu and Maertens 2009; Lall et al. 2010).

Our motivation of the chapter is guided by the following arguments. First, existing studies on regional growth in India mostly focus on real aspects. Financial development, however, receives less importance in analysis of growth. In Indian economy, financial intermediary development plays a pivotal role in facilitating economic growth as banks have been instrumental in mobilisation of savings and its effective disbursement as credit for investment.[1] India's financial system have been liberalised since second half of 1980s, gained momentum during 1990s and thereafter. Economic reforms played a significant role in augmenting Indian economy to higher growth trajectory. Although economic growth rate slowed down in initial years of the decade of 1990 due to contractionary fiscal as well monetary policies, it gained momentum in the second half of 1990s. Industrial sector played a significant role in accelerating economic growth through easing of various restrictions. It is worthy to mention that

[1]Recognising importance of banks in development process, Government of India took several initiatives such as (i) bank nationalisation: 14 largest commercial banks were nationalised in 1969 and six more banks were nationalised in 1980, (ii) priority sector lending targets under which a fraction of bank credit is channelised towards agriculture and small-scale sector, (iii) branch licensing policy under which a bank, willing to open a branch in already banked location, is required to open four new branches in unbanked locations. Under priority sector lending programme, 40% of adjusted net bank credit is provided to priority sectors of agriculture and small-scale sector industry, and separate targets are fixed for different sectors.

reforms in financial sector also became instrumental in facilitating intermediation in growth process. Several deregulation measures were introduced in Indian financial system during last three decades with the recommendations of the Narasimham Committee (GOI 1991, 1998). During pre-reform period, Indian credit market was mostly governed by public sector banks, interest rates were completely regulated, a substantial portion of credit was earmarked for priority sectors and banks were relatively less active in expansion of credit to wide range of borrowers such as retail customers. However, since 1990s, Indian banking system became relatively more competitive with the penetration of private and foreign banks. This fact is claimed to have substantially improved the operational efficiency of Indian banks and expanded the outreach of banking business. These phenomena are also reflected in changing composition of assets and liabilities of different bank groups (Mohan 2005). Developments in financial system are supposed to augment the pace of financial intermediation and foster the process of economic growth through greater mobilisation of savings and credit expansion across states. It is further expected to cater to the credit demand by micro-, small and medium scale enterprises (MSMSE) and services sector, which have great potential for growth and employment generation.

Second, existing studies on regional inequality in India focused mainly on state-level analysis. However, to gain better insights into sources of regional variation in growth and its relationship with financial intermediation, we carry out a further disaggregated analysis at the district level. It is argued that state-level analysis overlooks various dimensions of growth as well as financial development across different regions of a state. States are considered to be the dominant sub-national political units in India, with substantial power delegated by the Constitution of India. However, states are thought to be too large a unit to be used in analysing regional pattern of economic activity and development. Moreover, states in India are quite heterogeneous and major sources of heterogeneity are size, geographic features, degree of urbanisation, infrastructure and human development. While some states such as Madhya Pradesh, Rajasthan and Maharashtra are the largest in terms of area of land, few other states such as Uttar Pradesh and Bihar have the largest populations (Cashin and Sahay 1996).[2] States such as Uttar Pradesh, Bihar, Madhya Pradesh and Rajasthan register highest birth rates but lag far behind other states in terms of literacy rates and also in terms of reduction in death rates. One possible disadvantage of working with observations of heterogeneous entities of different sizes is that each receives equal contributory weight while estimating average effect (Singh et al. 2014). This limitation of state-level analysis is thought to be mostly overcome while using data pertaining to micro-regions within a state such as districts, which may be considered fairly uniform in terms of cultural, legal and regulatory framework. Districts within a state are assumed to be homogenous in terms of political, legal and monetary framework, there are no barriers to trade or capital flows between districts and stages of development across districts are considered to be similar (Kendall 2012).

[2]Even though states of Bihar and Uttar Pradesh were bifurcated in the year 2000, these states are still considered to be the most populous states of India.

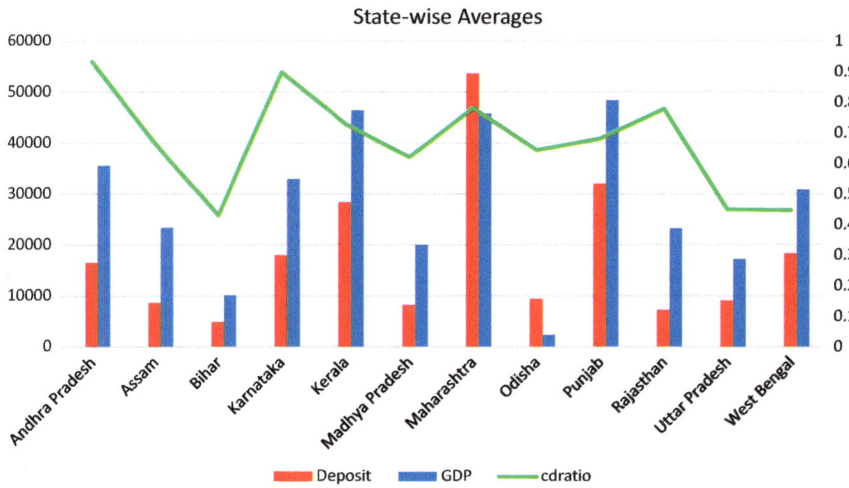

Fig. 12.1 Variation of growth and financial development indicators

Third, the advantage of using district-level micro-observations is that findings are supposed to be less confounded by the problem of *aggregation*. For instance, at constant prices, average gross district domestic product (GDDP) per capita varies from around INR 10,000 in the state of Bihar to INR 45,000 in the state of Maharashtra (see Fig. 12.1). State-level aggregates may also conceal important variations of income levels within the same state. For instance, average GDDP per capita varies from as low as INR 4086.4–32,389.9 in the state of Bihar.[3] Similar disparities are also observed in financial development indicators such as disbursement of credit which varies from INR 1418.7 to INR 16,556.5 in different districts of Assam.

Fourth, empirical evidence on finance–growth relationship based on cross-country studies is very often viewed with scepticism while drawing policy implications for the development of region and micro-regions within a country for reasons such as omitted variable bias. Cross-country studies frequently draw samples from different economies, and statistically significant financial indicators may partly be driven by excessively heterogeneous samples. In some sense, this is one source of omitted variable bias. Moreover, using disaggregated data, institutional, legal and cultural factors can be better controlled than in cross-country studies (Valverde et al. 2007). From methodological point of view, therefore, homogeneity across smaller economic units such as districts would imply the presence of fewer omitted variables compared to those in state-level or cross-country growth studies.

Against this background and motivations, we employ data at the district level to investigate finance–growth relationship and aim to draw certain policy implications on finance–growth relationship at the micro-level. In particular, we examine

[3]These inferences are drawn from our compiled data set.

finance–growth relationship using a sample of 355 districts of India over the period of 2004–05 to 2010–11.

The chapter contributes to the existing literature on finance–growth in several ways. *First*, unlike previous studies, the chapter utilises data of a large number of Indian districts to examine finance–growth relationship. Existing studies in the context of Indian districts mainly focus on various socio-economic issues such as poverty, backwardness (Kurian 2000; Debroy and Bhandari 2003; Sastry 2003; Singh et al. 2014). However, these studies hardly look specifically into the role of financial development on growth performance across districts. Further, district-level disparities may provide important clues regarding aggregate development at state/centre. Since independence, India followed a planned process of economic development in which five-year plans were formulated with devolution of funds as per plan provisions. However, policies designed at the centre or state level did not result in uniform economic development across the country.[4] With 73rd and 74th amendments, 1992 of Indian Constitution, a decentralised approach to development has been adopted in India. In this bottom-up approach to development, administrative units were created at district level. In particular, Panchayati Raj Institutions and Municipalities were created in rural and urban areas, respectively. Therefore, it is worthy to assess district-level disparities and analyse the effect of various factors such as financial depth, human capital and investment on district-level economic development. An understanding of the likely channels of economic development might help policy makers to devise appropriate policies for the balanced economic development. *Second*, we apply panel generalised method of moments (GMM) procedure (Arellano and Bond 1991; Blundell and Bond 1998) to estimate finance–growth relationship. Panel GMM methods are mostly used in micro-panels, *i.e.* large N, small T which is also the case in this chapter. Moreover, these methods also allow us to include lagged dependent variable in the regression and take care of endogeneity of the regressors by instrumenting endogenous variables using its own lags. *Third*, our study is expected to lay solid foundation for future studies involving district-level growth determinants, which can help us better understand as to why particular districts in a state are lagging behind others despite sharing a common state government, relatively uniform social and cultural attitudes among other common factors.

Remainder of this chapter is structured as follows. Section 12.2 presents an overview of existing literature relating to sub-national studies. Section 12.3 provides a description of Indian economic and financial system. Section 12.4 discusses data and methodology used in this chapter. Section 12.5 presents results and discussion. Section 12.6 presents concluding remarks.

[4]Ascani et al. (2012) in a review article emphasise the importance of studying the finance–growth relationship in regional framework. In Indian context, Das et al. (2015) finds evidence of income and growth divergence in the context of districts of India.

12.2 Literature Survey

Guiso et al. (2004) studied finance–growth relationship across Italian regions and found that a higher level of financial development at local level promotes the growth of local firms and fosters economic growth. Petersen and Rajan (2002) argued that location and the distance between small borrowers and their banks play an important role in the process of financial intermediation. On the other hand, for large enterprises, financial intermediation takes place centring around a major city with developed banking sector. The role of credit availability at regional or local level crucially depends upon the bank's ability to extend credit on the basis of superior local information and knowledge (Dow and Fuentes 1997; Fuentes 2005, pp. 61–65). Jayaratne and Strahan (1996), using generalised difference-in-difference approach observed that states in USA which allowed intra-bank branch reforms resulted in higher state-level economic growth. They also postulated that the channel through which deregulation in banking industry resulted in higher economic growth is possibly through increased quality of bank credit rather than increase in savings or through increased volume of credit. Liang and Jian-Zhou (2006) analysed causal relation between financial development and economic growth in China over the period 1952–2001 and find evidence of *demand-following hypothesis* which states that higher economic growth results in increased financial development).[5]

Existing studies in Indian context analysed the finance–growth relationship either at aggregate level or at state level (Demetriades and Luintel 1997; Bhattacharya and Sivasubramanian 2003; Misra 2003; Acharya et al. 2009; Sharma and Bardhan 2017a, b). Demetriades and Luintel (1997) found that restrictive policies such as interest rate controls, high reserve requirement and directed lending programme adversely affected financial deepening and hence growth. Bhattacharya and Sivasubramanian (2003) evaluated causal nexus between financial development (measured by ratio of broad money M3 to GDP) and economic growth and found evidence of supply-leading hypothesis. Misra (2003) took a micro-approach to analyse the credit–output relationship in Indian states using Granger causality framework and found significant support of demand-following hypothesis. Debroy and Bhandari (2003) analysed backwardness of 69 districts in India, in terms of poverty ratios, hunger, infant mortality rate, immunisation, literacy rate and enrolment ratios. The study found that poor infrastructure and connectivity between so-called backward districts and the rest of the economy largely contributed to this backwardness. Singh et al. (2003) uses NSS region-level data and examine issues of convergence, though performance measured by alternatives to income. Kurian (2000) examined intra-state disparities and observed that public policies in the face of wide variation of natural resources substantially reduced the disparity within a state. Dubey (2009) examined intra-state inequality across 47 districts in five Indian states during 1993–2005. Using

[5] Patrick (1966) characterised the finance–growth relationship in two hypotheses: demand-following and supply-leading. Under demand-following hypothesis, economic growth generates demand for financial services which leads to greater financial development; under supply-leading hypothesis, financial development leads to faster economic growth.

the Gini coefficient of per capita total consumption expenditure, and the coefficient of variation of headcount ratio of poverty, the author found evidence of increasing intra-state inequality. Raman and Kumari (2012) examined district level data for 13 indicators of agricultural development in Uttar Pradesh during 1990–2009 and found evidence of increasing intra-state disparities. Kendall (2012) used data of 209 districts corresponding to nine Indian states for the period 1991–2001 and identified that lack of banking sector development inhibited growth in many districts. Singh et al. (2014) found evidence of conditional convergence of growth across districts in terms of physical infrastructure, financial development and human capital. Das et al. (2015) explored the determinants of transitional growth across districts in terms of income and socio-economic characteristics and found evidence of absolute divergence across districts but conditional convergence in the presence of district-level characteristics, such as urbanisation Study also reveals significance of state-level effects to unbalanced growth.

12.3 Economic and Financial System

12.3.1 An Overview of District Economy

Districts are the local administrative units in India and form part of administrative set-up established in colonial period and continued even after independence in 1947. Districts constitute the third tier of governance in India below federal government (central government) and state/UT government. As per census 2011, there were 640 districts in India. A district comprises of several villages and cities and may be as big as Thane (in Maharashtra) with a population of 1.1 crores and as small as Dibang Valley (Assam) with population of 8004 in 2011. Through 73rd and 74th constitutional amendments, Panchayati Raj Institutions (PRIs) at rural level and municipalities at urban level, respectively, were given constitutional status, as means of decentralisation. In rural areas, three-tier Panchayati Raj Institutions consisting of Gram Panchayat (GP), Panchayat Samiti and Zilla Parishad were created. Following constitutional amendments, Gram Panchayats (GP) became primarily responsible to identify development needs of the villages and implement those programmes. Major responsibilities of the GPs comprised of administering local infrastructure (public buildings, water, roads, etc.) and identifying population for welfare programmes. Heads of Gram Panchayat must belong to the village and public policy decisions are taken by majority voting. Members of these bodies are elected through general elections and reservations are provided for women and under-privileged classes to maintain adequate representation of all sections of society in the participatory process of development. Previously, it was considered that uniform policies of federal government would result in egalitarian development for all sections of society. However, growing disparities between states and also at district level magnifies the importance of idiosyncratic factors, which affect development of heterogeneous regions and micro-regions in a different manner. As per Chattopadhyay and Duflo (2004), development programmes at local level are primarily determined by infrastructure needs, brought to the GP by male or female members of the GP. This bottom-up approach is aimed to mitigate the uneven growth patterns so that proper institutions are developed and policies are framed such that these micro-units grow in unison, thereby contribute towards the overall growth of states and hence the national economy.

12.3.2 Evolution of Financial System at Micro-Level

In India, commercial banks constitute the major sources of savings and external sources of financing of small and medium scale enterprises and agriculture sector. Indian government placed an increasingly important role of development to the scheduled commercial banks since independence. Banks were nationalised in two phases in 1969, and 1980, priority sector lending targets were set and branch licensing policy was adopted such that majority of population can be linked to the banking sector, banking access can be provided in rural and backward areas.[6]

In India, banks are required to obtain a licence from Reserve Bank of India (RBI) for opening a new branch. Branch licensing policy introduced by RBI in 1977 mainly focused on rural unbanked locations. Under this policy, a bank was granted a licence to open a new branch in an already banked location given that it opened new branches in four unbanked locations (Burgess and Pande 2005). The objective of this policy was to expand branch access in the most populated and rural regions, not served by banks, earlier. During 1969–1990, branches were opened in about 30,000 rural unbanked locations, and bank borrowing as a share of total rural household debt increased from 0.3 to 29% (Burgess and Pande 2005). However, this policy was replaced by a new policy under which branch location would be based on the 'need, business potential and financial viability of the location' (Government of India 1991).

Kendall (2012) argued that banks operating in a district are connected to regional and national markets via the money market and internal capital markets and capital can flow freely across district boundaries. One significant development to this direction is the introduction of Lead Bank Scheme (LBS) introduced in 1969 following the recommendations of Gadgil Committee and Nariman Committee (RBI 2014). The objectives of this scheme were to formulate plans and programmes for extending adequate banking and credit facilities for overall development of rural economy cities. Under this scheme, each public sector bank acts as a 'Lead Bank' which focuses on certain districts.

RBI made a comprehensive review of LBS in 2009, and this scheme was appraised to be successful in branch expansion, deposit mobilisation and lending to the priority sectors, especially in rural/semi urban areas. As a significant step to this development

---

[6]In 1969, 14 of the largest commercial private sector banks were nationalised followed by another round of bank nationalisation of six banks in 1980; it was primarily done to ensure timely and cost-effective availability of banking services to all sections of the society.

in post-reform period, private sector banks are also encouraged to actively participate in the process of implementation of district credit plan by leveraging on information technology. Although LBS initially aimed at all districts in India excluding districts in metropolitan areas, in 2013–14, 16 districts in metropolitan areas of Chennai, Delhi, Hyderabad, Kolkata and Mumbai were brought under the ambit of LBS. This policy change of RBI aimed at mitigating wide-scale financial exclusion among disadvantaged and low-income groups and urban poor in metropolitan areas (RBI 2014). It also provided an institutional mechanism for co-ordination between the government and bank. These policy initiatives of RBI, however, mainly focused on financial inclusion. As a major policy change to achieve 100% financial inclusion, a phase-wise approach was adopted by RBI in 2009 to extend banking facilities in all unbanked villages. Initially, banking services were aimed at villages with population of more than 2000, and subsequently, these services covered unbanked villages with population of less than 2000, following the road map created in June 2012, a road map was framed to provide banking services in unbanked villages with population less than 2000.

12.4 Data and Methodology

12.4.1 Description of Data

As per the availability, we use district-level data corresponding to 12 states providing us a data set of 355 districts in our sample for the period of 2004–05 to 2010–11.[7] Per capita gross district domestic product (GDDP) and growth rate of per capita GDDP (GDPGR) are considered as two alternate indicators of economic development.[8] Both the variables are measured in real terms. We consider per capita bank credit as the primary measure of financial development (King and Levine 1993a, b; Rioja and Valev 2004). We also consider bank deposit per capita as our second indicator of financial development in our empirical analysis (Luintel and Khan 1999; Christopoulos and Tsionas 2004). Importance of deposit mobilisation in financial intermediation can also be gauged from recent initiative of Government of India such as Pradhan Mantri Jan Dhan Yojna (PMJDY)—a comprehensive scheme of financial inclusion introduced in 2014. It is claimed to be immensely successful in terms of linking unbanked population with poor and also with respect to large deposit

[7]Sample consists of districts in twelve states of Andhra Pradesh, Assam, Bihar, Karnataka, Kerala, Madhya Pradesh, Maharashtra, Odisha, Punjab, Rajasthan, Uttar Pradesh and West Bengal. During the period under investigation, few new districts were created bifurcating existing districts. In order to maintain continuity in data set, we dropped those districts which were bifurcated or newly created during the study period.

[8]Gross district domestic product (GDDP) is defined as the money value of all goods and services produced during a given period of time, within the boundary of a district.

mobilisation.[9] Credit–deposit ratio (CDR) is our third alternative indicator of financial development, which is often considered as a measure of efficiency of financial intermediation process at given level of deposits.[10] CDR is important in that credit disbursement by banks in a given district depends on deposit mobilisation in that district and part of deposits, not disbursed as credit may be considered as cost of financial intermediation (Pagano 1993). The data pertaining to GDDP is extracted from *States of India* database, provided by Centre for Monitoring Indian Economy (CMIE). Statistical data of indicators of financial development is extracted from Reserve Bank of India (RBI) database as well as *States of India* database supplied by CMIE.[11]

In addition to the indicators of financial development, we also consider few control variables such as crime per 100,000 population,[12] real investment per capita and net enrolment ratio. The data corresponding to the crime rate pertains to the total crimes reported under Indian Penal Code (IPC). In many of the regions, different crimes such as domestic violence remain unreported. Therefore, data for crime may not actually reflect true picture of law and order situation. However, due to unavailability of any other reliable data, we use data of crime published by National Crime Records Bureau (NCRB), which is considered to be the most reliable and widely used source corresponding to the incidence of crime at district or state level. Following previous empirical growth literature, we consider *school enrolment ratio* as a close measure of human capital development (Barro 1991; Barro and Lee 1993). In particular, we considered net enrolment ratio (NER) in upper primary schools in this study.[13] For this purpose, we retrieve enrolment ratio data from District Information System for Education (DISE) which provides time series data at district level. District-wise

[9]Pradhan Mantri Jan Dhan Yojna (PMJDY) is scheme initiated by Prime Minister (Pradhan Mantri) of India for financial inclusion which is named on Public Money (Jan Dhan).

[10]Lower credit–deposit ratio may also indicate higher reserve requirements of RBI which leads to lower percentage of deposits, available for lending purposes as it happened during 1980s in Indian financial system.

[11]It is argued that district-level data across states are not strictly comparable. However, this problem is addressed partially by analysing available data state by state (Table 12.1). Indira et al. (2002) focused on income and poverty estimates at the district level and found that in some states, commodity producing sectors are considered as the sources of output in districts. In others states, both non-commodity producing sectors and commodity producing sectors are considered in order to get a measure of income and output. Services sector is also not considered due to non-availability of estimates of income accrued in a district. Due to these various conceptual differences, district-level data of GDP across states may not be strictly comparable.

[12]As bigger districts are expected to have higher number of crimes, we normalise the data by considering number of crimes per 100,000 populations such that meaningful comparisons can be obtained between districts of sample states.

[13]Net enrolment ratio (NER) is defined as ratio of number of children enrolled in school to total number of children in that age group. Number of enrolment in primary schools corresponds to enrolment in class I–V and upper primary enrolment includes enrolment in class VI–VIII. Although high enrolment is one of the policy targets of government, GER may be higher than 100 because of repeating students or underage students who are studying in higher classes as against their age category. Therefore, net enrolment ratio can be considered as a better proxy of human capital in comparison to GER.

data on investment per capita is procured from *CMIE*. For investment, we consider district-wise data for investment projects compiled by CMIE in its *States of India* database. We take natural logarithm of all the explanatory variables in panel data regression to take care of potential nonlinearity and also to take care of the effect of outliers in our estimation (see Table 12.7 of Appendix for definition of variables and sources of data).

Table 12.1 presents district-level average values of variables for each of our sample state, which illustrates that average GDDP per capita varies from Rs. 2500 per capita in Odisha to Rs. 48,000 in Punjab. This highlights the disparities at district level among different sample states. Further, average growth rate reveals that except highly growing districts of Maharashtra, other states recorded 5–8% growth rate during our sample period. District-level variation in financial development indicators also shows striking disparity across sample states where real deposit per capita in the state of Bihar at average Rs. 5009 appears to be close to one-tenth of average for districts in Maharashtra. We also observe disparities across districts in case of other indicators of financial development. Geographical heat maps of natural logarithm of per capita deposit (LNDEPOSIT), natural logarithm of per capita credit (LNCREDIT) and natural logarithm of per capita income (LNINCOME) for our sample districts are presented in Fig. 12.2. The maps exhibit the concentration pattern of deposits, credit and the level of income across districts indicated by colour intensity. With respect to net enrolment ratio (NER), we observe that districts of relatively backward states such as Bihar, Odisha and Uttar Pradesh, on an average, recorded significantly low NER compared to the districts of so-called developed states. This partially explains the income differentials in these states and relatively richer states. Investment per capita also exhibits similar picture with higher investments, on average, flown to richer states with an exception of Odisha. Odisha is considered to be one of the poorer states in India and yet has recorded the highest investment projects per capita. This may be due to large investment projects under different stages of implementation in the state which may be stuck due to various reasons.[14]

12.4.2 Econometric Methodology

We consider the following functional form to formlise the relationship between financial development and economic growth at the district level:

$$y = f(Fin\_Dev, X)$$

[14]Land acquisition policy in a state very often prevents infrastructure projects to be initiated and its effective implementation takes a long time. One notable example is POSCO steel project by South Korean steel firm to be started in Jagatsinghpur district of Odisha, worth INR 510 billion. The Memorandum of Understanding (MoU) for the project was signed in 2005 and this project is yet to take off even by 2017.

Source: http://www.thehindu.com/news/national/other-states/in-odisha-fresh-row-brewing-over-posco-land/article18516063.ece (Accessed: 31st May, 2018).

Table 12.1 State-wise averages of growth, financial development and other indicators

State	No. of districts	Real credit per capita	Real deposit per capita	Real GDDP per capita	GROWTH	CD ratio	NER	Crime per 100,000	Real investment per capita
Andhra Pradesh	23	16,684.6	16,607.3	35,691.5	0.0813	0.93	56.61	216.17	34,144.4
Assam	27	4014.92	8788.66	23,469.9	–	0.67	57.5	169.52	10,265.4
Bihar	38	1866.79	5009.30	10,220	0.0517	0.43	37.98	117.74	6245.68
Karnataka	24	14,582.8	18,032.50	33,028.8	0.0689	0.90	54.95	203.76	32,641.1
Kerala	14	17,890.6	28,373.6	46,502.5	0.0738	0.73	61.92	377.44	16,644.5
Madhya Pradesh	45	5184.62	8326.36	20,113.3	0.0565	0.62	58	285.47	14,279.7
Maharashtra	33	48,759.6	53,700.4	45,893.3	0.1427	0.78	66.94	195.18	47,303.5
Odisha	30	5770.03	9518.39	2484.18	0.0665	0.65	45.92	137.71	104,393
Punjab	11	19,754.2	32,076.7	48,451.9	0.0634	0.68	50.76	130.43	18,265.6
Rajasthan	29	6177.42	7313.02	23,309.4	0.0538	0.78	49.75	234.73	13,518.5
Uttar Pradesh	63	4134.82	9136.3	17,281.8	0.0710	0.45	41.59	79.06	15,535.7
West Bengal	18	12,468.8	18,353	30,936.6	0.0540	0.45	51.79	108.89	22,134.3

Notes Credit per capita, per capita deposit, GDDP per capita and investment are measured in rupee terms. Statistical data of real GDDP per capita for sample districts in the state of Assam is available only for 2009–10. Hence, growth rate of real GDDP per capita for Assam is not reported

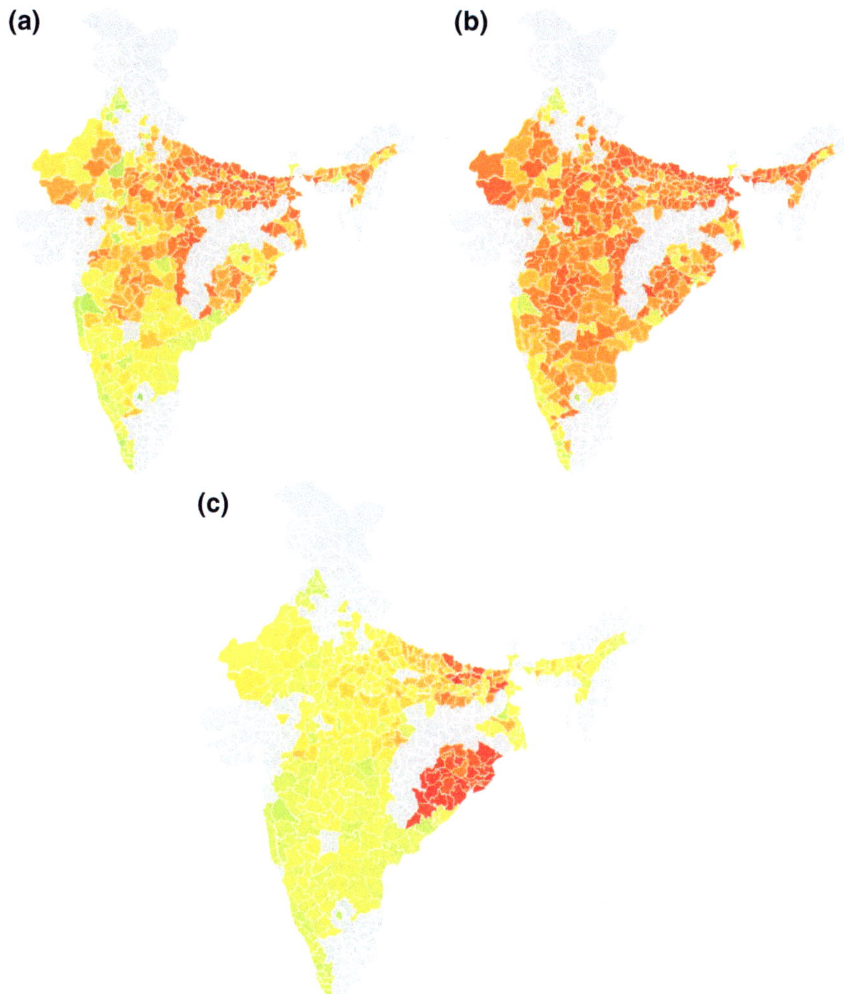

Fig. 12.2 District-wise geographical heat map over the period of 2004–05 to 2010–11. **a** Average LNDEPOSIT, **b** Average LNCREDIT, **c** Average LNINCOME *Note* (a) Average LNDEPOSIT, (b) Average LNCREDIT, (c) Average LNINCOME; LNDEPOSIT: natural logarithm of real deposit per capita; LNCREDIT: natural logarithm of real credit per capita; LNINCOME: natural logarithm of real income per capita. *Data Source* Authors' calculations based on the data generated from RBI database and states of India database (CMIE). Colour gradient: red indicates minimum

where Fin_Dev is the indicator of financial development; $\boldsymbol{y}$ represents district-level output or growth variable; and $\boldsymbol{X}$ represents the vector of control variables. Following empirical growth literature, our empirical model builds on Barro-type basic growth regression model:

$$y_i = \alpha_i + \beta_i X + \gamma FIN_i + \varepsilon_i \tag{12.1}$$

Our choice of empirical model is influenced by previous literature in that we consider a linear specification (King and Levine 1993a; Rajan and Zingales 1998; Beck and Levine 2004). In order to take care of individual heterogeneity along with time-varying effects across districts, we use dynamic panel data (DPD) model for empirical characterisation of model specified in Eq. (12.1). The panel data model is specified as follows.

$$Y_{i,t} = \alpha Y_{i,t-1} + \beta' X_{i,t} + \mu_i + \varepsilon_{i,t} \tag{12.2}$$

where $Y_{i,t}$ represents output variable (growth/real per capita GDDP); μ_i represents individual fixed effect; $X_{i,t}$ is the vector of explanatory variables, which also includes indicator of financial development and $\varepsilon_{i,t}$ is the error term. Since lagged dependent variable in (12.2) is correlated with error term, $\varepsilon_{i,t}$, OLS gives inconsistent estimates of Eq. (12.2) and OLS estimates suffer from dynamic panel bias (Nickell 1981). Therefore, we apply first-difference panel generalised method of moment (GMM) techniques proposed by Arellano and Bond (1991) and Arellano and Bover (1995). Following these methods, we take first differencing of Eq. (12.2) to remove fixed effects and obtain the following equation.

$$Y_{i,t} - Y_{i,t-1} = \alpha\left(Y_{i,t-1} - Y_{i,t-2}\right) + \beta'(X_{i,t} - X_{i,t-1}) + (\varepsilon_{i,t} - \varepsilon_{i,t-1}) \tag{12.3}$$

Equation (12.3) can also be rewritten as

$$\Delta Y_{i,t} = \alpha \Delta Y_{i,t-1} + \beta' \Delta X_{i,t} + \Delta \varepsilon_{it} \tag{12.4}$$

Although fixed effects are removed, new error term $\left(\Delta\varepsilon_{i,t}\right)$ is now correlated with $\Delta Y_{i,t-1}$ in first-difference Eq. (12.4). We apply GMM in Eq. (12.4) to estimate α and β', in which lagged values of dependent variable $Y_{i,t-2}$ and higher lags are used as instruments for $\Delta Y_{i,t-1}$. This is possible because $Y_{i,t-2}$ may be correlated with ΔY_{it-1} through $Y_{i,t-2}$ term being common. However, $Y_{i,t-2}$ is expected to be uncorrelated with $\left(\varepsilon_{i,t} - \varepsilon_{i,t-1}\right)$ if error term is serially uncorrelated at order 2. Therefore, using $Y_{i,t-2}$ and higher lags as additional instruments gives rise to following moment conditions:

$$\mathrm{E}\left[Y_{i,t-s}\left(\varepsilon_{i,t} - \varepsilon_{i,t-1}\right)\right] = 0 \text{ for } s \geq 2,\ t = 3,\ 4,\ \ldots,\ T \tag{12.5}$$

Additionally, if the explanatory variables $\left(X_{i,t}\right)$ are endogenous, we may use lagged values of X_{it} as instrument in same way as we did for lagged dependent variable. Therefore, we obtain following moment conditions.

$$\mathrm{E}\left[X_{i,t-s}\left(\varepsilon_{i,t}-\varepsilon_{i,t-1}\right)\right]=0 \text{ for all } s,t=3,4,\ \ldots,T \tag{12.6}$$

However, if explanatory variables are weakly exogenous, then two or more lags may be taken as instrument set giving rise to following moment conditions.

$$\mathrm{E}\left[X_{i,t-s}(\varepsilon_{i,t}-\varepsilon_{i,t-1})\right]=0 \text{ for } s\geq 2, t=3,4,\ldots,T \tag{12.7}$$

Equations (12.5)–(12.7) present the moments conditions which are applied depending upon the nature of variables. As noted earlier, two or more lags of dependent variables serves the purpose of instruments only if the error terms are serially uncorrelated of order 2. To test the second-order autocorrelation of error term, we conduct Arellano and Bond (1991) test.

12.5 Results and Discussion

12.5.1 Preliminary Observations

Before carrying out empirical estimations across districts, we present few observations about finance–growth relationship based on our sample states. In Figs. 12.3, 12.4 and 12.5, we present bi-variate scatter plot between natural logarithm of per capita income (INCOME) in real terms and alternative indicators of financial development (credit, deposit and credit–deposit ratio) for individual states in our sample. These illustrate that in majority of states, deposit and credit show discernible positive relation with income per capita whereas the relationship is not that clear in case of credit–deposit ratio. Figures 12.3, 12.4 and 12.5 indicate that although states diverge in terms of growth, state's financial development in terms of credit availability exerts significant positive impact on growth in most states. This finding is consistent with supply-leading hypothesis which postulate that causality runs from credit to output and establishes the evidence of finance led growth across Indian states. Availability of credit to a particular state, to a large extent, depends on the size of that state, availability of deposits, state's initial financial development, availability of infrastructure, etc. We also have similar observations in case of deposits. Deposits in states are taken as proxy representing availability of financial resources to support lending activities in line with arguments proposed by Beck et al. (2009). It is argued that higher the penetration of banking sector in a state through expansion of deposit base, greater would be credit extended through formal channels. These observations are consistent with existing studies on Indian states (Misra 2003; Sharma and Bardhan 2017a, b). However, for credit–deposit ratio, bi-variate scatter plots did not reveal clear

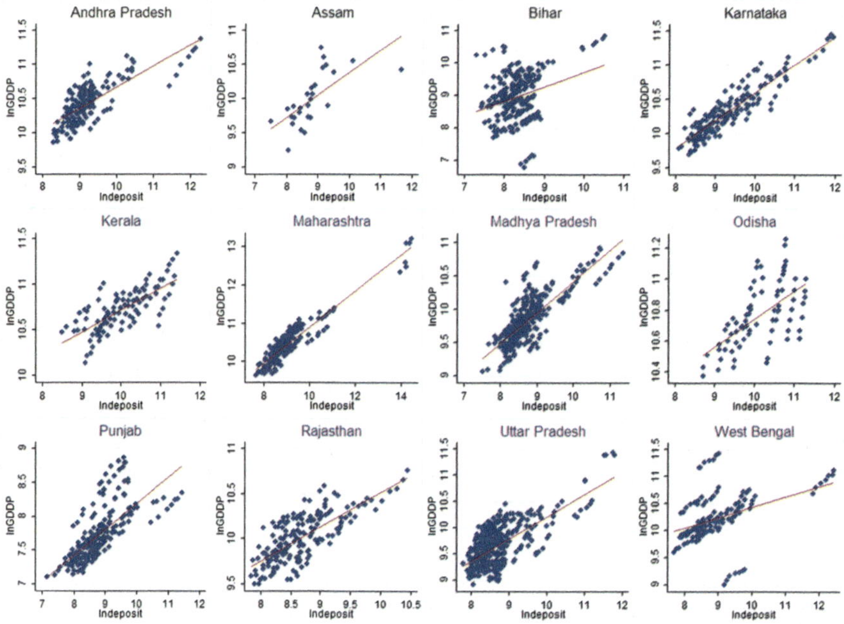

Fig. 12.3 State-wise lnGDDP versus lndeposit. lnGDDP: natural logarithm of district level real gross domestic product per capita; lndeposit: natural logarithm of real deposit per capita

positive relationship. Even if deposits mobilisation across states substantially increased, disbursement of credit did not keep pace until 2000. Therefore, supply side factors, perhaps, played a significant role behind low CD, arising out of unwillingness of banks to extend credit because of low credit worthiness of borrowers in states.

As against positive correlation between financial development and income (Figs. 12.3, 12.4 and 12.5), we also examine correlation between explanatory variables before carrying out panel GMM estimations. In Table 12.2, we present pairwise correlation between variables employed in empirical model to check for perfect multicollinearity. We observe that except high correlation between DEPOSIT and CREDIT, we do not observe very high correlation between other covariates which rules out misspecifications due to perfect multicollinearity.

12.5.2 Panel GMM Results

Table 12.3 presents results of first-difference GMM regression with growth of real per capita income (GROWTH) as the dependent variable. All explanatory variables used in our empirical estimation of GMM model are considered to be endogenous.

Table 12.2 Correlation matrix

	INCOME	GROWTH	DEPOSIT	CREDIT	CDR	INVEST	ENROL	CRIME
INCOME	1							
GROWTH	0.142***	1						
DEPOSIT	0.5248***	0.1155***	1					
CREDIT	0.5502***	0.1154***	0.8621***	1				
CDR	0.2132***	0.0291	0.061***	0.515***	1			
INVEST	0.1381***	0.0733***	0.4264***	0.4609***	0.1893***	1		
ENROL	0.3084***	0.0687***	0.1681***	0.2151***	0.1149***	0.1081***	1	
CRIME	0.3698***	0.0461*	0.4473***	0.5609***	0.2773***	0.2013***	0.3024***	1

Notes INCOME: logarithm of real per capita GDDP; GROWTH: growth of real per capita GDDP; DEPOSIT: logarithm of real per capita deposit; CREDIT: logarithm of per capita credit; CDR: ratio of real credit and real deposit; INVEST: logarithm of per capita investment; CRIME: logarithm of crime per 100,000 population; and ENROL: logarithm of net enrolment ratio. *, **, *** denote significance of correlation coefficient at 10, 5, 1%, respectively

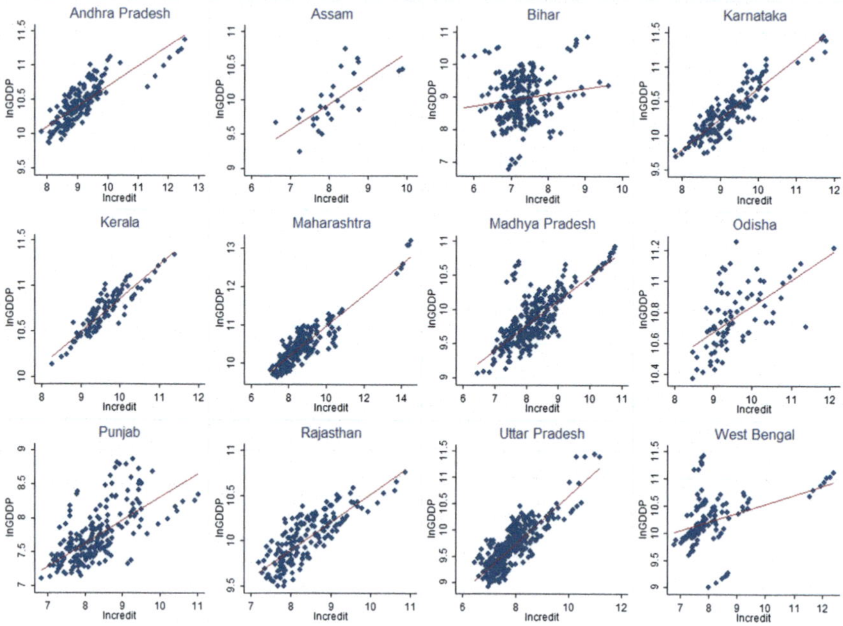

Fig. 12.4 State-wise lnGDDP versus lncredit. *Note* lnGDDP: natural logarithm of district level real gross domestic product per capita; lncredit: natural logarithm of real credit per capita

Following Arellano and Bond (1991), endogenous variables are instrumented using lagged values. We use the entire information set as instrument (i.e. use all available lags as instruments) for current observation as we have few observations to be used as instruments. Table 12.3 illustrates that financial development provide by DEPOSIT and CREDIT exert statistically significant effects on GROWTH ($p < 0.05$). The same, however, is not true for credit–deposit ratio (CDR). Effect of deposit per capita is much stronger than CREDIT. Natural logarithm of crime per 100,000 (CRIME) has statistically negative influence on GROWTH only with DEPOSIT. Logarithm of investment per capita (INVEST) maintains statistical significance in all the models involving different financial development indicators. District-level lagged income (INITIAL) has strong negative association with GROWTH which is in consonance with convergence hypothesis. This finding implies that districts with lower initial per capita income tend to grow faster than districts with higher initial per capita income. Human capital provided by net enrolment ratio (NER) exerts positive and statistically significant influence on GROWTH. This finding provides support to the hypothesis that human capital promotes economic growth. In the bottom of the table, we also report number of instruments as well as number of districts in each model which shows that number of instruments in each model is significantly lower than number of groups (i.e. districts). In all the models, model diagnostic test of Arellano–Bond test of error term ($p > 0.1$) indicates that errors are not serially correlated of order 2.

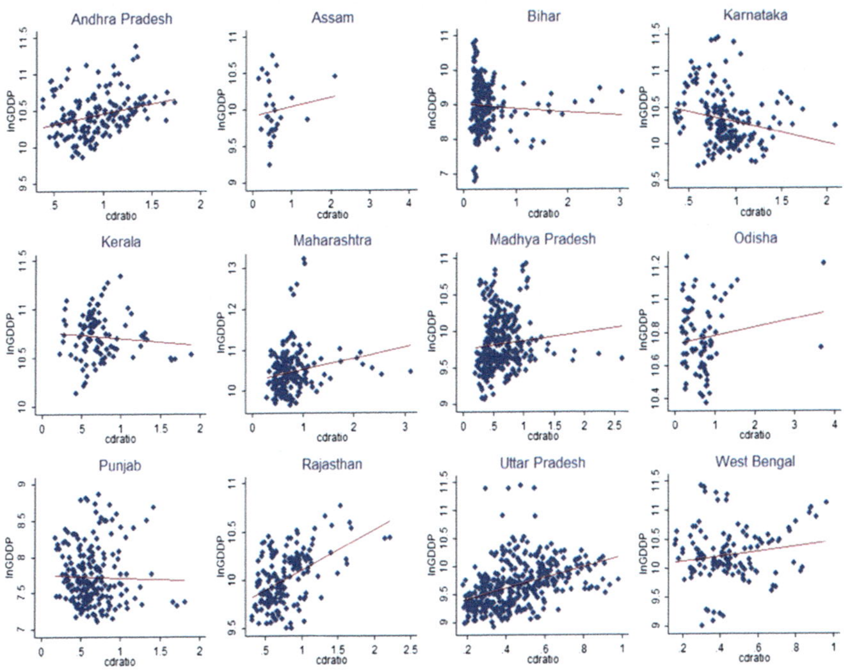

Fig. 12.5 State-wise lnGDDP versus lncdratio. *Note* lnGDDP: natural logarithm of district level real gross domestic product per capita; cdratio: ratio of real credit and real deposits

In Table 12.4, we present results with natural logarithm of real per capita GDDP (INCOME) as the dependent variable rather than district level growth. Rest of the model specifications remained the same as in Table 12.3. Considering INCOME as the dependent variable, we aim to examine whether higher degree of financial development is also associated with higher levels of income or not (as observed in Figs. 12.3, 12.4 and 12.5). We observe similar finding as observed in Table 12.3. From column I and II of Table 12.4, we observe that DEPOSIT and CREDIT exert positive and significant effects on per capita income. We also observe that the effect of DEPOSIT is much stronger than that of CREDIT. As the dependent variable as well as financial development indicators (DEPOSIT and CREDIT) is expressed in logarithmic terms, coefficient estimate is interpreted as the elasticity which implies that 1 *per cent* increase in DEPOSIT results in 0.37% increase in per capita income and 1 per cent rise in CREDIT results in 0.05% increase in per capita income. These findings indicate that districts are able to absorb funds locally either in terms of mobilisation of deposits or in terms of disbursement of credit. Local bank branches are considered to be the drivers of both credit and deposit services within a district. It is worthy to mention, however, that while banks generate supply for loans and deposits, demand for loans and deposits are largely governed by various factors such as infrastructure development and local business environment apart from the

Table 12.3 First-difference estimation results: GROWTH as dependent variable

Variable	I	II	III
INITIAL	−0.6726***	−0.2976***	−0.2591***
	(0.0574)	(0.0344)	(0.0256)
Fin_Dev	0.4374***	0.0607**	−0.0326
	(0.0608)	(0.0297)	(0.0285)
INVEST	0.0094***	0.0099***	0.0130***
	(0.0038)	(0.0036)	(0.0038)
CRIME	−0.2364***	−0.0349	−0.0310
	(0.0755)	(0.0575)	(0.0536)
ENROL	0.0960***	0.1309***	0.1377***
	(0.0339)	(0.0385)	(0.0374)
AR (2) test	−0.22	0.55	0.35
	(0.826)	(0.584)	(0.728)
No. of Obs.	1112	1111	1111
Number of groups	277	277	277
Number of instruments	90	90	90

GROWTH: growth of per capita real GDDP. INITIAL: real per capita GDDP in previous period; Fin_Dev: deposit, credit and CDR in column I, II and III, respectively; INVEST: per capita investment; CRIME: number of crimes per 100,000 population; and ENROL: natural logarithm of NER. Robust standard errors are presented in parentheses. One-step GMM estimation is applied and all lags are used as instruments. *, **, *** denote statistical significance at 10, 5, 1%, respectively

level of income of people at local level. In order to fasten the process of financial intermediation, however, banks are required to make sustained efforts to mobilise stable retail deposits by extending banking facilities and expanding their deposit base further. RBI's branch licensing policy and more recent initiatives of Pradhan Mantri Jan Dhan Yojna (PMJDY) introduced in 2014 played a significant role to this effect. Smaller coefficient of credit compared to that deposits, while explaining level of income across districts, indicate the possibility of less than full effect of financial intermediation. Credit–deposit ratio (CDR) exerts statistically insignificant effect on district level per capita income. CRIME has negative effects on income per capita which implies that crime rate not only affects economic growth adversely but has also results in lower per capita income at district level. Lagged income (INITIAL) has strong positive association with current income per capita implying high degree of income persistence. In this regression set-up too, number of instruments in each model is significantly lower than number of groups (i.e. districts). In all the estimated

Table 12.4 First-difference estimation results: LogGDDP as dependent variable

Variable	I	II	III
INITIAL	0.4209***	0.7353***	0.7695***
	(0.0509)	(0.0300)	(0.0226)
Fin_Dev	0.3684***	0.0533**	−0.0256
	(0.0510)	(0.0256)	(0.0246)
INVEST	0.0080**	0.0085***	0.0113***
	(0.0034)	(0.0033)	(0.0034)
CRIME	−0.1917***	−0.0262	−0.233
	(0.0632)	(0.0493)	(0.0310)
ENROL	0.0844***	0.1140***	0.1201***
	(0.0269)	(0.0316)	(0.0309)
AR (2) test	0.06	0.74	0.53
	(0.954)	(0.456)	(0.596)
No. of Obs.	1112	1111	1111
Number of groups	277	277	277
Number of instruments	90	90	90

Dependent variable, INCOME: per capita real GDDP. Explanatory variables are: INITIAL: per capita real GDDP in previous period; Fin_Dev: DEPOSIT, CREDIT and CDR in column I, II and III, respectively; INVEST: investment per capita; CRIME: number of crimes per 100,000 population; and ENROL: natural logarithm of NER. Robust standard errors are presented in parentheses. One-step GMM estimation is applied and all lags are used as instruments. *, **, *** denote statistical significance at 10, 5, 1%, respectively

models, AR (2) test of error term ($p > 0.1$) depicts that errors are not serially correlated of order 2.[15]

12.5.3 Robustness Check

First-difference GMM results are often sensitive to model specification and information set used for instrumenting the endogenous variables. In Tables 12.3 and 12.4, we used the entire instrumentation set (all available lags as instruments). However, as Roodman (2009a, b) pointed out that some of the instruments may be redundant

[15]We also conducted state-specific panel GMM regression corresponding to Tables 12.3 and 12.4. However, we present the coefficient estimates on financial development (DEPOSIT, CREDIT and CDR) with 90% CI in Figs. 12.6 and 12.7 of Appendix. We observe results similar to those observed in Tables 12.3 and 12.4 with DEPOSIT appearing as most strongly associated with INCOME and are statistically significant in majority of states with mixed results for CDR.

and may not provide useful information, we reproduce our results of Tables 12.3 and 12.4 by collapsing the instrument set, which effectively reduced the instruments count.[16]

Tables 12.5 and 12.6 did not reflect discernible change in sign of coefficients and significance of most of the explanatory variables as compared to Tables 12.3 and 12.4, which show that our findings are less sensitive to unusually high instrument count, which provides further robustness to our conclusion of finance-driven economic development at district level.[17]

12.5.4 Discussion

This study demonstrates that expanding banking sector outreach in local economy should be an important agenda of policy makers in order to enable economically disadvantaged districts to catch up. This may enable the districts to converge in terms of per capita income, over time. It is envisaged that through inclusion of all households under the ambit of formal financial system, there can be a mitigating effect on poverty and consequently, growth can be fostered. In addition to earlier policies of branch expansion in rural unbanked locations, recent initiatives by Government of India for greater financial inclusion such as Pradhan Mantri Jan Dhan Yojna (PMJDY) played a significant role towards this direction. The underlying optimism behind this strategy has been a vast amount of cross-country growth literature which shows that financial development is positively associated with high-income levels and growth (King and Levine 1993a; Levine et al. 2000; Rioja and Valev 2004, 2014).[18] This optimism is also supported by state-level analysis in India providing evidence of positive effect of financial development on economic growth (Demetriades and Luintel 1997; Bhattacharya and Sivasubramanian 2003; Misra 2003; Acharya et al. 2009; Sharma and Bardhan 2017a, b). However, these previous studies were based on either aggregate data set at the national level, or state-level. Current study, however, examines finance–growth relation at district level and demonstrates that financial development positively influences both per capita income and growth. It shows the importance of following a bottom-up approach in which local financial conditions are also

[16]Two commonly used ways of reducing instrument counts are: reducing number of lags taken as instruments and second by collapsing the instruments suggested by Roodman (2009b). We preferred second option in this paper as there were lesser time points available to be used as instruments.

[17]In Tables 12.8 and 12.9 of Appendix, we reproduce results of Tables 12.3 and 12.4, applying two-step estimation procedure along with collapse option and observe no noticeable change in coefficient sign and significance in majority of the explanatory variables. Tables 12.10 and 12.11 show the results of one-step estimation, without using collapse option and included year dummies as the explanatory variable. This observation is based on the premise that certain changes in income per capita and growth may be driven solely be temporal pattern irrespective of the effects of explanatory variables. This again shows robustness of the results corresponding to positive and significant effect of deposit per capita on per capita income and growth. Credit–deposit ratio is still statistically insignificant, and credit is no longer remains statistically significant.

[18]See Levine (1997, 2005) for extensive and detailed survey of finance–growth literature.

Table 12.5 First-difference estimation with GROWTH as dependent variable with reduced instrument count

Variable	I	II	III
INITIAL	−0.8988***	−0.4311***	−0.3281***
	(0.0674)	(0.0507)	(0.0319)
Fin_Dev	0.5976***	0.1444**	−0.0620
	(0.0747)	(0.0496)	(0.0460)
INVEST	0.0077	0.0103**	0.0091**
	(0.0046)	(0.0044)	(0.0044)
CRIME	−0.3014***	−0.0387	−0.0079
	(0.1115)	(0.0992)	(0.0950)
ENROL	0.1660***	0.2167***	0.2379***
	(0.0453)	(0.0414)	(0.0407)
AR (2) test	−1.09	−0.20	0.35
	(0.276)	(0.840)	(0.728)
No. of Obs.	1112	1111	1111
Number of groups	277	277	277
Number of instruments	28	28	28

GROWTH: growth of per capita real GDDP. INITIAL: real per capita GDDP in previous period; Fin_Dev: Deposit, Credit and CDR in column I, II and III, respectively; INVEST: per capita investment; CRIME: number of crimes per 100,000 population; and ENROL: natural logarithm of NER. Collapse option in xtabond2 (Roodman 2009a) is applied to reduce instruments count. Robust standard errors are presented in parentheses. *, **, *** denote statistical significance at 10, 5, 1%, respectively

considered important in addition to fostering financial development at a macro-level. Our results are in conformity to previous studies in the context of different countries (Guiso et al. 2004; Fafchamps and Schundeln 2013; Kendall 2012). However, unlike previous studies, we consider deposit and CD ratio along with credit as alternative indicators of financial development and found that deposit per capita exhibit strong association with district-level economic development.

The possible channels through which financial development may foster economic growth across districts are savings and hence investments. Nevertheless, human capital and productivity of existing capital also play a significant role in this regard. In fact, smaller entrepreneurs in local markets require access to cost-effective banking system and require localised banking solutions to cater to their needs. Moreover, having access to a bank account provides formal avenues of savings which boosts deposits having strong positive effect on economic growth. Therefore, having access to a bank account and hence saving and deposit in local banking markets are observed to be more strongly related to per capita income and economic growth. Perhaps, this also becomes instrumental in reducing the incidence of poverty in India. For instance,

Table 12.6 First-difference estimation: with LogGDDP as dependent variable with reduced instrument count

Variable	I	II	III
INITIAL	0.2362***	0.6213***	0.7116***
	(0.0599)	(0.0439)	(0.0285)
Fin_Dev	0.4972***	0.1261***	−0.0493
	(0.0626)	(0.435)	(0.0392)
INVEST	0.0063**	0.0087***	0.0079***
	(0.0040)	(0.0040)	(0.0039)
CRIME	−0.2364***	−0.0234	0.0046
	(0.0931)	(0.0857)	(0.0821)
ENROL	0.1427***	0.1846***	0.2028***
	(0.0345)	(0.0334)	(0.0330)
AR (2) test	−0.68	0.21	−0.29
	(0.495)	(0.833)	(0.775)
No. of Obs.	1112	1111	1111
Number of groups	277	277	277
Number of instruments	28	28	28

Dependent variable, INCOME: per capita real GDDP. Explanatory variables are: INITIAL: per capita real GDDP in previous period; Fin_Dev: DEPOSIT, CREDIT and CDR in column I, II and III, respectively; INVEST: investment per capita; CRIME: number of crimes per 100,000 population; and ENROL: natural logarithm of NER. Collapse option in xtabond2 (Roodman 2009a) is applied to reduce instruments count. Robust standard errors are presented in parentheses. *, **, *** denote statistical significance at 10, 5, 1%, respectively

PMJDY has been instrumental in this regard which ensured almost 100% banking sector coverage at the household level across Indian states and 316.7 million new bank accounts were opened and led to a deposit mobilisation to the tune of INR 811.57 billion[19] At individual level too, the World Bank Findex database reports that number of bank account of Indian adults has gone up from 35% in 2011 to 80% in 2017.[20]

An important policy question in this regard relates to whether opening a bank account ensures that an individual effectively operates that account. One problem that may inhibit financial development to have its full effect in intermediation process and hence economic growth and poverty at local level is the dormancy of bank accounts opened through financial inclusion schemes such as PMJDY. There may be few possible reasons for non-operation of bank accounts such as distance from bank branch, cost of operating bank account, time and travel costs and lack of money to be

[19]As on 23 May 2018. Source: www.pmjdy.gov.in (Accessed 31.5.2018).

[20]Source: https://globalfindex.worldbank.org/node (Accessed: 31.5.2018).

put into account. *Second*ly, while emphasising on the significance of financial development, we cannot undermine the role of other income and employment generating activities at the district level.

12.5.5 Limitations

First, due to limited availability of data, we were restricted to use data pertaining to a bunch of states. However, with increasing availability of more micro-level data, future analysis of finance–growth relationship at the district level is expected to become more rigorous and provide more robust evidence on finance–growth nexus. Second, period of analysis in this study is limited to 7 years during 2004–05 to 2010–11. Data availability for longer time series for larger set of districts is expected to unveil more robust conclusions and better policy implications. Third, there are quality issues with respect to district level data set of per capita income. Similarly, statistical data on few other indicators such as crime is also not foolproof and may not fully reflect the true picture of law and order situation in a district. Finally, GMM specification pertaining to this study is linear in nature. However, as found in previous literature, financial development may have nonlinear effect on growth (Cecchetti and Kharroubi 2012; Law and Singh 2014; Arcand et al. 2015). Therefore, future studies may explore nonlinear association between financial development and economic growth at local level too.

12.6 Concluding Remarks

This chapter examines finance–growth relationship in the context of Indian districts and attempts to provide policy implications on local access to financial services and hence growth of local economy. We find that both deposit and credit per capita have positive and significant association not only with district-level growth but also with income per capita. Effect of deposit mobilisation appears to be much stronger than that of credit per capita, which highlights the crucial role of branch access in intermediation process in local economy. As banks constitute the primary source of financing for agriculture and small-scale industries in local economy, the main channels through which financial development is ought to affect real output at district level are through the boost of savings and hence investment activity. Our findings implicate the importance of bottom-up approach of decision-making in which local financial conditions are considered as significant as fostering financial development at macro-level. Adoption of bottom-up approach is also supported by previous literature (Ascani et al. 2012). What seems to be more important is to enhance reliable access to bank credit to the local economy. Reserve Bank of India adopted several initiatives to extend the banking outreach in unbanked locations. As mentioned before, RBI's branch licensing policy favoured opening new branches in unbanked districts. Banks are also granted permission to use the services of business facilitators and business correspondents in outreach activities by extending savings and loan facilities to unbanked locations (RBI 2010). In particular, banks are encouraged to use the services of non-government organisations such as self-help groups (SHGs) and microfinance institutions (MFIs) to act as intermediaries to facilitate access to finance in local economy. High repayment performance and reduced transaction costs to lenders are some of the major advantages of microfinance programmes to bring people at the bottom of the pyramid under SHG. SHG–Bank linkage programme gained further importance with the initiative of NABARD to intensify these activities in 13 States, which accounted for 70.0 per cent of the rural poor population (RBI 2007). While *Debt and Investment Survey* (2002) revealed that role of institutional agencies in outstanding cash debts of the households declined from 66.3% in 1991 to 57.1% in 2002, *Key Indicators of Debt and Investment in India*, 2013 (GOI 2014), revealed that flow of credit by institutional agencies is recorded to be 86 per cent and the share of non-institutional agencies is recorded to be 69%. Therefore, in order to expand access of formal credit to local economies and expand financial inclusion and hence growth, banks are required to finance new entrepreneurs. This is expected to generate new income and employment opportunities in rural economy (Mohan 2006).

While emphasising the role of financial development, we also considered the role other growth determinants at district level such as net enrolment ratio (NER), as a proxy of human capital. In all of our empirical models, we find positive and significant effect of human capital. Previous studies predicted that higher levels of human capital may trigger alternative channels of growth and production which are less finance-intensive. Amin and Mattoo (2008) found that, during 1990s, areas with greater levels of human capital experienced much faster growth of the services sector which is less financially constrained. Kendall (2012) also found that improvement of human capital mitigates the effect of financing constraints on growth. We also observe that incidence of crime is negatively associated with economic growth as well as income per capita. Overall, we conclude that local conditions such as local financial development, human capital and crime rate matter for district-level economic development in India.

Appendix

See Tables 12.7, 12.8, 12.9, 12.10, 12.11 and Figs. 12.6, 12.7.

Table 12.7 Variable definition and data sources

Variables	Definition	Source
CRIME	Logarithm of total number of crimes reported per 100,000 population	NCRB (data.gov.in)
INITIAL	Ln (GDDP($t-1$)), where GDDP is per capita gross district domestic product	CMIE States of India
INVEST	Logarithm of total real per capita investments	CMIE States of India
DEPOSIT	Logarithm of real per capita deposit	CMIE States of India
CREDIT	Logarithm of real per capita credit	CMIE States of India
ENROL	Logarithm of net enrolment ratio	District Information System for Education
GROWTH	Per capita GDDP growth, calculated as Ln (GDDP(t)) − Ln (GDDP($t-1$))	CMIE States of India
CDRATIO	Ratio of real per capita credit to real per capita deposit	CMIE States of India

Table 12.8 First-difference estimation with growth as dependent variable (two-step estimation)

	I	II	III
INITIAL	−0.8972***	−0.4105***	−0.3215***
	(0.1199)	(0.0721)	(0.0544)
Fin_Dev	0.4934***	0.1128*	−0.0102
	(0.0947)	(0.0593)	(0.0468)
INVEST	0.0102*	0.0106**	0.0069
	(0.0057)	(0.0054)	(0.0052)
CRIME	−0.0603	0.0187	0.0243
	(0.1115)	(0.1069)	(0.1129)
ENROL	0.1696***	0.1827***	0.2499***
	(0.0383)	(0.0393)	(0.0431)
AR (2) test	−0.32	0.17	−0.74
	(0.751)	(0.862)	(0.547)
No. of Obs.	1112	1111	1111
Number of groups	277	277	277
Number of instruments	28	28	28

GROWTH: growth of per capita real GDDP. INITIAL: real per capita GDDP in previous period; Fin_Dev: DEPOSIT, CREDIT and CDR in column I, II and III, respectively; INVEST: per capita investment; CRIME: number of crimes per 100,000 population; and ENROL: natural logarithm of NER. Collapse option in xtabond2 (Roodman 2009a) is applied to reduce instruments count. Robust standard errors and are presented in parentheses. *, **, *** denote statistical significance at 10, 5, 1%, respectively

Table 12.9 First-difference GMM results with LogGDDP as dependent variable (two-step estimation)

Variable	I	II	III
INITIAL	0.2430**	0.6282***	0.7140***
	(0.1097)	(0.0644)	(0.0474)
Fin_Dev	0.4054***	0.1085***	−0.0080
	(0.0853)	(0.0551)	(0.0413)
INVEST	0.0093*	0.0096*	0.0066
	(0.0050)	(0.0049)	(0.0047)
CRIME	−0.0392	0.0166	0.0385
	(0.1071)	(0.0952)	(0.0988)
ENROL	0.1483***	0.1591***	0.2120***
	(0.0345)	(0.0322)	(0.0343)
AR (2) test	−0.68	0.49	−0.33
	(0.495)	(0.833)	(0.739)
No. of Obs.	1112	1111	1111
Number of groups	277	277	277
Number of instruments	28	28	28

Dependent variable, INCOME: per capita real GDDP. Explanatory variables are: Initial: per capita real GDDP in previous period; Fin_Dev: DEPOSIT, CREDIT and CDR in column I, II and III, respectively; INVEST: investment per capita; CRIME: number of crimes per 100,000 population; and ENROL: natural logarithm of NER. Robust standard errors and are presented in parentheses. *, **, *** denote statistical significance at 10, 5, 1%, respectively

Table 12.10 First-difference GMM results with growth as dependent variable and year dummies

	I	II	III
INITIAL	−0.5652***	−0.5258***	−0.5452***
	(0.0584)	(0.0461)	(0.0409)
Fin_Dev	0.2736**	0.0380	0.0073
	(0.1172)	(0.0253)	(0.0262)
INVEST	0.0069**	0.0027	0.0011
	(0.0033)	(0.0031)	(0.0031)
CRIME	−0.2169***	−0.2248***	−0.2533***
	(0.0633)	(0.0687)	(0.0699)
ENROL	0.0238	0.0329	0.0294

(continued)

Table 12.10 (continued)

	I	II	III
	(0.0243)	(0.0251)	(0.0256)
AR (2) test	−1.09	−1.22	−1.30
	(0.274)	(0.224)	(0.194)
Year dummies	Yes	Yes	Yes
No. of Obs.	1112	1111	1111
Number of groups	277	277	277
Number of instruments	95	95	95

GROWTH: growth of per capita real GDDP. INITIAL: real per capita GDDP in previous period; Fin_Dev: DEPOSIT, CREDIT and CDR in column I, II and III, respectively; INVEST: per capita investment; CRIME: number of crimes per 100,000 population; and ENROL: natural logarithm of NER. Robust standard errors and are presented in parentheses. *, **, *** denote statistical significance at 10, 5, 1%, respectively

Table 12.11 First-difference GMM results with LogGDDP as dependent variable and year dummies

Variable	I	II	III
INITIAL	0.5090**	0.5357***	0.5196***
	(0.0524)	(0.0435)	(0.0391)
Fin_Dev	0.2187***	0.0323	0.0078
	(0.0989)	(0.0218)	(0.0227)
INVEST	0.0055*	0.0022	0.0009
	(0.0029)	(0.0028)	(0.0029)
CRIME	−0.1843***	−0.1967***	−0.2201***
	(0.0542)	(0.0593)	(0.0596)
ENROL	0.0206	0.0286	0.0253
	(0.0197)	(0.0202)	(0.0206)
AR(2) test	−0.81	−0.88	−0.95
	(0.419)	(0.380)	(0.340)
Year dummies	Yes	Yes	Yes
No. of Obs.	1112	1111	1111
Number of groups	277	277	277
Number of instruments	95	95	95

Dependent variable, INCOME: per capita real GDDP. Explanatory variables are: INITIAL: per capita real GDDP in previous period; Fin_Dev: DEPOSIT, CREDIT and CDR in column I, II and III, respectively; INVEST: investment per capita; CRIME: number of crimes per 100,000 population; and ENROL: natural logarithm of NER. Robust standard errors are presented in parentheses. *, **, *** denote statistical significance at 10, 5, 1%, respectively

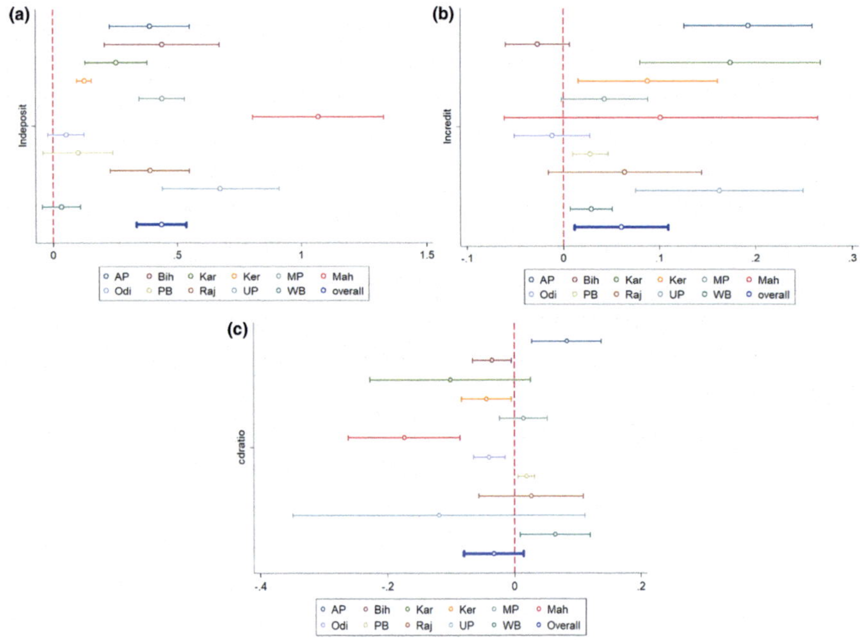

Fig. 12.6 State-wise verses overall coefficient plots of financial development (**a** lndeposit, **b** lncredit, **c** cdratio) on growth. *Note* lndeposit: natural logarithm of district-wise deposit per capita; lncredit: natural logarithm of district-wise credit per capita; cdratio: credit-deposit ratio. Above coefficients correspond to state-specific panel GMM regression as specified in Table 12.3, only the coefficients of financial development are shown along with 90% confidence interval. As the data for Assam was available for one year, its panel estimation results are not available. Coefficient estimates are plotted using coefplot command (Jann 2014)

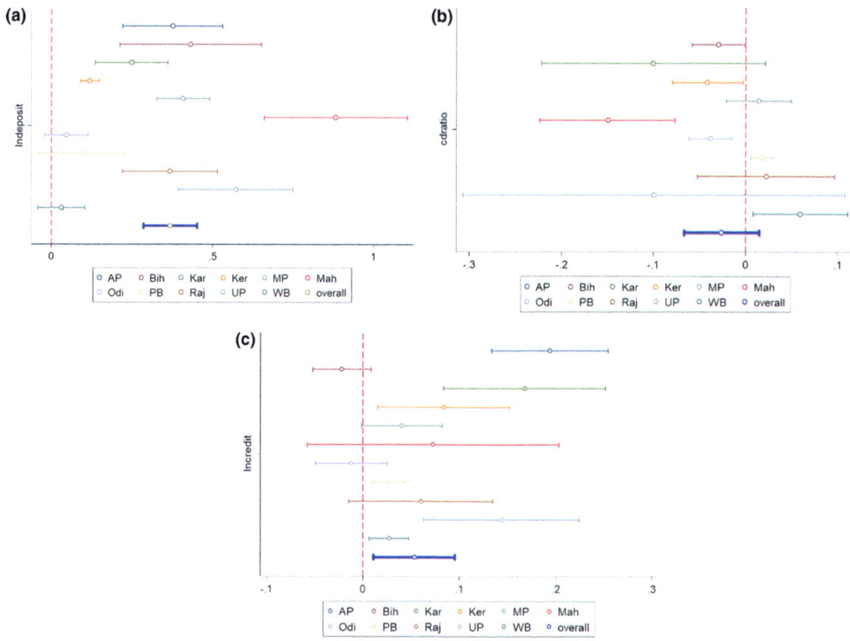

Fig. 12.7 State-wise verses overall coefficient plots of financial development (**a** lndeposit, **b** lncredit, **c** cdratio) on income. *Note* lndeposit: natural logarithm of deposit per capita; lncredit: natural logarithm of credit per capita; and cdratio: credit-deposit ratio. Above coefficients correspond to state-specific panel GMM regression as specified in Table 12.4, only the coefficients of financial development are shown along with 90% confidence interval. As the data for Assam was available for one year, its panel estimation results are not available. Coefficient estimates are plotted using coefplot command of Jann (2014)

References

Acharya, D., Amanulla, S., & Joy, S. (2009). Financial development and economic growth in Indian states: An examination. *International Research Journal of Finance and Economics, 24*(2), 117–130.

Amin, M., & Mattoo, A. (2008). *Human capital and the changing structure of the Indian economy*. World Bank Working Paper Series 4576.

Arcand, J. L., Berkes, E., & Panizza, U. (2015). Too much finance? *Journal of Economic Growth, 20*(2), 105–148.

Arellano, M., & Bond, S. (1991). Some tests of specification for panel data: Monte Carlo evidence and an application to employment equations. *Review of Economic Studies, 58*(2), 277–297.

Arellano, M., & Bover, O. (1995). Another look at the instrumental-variable estimation of error-components models. *Journal of Econometrics, 68*, 29–52.

Ascani, A., Crescenzi, R., & Iammarino, S. (2012). *Regional economic development: A review*. 7th European community framework programme. SEARCH Working Paper 1(03).

Bandyopadhyay, S. (2012). Convergence club empirics: Evidence from Indian states. In J. A. Bishop, R. Salas (Eds.) *Inequality, mobility and segregation: Essays in honor of Jacques Silber* (Research on Economic Inequality), Vol. 20 (pp. 175–203). Emerald Group Publishing Limited.

Bardhan, P. (2010). *Awakening giants: Feet of clay*. Princeton N. J.: Princeton University Press.

Barro, R. J. (1991). Economic growth in a cross section of countries. *Quarterly Journal of Economics, 106*(2), 407–443.

Barro, R. J., & Lee, J. W. (1993). International comparisons of educational attainment. *Journal of Monetary Economics, 32*(3), 363–394.

Basu, K., & Maertens, A. (2009). The growth of industry and services in South Asia and its impact on employment. In A. Sadiq & E. Ghani (Eds.), *Accelerating growth and job creation in South Asia* (pp. 81–140). Washington, DC: World Bank, Washington.

Beck, T., & Levine, R. (2004). Stock markets, banks, and growth: panel evidence. *Journal of Banking & Finance, 28*(3), 423–442.

Beck, T., Levine, R. E., & Levkov, A. (2009). Big bad banks? The winners and losers from bank deregulation in the United States. *Journal of Finance, 65*(5), 1637–1667.

Bhagwati, J., & Panagariya, A. (2013). *Why growth matters: How economic growth in India reduced poverty and the lessons for other developing countries*. UK: Hachette.

Bhattacharya, P. C., & Sivasubramanian, M. N. (2003). Financial development and economic growth in India: 1970–1971 to 1998–1999. *Applied Financial Economics, 13*(12), 925–929.

Blundell, R., & Bond, S. (1998). Initial conditions and moment restrictions in dynamic panel data models. *Journal of Econometrics, 87*(1), 115–143.

Burgess, R., & Pande, R. (2005). Do rural banks matter? Evidence from the Indian social banking experiment. *American Economic Review, 95*(2), 780–795.

Cashin, P., & Sahay, R. (1996). Regional economic growth and convergence in India Finance and Development. *International Monetary Fund, 33*(1), 49–52.

Cecchetti, G., & Kharroubi, E. (2012). *Reassessing the impact of finance on growth*. BIS Working Papers No. 381, Bank for International Settlements.

Centre for Monitoring Indian Economy (CMIE) States of India database. http://statesofindia.cmie.com.

Chattopadhyay, R., & Duflo, E. (2004). Women as policy makers: Evidence from a randomized policy experiment in India. *Econometrica, 72*(5), 1409–1443.

Christopoulos, D. K., & Tsionas, E. G. (2004). Financial development and economic growth: Evidence from panel unit root and cointegration tests. *Journal of Development Economics, 73*(1), 55–74.

Das, S. (2012). The convergence debate and econometric approaches: Evidence from India. In C. Ghate (Ed.), *The oxford handbook of the Indian economy* (pp. 766–782). New York: Oxford University Press.

Das, S., Ghate, C., & Robertson, P. R. (2015). Remoteness, urbanisation and India's unbalanced growth. *World Development, 66,* 572–587.
Debroy, B., & Bhandari, L. (2003). *District-level deprivation in the New Millennium.* Delhi: Konark Publishers.
Demetriades, P. O., & Luintel, K. B. (1997). The direct costs of financial repression: Evidence from India. *Review of Economics and Statistics, 79*(2), 311–320.
Dow, S. C., & Fuentes, C. J. R. (1997). Regional finance: A survey. *Regional Studies, 31*(9), 903–920.
Drez, J., & Sen, A. (2013). *An uncertain glory: India and its contradictions.* Princeton: Princeton University Press.
Dubey, A. (2009). Intra-state disparities in Gujarat, Haryana, Kerala, Orissa and Punjab. *Economic and Political Weekly, 44*(26/27), 224–230.
Fafchamps, M., & Schündeln, M. (2013). Local financial development and firm performance: Evidence from Morocco. *Journal of Development Economics, 103,* 15–28.
Fuentes, C. J. R. (2005). *Regional monetary policy.* Routledge.
Ghate, C., & Wright, S. (2012). The V-factor: Distribution, timing and correlates of the great Indian growth turnaround. *Journal of Development Economics, 99*(1), 58–67.
Ghosh, M. (2008). Economic reforms, growth and regional divergence in India. *Margin, Journal of Applied Economic Research, 2*(3), 265–275.
Guiso, L., Sapienza, P., & Zingales, L. (2004). Does local financial development matter? *Quarterly Journal of Economics, 119*(3), 929–969.
Government of India. (1991). *Report of the Narasimham Committee on the financial system (Narasimham Committee I).* New Delhi: Ministry of Finance.
Government of India. (1998). *Report of the Narasimham Committee on the banking sector reforms (Narasimham Committee II).* New Delhi: Ministry of Finance.
Government of India. (2014). Key Indicators of Debt and investment in India. Ministry of Statistics and Programme Implementation.
Indira, A., Rajeev, M., & Vyasulu, V. (2002). Estimation of district income and poverty in Indian states. *Economic and Political Weekly*, 2171–2177, June 1.
Jann, B. (2014). Plotting regression coefficients and other estimates. *Stata Journal, 14*(4), 708–737.
Jayaratne, J., & Strahan, P. E. (1996). The finance-growth nexus: Evidence from bank branch deregulation. *Quarterly Journal of Economics, 111*(3), 639–670.
Lall, S. V., Wang, H. G., & Deichmann, U. (2010). *Infrastructure and city competitiveness in India.* Working paper No. 22/2010, World Institute for Development Economics Research.
Kendall, J. (2012). Local financial development and growth. *Journal of Banking & Finance, 36*(5), 1548–1562.
King, R. G., & Levine, R. (1993a). Finance and growth: Schumpeter might be right. *Quarterly Journal of Economics, 108*(3), 717–737.
King, R. G., & Levine, R. (1993b). Finance, entrepreneurship, and growth: Theory and evidence. *Journal of Monetary Economics, 32*(3), 513–542.
Kurian, N. J. (2000). Widening regional disparities in India: Some indicators. *Economic and Political Weekly, 35*(7), 538–550.
Law, S. H., & Singh, N. (2014). Does too much finance harm economic growth? *Journal of Banking and Finance, 41*, 36–44.
Levine, R. (1997). Financial development and economic growth: Views and agenda. *Journal of Economic Literature, 35*(2), 688–726.
Levine, R. (2005). Finance and growth: Theory and evidence. In A. Philippe & N. D. Steven (Eds.), *Handbook of economic growth* (Vol. 1, pp. 865–934). Amsterdam, North–Holland: Elsevier.
Liang, Q., & Jian-Zhou, T. (2006). Financial development and economic growth: Evidence from China. *China Economic Review, 17*(4), 395–411.
Luintel, K. B., & Khan, M. (1999). A quantitative reassessment of the finance–growth nexus: Evidence from a multivariate VAR. *Journal of Development Economics, 60*(2), 381–405.
Misra, B. S. (2003). Analytics of credit-output nexus in India. *Reserve Bank of India Occasional Papers, 24*(1–2), 145–171.

Mohan, R. (2005). Financial sector reforms in India: Policies and performance analysis. *Economic and Political Weekly, 40*(12), 1106–1121.

Mohan, R. (2006). Agricultural credit in India: Status, Issues and future agenda. *Economic and Political Weekly, 41*(11), 1013–1023.

National Crime Records Bureau (NCRB): Available http://ncrb.gov.in/.

Nickell, S. (1981). Biases in dynamic models with fixed effects. *Econometrica, 49*, 1417–1426.

Pagano, M. (1993). Financial markets and growth: an overview. *European Economic Review, 37*(2), 613–622.

Patrick, H. T. (1966). Financial development and economic growth in underdeveloped countries. *Economic Development and Cultural Change, 14*(2), 174–189.

Petersen, M. A., & Rajan, R. G. (2002). Does distance still matter? The information revolution in small business lending. *Journal of Finance, 57*(6), 2533–2570.

Raman, R., & Kumari, R. (2012). Regional disparity in agricultural development: A district level analysis for Uttar Pradesh. *Journal of Regional Development and Planning, 1*(2), 71–90.

Rajan, R., & Zingales, L. (1998). Financial dependence and growth. *American Economic Review, 88*(3), 559–586.

Reserve Bank of India. (2007). *Credit market.* http://rbidocs.rbi.org.in/rdocs/PublicationReport/Pdfs/77575.pdf, http://www.rbi.org.in. Accessed on December 10, 2018.

Reserve Bank of India. (2010). *Master circular on branch authorisation.* https://rbidocs.rbi.org.in/rdocs/notification/PDFs/58MCCB010710_F.pdf. Accessed on February 5, 2019.

Reserve Bank of India. (2014). *Master circular: Lead bank scheme.* http://www.rbi.org.in.

Rioja, F., & Valev, N. (2004). Does one size fit all? A reexamination of the finance and growth relationship. *Journal of Development Economics, 74*(2), 429–447.

Rioja, F., & Valev, N. (2014). Stock markets, banks and the sources of economic growth in low and high income countries. *Journal of Economics and Finance, 38*(2), 302–320.

Roodman, D. (2009a). How to do xtabond2: An introduction to difference and system GMM in stata. *Stata Journal, 9*(1), 86–136.

Roodman, D. (2009b). A note on the theme of too many instruments. *Oxford Bulletin of Economics and Statistics, 71*(1), 135–158.

Sharma, R., & Bardhan, S. (2017a). Finance growth nexus across Indian states: Evidences from panel cointegration and causality tests. *Economic Change and Restructuring, 50*(1), 1–20.

Sharma, R., & Bardhan, S. (2017b). Does regional financial development matter for growth? Evidence from Indian states. *International Economic Journal, 31*(4), 621–646.

Sastry, N. S. (2003). District level poverty estimates—Feasibility of using NSS household consumer expenditure survey data. *Economic and Political Weekly, 38*(4), 409–412.

Singh, Nirvikar, Bhandari, Laveesh, Chen, Aoyu, & Khare, Aarti. (2003). Regional inequality in India: A fresh look. *Economic and Political Weekly, 38*(11), 1069–1073.

Singh, N., Kendall, J., Jain, R. K., & Chander, J. (2014). Regional inequality in India in the 1990s: A district-level view. *Economic and Political Weekly, 49*(15), 71–76.

Valverde, C. S., Lopez, D. P. R., & Rodríguez, F. F. (2007). Financial innovations in banking: Impact on regional growth. *Regional Studies, 41*(3), 311–326.

Part VII
Social Sector

Chapter 13
A Neoliberal Approach to Policy Making in Indian Higher Education During the Post-liberalization Era

Saumen Chattopadhyay and Aishna Sharma

Abstract It looks at the series of higher education reforms which have been mooted and implemented since the beginning of the liberalization phase in India. It unravels the rationality behind the reform measures and traces its evolution over the last two and half decades. It then questions whether the rationale of promoting market in higher education, changing governance of public institutions and the increased role of the private sector based on the concept of efficiency are tenable or not in the context of higher education in a developing country like India.

13.1 Introduction

Policy making in the education sector and in particular in the higher education sector gradually came under the influence of the new economic policy which consisted of the Structural Adjustment Program (SAP) advocated by the World Bank and the stabilization package advised by the International Monetary Fund (IMF). While the loans from the World Bank sought to foster competitiveness at the sectoral level by encouraging private sector participation in a regulated market, the stabilization package targeted fiscal deficit in terms of gross domestic product (GDP) to stabilize the macro-economy by reining in the expenditure growth and mobilizing more revenue.[1] Initially the Centre and later the states were required to enact the Fiscal Responsibility and Budget Management (FRBM) Act to keep the fiscal deficit within the limit of 3% of GDP. Higher education policy making gradually started reflecting the major tenets of the new economic policy like budget cut, restructuring of the public sector,

[1] Revenue augmentation measures included encouraging tax compliance, hike in user charges to mobilize more non-tax revenue and disinvestment of public assets.

S. Chattopadhyay (✉)
Zakir Husain Centre for Educational Studies, Jawaharlal Nehru University, New Delhi, India
e-mail: saumen@mail.jnu.ac.in

A. Sharma
Visiting Faculty, Shiv Nadar University, Noida, India
e-mail: aishnas@gmail.com

P. K. Biswas and P. Das (eds.), *Indian Economy: Reforms and Development*, India Studies in Business and Economics, https://doi.org/10.1007/978-981-13-8269-7_13

facilitating the entry of the private sector and a move towards construction of a higher education market.[2]

Reforms could broadly be categorized into two kinds: one, funding reforms and two, non-funding regulatory and/governance reforms. The undertones of all these reforms have been efficiency—both allocative and technical, in the higher education system.

This chapter seeks to chronicle the reform measures mooted and implemented for the higher education sector as India geared up for embracing the gradual unfolding of the new economic policy in three phases. The chapter then assesses the implications of these recommendations on excellence or quality, and juxtaposes the objective of efficiency with achieving excellence or quality.

The chapter is structured as follows: at the outset, it highlights the nature of higher education. In the sections that follow from there, it discusses reforms under the four categories: trends in public funding, infusion of private players, governance reforms and construction of regulated markets, during different phases beginning with the new economic policy. The chapter concludes with an appraisal of these reforms on quality of higher education in India.

13.2 Higher Education as a Public Good

The new economic policy questions the role of the public sector and argues for a larger role of the private sector. The Indian Higher Education has seen a profusion of either market principles in the functioning of public universities or direct privatization with the rampant growth of private sector in the system (as we would also see in the sections that ensue). There has also been a tendency to move from input based funding to output based funding and channeling funds through market like vouchers, fee reimbursement scheme, industry funding, and more recently through Higher Education Funding Agency[3] (HEFA). The nature of higher education is put to question as a result of these changes; is it a public good or a private good? In a way, the reform measures can be viewed as a debate on the nature and extent of public-private divide in funding of higher education and regulatory intervention of the government.

Higher education is often classified as a public good which forms the basis for arguing in favour of public funding of higher education. But we need to distinguish between the positive and the normative approach. In terms of specific characteristics, higher education is not a pure public good. This is also evident from the fact that there has been an increase in private participation in higher education world

[2]SAP and the stabilization package together constitute the Washington Consensus as both the institutions are located at the Washington D.C. Neoliberalism as an ideology, arguably, informs Washington Consensus.

[3]Higher Education Funding Agency was set up in 2016, in order to finance infrastructure and research in universities through loans. The principal portion of the loan would be repaid through internal receipts, generated through fee receipts, research earnings, etc.

over. This is different from saying that higher education should be a public good to capitalize on publicness of higher education to inculcate responsible citizenship and build an inclusive society. If we go strictly by the definition of public good as given by Samuelson (1954), higher education is excludable as access to higher education is regulated depending on eligibility and paying capacity. Higher education is both rival in its consumption and excludable in benefits[4] as admission is not assured for all in view of the limited number of seats in the HEIs and merit as one has to become eligible for admission in a HEI. Non-rivalry is essentially a case of externalities. However, those who take admission and pursue higher studies undergo transformation to generate externalities for the society. There arises a case for public funding because these externalities account for the difference between the social demand and private demand. Should there be public funding only because of the positive externalities that HE generates? The portrayal of the private demand and social demand does not include those who cannot pay for education and hence they remain outside the realm of the market. For the purpose of social mobility, inclusiveness needs to be ensured. Those who are meritorious need to be supported by scholarship otherwise they would end up investing less on their education and the nation as a whole would suffer. There is a transformation that education brings about in the individuals to create a public sphere to build up a society of concerned and responsible citizens. Without scruples and morality, no economic system can function at its best as corruption erodes the fundamentals of the society. The outcome of education in the form of human capital formation is embodied in an individual who stands to gain in terms of higher stream of future earnings as a reward for higher productivity.

Higher education is therefore best argued as a quasi-public good (Marginson 2007; Chattopadhyay 2012) as it combines the features of both private and a public good. The development of scientific literacy is essential for, distribution of knowledge and promotion of arts and culture (Marginson 2016). This is not only necessary to achieve participatory and inclusive development but also to gain from merit and cultivate talent to build up a knowledge based competitive economy.

Higher education should not be considered as a merit good either as graduates do not suffer from the same kind of deficiencies as the school going children and their parents do.[5] Generally primary education is considered to be a merit good which warrants full public support for the schools as the Right to Education (RTE) Act exemplifies. There is one more dimension to the public funding of higher education and that is the mode of funding. While it is widely recognized that higher education needs to be publicly funded, the issue of poor governance has been a matter of concern for the policy makers. Despite 'higher education' being a quasi-public good,

[4]By excludability in consumption of higher education is meant that the consumption of higher education, in terms of vacancy/admission, by one individual diminishes the possibility of admission/availability of that very vacancy for the other individual. Rivalry in benefits arises from the fact that the benefits of higher education, in terms of higher future income stream, is enjoyed only by the individual who invests in education, and not others.

[5]This is as per the definition of merit good given by Musgrave and Musgrave (1989) which argues that the preferences suffer from myopia and information asymmetry and hence the government should intervene instead of banking on people's choices.

the Indian higher education policy has been steered by the neo-liberal principles which has sought to undermine the public good character of higher education. We would now examine the policy trail in the rest of the paper and try to understand the ramifications on equity, excellence and quality, the three often-quoted objectives for the higher education sector as a whole.

13.3 The Neoliberal Elements of Higher Education Reform Measures

The entire gamut of new economic policies framed under the neoliberal influence can be classified into four categories (i) a cut in public sector funding, (ii) facilitation of entry of the private sector, (iii) restructuring of the public sector and measures to improve governance; and (iv) construction of a regulated quasi-market. Public sector governance reform upholds the principle of technical efficiency and the rationale for market construction is based on achieving allocative efficiency (Jongbloed 2004). The governance reform is advocated in line with the new public management (NPM), which is based on corporate principles. Public-private partnerships (PPP) can also be viewed as one way of governance reform. Under the NPM as well as PPP, public HEIs are governed in the corporate style to make them efficient and productive. The governance reforms aim at improving technical efficiency, by making the institutions cost conscious. Technical efficiency essentially focuses on the strengthening of the use of input and production of output/service with the purpose of restoration and consolidation of the educational production function. This entails institutional governance reform. The other strand is a cut in the public expenditure, coupled with exploring other modes of funding, which is often argued to curb wastage and ensure accountability in the HEIs. Accountability brings in efficiency in public institutions (Mortimer 1972; Berdahl 1990; Alexander 2000; Huisman and Currie 2004; Kai 2009) by reduction in wastage of resources and by providing justification for expending public money by registering their performance. It was argued that funds be reallocated from higher education to school level education, which was thought to be conferring greater externalities on the society. A cut in public expenditure, thus, is a case of allocative efficiency within the education sector. Table 13.1 shows the relative shares of GDP spent on school level education and higher education over years. It can be seen that the share of school level education (elementary and secondary combined) has been consistently above that of higher education. On an average the expenditure on school level education constituted 2.5% of the GDP from 2005–06 to 2012–13, while the expenditure on higher education as a proportion of GDP stood at 0.74% on an average during the same period.

Table 13.1 Public expenditure on education as a percentage of GDP

Education level	Year							
	2005–06	2006–07	2007–08	2008–09	2010–11	2011–12	2012–13	Average
Higher education	0.67	0.7	0.83	0.87	0.86	0.62	0.63	0.74
School level	2.5	2.49	2.3	2.37	2.68	2.69	2.5	2.5

Source Annual Budget, various years (GoI)

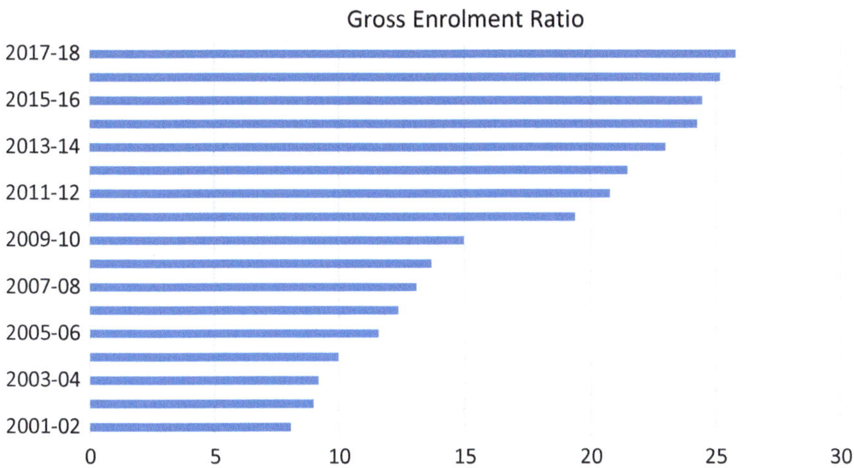

Fig. 13.1 Gross enrolment ratio over years. *Source* Education Statistics at a glance (2016). Report on All India Survey of Higher Education, various years

Despite the abysmal public expenditure on higher education vis-à-vis school education, the gross enrolment ratio (GER)[6] has shot up from 8.1% in 2001–02 to 25.8% in 2017–18, as shown in Fig. 13.1.

As would be seen in the ensuing sections, much of this enrolment is catered to by the private sector (privately managed colleges). It was an outcome of the other two reform measures, that is private sector participation and construction of a regulated market which are presumed to bestow sovereignty on the market participants to make choices, providing freedom to the providers as well as to the students who are viewed as consumers, changing thereby the role of the State to only that of a regulator or facilitator' of the market conditions and foster competitiveness. These two measures seeking to achieve allocative efficiency in the system improve, arguably both quality of service delivery of the HEIs and saving of government resources. These claims are however highly contestable. Given that efficiency in an education

[6]Gross Enrolment Ratio refers to the total enrolment in higher education, regardless of age, expressed as a percentage to the eligible official population (18–23 years) in a given school year.

market is selection based or S-efficiency rather than exchange based or E-efficiency, the role of free choices and competition is limited (Glennerster 1991). Further, the typical forces of market are required to be regulated to give more space to merit and the deserving rather than those who can afford to pay for the sake of quality and equity (Chattopadhyay 2012).

Though the market for higher education is an imperfect one by all counts, a market is still desired because it gives freedom to the students and the education providers to choose from and foster competitiveness as an instrument of realizing the potential of human capital embodied.

Since 1991, higher education policies reflect both the attempts, construction of a regulated higher education market as suggested by various commissions and committees and its culmination in the repeal of the UGC Act proposed on 30 June 2018. The various kinds of freedom to the providers and the consumers which are required to install market like conditions can be summed up as given in Table 13.2.

Market entails that both the consumers and the producers respond to the signals in terms of the prices and the composition of demand. However, there is an internal contradiction if we juxtapose freedom to determine prices with that of freedom to determine courses to be offered. Cost recovery would mean that the HEIs would be required to customize their courses and admit students who can pay rather than who deserve to be given admission based on their merit and societal and economic backgrounds to ensure equal accessibility.

Students, as consumers, are to be provided with freedom to choose not only the institution they would like to pursue studies from but also freedom to choose the courses (credits) they would like to opt for. The students are provided information regarding the course-wise price in the institution brochure and also with the information on ranks of HEIs as a guide to the relative quality of HEIs. Following the World Bank argument, students should be charged high price for their education because the private rates of return for students, in terms of future income streams, are higher than the social rates of return (Psacharopolous 1986) and thereby role of prices in generating signals would be restored.[7] Giving freedom to the students begs the questions whether the students are really the customers. Both in teaching-learning and research, students and the teachers are the co-producers of quality knowledge. This

Table 13.2 Eight conditions for market

'Four freedoms' for providers	'Four freedoms' for consumers
Freedom of entry	Freedom to choose provider
Freedom to specify products	Freedom to choose product
Freedom to use available resources	Adequate information on prices and quality
Freedom to determine prices	Direct and cost-covering prices paid

Source Adapted from Jongbloed (2004)

[7]Higher education can be considered to be a quasi-public good which is assumed to have both the 'privateness' and 'publicness'. It is a public good because the externalities are generated but at the same time it is exclusive.

entails that the students have to work hard for the degrees as degrees are not for sale as paying fees ensures admission to a program of study. These are the fundamental flaws in the application of market principles to undertake governance reform. Not only these freedoms are internally inconsistent, these freedoms do not do justice to the principles higher education should seek to uphold for societal and economic benefits.

Starting from the early 1990s, the entire reform phase can be categorized into three periods as (1) 1991–2007, (2) 2007–08 to 2013–14 and (3) 2014–2018. Here the beginning of the second and the third phase had a major policy break from the previous one. We would like to discuss policy making under the four aspects of new economic policy during these three phases. As shall be discussed subsequently, such a paradigmatic shift, with a growing role for the private sector, has serious ramifications for all the three objectives, namely, expansion, inclusion and quality.

13.4 Policy Making During First Phase of Reform (1991–2007)

During this phase, there was an emphasis on only cutting public funds, exploring other modes of funding, and entry of private sector in the system, but no concrete regulatory framework to usher in markets in higher education sector, in true sense.

13.4.1 Public Funding

The policy during this phase, kick started by exploring other sources of funding higher education, than relying on public funding only. To begin with, the Punnayya Committee Report (1992–93) (GOI 1993) argued that the central universities should supplement the state efforts by raising their own resources and thus stabilize their functions and development. To promote internal efficiency and quality, negotiated mode of funding should be discontinued with.[8] It was proposed that the Central universities shift to a mix of input-funding and a student based funding system. This was argued to be promoting cost efficiency and competition amongst the universities.

The Birla-Ambani Report (GOI 2000) on reforms in education, also suggested for a creation of a market oriented competitive environment for higher education institutions. It proposed that funds be reallocated to primary education and user-pay principle must be applied in case of higher education, supported by loan provision. Basically, the Report argued for treating higher education more as a private good and creating a level playing field for larger private sector participation without giving any specific directions for the extent of regulation the market would need. There was

[8]Negotiated mode of funding involves allocation on the basis of previous year and providing incremental funds on the broadly laid formula.

opposition to the role of the private sector and the stage was not set for ushering in the market, albeit quasi-market in the context of higher education with adequate safeguards.

The Tenth Five Year Plan (2002–07) proposed rationalization of tuition fees, generation of internal sources of funding, and exploration of other avenues for receipt of contributions, donations, gifts, and sponsorships from the alumni, trusts, private sector and industries.

The CABE Committee (2004–05) (GOI 2005) contended that universities should have freedom to bring in entrepreneurial education, self-financed and job-oriented courses and to look for alternative sources of funding higher education, which would incentivize them to perform better. The level of funding should be enhanced by charging high and differentiated fees, to cover the cost of provision to generate reasonable amount of surplus. The Committee noted that financial aid acted as a tool to curtail freedom of the providers, both academic as well as financial. Thus there was a focus on improving the governance of the public funded institutions and be more responsive to the demand through changes in the mode of funding. The Committee also suggested to set up an Internal Quality Assessment Cell (IQAC) to ensure quality improvement.

Let us look at the trend in public funding during this phase. During the early 1990s, there was a cut in the public expenditure for the universities. The plan and non-plan expenditure registered a decline in real terms from 1990–91 to 1995–96, with expenditure on higher education as a percentage of GDP by the Centre was hovering around 0.4% (on an average) from 1990–91 to 2000–01 (Tilak 2004). This reduction was mostly felt in the maintenance grants, which is meant for recurring expenditures, including teachers' salaries. That the higher education was relegated as compared to school level education can be seen by the fact that the share of expenditure on higher education as a percentage of total expenditure on education was only 11.5%, on an average, during the same period (Tilak 2004). It was also a period when the White Paper (GOI 1997) on government subsidies branded higher education as a non-merit good which was used as a justification for compression of government subsidies[9] (Chattopadhyay 2009). The annual growth rate of the HEIs and the enrolment during 1995–96 to 2005–06 were 7–8 and 8% respectively (Duraisamy and Duraisamy 2015).

The Punnaya Committee (GOI 1993) suggested funding via cash support to the students as a part of this approach. The CABE Committee (GOI 2005) recommended choice-based credit courses which would bring in flexibility in the academic structure besides promoting students' mobility both within the country and abroad, thus ensuring academic parity with international standards. Though educational loans were made available for the students, the demand was low. During 1990–91 to 1999–2001, the annual growth rate in the loans accounts was 5.5% with a growth rate in outstanding loans amounting to 23.8% (Duraisamy and Duraisamy 2015).

---

[9]Though faced with criticism, higher education was later admitted to be a merit good but of lower merit compared to school education.

13.4.2 *Private Providers*

The number of private providers in the first phase was very few. However, the 10th FYP gave an indication towards increased private participation in the management of colleges and the deemed to be universities, with the two key words of liberalization and internationalization of higher education constituting the overall thrust of education policy reform. The period could be characterized by installation of concrete policy regarding the role of the private sector, as argued by Tilak (2014).

13.4.3 *Governance Reforms*

Governance reforms were rather subtle during this phase. Drawing on the Academic Audit practised in the then UK higher education system, the Punnayya Committee in early 1990s, suggested introduction of a monitoring system for the Indian Universities, which required developing indicators on their academic, financial and administrative operations. This was suggested to have information about the functioning of universities, which was expected to result into internal pressures for improved performance. It was also during this phase that National Assessment and Accreditation Council (NAAC) was set up, in 1994, to assess the performance at the institutional level. The NAAC didn't make a dent on internal life of universities because (a) accreditation was discretionary, and (b) it did not directly affect individual faculty behaviour; not every faculty was mandated to perform and deliver outputs every year. The CABE (Central Advisory Committee on Education) (GOI 2005) recommended implementing of academic audit and setting up on Internal Quality Assessment Cell (IQAC) and improve accountability of faculty thereof. But in the aggregate, the governance reforms were at a nascent stage during this phase.

13.4.4 *Construction of Market*

While this period did not witness any significant regulatory changes to construct markets in higher education, the CABE report recommended the Ministry of Human Resource Development (MHRD) to streamline the establishment and governance of private sector institutions and Self-Financing Institutions. The role of State was clearly mentioned to be that of a facilitator of self-financing courses.

In sum, we can say that this phase had set in the stage for a shift towards market-like condition in the Indian higher education, with a strong emphasis being placed on diversification of funding base by exploring other sources. The typical neoliberal governance reforms did not take off during this period, although the policy witnessed a move towards recommending such reforms in the form of having IQAC, or having performance indicators. It was in the next phase that there was a furore in the policy about privatization and market-based governance reforms.

13.5 Policy Making During Second Phase of Reform (2007–08 to 2013–14)

13.5.1 Public Funding

With respect to mode of funding, the 11-th FYP proposed that the government must ensure that fee levels are not profiteering and beyond this the State should not interfere in institutional governance (GOI 2008). The FYP therefore did not question setting up fees at levels which meets the costs. In order to meet the need for an expansion in HEIs, the National Knowledge Commission (NKC) (GOI 2009a) recommended that the funding should be enhanced from both the public and the private modes. It reiterated that the HEIs should look for alternative sources of funding.

During this phase, the share of public expenditure on higher education in GDP showed only a marginal improvement, at 0.83 during 2007–08 to 2010–11 (GOI 2012a)[10] caused by an increase in the number of public funded universities[11] from 253 in 2007–08 to 308 in 2010–11.[12] At the same time, the average share of school level education in GDP for the same period was higher at 2.31%. The annual growth rate of the HEIs and the enrolment were higher compared to the first period at 13 and 14% respectively during 2005–06 to 2010–11 (Duraisamy and Duraisamy 2015).

The 11th FYP clearly spelt out the three major objectives of higher education reform: expansion, inclusion and quality. The budgetary provision was raised significantly with a larger role for the government to achieve all the three without there being any trade-off between them. To mitigate the adverse impact on inclusiveness because of rising private sector participation, scholarship was to be largely relied upon. The 11th FYP vision document, however, sought to make it clear that public sector based expansion could deliver on inclusive expansion if corrective measures are adopted to improve quality. Setting up of central universities in all the states was proposed. The 11th FYP budgeted for a massive rise of around 4.6 times in its budgetary allocation in comparison with the 10th FYP (GOI 2008).

[10]Retrieved from Reference Note, Lok Sabha Secretariat (2014), No.21/RN/Ref./2014.

[11]Central Universities and State Universities combined.

[12]Annual Reports, UGC, various years.

Table 13.3 Number of state private universities over years

Year	Number of state private universities
2007–08	14
2008–09	21
2009–10	60
2010–11	80
2011–12	111
As on 23.02.2015	201
As on 31.03.2016	235
As on 31.03.2017	262

Source UGC Annual Report, various years

Table 13.4 Proportion of privately managed universities in total universities (in percentage)

	2010–11	2011–12	2012–13	2013–14	2014–15	2015–16	2016–17	2017–18
Total universities	621	642	667	723	760	799	864	903
Privately managed	178	195	209	219	261	277	277	343
Proportion (%)	28.7	30.4	31.3	30.3	34.3	34.7	32.1	38

Note Privately Managed Universities include State Private Universities (regular and open) and Deemed Private Universities
Source All India Survey of Higher Education, MHRD, GOI, various years

13.5.2 Private Providers

In addition, this phase witnessed a sharp rise in the state private universities. The number went up from 14 in 2007–08 to 262 (as on 31.03.2017), with a sudden shoot up in the year 2009–10 (Table 13.3).

Table 13.4 shows the growth of privately managed universities during this period, along with the growth of total number of universities in the country. It needs to be noted that the number of privately managed universities increased from 178 in 2010–11 to 343 in 2017–18, which is a 93% jump in a span of just 7 years. The proportion of privately managed universities to the total universities increased from 28.7 to 38.0% during this period.

Colleges cater to a large chunk of student in the higher education. Across the country, a majority of colleges are privately managed, with a significant proportion of that belonging to the unaided category, reflecting a support given by the State to the establishment of pure private institutions. These privately managed have as much as 67.3% of the total students in all the colleges. This can be seen from Fig. 13.2.

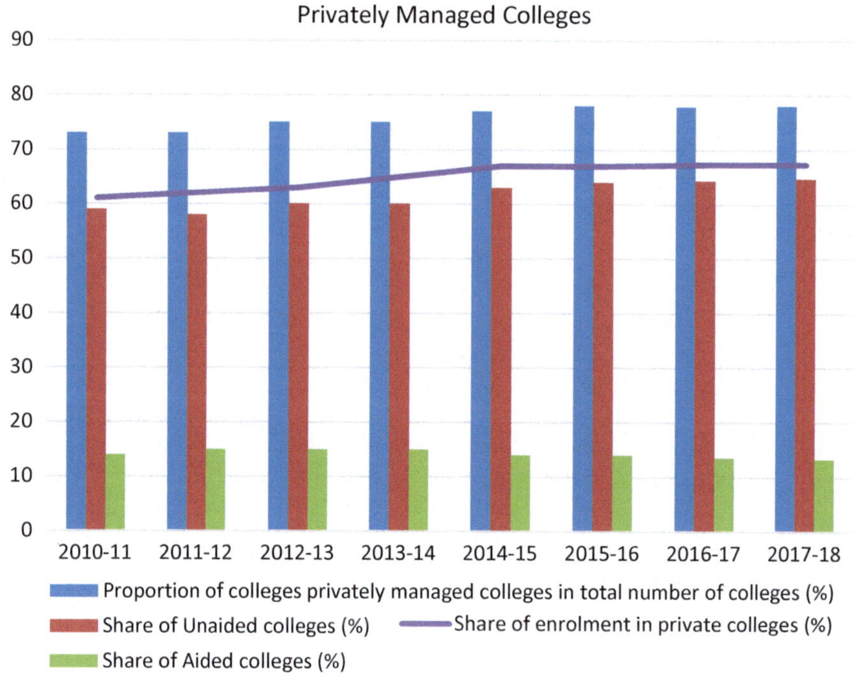

Fig. 13.2 Share of privately managed colleges and enrolment in privately managed colleges over years (in percentage). *Source* All India Survey of Higher Education (GoI), various years

During this period, the cost recovery by the public HEIs went up to nearly 40% (CABE), partly contributed by the self-financing courses, rise in tuition fees and other incomes (GOI 2005).

13.5.3 Debate on Public-Private Divide

There was apparently a clash of ideas towards higher education reform between the 11th FYP and the National Knowledge Commission (NKC). While the 11th FYP favoured a larger role for the public funding in achieving the higher education objectives, the NKC argued for a larger role for the private sector. The other major contention was the role of the UGC in the emerging context and installation of a regulatory body. Possibly to negotiate between the pro-public sector role envisaged in the 11th FYP and pro-market pro-private sector role as envisaged in the NKC, the central government set up the Yashpal Committee apparently to revisit the debate in policy approaches and resolve to suggest policies for possible implementation. The Yash Pal Committee Report sought to reverse the trends of fragmentation and compartmentalization in the system of knowledge generation and knowledge dissemination and suggested setting up of research networks for fostering collaborations.

The 12th FYP favoured participation of the private higher education while at the same time, advocating policies for access, equity and quality with an objective of meeting the international standards. It highlighted a need for an improved governance system with the application of new management principles. As a measure to enhance inclusion as well as to support the private self-financing institutions and move closer towards market, voucher system was recommended to meet the financial needs of the students from marginalized group (GOI 2013b). However, implementation of the voucher scheme raised two concerns, (a) the students suffer from lack of information on the quality of courses or the institutes, making them vulnerable to uninformed or poor decision making, (b) the voucher system will infuse demand driven mechanism wherein the institutes of higher education would compete with each other resulting in stratification of the market.

The 12th FYP advocated strongly Public-Private Partnership (PPP) in higher education, for setting up new universities and colleges and for creating quality infrastructure and physical facilities in the existing colleges. Under this system, the investment is shared in varying degrees between public and the private sector with respect to management of the HEIs and their infrastructure. Further, it recommended models for industry-institute interface whereby large education hubs can be set up with the active support by the state government concerned including provisioning of land (ibid.).

The National Higher Education Mission (*Rashtriya Uchchatar Shiksha Abhiyan*, RUSA) (GOI 2013a) also sought to generate competition amongst the HEIs by recommending performance based funding of the state universities. It recommended financial as well as academic autonomy in order to prevent further deterioration. For rendering financial autonomy, the RUSA suggested that every state should set up State Higher Education Council (SHEC), which would disburse funds to the state universities. Also the Committee suggested that by providing freedom to the state universities, they would enhance their quality.

13.5.4 Private Providers

The NKC argued that private investment in education should be encouraged. For this purpose, public resources like land should be leveraged especially in the form of land grants to attract more private investment. It also recommended that 1500 new universities be set up, which would be accorded autonomy to fix student fees and tap other sources for generating funds. These new universities should develop strong interfaces with industry.

As mentioned earlier, the 12th FYP had argued for a larger role private sector should play in raising the Gross Enrolment Ratio (GER) to 30% by 2020. The amount of resources required was five times the current expenditure. The private sector was envisaged to emerge as a massive investor particularly in the professional and technical education. The Narayana Murthy Committee (GOI 2012b) suggested a larger role of the private sector, university-corporate link up in order to enhance the relevance of education and as also to explore an alternative mode of funding research in the universities.

13.5.5 Supply of Skill

In addition to all this, the 11th Plan sought to address the deficiency of skilled manpower in the labour market by introducing the National Skill Development Mission. The goal was to create skilled and employable personnel in line with the requirement of the economy. It aimed at generating 500 million skilled people by 2022. This was to ensure that the supply-side responses are perpetually in sync with the demand side impulses both from domestic as well as global economies and therefore both private and public sector need to be involved via a public-private partnership (PPP) mode. Two Bills were introduced in the Parliament to set up 8 new IITs and 5 new Indian Institute of Science Education and Research (IISER). A scheme was also framed to set up colleges in 374 educationally backward districts with lower than the average GER for India.

The integration of skill development with the conventional education has also been proposed by the State under the 'Minimum course curriculum for undergraduate courses under choice based credit system'.[13] This would confine the learning of students to getting trained in certain skills only, in order to become employable.

13.5.6 Governance Reforms

As compared to the previous period, the policy in this period was emphatic about increasing monitoring mechanism in the higher education sector, which marks the beginning of NPM based governance reform. In 2010, to ensure credible recruitment of teachers and their performance in higher education institutions, the UGC advocated minimum qualifications for appointment of teachers and other academic staff in universities and colleges by way of Performance Based Appraisal Scheme (PBAS) (GOI 2010). As argued by Das and Chattopadhyay (2014), implementation of PBAS amounts to straight-jacketing of regulatory interventions with disregard for individual differences in conceptualization of performance, disciplinary differences and differences in university mandates. The National Assessment and Accreditation Council (NAAC) was set up in 1994. But only in 2013 that it was made mandatory for universities to get themselves accredited. It can be seen from Fig. 13.3, that there has been a drastic increase in the number of institutions getting accreditation over the years. In 2016–17 a total of 1640 institutions got accreditation.

---

[13]http://www.ugc.ac.in/pdfnews/8023719_Guidelines-for-CBCS.pdf.

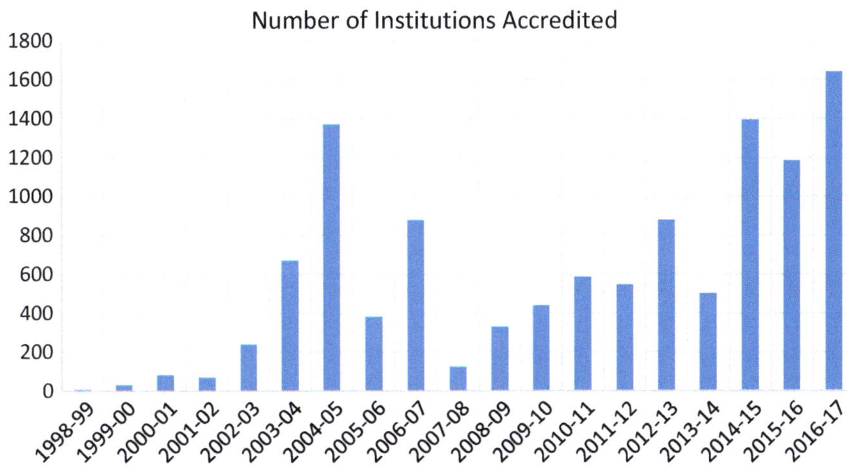

Fig. 13.3 Number of institutions accredited over years. *Source* NAAC Annual Report, various years

In the same year, 2013, there was an attempt to make funding contingent upon relative performance of the state universities under RUSA.

During the first phase of reform the focus was more on the reform of the government funded institutions through changes in the mode of funding what is called endogenous privatization[14] (Ball and Youdell 2007). In a way, this pursuit for technical efficiency was deemed necessary to enable the public funded institutions to enter the market and compete with the private in due course of time and to expand the choices faced by the students.

The second phase can be named as the phase of endogenous as well as exogenous privatization[15] (Ball and Youdell 2007) because the government aims to realize expansion of higher education by (a) bringing in financial form of privatization of public HEI through fees, student loans, self- financed courses and also (b) by both active involvement of private sector and through different modes of public-private partnership (Tilak 2012, 2014). Only with the emergence of a strong and credible private sector in higher education, the government could start veering towards the construction of the market. The presence of the private sector was rather small during the 1990s.

[14]It involves importing of ideas, techniques and practices from the private sector in order to make the public sector more business-like.

[15]It entails opening up of public education services to private sector participation on a for-profit basis and using the private sector to design, manage or deliver aspects of public education.

13.5.7 Construction of a Regulated Market

The period saw a rampant change in nature of regulatory bodies in a manner/installation of new regulatory bodies, with an objective of constructing markets in the higher education sector. The NKC (GOI 2009a) argued for the formation of an Independent Regulatory Authority of Higher Education (IRAHE), which would be an overarching body, under which all the bodies would be subsumed. A single body would lead to hassle-free establishment of HEIs, particularly private. Thus, there were indications clear enough towards implementation of a full-fledged neoliberal reform agenda. It was also felt by the NKC that all three objectives of expansion, inclusion and quality cannot be pursued unless the private sector is brought in view of poor governance of the publicly funded institutions. The idea of setting up a new regulatory body called National Council for Higher Education and Research (NCHER) in place of multiple regulatory body, with an objective to reduce bureaucratic interference in the working of higher education system was put forth also by the Yash Pal Committee in 2009.

The year 2010 introduced certain Bills in the higher education sector. It was argued that the Bills sought to address certain problems that higher education sector was found to be suffering from, like information asymmetry, abuse of freedom amounting malpractices in the delivery of education, and irreversibility of educational choices (Chattopadhyay 2012). All these factors lead to market failure, which were sought to be corrected by the Bills. The Bills introduced were the Foreign Education Institutions (Regulation of Entry and Operations) Bill, Bill on Prohibition of Unfair Trade Practices, Educational Tribunals Bill, Universities for Innovations Bill, National Accreditation Regulatory Authority for Higher Education Institutions Bill and National Commission for Higher Education and Research. The underlying rationale was to correct the sources of market failure and infuse competition within the higher education sector.

But the competition would be amongst the unequals and might accentuate the prevailing hierarchy and dualism in the higher education sector (Glennerster 1991; Winston 1999). It would lead to a loose framework of regulations particularly for the agricultural institutes and for innovation universities, rather than addressing the issue of quality (Tilak 2010). The Unfair Trade Practices bill may not have addressed the issue of low quality of education being delivered even at high costs (Sharma 2010). Establishing the overarching National Council for Higher Education and Research (NCHER) was thought to be expediting setting up of private universities, without having to seek permission from a plethora of regulatory bodies (Sharma 2010). They may not help address all the three major objectives of expansion, inclusion and quality simultaneously in the wake of rising participation of the private providers (Chattopadhyay 2012).

The UGC during this phase also encouraged Choice Based Credit System (CBCS) from July 2015, allowing students to transfer their credits amongst the universities recognized by the UGC. This was also suggested in the RUSA (GOI 2013a) which was supposed to give a boost to student mobility and expand student choices to let them reign supreme in such a system.

But the idea of a regulatory body to oversee the entire higher education system and ward off political intervention and confusions arising out of overlapping jurisdictions continued to be considered as a very important policy measure by the policy makers (which primarily led to the formation of a committee headed by Prof. Yash Pal).

13.6 Policy Making During the Third Phase of Reform (2014–2018)

13.6.1 Public Funding

It was reiterated by the NKC to dedicate 6% of GDP to education and 1.5% to higher education. It is yet to be materialized. Though there was a significant jump during the 11th FYP, in real per capita terms, the higher education budget has not seen any rise. In fact, as argued by Tilak (2016), it even declined. It has to be noted that an increase in budgetary allocation is not a guarantee for good quality as long as internal governance remains an issue of concern. A significant portion of the budget is earmarked for an increase in the salaries of the teachers. Resources are scarce for development of the infrastructure and augmentation of facilities. Further, given the huge size of the higher education sector, public funding for research is minimal. The students' loan has gained importance but at the same time, loan recovery has emerged to be a problem (Krishnan 2017). As per the latest news report, the growth in outstanding educational loans slowed down to only 0.02% during 2017–18. There has been an overall tendency to move towards output-based funding to be routed through the market to effect improvement in governance (Chattopadhyay 2016) by linking funding to accreditation, world ranking, financial autonomy to the Category I HEIs under the new scheme of graded autonomy.

A drastic shift towards market as a source of funding has happened as a result of setting up of Higher Education Funding Agency (HEFA), for providing additional funds for research and infrastructure in Universities through 10-year loans. The principal of the loan would be repaid through internal receipts, to be earned by HEIs through fee receipts and research earnings. The sources for internal receipts include tuition fees and research receipts. It is not hard to argue to such a measure would cause exclusion of students who are meritorious but cannot afford to pay for their education. Also, the nature of knowledge generated would be restricted to the one that can generate resources without much risks involved; fundamental research/basic research, the outcome of which is uncertain and time consuming, would suffer and applied research or reproduction of the same principles in research, would be reined in. Autonomy of researcher in the universities could also get hampered, as output might get structured as per the needs of the funders providing resources for research.

13.6.2 Governance Reform

The third phase marks a major departure from the earlier two phases in terms of major policy changes which seeks to overhaul the entire higher education system in line with the neoliberal principles. The major policy initiatives are graded autonomy (GOI 2018) and setting up of institutes of eminence (GOI 2017) or what are called World Class Universities.

The policy of graded autonomy is expected to usher in a sea change in the way the universities are regulated and funded. This new policy shows very clearly what does the government think about the possible relationships amongst regulation, autonomy and quality. These are as follows: one, that the government believes that autonomy is crucial for achieving quality; two, autonomy can be bestowed on those institutions who have performed well and hence are trust worthy and capable of exercising autonomy to achieve quality and three, the role of regulations is to help attain minimum standard as stated in the UGC Regulations.

The way the categorization of the Universities has been conceived of are as follows for the grant of graded autonomy. Category I HEIs should have NAAC score of 3.5 and above or it has been awarded a corresponding grade/score by a reputed accreditation agency empanelled by the UGC or it has been among the top 500 of reputed world rankings such as the Times Higher Education or Quacquarelli Symonds (QS). Category II HEIs should have a NAAC score between 3.01 and 3.49 or it has received a corresponding accreditation grade/score from a reputed accreditation agency empanelled by the UGC. Category III HEIs are neither I nor II as above (GOI 2018). PPP and financial autonomy under graded autonomy to the public institutions amount to infusion of private sector principles in the functioning of the public sector institutions.

The conditionalities attached to funding show that autonomy has to be defined carefully. Autonomy for the institutions need not get translated to autonomy for the teachers to exercise their academic freedom. Autonomy to the institutions to pursue goals in line with what the UGC has recommended does not imply of course that the teachers will be autonomous. Further, in the name of financial autonomy, the greatest casualty is likely to be the academic freedom and the institutional autonomy.

13.6.3 Selective Autonomy

That the Category I institutions are trust worthy is evident in the very first dimension of autonomy to be given to the institutions regarding the review process. For these HEIs, there will be no external review and only internal review will do. For Category II, however, external review is required. Autonomy comes in the form of permission given to offer new courses/department in self-financing mode including skill development courses under the Ministry of Skill Development. Development of research parks, incubation centers, university-society linkage centers, under PPP or self-financing mode are to be encouraged and the institutions need not seek any prior approval. The most important change which is in a way a path breaking one is to allow the universities to hire foreign faculty up to 20% of its total faculty strength with the provision to allow for arriving at the remunerations through mutual agreement. This marks a departure from the determination of the pay scales in line with the recommendation of the Pay Commission. The institutions can admit foreign students up to 20% of its total strength based on merit. The scope for incentivization is in the form of career advancement if the basic minimum as prescribed by the PBAS-API system is complied with. There is no provision for the reward at the margin for the extra points that the faculty accumulates. Now the university is allowed to provide for building in an incentive structure to attract talented faculty as long as incentives are paid out of own funds. Autonomy is being given as long as the HEIs can raise resources. This will foster competition among the HEIs. So, the extent of competition will be regulated depending on the categorization of the HEIs because competition presupposes ability to compete and the ability will now be determined by their respective performances as measured in terms of ranking and NAAC score. Eventually the Category I will be moving farther from the remaining set of institutions and the extent of differentiation that exist today among the institutions, which is, in a way, systemic and inevitable, will get more and more accentuated. This will render the credentials more differentiated depending on the category of the institution it belongs to. Given the uniqueness of the human capital, this competition in the education market is a zero-sum game.

This is one way of privatization of the governance structure of the publicly funded universities. The teachers at the individual level will not be able to exercise much autonomy as the universities will be keen to offer courses and programs on skill development. The infusion of funding conditionalities will circumscribe the academic freedom and accentuate hierarchy between the university authority and the faculty.

The basic idea is to invoke Regulations to govern the HEIs to optimize its full potential to get the best of an institute and attain at least a minimum standard. At the same time, the universities within a set of defined rules of the game, are required to compete with each other to achieve higher ranking. There are certain implications we would like to point out. Market competition requires a level playing field to exist. Increasing importance of quality assurance and ranking not only in measuring but guiding by changing evaluation mechanism. The foreign faculty and incentive based pay structure will mean that the Category I institutions will no longer be under any compulsion to follow the PBAS-API system. Opening the doors to the foreign students and foreign faculty is a step towards internationalization of the Indian higher education program. This will be extremely crucial both for the academic program, collegiality that prevails among the faculty. This is also privatization of the publicly funded universities. As more and more courses are offered in the self -financing mode, fees would go up.

13.6.4 Private Providers

The growth of the privately funded institutions continues. Within this period the State Private Universities grew from 201 as on 23rd February 2015 to 262 as on 31st March 2017 (Table 13.2). Public-Private Partnership has also led to an expansion in the provision of education by private sector.

13.6.5 Construction of Market

Much in line with the previous phase, in 2017, it was again proposed that the UGC and the AICTE should be replaced by a new body called Higher Education Empowerment Regulation Agency (HEERA). It was felt that multiple regulatory bodies led to excessive and restrictive regulations.

In 2018, government again proposed to repeal the UGC Act and set up Higher Education Commission of India (HECI), which is apparently a step towards regulation of market. But the way the draft of the HECI has been prepared, a selective set of public funded institutions are enabled to participate in the market. The issue is can the policy makers gradually move towards setting up of a market for higher education? Market is a central piece in the architecture of the economy the neoliberals envisage. However, as pointed out by Marginson (2016) that the neoliberal construction of market has failed world over as it is very much intrinsic to the functioning of a higher education market that a full-fledged market construction will remain incomplete due to the public good nature of knowledge and political impediment.

13.7 Concluding Remarks

As the policy making in higher education sector continues to be guided by the neoliberal principles the sector has to grapple with the aims of achieving three objectives of equity, quality and expansion as discussed above. However, by leaving higher education to the vagaries of market, which is premised on the logic of efficiency, it is unlikely that these objectives would be met (See Appendix Table 13.5). This is because the economic principles that guide neoliberal policy making are not readily applicable for the functioning of a university and higher education market. It is discussed how the idea of efficiency clashes with the aforementioned objectives of policy.

13.7.1 Can Construction of a Market Overcome Market Failure in Education?

The overall thrust of policy making has been to construct market for higher education which entailed corporate style governance reform of the publicly funded institutions, make scope for the private sector to play a larger role. The question is whether market can help overcome the intrinsic deficiencies of an education market. Policy reform also should take note of the specificities of education in creating conditions for growth and inclusive development by promoting talent and widening access. As the market for higher education seeks to achieve S-efficiency rather than exchange based E-efficiency, competition has a tendency to attenuate the hierarchy as the ranking order particularly at the top remains stable. However, market as an institution to guide reform is favoured for its ability to generate competition by giving freedom to the institutions and the students in what they seek to do and to improve quality which remains constrained by the availability of human capital and financial resources. Accountability to market is also thought to be reflective of the demand society generates for higher education and the society expects the universities to cater to. But marketization is inherently problematic for another reason. The students and the education providers (or the teachers) are the co-producers as the students cannot buy the degrees but they have to earn it and hence treating them as customers leads to dilution of quality the teachers would strive to deliver.

13.7.2 Politics and Market Failure in the Indian Higher Education

In the Indian context, the intrinsic problems of an education market have appeared to be very pronounced after three decades of neoliberal reform. Though there are a few good quality private universities, overall privatization has not led to any major improvement in quality. The majority of the public funded institutions suffer from typical government failure. The bad quality private institutions continue to cater to a large community of students because the students have no option as the subsidized publicly funded institutions have not grown commensurate with growing demand particularly for the professional courses. Students in a good number of colleges and universities exercise no agency to infuse vibrancy into the system. On the other hand, where they pay high fees, their consumerist approach to learning and research has led to serious dilution of quality. Most of the privately funded ones which run on commercial basis, cut costs at the expense of quality, appease students and end up delivering poor quality of education. The students want degrees and not necessarily quality education, which make things easier for the unscrupulous providers to mint money. It is often argued that the State fund goes waste and/or inefficiently allocated in public institutions. Whatever fund that they receive from the State is found to be insufficient, which makes it difficult for them to support their activities. Another problem that could be found, particularly in many state universities/colleges is the lack of motivation among the faculty to perform. The nexus between the universities and the political parties is a common place, along with political interference in appointment and academic matters of the universities. When this is coupled with stagnant funding to a large number of public universities, it throws up a new dimension to the entire set of challenges for the policy makers. These policy makers are themselves not above boards always. Amidst all these, the role of teachers and the students needs deeper probe for blunting the efficacy of reforms, even if they are founded upon misconceived notion of education as a commodity. Employability of the students has become a major concern. Further, privatization conflicts with the promotion and nurturing of merit, and hinders accessibility as fees become cost determined.

To tackle government failure in the government funded education system and reward those who have performed better relatively speaking, the introduction of graded autonomy has the potential to be a path changer. But it is unlikely to be so. Three categories have been created for differential treatment of regulation. The best ones are supposed to be liberated from the clutches of regulation while the Category III HEIs should continue to be regulated to bring out the best from them before they are set free. But academic autonomy requires public funding based on cost of education rather than market based funding which robs the universities of their academic autonomy. The institutional autonomy has ceased to exist as both market pressure and ranking have led to erosion of academic freedom in the name of accountability and sustainability. A move towards output-based funding and market based funding, loss of academic freedom, and a move towards professional conduct and commercialization have determined the kind of values which are inculcated, as well as teaching and research. According the status of Institutions of Eminence to a set of universities, ostensibly with the purpose of enabling them to acquire the status of world class universities in terms of global ranking means lower funding for the rest in view of stagnancy in the higher education budget.

Massification of higher education in India has not been accompanied by a concomitant improvement in quality. Kapur and Mehta (2017) have sought to explain this in terms of a 'trilemma' among scale (expansion), cost and quality where only two of three objectives can be realized. They argue that the transformation in the landscape of Indian higher education has been one of expansion with cost constraint. While it is true that public fundung remained inadequate, the private sector too did not pump in adequate resources as they contributed in a big way to the process of expansion. Tilak (2005) has favoured a larger role of state in funding. One way of negotiating with the 'trilemma' would be to ensure good governance in public funded HEIs and setting up of a regulatory framework for the HE system as a whole. The neoliberal policy reforms have tried to tackle government failure through the construction of market upholding the principles of allocation and technical efficiency. But the Indian higher education system continues to grapple with the challenges which have multiplied rather than getting mitigated. While market failures are systemic for education as evident from the lack of success of neoliberal policy reforms, public funded institutions need more funds and autonomy to chart out their paths.

Table 13.5 Framework for looking at the implication of reforms/efficiency on Equity, Excellence and Expansion

Category of reforms	Efficiency	Implications		
		Equity	Quality	Expansion
Cut in Public Expenditure and exploring alternative sources of funding education	Allocative Efficiency/technical efficiency	Negative	Uncertain	Uncertain
Governance reforms	Technical efficiency	Uncertain	Positive	Uncertain
Private sector participation	Allocative efficiency/technical efficiency	Negative	Uncertain	Positive
Construction of regulated markets	Allocative efficiency	Unlikely	positive	Uncertain

Appendix

See Table 13.5.

References

Alexander, F. K. (2000). The changing face of accountability: Monitoring and assessing institutional performance in higher education. *The Journal of Higher Education, 71*(4), 411–431.

Ball, S., & Youdell, D. (2007). Hidden privatisation in public education. *Education International*. University of London: Institute of Education.

Berdahl, R. (1990). Academic freedom, autonomy and accountability in British Universities. *Studies in Higher Education, 15*(2), 169–180.

Chattopadhyay, S. (2009). The market in higher education: Concern for equity and quality. *Economic and Political Weekly, 44*(29), 53–61.

Chattopadhyay, S. (2012). *Education and economics*. New Delhi: Oxford University Press.

Chattopadhyay, S. (2016). New modes of financing higher education: Cost recovery, private financing and education loans. In N. V. Varghese & G. Malik (Eds.), *India Higher Education Report 2015* (pp. 333–351). Routledge.

Das, D. N., & Chattopadhyay, S. (2014). Academic performance indicators. *Economic and Political Weekly, 49*(50), 68–71.

Duraisamy, P., & Duraisamy, M. (2015). On the privatization, economic burden of expenditure on households, and role of student loan in financing higher education in India. Paper presented at an international seminar on *Innovative Methods of Financing of Higher Education During February 23–25, 2015* at NUEPA. New Delhi (Draft).

Glennerster, H. (1991). Quasi-market for education? *The Economic Journal, 101*(408), 1268–1276.

GoI. UGC. Various years. *Annual reports*.

GOI. (1993). *UGC Funding of the institutions of higher education. Report of Justice Punnayya Committee 1992–93*. New Delhi: University Grants Commission.

Government of India. (1997, May). *Government subsidies in India. Discussion Paper*. New Delhi: Ministry of Finance. Department of Economic Affairs.

Government of India. (2000, April). *Report on a policy framework for reforms in education*. New Delhi.

Government of India. (2005). *Report of the Central Advisory Board of Education (CABE) committee on Autonomy of Higher Education*. New Delhi: Ministry of Human Resource Development.

Government of India. (2008). *Eleventh five year plan (2007–12). Social sector* (Vol. 2). *Planning Commission of India*. New Delhi: OUP.

Government of India. (2009a). *National knowledge commission: Report to the nation 2006–09*. New Delhi: Ministry of Human Resource Development.

Government of India. (2009b). *Report of the Committee to Advise on Renovation and Rejuvenation of Higher Education*. Delhi: UGC.

Government of India. (2010, September 18). *UGC Regulations on Minimum Qualifications for appointment of teachers and other academic staff in universities and colleges and measures for maintenance of standards in higher education*. Delhi: The Gazette of India.

Government of India. (2012a). *Analysis of budgeted expenditure on education*. New Delhi: Ministry of Human Resource Development.

Government of India. (2012b). *Committee on report of participation in higher education. Report of NR Narayana Murthy Committee*. New Delhi.

Government of India. (2013a). *Rashtriya Uchchatar Shiksha Abhiyan*. Ministry of Human Resource Development.

Government of India. (2013b). *Twelfth Five Year Plan (2012–17). Social Sectors. Vol. 3. Planning Commission of India*. New Delhi: Sage Publication.

Government of India. (2013c, January). *UGC regulations for mandatory accreditation*. Delhi: The Gazette of India.

Government of India. (2014). *All India survey of higher education*. New Delhi: Ministry of Human Resource Development.

Government of India. (2017). *UGC (Institutions of Eminence Deemed to be Universities) Regulations 2017*. New Delhi: University Grants Commission.

Government of India. (2018). *UGC [Categorization of Universities (only) for Grant of Graded Autonomy] Regulations, 2018*. New Delhi: Ministry of Human Resource Development.

Huisman, J., & Currie, J. (2004). Accountability in higher education: Bridge over troubled waters? *Higher Education, 49*, 529–551.

https://mygov.in/new-education-policy-group.html.

http://www.ugc.ac.in/pdfnews/8023719_Guidelines-for-CBCS.pdf.

Jongbloed, B. (2004). Regulation and competition in higher education. In Pedro Texeira, Ben Jongbloed, David Dill, & Alberto Amaral (Eds.), *Markets in higher education: Rhetoric or reality?*. London/Boston/Dordrecht: Kluwer Publishers.

Kai, J. (2009). A critical analysis of accountability in higher education. *Chinese Education and Society, 42*(2), 39–51.

Kapur, D., & Mehta, P. B. (2017). Introduction. In D. Kapur & P. B. Mehta (Eds.), *Navigating the labyrinth: Perspectives on India's higher education* (pp. 1–37). Hyderabad: Orient Blackswan.

Krishnan, K. P. (2017). Financing of higher education in India: The way forward. In K. Devesh & P. B. Mehta (Eds.), *Navigating the labyrinth: Perspectives on India's Higher Education*. Hyderabad: Orient Blackswan.

Lok Sabha Secretariat. (2014). *Budget for education sector in India*. Reference Note. No. 21/RN/ReF./2014.

Marginson, S. (2007). The public/private divide in higher education: A global revision. *Higher Education, 53*(3), 307–333.

Marginson, S. (2016). *Higher Education and the common good*. Melbourne: Melbourne University Press.

Mortimer, K. P. 1972. *Accountability in higher education*. Washington D.C.: American Association for Higher Education.

Musgrave, R. A., & Musgrave, P. (1989). *Public finance in theory and practice* (5th ed.). New Delhi: McGraw-Hill Book Company.

Psacharopoulos, G. (1986). *Financing education in developing countries: An exploration of policy options*. Washington, DC: The World Bank.
Samuelson, Paul A. (1954). The Pure Theory of Public Expenditure. *The Review of Economics and Statistics, 36*(4), 387–389.
Sharma, V. (2010, September–December). *UPA's agenda of Academic 'Reforms' facilitating trade in Higher Education. Social Scientist, 38*(9–12).
Tilak, J. B. G. (2004, January). Public subsidies in education in India. *Economic and Political Weekly, 39*(4), 343–359.
Tilak, J. B. G. (2005). Higher education in Trishanku: Hanging between state and market. *Economic and Political Weekly, 40*(37), 4029–4037.
Tilak, J. B. G. (2010). Policy crisis in higher education: Reform or deform? *Social Scientist, 38*(9–12), 61–90.
Tilak, J. B. G. (2012, March 31). Higher education policy in India in transition. *Economic and Political Weekly*, 36–40.
Tilak, J. B. G. (2014, October 4). Private higher education in India. *Economic and Political Weekly, 49*(40), 32–38.
Tilak, J. B. G. (2016). A Decade of ups and downs in public expenditure on higher education in India. In N. V. Varghese & Garima Malik (Eds.), *India Higher Education Report 2015*. New York and Oxon: Routledge Taylor and Francis Group.
Winston, G. C. (1999). Subsidies, hierarchy and peers: The awkward economics of higher education. *The Journal of Economic Association, 13*(1), 13–36.

Reports

All India Survey of Higher Education (various years), Ministry of Human Resource Development.
Education Statistics at a glance (2016), Ministry of Human Resource Development.
NAAC Annual Reports, various years.

Chapter 14
Finance and Health

Parthasarathi Banerjee

Abstract The business of health care is currently undergoing a profound transformation. Global finance is forcing transformation of the public policies as well as of the private business of health care. Key to this strategic leverage is financialisation of the personal body. As it is evident from the early modern state in Europe under the received practices of health sciences, it would take hold of personal body for disciplining, regimenting and shaping the unseemly mass through public provisioning of health services. Public hygiene, public health provisioning with minimum health care attempted capture of massed bodies in order that the mass bodies could obey rules and codes of mass body politics. Personal health is reconstructed as emergent envelopes of information getting generated ever continuously with ever-increasing risks and uncertainty. Palliative goals are now replaced with elusive envelopes of probable health status. These bodily states of affairs being inherently risky are profoundly financialisable. Postmodern state, postmodern business and the postmodern person are no longer incorporated. They have translated into flux of finance. Inter-bodily relations are passe.

14.1 Introduction

Years back an ailing person in India could walk up to the local Primary Healthcare Centre (PHC) or to the nearby general practitioner (GP) (see Bhat 1999) with the wish to get well and while the PHC often would not have a physician or medicines the ramshackle system of health delivery could sometimes alleviate the ailments and offer health recovery. Diagnoses often remained elusive and yet, as it were due to bodily resilience and as though through miracle some patients could recover health. Expenses at PHC used to be taken care of by public funding and with the GP by way of private out-of-pocket (or private savings) withdrawals. This system had the goal of alleviating ailment and took care of personal integrated body as an integral system and physician practices derived from a system of knowledge and practices that cared

P. Banerjee (✉)
International Management Institute, New Delhi, India
e-mail: psb_nist@yahoo.com

P. K. Biswas and P. Das (eds.), *Indian Economy: Reforms and Development*, India Studies in Business and Economics, https://doi.org/10.1007/978-981-13-8269-7_14

for the recovery from ailment as its goal while remaining deficient often in specific diagnosis (Banerjee 2010). This system did not differentiate between criticality of ailments and remaining geographically very close to the residence of a patient the entire medical system then was highly geographically dispersed, least integrated by any controlling authority and necessarily was also least vitiated by corruption owing to multiple types of agency opportunism. The lone GP or the PHC with poor infrastructure could not offer systematic diagnostic tests both because of poverty of knowledge of contemporary medical practices and because of the absence of a system of medical machinery oiled by systemic cash flows.

Increasingly and over the years the PHC as well as the GP lost their place in private health care and also lost local autonomy. New institution of health care has been growing primarily through major public programmes of the Indian central government as also of several state governments and by several global financing agencies. This new institution has as its foundation not health insurance alone but more importantly the substitution of the previous health services market that was dominated by public delivery by another market organised by large and rather often global finance. Necessarily, this new market has new defining rules and products and new ways of defining efficiency. This new medical institution has as its infrastructure the highly integrated system of hospitals including specialty hospitals and medical diagnostics (Business Standard 2018b) that gets fuelled by insurance and large finance and that singularly targets identified and structured categories of ailments defined as critical. Further, the new market is founded upon two central principles, diagnosis and medical practice as defined as well as standardised sets of investigative procedures. Ailment has been substituted by investigative risk profiling and integrated body of a patient has been broken down into large sets of disparate parameters. Private providers have largely replaced the PHC-centric system while the insurance, financing system, private providers together and between them set up this new market institution (Relman 1980; Clarke et al. 2003; Stein and Sridhar 2018), based as it is on risk engenderment and moral hazards.

This departure to a new structured and organised market was marked by generation of medical scientific evidences through plethora of diagnostic tests and images with emphases shifting from alleviation of pain to documenting and researching in order to generate larger evidences of bodily instances of facts that would help potential and probabilistic estimation of specific and acutely captured diagnosis of diseases and would only thus generate potential solutions to probabilistic diseases while often neglecting the integral body ailments (Gelijns and Rosenberg 1995; Robinson 2014). The modern system thus systemically increased the risk to the ailing person. Opportunistic behaviours in the new institution of health care along with the emergence of quantifiable and parametrised dimensions of public health that are tradable in the global financial market together render this new health service institution as generative of systemic risk. This new market institution of health services generates systemically at least two categories of risks first of the private body and secondly of the body of the population. The claim of this article is that risk generation provides the foundation to financialisation of health and personal body and a build-up of risks to the personal and population bodies threaten both the financial stability and bodily integrity. Material anatomical processes as well as the financial expectations introduce uncertainty and volatility including the potentiality of break down in the Minskian sense (Minsky 1989).

Sound health as the only desert while could have been the goal of the GP/PHC laggards, the contemporary system has no claim to any desert and the latter generates evidences which in turn advance medical sciences and its innovative practices. The former has not been organised part of a global system, while the latter is structural part of a global science standing principally upon global system of financing including of medical insurance as also upon the infrastructure of medical diagnostics. The state and the political systems have been bought into by this powerful scientific narrative. The PHC-based state forming political processes had developmental nation-state narratives while the contemporary medical market-based services provisioning draws upon risk-engendering sciences of bodily parts which in turn undermines developmental nation state and offers a post-liberal globalised financial-political structure.

The business of health care in India is currently undergoing a profound transformation (The Wire 2017). Global finance is forcing transformation of the public policies as well as of the private business of health care. Key to this strategic leverage is financialisation of the personal body. Financialised body poses direct challenges to person incorporated bodily integrity and bodily authority as also confronts the received practices and institution of health sciences.

In the following parts of this article, the above theme gets corroborated. The next section describes the political challenges, followed by a discussion on defining financialisation. Further ahead discussions address the facts of health needs and services in India, in brief, along with a brief discussion on instruments of financialisation of health and body. In the concluding part, health market institutions are compared and the arguments get summed up.

14.2 Political Challenges to Body and Transformation of Health Services

Formation of the early modern state in Europe to recall took hold of the personal body through its capture at the hospitals and asylums. Personal body as an integral whole was constitutive of the political structure and its processes, and this integral body the anatomical whole was the body corporate, as was the kingship and as was the business company and as was the democratic political structure. Captured bodies corporate yielded information through dissection about mechanisms that proposedly incorporated personal bodies, as was the reconstituted state and the society who as bodies corporate was claimed to have been constituted by finite and countable integrally whole personal bodies. The body of the state thus designed political structures and processes that using corpore corpori principles could claim sovereignty over personal body corporate. By late nineteenth and early twentieth century, legitimacy of the political state was to be constituted and justiciated through for example, by way of providing health care to the anatomical whole personal body. Palliative care then thus became the constitutive goal of the health politics of the state body. The early modern state body thus designed politics and the health in manners that forced separation of a personal physician from the patient and transformed personal physician knowledge to an art and science of palliative mechanisms, the medical science and the professional doctor thus emerged. Neighbourhood physician magician migrated to professional practitioner.

The modern state in command of seized personal bodies undertook the task of disciplining regimenting shaping the unseemly mass of multiple unique bodies (Bevir 1999), sometimes even through wars alternately through public provisioning of health services or by way of searching for organised public provisioning of ways and means to control epidemic or famine. Public hygiene, public health provisioning with minimum health care attempted capture of massed bodies in order that the mass bodies could obey rules and codes of mass body politics. Insurance design appeared based on gathered knowledge of statistical risk profiling of massed bodies. Insurance amongst other instruments took care of health code allegiance. Mass vaccination trained up paramilitary preparedness of state body to retain control over massed bodies while ensuring a profitable business for private capital out of the public domain of health for all and by the state body. The emergence of modern state paralleled authentication of justice provided amongst others by way of public provisioning of health care. The liberal ideology thus proposed a healthy mass of population as an economic asset as it were. This political process and its structuration necessarily remained territorial-based as this was founded upon bodily territories. Stability of bodily and state territories necessarily remained crucial and risk-reduction remained pivotal.

Postmodern and post-liberal state is in the business of risk and uncertainty. Finance is where the risk is. Financialised state undertakes journey in uncertainty through risking the giving up of bodily political structures and processes and enplacing information in situ. Personal bodies that were there as en masse now get thrown away as dismembered and disembodied entities. Personal health is reconstructed as emergent envelopes of information getting generated ever continuously with ever-increasing risks and uncertainty. Palliative goals are now replaced with elusive envelopes of probable health status. Incorporated body had proved relatively more impenetrable to information generative health business which now with satisfaction reconstitutes health images and envelopes as possible states of health. These bodily states of affairs being inherently risky are profoundly financialisable.

Postmodern state disembodies itself and so does the political and business structure and process. Global finance inheres through these states through continuous generation mapping and tracking profiling of information. Personal bodies as also the state body together are immersed in this transformative flux. Translational science of health as part of this flux is the financialised practices on health. Health politics and health insurance are accordingly being redesigned. Contemporary state necessarily gives up the care of corporate body or massed body.

Postmodern state, postmodern business and the postmodern person are no longer incorporated. The residence has been lost and geographic co-locational ties as building up a political process and structures have been lost to the non-locational flux of shared groups. Consequently, political structures and processes are getting increasingly de-centred and are continuously gyrating outside the campus of integrated personal bodies. Health politics is transmuting integral bodies into flux of bodily data, and the political processes as well as political structures are designing health policies and instruments that would control bodily states of data. Bodily health is then transfigured into states of health of indistinguishable possible bodies. Integrity gets given up. Risks amass. Bundling controlling distributing and marketing of bodily data gets described as health deliveries and necessarily this entire process of risk engendering happens by way of financialisation. This assumes foundational shift for political structures and for postmodern state. The bodily corporate state has translated into flux mediated through finance. Inter-bodily relations are passed.

14.3 Financialisation Beyond Health Insurance

The principle of corpore corpori involving transactions between corporeal bodies need money, however, with the giving up of corporeal unity, there must emerge a virtual controller to piece, transmute and reorder sets of bodily pieces or images (Deleuze 1992). Finance alone can take up that role. Money mediates transaction while finance assumes control. Thus, as the body fails to command over its images or multiplicities of states, a controller appears as in finance to undertake trades between several states of bodies. Finance is thus absolute necessity for this new flux. Conversely, foundation for financialisation is the generation of flux of states.

The other dimension is that as the body breaks into fragments of images or state data, and as data generation gets frothier and randomised, risk and uncertainty seeps into. In other words, risk becomes fundamental to such existence. Each person suffers from increasingly perceived risk. Such risk provides the foundation to financialisation (Robinson 2014). All integral bodies including the human body thus while getting fragmented provide the new foundation to financialisation. Fragmented pictures of a single corporeal person the severalties of medical images and the risky pathway not to convalescence but to sharper diagnosis and possible medical management of increasing risk and all this together provide the foundation to financialisation of body and health.

As in the dissertation on translational neuroscience, Robinson (2014) puts it "Yet, as Jones continues to expound, she begins to articulate the ways that the value that she had just articulated, values predominantly about information and explanation, are not the same as improved therapeutics and better outcomes. The complicated role of information in the biomedical encounter is made clear in the complicated morass of diagnostics. Verging towards a more discursive frame, she continued to think through and deconstruct the impacts of an increasing emphasis upon diagnostics for her practice:

> The cost of certain technologies is a problem and even though now we're able to make a different diagnosis, it doesn't change what we will do, we spend a ridiculous amount of money diagnosing something and the outcome for the patient isn't any different and that is a biggest [sic] issue. There's more emphasis on diagnosis and not more [emphasis] on

> treatment. We're able to have an exact diagnosis, but a lot of healthcare dollars are going where it isn't changing the outcomes. (Interview 08 May 29, 2010) … (Robinson 2014, p. 95)

Further "According to Shana, she didn't really experience risk *any more.* As Shana told me, "Every thing they give Jawan has risks." "A risk that is "everywhere" and in "everything" creates questions about the social and political ubiquity, especially in speculative economic regimes…" (Robinson 2014, pp. 105–06).

Gelijns and Rosenberg (1995) too noted that with advancing medical technologies, risk increases. Robinson, though, puts this increased risk as the foundation for financialisation, an impregnating mode whence risk interplays as the medium between advanced medical intervention and finance, and that thereby sets up the institution on risk. This new institution of health delivery obtained through new medical sciences and technologies are also the instruments to 'ingest as Robinson puts it "Under the specificities of neoliberalism, there are new questions about how risk gets ingested by the public via the state—through the machinations of public-private partnerships and via the privatization of public resources … The increasing resocialization of risks onto the public that increasingly comes with privatization … as well as the increasing interdependence of international economies under financialization… thusly require an examination into an increasingly *public* ingestion of risk and/or the production of new forms of digestibility and new banalities via the inurements of neoliberalism …" (Robinson 2014, pp. 106–07).

Another group of anthropologists termed this emerging mode as "Biofinance", "the financialisation of life" as based on "Speculation, Risk, Debt, and Value from Bios" (the Blog "Somatosphere" in 2016) and as evidence of new means of producing "value in modern technoscience", a kind of value that Robinson grasped as "difficulty of reconciling different constitutions of value—pharmacological, biotechnological, and molecular, global, community, public or individual measures of health. Thus, I wanted to track the discourses articulating grand transformations in health in which a molecular emphasis stands in for health itself. …" (Robinson 2014, p. 109). These are the molecules and the genetic ordering of the self, and of the medicines (Rose 2003, called that "Neurochemical selves"; also see, Triggle 2007).

The system of public ingestion that Robinson referred to had its early journey in the medical insurance system, designed a century back but saw its rapid growth especially in India only during last fifteen years, initially with RSBY (Rashtriya Swasthya Bima Yojana; Raza et al. 2016) providing hospitalisation insurance to persons below the poverty line (BPL) (Conti et al. 2016) now extended by the Auyshman Bharat scheme which is several folds larger in quantity and depth. However, the system of public ingestion refers to many levels from individual to small communities to larger metropolitan living and from medicine through physicians in professionalised forms to diagnostic sciences including its multiple providers at the public, private and public–private forms of organizations. This large edifice going much beyond the Latourian technoscience (2003) to what Clarke et al. (2003) called "biomedicalisation", characterised by a shift from control over biomedical phenomena to a system of biomedical transformation. What started out in the USA as "the new medical–industrial complex" (Relman 1980) and rolled out amongst others through a transformative system of biomedical knowledge, medicine including the evolution of blockbuster drugs and imaging systems in diagnostics (Iriart et al. 2011; Havighurst 2001) and the profit-seeking instruments in the new forms of corporate governance (Nik-Khah 2014), this biomedicalisation as Clarke et al. put it, also induced a transformation of bodies to include new properties and to exhibit the production of "new individual and collective technoscientific identities" (Clarke et al. 2003, p. 161).

On this path of diagnosis or otherwise on the way to preventive health care and the vaccinating state, what fell by the wayside was the curative dimension, the luxury of recovering, as Petryna argued on "the right to recovery" (2013), and in India which Nandraj argued (1994) led to unregulated growth of private healthcare providers. The insurance to recall addresses only the hospitalisation or what the contemporary narrative has defined as the "critical" health care, paid through the public and private cash expenses. Much larger in canvas is the financing of healthcare information, health media, health professionalisation including costs on conferences for example, of health providers especially on their instrumentation and on real estates, medical innovations in both medicines and instruments including procedures, setting up medical protocols and standards, and in medical education and in many similar others. Medical insurance constitutes a small fragment of this entire episode of financing.

This is about "capitalisation of almost everything" (Leyshon and Thrift 2007), a voracious appetite of the finance to infiltrate and transform every dimension of body and health. Leyshon and Thrift defined that as financialisation. Stein and Sridhar defined this "financialisation of global health" (2018) in terms of "financial motives, markets, actors and institutions …determine which kinds of healthcare are available to people in need" (p. 2) and exemplified amongst others by rise in parallel with domestic institutions, of the global institutions such as The World Bank's Pandemic Emergency Financing facility or of the initiatives to turn "Indicators of Health" of a population group or of a province or of a country amongst others into an indicator of financial market—comparable to current "Delta" ranking of "Aspirational Districts" in India which ranks districts in terms of health outcome (GOI 2015b; ICMR et al. 2017), amongst others. The rise of Gavi and the Global Fund is also another example. A recent publication comparing health indicators of states of India (ICMR et al. 2017) is a step in this direction. This publication was co-researched by two institutions from India and one from the USA and the report detailed out health performances of states of India captured in terms of multiple indicators of health outcome.

The question that faces India is whether its people are to be provided public provisioning of health care including both the curative and the preventive or a healthcare publicly supported and provided mostly by private providers! The National Health Policy (2017) adumbrated "The health policy recognises that there are many critical gaps in public health services which would be filled by "strategic purchasing". Such strategic purchasing would play a stewardship role in directing private investment…The main mechanisms of strategic purchasing are insurance and through trusts…Payment is by reimbursement on a fee for service basis and many private providers have been able to benefit greatly by these schemes …For achieving the objective of having fully functional primary healthcare facilities … Government would collaborate with the private sector for operationalising" (NHP 2017, p. 20). The Draft National Health Policy, on the contrary, had stated "The experience is that insurance mechanisms are unable to act against the denial of services, supply driven irrational care, unethical practices, and charging patients for what should be cashless services. It is clear that without a regulatory structure in place, it would be difficult to ensure that public–private partnerships or insurance based purchasing would deliver on either health outcomes or financial protection." (Sengupta, Scroll.in, 20/03/2017).

The public–private model in the present policy surely overlooked what the previous Draft Policy had proposed and the experience, as for example with the cautionary tale on PPP with the Apollo Hospital (Thomas and Krishnan 2010) amongst several similar others too were overlooked. Indeed, the NITI Aayog reportedly proposed another model of partnership between district government hospitals and private providers where the latter would take care of patients of the former, at a fee and at the public land facility (ET, 24 July 2017). One state government, the Government of Chhattisgarh, reportedly came forward to implement this scheme as well. Several news reports during this period, covering the beginning of the new Ayushman Bharat-National Health Protection Mission (AB-NHPM) (for example, the LiveMint on 20 March 2018; The ET on 24 May 2018; The ET on August 2018) pointed out this new direction in implementation of health care on both insurance and private provisioning.

Beyond the importance of AB-NHPM, there have been major and substantive changes in the health care in India. Beginning with the acquisition of Ranbaxy, about a decade back, a significant number of domestic manufacturers of medicine have gone through mergers and acquisitions (M&A) by global majors. With AB-NHPM the hospitals and diagnostics sectors too, have been going through transformations—several private equity (PE) providers have made financial entry. One report suggests that between 2007 and 2017, the PE's have invested a total of US$3.4 billion in hospitals (Indian Express 3/4/2018). Major global private equity firm such as the KKR (Kohlberg Kravis and Roberts) has invested strongly in the providers segment; a few M&A deals with hospitals experienced breaking up of diagnostics and care provisioning. The import of medical devices has gone up very significantly over the last few years and the PE's have also invested in the domestic diagnostics and devices market (The ET, 20 December 2017). In parallel, powerful narratives have been woven around "critical" health issues, sometimes under non-communicable diseases category, to picturise the pain and trauma associated with diseases such as cancer. One state government, the Government of Assam, for example, in its advertisement, in national newspapers on "Atal Amrit Abhiyan" (AAA) mission of health insurance scheme, described the AAA as "one of the largest health insurance schemes …to provide medical benefits for critical care illness under cashless mode." for "**(a) Cardiovascular diseases, (b) Cancer, (c) Kidney diseases, (d) Neurological conditions, (e) Neonatal diseases, and (f) Burns**. Treatment is available for **438** procedures …. At **empanelled hospitals** …" (emphases original, The Indian Express, 18/4/2018). While a deconstruction of "critical" is beyond the scope of this paper, we could learn from a reading on the narrative of making of "pain" and the making of an empire and a dynasty through that by the now infamous "Sackler dynasty" from the USA (Keefe, in The New Yorker, 30.10.2017).

Recent report suggests that "critical" diseases, such as "angioplasty"—the cardiovascular, have earned the topmost rank in insurance claims under the AB-NHPM or known otherwise as PMJAY (Pradhan Mantri Jan Arogya Yojana). Out of about 6,40,000 claims till late December 2018, angioplasty took 22% of the admissions, followed by coronary artery bypass graft (nine per cent), valve replacement and repair (six per cent), polytrauma (four per cent) and joint replacement (three per cent), and of all the claims 65% are from private providers (Business Line, December 26 2018). Another report points out sharp increase in the C-section delivery, the Indian Parliament was reported (Business Standard, 30 December 2018) that C-sections rose sharply and the state of Telangana reported the highest proportion of 58% of C-sections in all deliveries. In parallel, the capture and monopolisation of pharmaceutical retail sales direct to the consumer by large online pharmacies, where in turn the PE/VC (venture capital) investments rose sharply, have been redefining the drugs that should be in use. A recent report suggests that between 2013 and 2018, there have been ten deals by the PE-VC investing 140 mn US$ in large online drugs retail such as in the company Pharmeasy (Business Standard, 30 December 2018).

This brief detour of the transformations in the biomedical of India indicates that new ingesting public spaces of medical insurance, private hospitals, pharmaceutical companies, pharmaceutical online sales or privatised medical education along with reformations in medical education syllabus, and similar others have been bolstered and encouraged to grow with massive input of finance; and all these changes in public spaces have been paralleled by great transformations in the private spaces of persons through flipping up of critical diseases or through marathon runs or vaccinations on war footing or even through WhatsApp and similar other narratives and video clips. The modern state separated the public and private spaces and the postmodern state breaks down barriers separating these two spaces by transforming the notion of public and private spaces. Space is now imageries and semiotic symbols, catapulted in several series whence the corporeal holding person has to give up ownership and control of bodily things and take upon flights of floating images and information.

Financialisation breaks down the private and the earlier mode of public by generating dynamically floating flights of rootless images and information on states of matter. Robinson argued (2014) that financialisation generates new ingesting public spaces financed by the state and finance. We argue that financialisation goes further. The private space too gives up and a dread as in Kirkegaardian (1957/1944) sense ratcheted by ever-increasing risks and uncertainties of holding private bodies and captures all the flights of images and numbers.

This mode of grasping financialisation, where risks and uncertainties become the actuator as well as the ontological foundation for deepening and widening of finance in all private and public and also by the erasement of separations of public and private and as evidenced in the domain of health is, we claim, the politics of postmodern state that goes much beyond narrow boundaries of nation. What we argued goes beyond definitions that financialisation is "the process by which the various forms of capital in exchange …have not only expanded in extent and diversity but become increasingly articulated with one another … in particular interest-bearing capital has increasingly appropriated activities … Consequently, economic activity in general has become subject to the logic and imperative of interest-bearing capital" (Fine 2010, pp. 98–99). Similarly, facets of financialisation as captured by Froud, for example (Froud 2003) that managing risks and uncertainty through private finance initiative is mistaken, or by Lazonick and Tulum (2011) and by Froud et al. (2002) that financialisation brought manufacturing to its end or by Epstein (2005) that financialisation is necessarily global or macroeconomic (Van Treeck 2009) are all and together descriptions of this massive transformation.

This discussion on financialisation of health began with two dimensions, the breakdown of intra- and inter-corporeal relations and the body breaking down into volatile images and state-data. Through this discussion, we probed the interrelations between these two dimensions as founded upon engendering of risks and uncertainty and thus necessarily of finance. The ever-increasing risk and uncertainty of personal body of a collective or of human species in general bring together these two dimensions of financialisation. It is as it were the ontological as well as the foundational claim that enhanced risk engenders finance deepening and widening. This transformation by finance takes over all public institutions, all private institutions and beyond that, all personal bodies. It is also worth noticing that science and technologies of biomedical prove to be the great intermediary in this engenderment of risks. The desert of elevation of bodily integrity is lost to this scientific enterprise (McIntyre 2007). Important also to notice that technoscience as of Latour et al. does not offer any ethical import and is descriptive of material situations. The desert argument is both political and ethical. The political and ethical are necessary because, as we saw happening in India, it is now a question of recapturing personal body.

14.4 Health Needs and Services in India

Palliative health care is being forced now to become increasingly more elusive with every new politically directed and finance impelled sets of actions and policies. In short, every bit of previous institution of health care that was largely based on local autonomy getting if not directly delegalised otherwise as unkempt and unsupported and irregularised the vestiges of that autonomous institution barely lingers on. The GP and PHC are thus getting into oblivion (Rao and Chadhury 2012). Organised health offerings, especially for ailments that have been accredited "critical" status, bound now by several court rulings that borrowed largely from US/UK legal traditions often from tort, and that are on consumer redressal as well as what follows globally set down protocols and standards (Banerjee 2014), find favourable responses from insurance and public systems.

The mass of data generated by national statistical system, such as the NSS (National Sample Surveys, several rounds) (GOI 2015a), however, disputes the "critical" status provided as these diseases are less prevalent in terms of number of persons affected or in terms of number of days that a person ordinarily remain affected and

Table 14.1 Number per 1,00,000 of persons reporting onset of specific ailments during last 15 days and average duration of ailment by broad ailment type and for all India

Type of hospital	Rural			Urban		
	2004 (60th)	1995–96 (52nd)	1986–87 (42nd)	2004 (60th)	1995–96 (52nd)	1986–87 (42nd)
Government	417	438	597	382	431	603
Non-government	583	562	403	618	569	397
All hospitals	1000	1000	1000	1000	1000	1000

Source Report No. 507: Morbidity, Health Care and the Condition of the Aged. NSS 60th Round (January–June 2004). NSSO. GoI. March 2006

disoriented, or even in terms of causes of death or severe morbidity. A simple observation in terms of prevalence as exhibited in Table 14.1 which is a select listing of prevalence of ailments definitely contradicts criticality of diseases such as cancer or joint replacement as most prevalent or most debilitating or that causes most economic and bodily ruin. Diseases such as diarrhoea, typhoid, malaria, tuberculosis, respiratory/bronchial, whooping cough, fever of unknown origin, accidents and injuries and many similar others as listed in Table 14.1 are highly prevalent, causes great disability and causes greatest economic ruin and while these could have been considered "critical" another set of diseases for what imported machines systems and medical practices and protocols or standards are available receives the status since this new set is amenable to greater financial control and can be indexed monitored as well as speculated on. The NSSO (2004/06) also reported that number of persons affected out of every 1000 persons hospitalised the categories—diarrhoea/dysentery, gastritis/ulcer, respiratory including of ENT, tuberculosis, bronchial asthma, gynaecological disorders, accidents with locomotor disability, other diagnosed ailments, malaria, fever of unknown origin, etc., for example, were, respectively, 76, 48, 35, 30, 34, 52, 101, 164, 32 and 79; while for cancer and other tumours to cite one example, this figure was 28. Exhibit at Table 14.2 from NSSO (2014/15) indicates that criticality when defined in terms of expenditure in cash and at hospital only and that too at private hospitals refers to cancer as the most critical, followed by cardiovascular, followed by injuries and then psychiatric-neurological, and similarly. However, criticality in terms of the debilitating effect or in terms of loss of economic earnings or loss of days and similar others including and no less importantly, in terms of statistical prevalence would indicate that cash cost at private hospitals alone cannot be sufficiently defining parameter.

Another set of statistics (GOI/AHS 2015a, b) that classifies illness under two categories, namely "acute" as that with abrupt onset and is short-lived, and "chronic" as that with persistence lasting longer and cannot be cured completely, and was undertaken for select states of India, reported that per 1,00,000 population of acute illness there had been an overall increase and was similarly so for every 1,00,000

Table 14.2 Average medical expenditure, in INR, per hospitalisation case for each broad ailment category in different types of hospital

Broad ailment category	Average medical expenditure in INR per hospitalisation case (AME)—public	AME—private	AME—all
Infections	3007	11,810	8134
Cancers	24,526	78,050	56,712
Blood diseases	4752	17,607	13,313
Endocrine, metabolic and nutrition	4625	19,206	14,117
Psychiatric and neurological	7482	34,561	23,984
Eye	1778	13,374	9307
Ear	6626	19,518	15,285
Cardiovascular	11,549	43,262	31,647
Respiratory	4811	18,705	12,820
Gastrointestinal	5281	23,933	17,687
Skin	3142	14,664	10,438
Musculo-skeletal	8165	23,896	21,862
Genito-urinary	9295	29,608	24,525
Obstetric and neonatal	2651	21,626	11,707
Injuries	6729	36,255	23,491
Other	14,030	35,572	28,003
All	6120	25,850	18,268

Source NSSO 2014. 71st Round (January–June 2014). Key indicators of social consumption in India—Health. Ministry of Statistics and Program Implementation, NSSO, Government of India. June 2015

population with chronic illness. The state of Bihar, for example, reported 12,898 acutely ill and 8755 chronically ill persons in 2010–11, that rose to 14,923 under acute category and to 19,219 under chronic category, per 1,00,000 population. The same state reported that treatment received from public sources stood at 10.3% in 2010–11 and at 5.2% in 2012–13 out of all cases of acute illness, and this was 8.8% in 2010–11 and was 9.2% in 2012–13 for all chronic illness. The illnesses that affected mostly were under the categories—diarrhoea/dysentery, fever, hypertension, diabetes, tuberculosis, asthma, arthritis, and injuries from severe to major. Previously the PHC's and the GP's had the wherewithal of knowledge of treating these prevalent diseases and the local pharmaceutical companies had locally researched cheap solutions of medicines. However, with M&A of local pharmaceutical companies, and the closure of PHC's and delegitimisation of GP's and the delegalisation of unrecorded medical techniques of the GP's which mostly based on touch and feel and did use the least of medical devices—and in parallel, with the emergence of new narratives on

Table 14.3 Distribution of hospitalised treatment, by public and private during 2004, 1995–96 and 1986–87

All MPCE classes	Source of finance			
	hhd income/savings	Borrowings	Others	Total
Rural	772	172	56	1000
Urban	865	71	64	1000

Source Report No. 507: Morbidity, Health Care and the Condition of the Aged. NSS 60th Round (January–June 2004). NSSO. GoI. March 2006

health that circulates on social media and the new politics of health as justice have together unmade the reality of ailments that suffer common Indian.

Decreasing availability of public hospitals (Ellis et al. 2000; Sodhi and Rabbani 2014) as exhibited in Table 14.3, and of course, for non-hospitalising diseases (to recall, most ailments fall under this category) the PHC's and the GP's, have forced two outcomes: increase in the out-of-pocket expenditure (Karan et al. 2014; Selvaraj and Karan 2009) and consequential indebtedness as well as loss of the right and capability to recovery (Patel et al. 2015). Table 14.4 exhibits how privatised medical care gets financed, foremost and increasingly from family savings and otherwise by sales/mortgaging jewellery or livestock or even land or otherwise borrowing (Ghosh 2011; Berman et al. 2010). Data from the 2014 NSS 71st Round (NSSO 2014/15) exhibits that percentage of spells of ailment treated at public system during last 15 days of reporting, was 11.5 and 3.9%, respectively, in rural and urban public healthcare systems excluding hospitals, and that from public hospitals was 16.8% for rural and 17.3% for urban, and all the rest got treated from private doctors/clinics or private hospitals. Amongst the hospitalised cases of treatment (NSSO 2014/15), the public hospital system treated only 41.9, 41.7 and 43.8% in years 2014, 2004 and 1995–96, respectively, from rural areas, and this figures were 32, 38.2 and 43.1%, respectively, for the same years but for urban persons.

The importance of both pre-hospitalisation and post-hospitalisation as well as the importance of non-hospitalisation yet severely debilitating ailments in the complete annual life cycle of an Indian cannot be overlooked. Insurance and the private hospitals especially those categorised as specialty hospitals cannot and do not provide services to these three types of pre-, post-hospitalisation and non-hospitalising severe disability. To record that these are most prevalent and are also most ruining, one would wonder whether the financialisation is also simultaneously the politics of dispossession of capability of a bodily person and that of bodily community or collective to achieve health recovery! The politics of financialisation appears thus to be both a loot of wealth and robbing off the corporeal capability (Boerma 2018; Business Standard 2018a).

Most disconcerting aspect is that, and as reported in the NSSO (2004/06), average loss of household income due to ailment, during the last 15 days, is most despairing and acute amongst the bottom MPCE classes, such as in classes of 0–235, 235–265, and so on up to even the class of 730–980 (which is third from the top of all MPCE

Table 14.4 Distribution per 1000 of household total expenditure on treatment during the last 15 days by source of finance

Broad ailment type	Incidence rate of ailment during last 15 days—no. of persons	Average duration of ailment in days (0.0)—no. of persons	Persons reporting onset of ailment during last 15 days—Estd. No. (00)	Persons reporting onset of ailment during last 15 days—sample
Diarrhoea/dysentery	381	5.6	36,701	1326
Gastritis/gastric or peptic ulcer	120	21.6	11,503	456
Hepatitis/jaundice	14	11.8	1358	60
Heart disease	19	91.0	1863	120
Respiratory including ENT ailments	443	7.8	42,659	1579
Tuberculosis	6	127.1	577	41
Bronchial asthma	61	80.1	5908	220
Disorders of joints and bones	91	72.3	8756	363
Gynaecological disorders	32	16.6	3124	148
Neurological disorders	36	45.8	3472	122
Diseases of skin	68	15.1	6515	206
Diabetes mellitus	16	253.6	1508	67
Malaria	119	6.8	11,484	370
Eruptive	35	9.7	3324	70
Whooping cough	166	10.5	15,496	525
Fever of unknown origin	1484	5.3	142,795	4645
Locomotor disability	18	122.2	1730	79
Hearing/diseases of mouth/teeth	11	25.6	1062	37
Gum	61	41.4	5842	199
Cancer and other tumours	8	47.4	775	41
All	4444	17.3	427,727	15,292

Source Report No. 507: Morbidity, Health Care and the Condition of the Aged. NSS 60th Round (January–June 2004). NSSO. GoI. March 2006

classes). The group with 0–235 would lose INR 569! Therefore, a large number of ailments remain untreated, and often owing to financial reasons, for example, the 60th Round of NSS reported that 28% of spells of ailment remained untreated owing to financial reasons, while the 52nd Round of NSS reported a lower figure of 24% of untreated spells of ailment owing to the same reason. The share of public provisioning of non-hospitalised treatments the NSSO (2004/06) reported was only 22.3% for all rural ailment spells and 19.2% for all urban ailment spells. The NSS 71st Round of 2014 consumption data exhibits that out of the quintile classes of UMPCE, the bottommost class did not have any kind of insurance coverage and only 10.1% of such persons enjoyed government-funded insurance scheme, while 89.1% were not covered at all in the rural areas. The same data also exhibited that the severity of non-coverage was higher for urban bottommost class, which stood at 91.4% with no coverage and 7.7% with government-funded insurance scheme while none with any coverage from insurance. The figures for all UMPCE classes and for all India showed that 82% persons were not covered by any financial support, 12% enjoyed government-funded insurance scheme, and only 3.5% enjoyed coverage from insurance (see also Dilip 2012; Raza et al. 2016). IRDA Annual Reports as reported in the Economic Times (ET 16-08-2018) showed that health insurance rose from lives covered at 216.2 million in 2013–14 to 437.5 million in 2016–17.

The trend is definite that there is an increasing withdrawal from public system on the ground and especially, from such public grounded systems that are under the control of local community or the local government. This withdrawal is happening in parallel with increasing institutional collapse as well as delegitimisation of all facets of community-controlled locally grounded institution of healthcare. Financial control of ungrounded healthcare institution is easy. Parameters of health outcome are pre-determined, indexed, capitalised and speculated as well as traded. The politics of justice creates new narratives of statistics, statistical outcome in health parameters and it is this politics that undermines sovereignty of the category of body.

14.5 Concluding Remarks

De-grounding of body corporate is the politics of finance. From personal body to several varieties of community bodies are increasingly getting de-grounded, and foot-loose, such bodies break down into plethora of floating images, information and semiotic symbols that the financialising politics bundles as well as unbundles generating risks and uncertainties. Ungrounded risky imageries and information provide the foundation to financialisation.

India with its billion over poor population is the coveted ground for financialisation of bodies broken down. The politics of financialisation of body and health is about unfreedom and inidentity. A politics of liberation of body should open up a new chapter in the politics of sovereignty. Bodily sovereignty could be a promising ground of exploration.

References

Banerjee, P. (2010). Consuming body and shaping policy on the science of healing. In A. Jain (Ed.), *History of science, philosophy and culture in Indian civilization: Vol. XV, Part 2—Science and the public* (pp. 225–252). New Delhi: Centre for Studies in Civilizations-PHISPC.

Banerjee, P. (2014). Medical consumption and clinical practice: India at the crossroads. In K. Das (Ed.), *Globalization and standards: Issues and challenges in Indian Business* (pp. 165–178). Berlin: Springer.

Berman, P., Ahuja, R., & Bhandari, L. (2010). The impoverishing effect of healthcare payments in India: New methodology and findings. *Economic and Political Weekly*, *17*, 65–71.

Bevir, M. (1999). Foucault and critique: Deploying agency against autonomy. *Political Theory, 27*(1), 65–84.

Bhat, R. (1999). Characteristics of private medical practice in India: A provider perspective. *Health Policy and Planning, 14*(1), 26–37.

Boerma, T., et al. (2018). Global epidemiology of use of disparities in caesarean section. *The Lancet, 392*(10155), 1341–1348.

Business Standard. (2018, December 30). https://www.business-standard.com/article/companies/investment-surge-in-online-pharmacy-six-year-high-in-2018-observers-118123000598_1.html.

Business Standard. (2018a, December 20). https://www.business-standard.com/article/current-affairs/blame-private-hospital-boom-for-rising-caesarean-delivery-rate-says-report-118122000164_1.html.

Business Standard (2018b, June 11). https://www.business-standard.com/article/companies/import-of-medical-devices-from-us-on-the-rise-here-s-all-you-need-to-know-118061000756_1.html.

Clarke, A. E., et al. (2003). Biomedicalization: Technoscientific transformations of health, illness, and U.S. Biomedicine. *American Sociological Review, 68,* 161–194.

Conti, G., et al. (2016). Expanding Indian Public Health Insurance above the Poverty Line. *International Growth Centre (IGC).* http://www.theigc.org/blog/expanding-indian-public-health-insurance-above-the-poverty-line/.

Deleuze, G. (1992, October). Postscript on the societies of control (Vol. 59, pp. 3–7).

Dilip, T. R. (2012). On publicly financed health insurance schemes: Is the analysis premature? *Economic and Political Weekly, 47*(18), 79–80.

Economic Times. (2017, July 24). https://economictimes.indiatimes.com/industry/healthcare/biotech/healthcare/niti-aayogs-healthcare-ppp-needs-clarity-hospitals/articleshow/59728377.cms.

Economic Times. (2017, December 20). https://economictimes.indiatimes.com/industry/healthcare/biotech/healthcare/niti-aayogs-healthcare-ppp-needs-clarity-hospitals/articleshow/59728377.cms?utm_source=Colombia&utm_medium=OrganicNative&utm_campaign=CTN&utm_content=21.

Economic Times. (2018, May 24). https://economictimes.indiatimes.com/industry/healthcare/biotech/healthcare/modicare-govt-sets-rates-for-1354-treatment-packages-to-implement-ayushman-bharat-scheme/articleshow/64297506.cms.

Economic Times. (2018, August 16). https://economictimes.indiatimes.com/industry/healthcare/biotech/healthcare/can-indu-bhushan-deliver-pm-modis-promise-of-healthcare/articleshow/65418323.cms.

Ellis, R. P., Alam, M., & Gupta, I. (2000, January 22). Health insurance in India: Prognosis and prospectus. *Economic and Political Weekly*, 207–217.

Epstein, G. A. (2005). *Financialization and the world economy*. Cheltenham, UK: Edward Elgar.

Fine, B. (2010). Locating financialisation. *Historical Materialism, 18*(2010), 97–116.

Froud, J., et al. (2002). Cars after financialisation: A case study in financial under-performance, Constraints and Consequences. *Competition and Change, 6*(1), 13–41.

Froud, J. (2003). The private finance initiative: Risk, uncertainty and the state. *Accounting, Organizations and Society, 28,* 567–589.

Gelijns, A. C., & Rosenberg, N. (1995). The changing nature of medical technology development. In N. Rosenberg, et al. (Eds.), *Sources of medical technology: Universities and industry* (pp. 3–114). Washington D.C.: The National Academies Press.

Ghosh, S. (2011). Catastrophic payments and impoverishment due to out-of-pocket health spending. *Economic and Political Weekly, 46*(47), 63–70.

GOI/AHS. (2015a). *Report on medical certification of cause of death 2015*. New Delhi: Office of the Registrar General, India, Ministry of Home Affairs. Government of India.

GOI/AHS. (2015b). *Annual health survey report. A report on core and vital health indicators. Part I*. New Delhi: Office of the Registrar General and Census Commissioner, India. Ministry of Home Affairs. Government of India.

Havighurst, C. C. (2001). Health care as a (big) business: The antitrust response. *Journal of Health Politics and Law, 26*(5), 939–955.

Indian Council of Medical Research (ICMR), et al. (2017). *India: Health of the nation's states—The india state-level disease burden initiative*. New Delhi: ICMR, PHFI, and IHME.

Indian Express. (2018, April 3). http://indianexpress.com/article/business/business-others/the-business-of-hospitals-big-ticket-deals-dominate-pe-vc-investment-flows-5121093/.

Indian Express. (2018, April 18). http://indianexpress.com/article/india/chhattisgarh-move-for-ppp-health-centres-draws-flak-5110382/.

Iriart, C., et al. (2011). The creation of the health consumer: Challenges on health sector regulation after managed care era. *Globalization and Health, 7*, 2. http://www.globalizationandhealth.com/content/7/1/2.

Karan, A., Selvaraj, S., & Mahal, A. (2014, August). Moving to universal coverage? Trends in the burden of out-of-pocket payments for health care across social groups in India, 1999–2000 to 2011–12. *PLoS-ONE, 9*(8).

Keefe, P. R. (2017, October 30). The family that built an empire of pain. *The New Yorker*. https://www.newyorker.com/magazine/2017/10/30/the-family-that-built-an-empire-of-pain.

Kirkegaard, S. (1957/1944). *The concept of dread* (Walter Lowrie, Trans.). Princeton: Princeton University Press.

Latour, B. (2003). The promises of constructivism. In I. Don & S. Evan (Eds.), *Chasing techno-science: Matrix for materiality* (pp. 27–46). Indiana University Press.

Lazonick, W., & Tulum, O. (2011). US biopharmaceutical finance and the sustainability of the biotech business model. *Research Policy, 40*(2011), 1170–1187.

Leyshon, A., & Thrift, N. (2007). The capitalization of almost everything: The future of finance and capitalism. *Theory, Culture and Society, 24*(7–8), 97–115.

LiveMint. (2018, March 20). https://www.livemint.com/Opinion/qsEMS2Y5uD6Deckt6g6EjN/Modicare-is-both-a-social-cause-and-a-political-gamble.html.

McIntyre, A. (2007). *After virtue: A study in moral theory*. Notre Dame: University of Notre Dame Press.

Minsky, H. P. (1989). *The financial instability hypothesis: A clarification*. Hyman P. Minsky Archive. Paper 145. http://digitalcommons.bard.edu/hm_archive/145.

Nandraj, S. (1994). Beyond the law and the lord: Quality of private health care. *Economic and Political Weekly, 29*(270), 1680–1685.

National Health Policy. (2017). Ministry of Health and Family Welfare, Government of India 2017, New Delhi.

Nik-Khah, E. (2014). Neoliberal pharmaceutical science and the Chicago School of Economics. *Social Studies of Science, 44*(4), 489–517.

NSSO. (2004/06, June). *Morbidity, health care and the condition of the aged*. Report No. 507 (60/25.0/1) NSS 60th Round (January–June 2004) Ministry of Statistics and Program Implementation, NSSO, Government of India.

NSSO. (2014/15, June). Key indicators of social consumption in India: Health. (January–June 2014) Ministry of Statistics and Program Implementation, NSSO, Government of India.

Patel, V., et al. (2015, December 12). Assuring health coverage for all in India. *The Lancet, 386*, 2422–2435.

Petryana, A. (2013, October). The right of recovery. *Current Anthropology, 54*(Suppl 7), S67–S76.
Rao, G., & Chaudhury, M. (2012). Health care financing reforms in India. *Working Paper No. 2012-100.* New Delhi: NIPFP.
Raza, W., et al. (2016, January). Analyses of enrolment, dropout and effectiveness of RSBY in northern rural India. *MPRA. Paper No. 70081*. https://mpra.ub.uni-muenchen.de/70081/.
Relman, A. S. (1980). The medical-industrial complex. *The New England Journal of Medicine, 303*(17), 963–970.
Robinson, M. D. (2014, June). *Neuro-innovation: translational science, ethics and the financialization of health*. A Dissertation for Ph.D. to Princeton University.
Rose, N. (2003, November–December). Becoming neurochemical selves. *Society*, 46–59.
Sengupta, A. (2017, March 20). Scroll.in. https://scroll.in/pulse/832245/indias-new-national-health-policy-sets-a-very-low-bar-for-better-public-health.
Selvaraj, S., & Karan, A. K. (2009). Deepening health insecurity in India: Evidence from national sample surveys since 1980s. *Economic and political weekly, 44*(40), 55–60.
Sodhi, C., & Rabbani, A. (2014). Health service system in India: Is insurance the way forward? *Economic and Political Weekly, 49*(35), 26–28.
Somatosphere. (2016). http://somatosphere.net/2017/02/biofinance-speculation-risk-debt-and-value-from-bios-a-conference-report.html.
Stein, F., & Sridhar, D. (2018). The financialisation of global health. *Wellcome Open Research 2018, 3*:17. Last updated February 26, 2018.
The Wire. (2017, July 25) https://thewire.in/160920/niti-aayog-ppp-model-healthcare/.
Thomas, G., & Krishnan, S. (2010, January–March). Effective public-private partnership in healthcare: Apollo as a cautionary tale. *Indian Journal of Medical Ethics, 7*(1).
Triggle, D. J. (2007, February). Treating desires not diseases: A Pil for every ill and an ill for every pill? *Drug Discovery Today, 12*(3–4), 161–166.
Van Treeck, T. (2009, December 5). The political economy debate on 'financialization'—A macroeconomic perspective. *Review of International Political Economy, 16*, 907–944.

Printed by Printforce, the Netherlands